German
for Reading
Knowledge

Sixth Edition

JANNACH'S

German for Reading Knowledge

Sixth Edition

Richard Alan Korb
Columbia University

HEINLE
CENGAGE Learning

Australia • Brazil • Japan • Korea • Mexico • Singapore • Spain • United Kingdom • United States

HEINLE
CENGAGE Learning™

Hubert Jannach's German for Reading Knowledge, Sixth Edition
Richard Alan Korb

Executive Editor: Lara Semones

Assistant Editor: Catharine Thomson

Editorial Assistant: Julie Foster

Technology Project Manager:
Morgen Murphy

Marketing Manager: Lindsey Richardson

Marketing Communications Manager:
Stacey Purviance

Project Manager, Editorial Production:
Tiffany Kayes

Creative Director: Rob Hugel

Art Director: Cate Barr

Senior Print Buyer: Elizabeth Donaghey

Permissions Editor: Mollika Basu

Production Service/Compositor:
ICC Macmillan Inc.

Text Designer: Meral Dabcovich/Visual
Perspectives

Copy Editor: Tunde Dewey

Cover Designer: Dick Hannus

Cover Image: istockphotos.com
© Torsten Lorenz

For product information and technology assistance, contact us at **Cengage Learning Customer & Sales Support, 1-800-354-9706**

For permission to use material from this text or product, submit all requests online at **cengage.com/permissions.** Further permissions questions can be e-mailed to **permissionrequest@cengage.com**.

Library of Congress Control Number: 2008920884

ISBN-13: 978-1-413-03349-6
ISBN-10: 1-413-03349-0

Heinle Cengage Learning
25 Thomson Place
Boston, MA 02210-1202
USA

Cengage Learning products are represented in Canada by Nelson Education, Ltd.

For your course and learning solutions, visit **academic.cengage.com**.
Purchase any of our products at your local college store or at our preferred online store **www.ichapters.com**.

Printed in the United States of America
1 2 3 4 5 6 7 14 13 12 11 10 09 08

PREFACE

When I was a college senior in the early 1970s, *Jannach's German for Reading Knowledge* was the required textbook in a course called "Scientific German." That first edition of "Jannach" was filled with exercises and readings on acids, chemical compounds, and World War II. The step-by-step grammar outline provided our class with all the basics to translate German texts, which back then was nearly the sole purpose for learning the language.

Much has changed in the meantime. *Jannach's German for Reading Knowledge* has developed into a tool intended to meet the needs of students in the humanities, arts, and social sciences who have decided to concentrate on the skills of translating and reading German for academic purposes. This sixth edition continues to provide 1) clear grammar explanations focused on non-speaker perceptions and 2) approaches to negotiating meaning. The exercises and readings have been chosen with thought to both "bottom-up" and "top-down" reading approaches: From the bottom up, they build on and recycle grammar and vocabulary from chapter to chapter in ways that encourage attention to individual words and functions, as well as to the importance of using a dictionary effectively. From the top down, the variety of topics reflects multiple facets of contemporary German-language cultures promoting interpretive thinking, reflecting, guessing, and further reading by students from a wide range of academic fields.

Users who liked the fifth edition will be glad to find the style and even a good deal of the content of the sixth edition unchanged but much refreshed. Changes to the new edition include:

- An introduction to students and instructors on "how to use this book," plus added reading strategy tips on learning vocabulary and using a dictionary have been added to early chapters. Further suggestions can be found in a new version of Appendix C: "How to choose and use a dictionary."

- **Grundwortschatz** (basic vocabulary) and text glosses have been streamlined by clarifying their role in the learning process and removing repeat entries; basic definitions reflect usage in a given chapter or text.
- Glosses to **Lesetexte** (readings) and **Wiederholungen** (review texts) have been revised and reduced in volume; emphasis has been placed on idioms, unfamiliar terms/forms, and text-specific meanings. Reduced glosses also encourage reading strategies (form recognition, vocabulary learning, contextual intuition, background knowledge, and/or dictionary skills).
- **Übungssätze** (exercise sentences) were checked for standard German usage and content and about 40 sentences were updated, rewritten, or added. Updated translations of all the nearly 550 **Übungssätze** are available as an online exercise sentences key at academic.cengage.com/german/korb.
- Three new **Lesetexte** provide fresh perspectives on Europe's view of the AIDS pandemic, mobility in Eastern Germany, and "Ostler" as immigrants. Six **Lesetexte** were updated and/or supplemented with additional historical background.
- Updated online reading comprehension guides with pre-reading, reading, and post-reading activities for the 30 **Lesestücke** are also on the companion website at academic.cengage.com/german/korb. All website links suggesting further reading are regularly reviewed and updated.
- Based on instructor and student feedback, grammar presentations including the following were expanded or revised: nominative interrogatives, N-nouns, possessive pronouns, **es gibt**, prepositions following nouns, adjectival nouns, reflexive verbs, and subjunctive II.
- A new presentation of **es** used in weather expressions has been added to **Kapitel 30** and metric conversions were removed from **Kapitel 2**.
- Grammar tables, also available for review on the companion website at academic.cengage.com/german/korb, have been made user-friendlier throughout the new edition.

Readings and exercises in *Jannach's German for Reading Knowledge*, Sixth Edition, have been tested on graduate students and scholars preparing for exams or research involving German-language texts. Additions and revisions to the new edition have been made with those readers in mind.

Acknowledgments

I should like to thank my colleagues in the Department of Germanic Languages at Columbia University for their support and to express my gratitude to Columbia students and instructors for invaluable input in revising the sixth edition. Heinle/Cengage would also like to thank Tunde Dewey for her native read of the sixth edition.

Thanks as well to the following colleagues for their thoughtful reading and guidance throughout the writing process:

Anne Green, *Carnegie Mellon University*
Angela Lin, *Vanderbilt University*
Frederick Schwink, *University of Illinois at Urbana-Champaign*
Margrit Zinggeler, *Eastern Michigan University*

Special thanks are due to Robert K. Bloomer (SUNY, Stonybrook), Kai Artur Dies (Rutgers University), and Samuel J. Spinner, Simona Vaidean, and Julia Nordmann (all of Columbia University) for their invaluable suggestions, and to my partner, Donald Downs, for reading, cooking, cleaning, and being so patient.

CONTENTS

How to Use *German for Reading Knowledge*

This book provides guidance and practice in applying basic German grammar and vocabulary to reading and translating progressively more complex texts. The basic components are: grammar outlines, vocabulary lists, exercise sentences, chapter readings, and review readings after every five chapters. The companion website adds exercise keys, grammar review charts, and reading guides.

Here are suggestions for how best to utilize these features.

1. **Grammatik** (grammar outline): Use outlines for reference purposes. Compare explanations and examples to structures in the exercise sentences. Bring comments and questions on the grammar for class discussion. Refer to the companion website's grammar charts for review (academic.cengage.com/german/korb).

2. **Grundwortschatz** (basic vocabulary): These common words recur throughout the book and are listed with basic meanings and forms. They are the basis for your personal active vocabulary list, and they appear again in the end vocabulary (pp. 301–324).

3. **Übungssätze** (exercise sentences): Daily practice translating and then reviewing these sentences builds vocabulary and skills in recognizing word function and context. After translating all the sentences, check your accuracy using the online exercise key (academic.cengage.com/german/korb). Note both errors in your translation—to facilitate feedback and avoid future errors—and idiomatic expressions. The online key strives for idiomatic translations instead of word-for-word renderings. Bring questions and comments for class discussion.

4. **Kapitel Lesestücke** (chapter readings): These passages can be used to practice reading strategies and/or translating contextualized material. The online reading guides (academic.cengage.com/german/korb) have three components: pre-reading activities activate background knowledge and help organize an approach to reading, skimming, and scanning activities help readers understand the gist and key elements of the text, intensive reading activities promote thinking about information in the text and provide suggestions for further reading. Links are reviewed and updated regularly.

5. **Wiederholungen** (review readings): After every five chapters, a
   review reading recycles grammar and vocabulary, and challenges
   students to develop individual reading strategies and to improve
   dictionary skills. Glosses in both the review readings and the
   readings after **Kapitel 7** concentrate on idioms and text-specific
   terminology. Pay attention to context and to functions as you
   read, and when necessary use your dictionary. For suggestions on
   dictionary use see Appendix C (296–298).

KAPITEL 1

1.1 German Nouns and the Definite Article

One of the most salient features of the German language is the indication of gender (and case) by means of the definite article. Whereas English has only one form of the definite article, *the,* which does not differentiate gender or number, German has four forms of the definite article: three singular and one plural. Dictionaries and the vocabulary lists in this book indicate nouns as *m.* (masculine), *f.* (feminine), *n.* (neuter), or *pl.* (plural). The corresponding German definite articles are as follows.

Masculine:	der
Feminine:	die
Neuter:	das
Plural, all genders:	die

1.2 Gender of Nouns

German nouns are masculine, feminine, or neuter. Because of the synthetic nature of German, it is essential from the beginning to learn each noun together with its gender-specific article.

Masculine:	der Mann, der Student, der Tisch *(the table)*, der Stuhl *(the chair)*
Feminine:	die Frau *(the woman)*, die Studentin, die Universität, die Lampe *(the lamp)*
Neuter:	das Haus, das Bett, das Kind *(the child)*, das Buch *(the book)* *the bed*

Note that all German nouns are capitalized.

To be able to read German with accuracy it is essential to learn the gender of each noun, since recognizing the gender of a noun is key to deciphering overall meaning and recognizing the function of the noun in a given situation. The general aids given in the following sections and in subsequent chapters will help you learn and remember the genders of German nouns; otherwise, consult a dictionary for assistance. The following aids are starting points to help you determine the gender of a noun.

A. Masculine

The following nouns are always masculine.

1. Nouns denoting male beings (people, animals, professions):

der Vater	*father*	der Stier	*bull*
der Freund	*friend*	der Gott	*god*
der Hahn	*rooster*	der Künstler	*artist*

2. Most nouns ending in **-er** that are agents of a specific activity:

der Arbeiter	*worker*	der Computer	*computer*
der Wissenschaftler	*scientist*	der Kugelschreiber	*(ballpoint)*
der Schriftsteller	*writer*		*pen*

3. The days, months, and seasons:

der Montag	*Monday*	der Dezember	*December*
der Mittwoch	*Wednesday*	der Winter	*winter*
der Oktober	*October*	der Sommer	*summer*

4. Nouns ending in **-ig, -ich, -ing, -ast, -mus**:

der König	*king*	der Palast	*palace*
der Teppich	*carpet, rug*	der Sozialismus	*socialism*
der Sperling	*sparrow*		

5. Points of the compass:

der Norden	*north*	der Osten	*east*
der Süden	*south*	der Westen	*west*

B. Feminine

The following nouns are always feminine.

1. Nouns denoting female beings (people, animals, professions):

die Mutter	*mother*	die Kuh	*cow*
die Freundin	*friend*	die Göttin	*goddess*
die Henne	*hen*	die Künstlerin	*artist*

2. Names of most trees, fruits, and flowers:

die Eiche	*oak*	die Tomate	*tomato*
die Kastanie	*chestnut*	die Rose	*rose*
die Birne	*pear*	die Orchidee	*orchid*

3. Nouns ending in **-ei, -ie, -ik, -in, -ion, -heit, -keit, -schaft, -tät, -ung, -ur**:

die Bäckerei	*bakery*	die Gesundheit	*health*
die Industrie	*industry*	die Gesellschaft	*society*
die Musik	*music*	die Universität	*university*
die Architektin	*architect*	die Hoffnung	*hope*
die Version	*version*	die Literatur	*literature*

C. Neuter

The following nouns are always neuter.

1. Nouns (including male/female beings) with diminutive endings **-chen** or **-lein**:

   das Buch → das Büchlein   *book → small book*
   der Teil → das Teilchen   *part → particle*
   der Mann → das Männlein   *man → little man*
   der Tisch → das Tischchen   *table → little table*

   Diminutive forms usually have an umlaut if the stem vowel is **a**, **o**, **u**, or **au**, for example: **Büchlein, Häuschen**.

2. Most nouns of foreign origin that end in **-o**:

   das Auto   *auto*   das Embargo   *embargo*
   das Radio   *radio*   das Video   *video*

3. Infinitives used as nouns:

   das Kommen   *coming*   das Lernen   *learning*
   das Gehen   *going*   das Denken   *thinking*
   das Wissen   *knowledge*   das Sein   *being*

4. Nouns ending in **-ium** and **-um**:

   das Studium   *study*   das Evangelium   *gospel*
   das Universum   *universe*   das Visum   *visa*

1.3 Present and Past Tenses of the Verb *sein* (to be)

Since the verb **sein** is one of the most frequently used words in the German language, memorizing its forms from the very start will facilitate all your future reading and translating endeavors. Note that the forms of the verb **sein** are irregular in both the present and the past tense; no other verb follows the pattern of **sein** in the present tense. (See **Kapitel 2**.)

A. Present tense of *sein*

Singular		Plural	
ich bin	*I am*	wir sind	*we are*
du bist	*you are*	ihr seid	*you (guys/all) are*
er ist	*he is/it is*	sie sind	*they are*
sie ist	*she is/it is*	Sie sind	*you are*
es ist	*it is*		

Pay close attention to the subject and verb in each of the following examples, and ascertain *who* is **jung** *(young)*, **alt** *(old)*, **gesund** *(healthy)*, or **krank** *(ill)*.

Ich bin der Professor. Ich bin 40 Jahre alt. Ich bin gesund.

Du bist die Studentin. Du bist 21 Jahre alt. Du bist jung und
gesund.

Der Mann ist der Arzt. Er ist gesund, aber der Patient ist krank.

Die Patienten sind im Krankenhaus *(in the hospital)*. Sie sind
nicht gesund, sie sind krank.

–Armin und Jörn, seid ihr krank? –Nein! Wir sind gesund.

–Frau Meyer, sind Sie krank? –Nein, ich bin gesund. Herr Meyer
ist krank. Er ist im Krankenhaus.

–Herr und Frau Stein, sind Sie gesund? –Ja, wir sind gesund.
Dr. Schmidt ist unsere Ärztin. Sie ist sehr intelligent.

Note that German has three words for *you:* **du, ihr,** and **Sie.** When
speaking or writing to children, relatives, colleagues, and close friends,
Germans use the familiar form of address: **du** for the singular, **ihr** for
the plural (the second and fifth examples). In all other situations, the
formal **Sie** (always capitalized) is used for both the singular and plural
(the last two examples).

B. Past tense of *sein*

The lack of endings in the first- and third-person singular forms in
the past tense of **sein** is common only to irregular verbs; a different
set of endings is to be found with regular verbs. (See **Kapitel 3** and
Kapitel 4.)

Singular		**Plural**	
ich war	*I was*	wir waren	*we were*
du warst	*you were*	ihr wart	*you (guys/all) were*
er war	*he was/it was*	sie waren	*they were*
sie war	*she was/it was*	Sie waren	*you were*
es war	*it was*		

Helmut Kohl war 1982–1998 Bundeskanzler. Er war Christ-
demokrat.
Helmut Kohl was *Federal Chancellor 1982–1998. He was a
Christian Democrat.*

Willi Brandt und Helmut Schmidt waren auch Bundeskanzler.
Sie waren Sozialdemokraten.
*Willi Brandt and Helmut Schmidt were also Federal Chancel-
lors. They were Social Democrats.*

Das Buch von Günther Grass war lang. Die Bücher von Thomas
Mann waren sehr lang.
*The book by Günther Grass was long. The books by Thomas
Mann were very long.*

Examine the two verb forms in the last example. **Das Buch**, a singular
noun, is the subject of the first sentence; **war** is the singular form of
the verb in the third person, corresponding to the singular third-
person subject. **Die Bücher**, a plural noun, is the subject of the second
sentence; **waren** is the plural form of the verb and corresponds to the
plural subject. These examples illustrate an important rule: *subject and
verb agree in number*. Whenever you see a verb ending in **-en** or **-n** (or
the form **sind**), you know immediately that the subject is plural, with
the exception of the formal **Sie** with singular meaning. Which other
sentences above exhibit a plural subject and verb?

In all conjugations, pay particular attention to verb forms in the third-
person singular or plural; these forms constitute the vast majority of the
verb forms encountered in academic reading.

1.4 Interrogatives

A. Common interrogatives

wann?	*when?*	wie?	*how?*
warum?	*why?*	wie viele?	*how many?*
was?	*what?*	wie viel?	*how much?*
was für ein?	*what kind of?*	wo?	*where?*
welcher?	*which, what?*	wohin?	*where to?*
wer?	*who?*		

B. Word order in information questions

Interrogatives seek information specifically related to the question
word that initiates the question. The main verb of the sentence follows
the interrogative in second position. In the case of such questions as
was für ein?, **welcher?**, **wie viel?**, and **wie viele?**, qualifiers accompany
the interrogative and also precede the verb. Note the position of each
interrogative and verb in the following questions.

Wo ist die Universität? *Where is the school (university)?*
Wohin gehen Sie? *Where are you going (to)?*
Was für ein Buch ist das? *What kind of a book is that?*

Was für Bücher sind das?	*What kind of books are these?*	
Wie viel kostet das Buch?	*How much does the book cost?*	
Wie viele Studenten sind hier?	*How many students are here?*	

1.5 Cognates and Loanwords

Cognates are words from different languages that are related in origin. Since German and English developed from the same ancestral roots, they have a great number of words that are identical and/or similar in their spellings and sound. In addition, loanwords are words that have been adopted from another language and completely or partially naturalized. Here is a list of some of the many German words that are so similar to the English that you will recognize them with little or no effort.

all	die Geographie	die Million
der April	die Geometrie	die Minute
analog	das Gold	modern
die Anarchie	die Hand	das Museum
die Architektur	das Happy End	die Musik
der Arm	das Hotel	der Name
der August	der Hunger	national
das Auto	der Index	der November
der Ball	die Informatik	das Opium
der Beginn	das Instrument	der Oktober
die Biologie	der Januar	die Opposition
bitter	das Kilometer	original
der Bus	der Kindergarten	der Park
die Butter	die Klarinette	die Philosophie
der Clown	der Knoten	die Physik
der Computer	das Know-how	die Politik
der Dezember	konservativ	das Problem
die Diskette	der Kompromiss	der Professor
die Division	die Kultur	progressiv
die E-Mail	das Labyrinth	das Programm
das Experiment	das Land	das Projekt
der Februar	die Linguistik	der Prozess
der Film	die Literatur	die Prozession
der Finger	die Madonna	der Pullover
das Foto	die Mathematik	die Psychologie
die Garage	die Migration	das Quartal
der General	mild	quick

das Radio	der Tank	die Villa
real	das Taxi	die Viola
die Reform	das Team	virulent
das Restaurant	die Technologie	warm
der Ring	der Text	wild
die Rose	das Theater	der Wind
der Sand	das Thermometer	der Winter
das Semester	transparent	der Wolf
der Senator	die Tube	die Xenophobie
der September	die Tundra	die Yacht
so	der Tunnel	der Yak
das Sofa	der Turban	der Yankee
die Soziologie	die Turbine	der Yen
der Sport	das Ultimatum	das Yoga
die Story	der Umlaut	die Yucca
still	die Vendetta	das Zebra
der Student	die Veranda	die Zero
das Talent	das Verb	der Zoo
der Tango	das Video	

For a list of related German and English verb infinitives, go to pages 15–16. A list of "False Friends," or German words that look like English words but have different meanings, can be found on page 178.

Grundwortschatz means *basic vocabulary*. Under this rubric in each chapter you'll find common, recurring vocabulary and their basic meanings and forms. Learning these basic words with each chapter facilitates efficient reading. Basic vocabulary words are not glossed in exercises or texts, but are listed in the end Vocabulary (pages 301–324).

Learning Strategy 1: Highlight basic vocabulary in the end vocabulary list and in your dictionary; note each subsequent time you look up the same word. If you've looked up the same word several times, commit it to memory and add it to your active personal vocabulary list.

Learning Strategy 2: When using your dictionary, note related words and word families. Add word families to your personal vocabulary list. Suggestions for choosing and using a dictionary can be found in Appendix C (pages 296–298).

Grundwortschatz

aber	but, however	**natürlich**	of course, naturally
alt	old		
Anfang (m.)	beginning, start	**nicht**	not
auch	also, too	**Österreich** (n.)	Austria
berühmt	famous	**österreichisch**	Austrian
deutsch	German	**sagen**	to say
Deutschland (n.)	Germany	**schön**	beautiful, nice
dort	there	**sehr**	very
ein	a, an, one	**sein**	to be
einige	some, several	**Stadt** (f.)	city
Erde (f.)	earth	**studieren**	to go to college/ university
Frage (f.)	question		
Frau (f.)	Mrs., Ms., woman, wife	**Tag** (m.)	day
		und	and
Freund (m.), **Freundin** (f.)	friend	**Universität** (f.)	university
		Vater (m.)	father
Geographie (f.)	geography	**wann**	when
Geschichte (f.)	history	**was**	what
groß	large, great	**wer**	who
gut	good	**wie**	how
Herr (m.)	Mr., gentleman	**wie viele**	how many
hier	here	**wie viel**	how much
ja	yes	**Wissenschaft** (f.)	science, scholarship
Jahr (n.)	year		
kein	no, not any	**Wissenschaftler** (m.)	scientist, scholar
Kunst (f.)	art	**wo**	where
Land (n.)	land, state, country	**Wort** (n.)	word
		ziemlich	fairly, rather
Mutter (f.)	mother		

 Lösungen zu Übungssätzen auf **academic.cengage.com/german/korb**

Übungssätze

Many cognates occur in the first few chapters. If a word is not listed in the chapter vocabulary list, employ "intelligent guessing" and try to infer its meaning from the context before consulting the vocabulary list at the end of the book.[1] Be careful of singulars and plurals—remember the rule about **sind** and verbs ending in **-en** or **-n**. Adjectives and nouns

---

1 Numbers on vocabulary items beneath exercises refer to the corresponding practice sentence.

may have endings added to the form given in the vocabulary. For the time being disregard these endings; they will be explained in later lessons.

1. Die Erde hat sieben Kontinente: Afrika, Asien, Australien, Europa, Nordamerika, Südamerika und die Antarktis. Wie viele Studenten studieren Geographie?
2. Deutschland liegt in Europa. Es hat neun Nachbarländer. Die Hauptstadt ist Berlin.
3. München ist eine schöne, alte Stadt im Süden von Deutschland. Sie ist die Hauptstadt von Bayern.
4. Österreich ist auch ein sehr schönes Land. Wie heißt die Hauptstadt von Österreich? –Sie heißt Wien.
5. Wann waren Sie in Wien, Frau Motyl? –Ich war diesen Sommer in Wien. Es ist eine fantastische Stadt. Meine Mutter und ich waren sehr oft in der Oper.
6. Ich studiere Kunstgeschichte und Architektur. Oskar Kokoschka war ein berühmter österreichischer Künstler. Otto Wagner war ein großer Wiener Architekt.
7. Die Max-Planck-Gesellschaft (MPG) hat vierundsechzig (64) Institute. Die MPG ist ziemlich neu–1948 gegründet, aber heute ist sie sehr berühmt für Chemie und Biologie.
8. –Wer war Max Planck? –Er war ein berühmter deutscher Physiker. Die Physik ist eine Naturwissenschaft.
9. Die Universitäten in Deutschland sind gut. Einige sind auch sehr alt.
10. Die Universität Heidelberg ist sehr alt. Im Jahre 1986 war die Universität 600 Jahre alt. Sie liegt natürlich in Heidelberg.
11. Die Studenten studieren dort Naturwissenschaften, Politik, Geschichte, Musik und Kunst. Was studieren Sie?
12. Ich studiere Philosophie. Platon und Sokrates waren Philosophen. Sie waren Griechen.

2. **liegen** *to lie*
   Nachbarland (*n.*), ⁻er *neighboring country*
   Hauptstadt (*f.*) *capital city*
3. **im Süden von** *in the southern part of*
   Bayern *Bavaria*
5. **diesen Sommer** *this summer*
   Oper (*f.*) *opera*
6. **Kunstgeschichte** (*f.*) *art history*
   österreichisch *Austrian*
   Wiener (*city names used as adjectives end in* -er) *Viennese*
7. **Gesellschaft** (*f.*) *society*
   gegründet *founded*
12. **Grieche** (*m.*) *Greek*

13. Mein Freund studiert Religion an der Universität. Er liest den Koran und die Bibel.
14. Germanistik ist das Studium von deutscher Sprache, Literatur und Kultur. Das beste Buch von Goethe ist *Faust*.
15. Der Geist ist willig, aber das Fleisch ist schwach.
16. Der Student ist willig, aber er ist nicht sehr intelligent.
17. Ich bin zehn Jahre alt. Wie alt bist du, Fritz? Wie alt ist dein Freund?
18. Wie alt sind Sie, Herr Müller? Wann ist Ihr Geburtstag?
19. Hamlet war ein dänischer Prinz. Die Geschichte ist tragisch. Shakespeares Theaterstück ist eine Tragödie.
20. „Sein oder nicht sein, das ist hier die Frage." Hamlet, V.1.

13. **an der** *at the*
    lesen (liest) *to read (reads)*
    Koran (*m.*) *Koran*
    Bibel (*f.*) *Bible*
14. **Sprache** (*f.*) *language*

15. **Geist** (*m.*) *spirit*
    willig *willing*
    Fleisch (*n.*) *flesh*
    schwach *weak*
18. **Geburtstag** (*m.*) *birthday*
19. **Theaterstück** (*n.*) *theater play*

 Leitfragen zum Lesetext auf **academic.cengage.com/german/korb**

ALLER ANFANG IST SCHWER

„Aller Anfang ist schwer." Das heißt: Es ist hart zu beginnen; der Beginn ist nicht einfach. „Im Anfang war das Wort." Das ist der Beginn vom Johannes Evangelium im Neuen Testament. Johannes 1
5 beginnt: „Im Anfang war das Wort (Logos), und das Wort war bei Gott, und das Wort war Gott. Dieses war im Anfang bei Gott." (Jh. 1, 1–3) Hier ist die englische Version vom Anfangstext des Johannes Evangeliums: „In the beginning was the Word, and the

1 **aller Anfang** *getting started, the first step*
  Anfang (*m.*), ̈-e *beginning, start*
  schwer *difficult, weighty*
  das heißt *that means*

2 **beginnen** *to begin*
  nicht einfach *not easy; difficult*
3 **im Anfang** *in the beginning*
  Wort (*n.*) *word*
4 **von; vom** *of; of the*

Word was with God, and the Word was God. The same was in the beginning with God." (John 1: 1–3) 10

„Im Anfang war das Wort", der erste Satz vom Johannes Evangelium in der Bibel, ist auch der Anfang von der Szene „Im Studierzimmer" aus Goethes *Faust I*. Faust sitzt und lernt in seinem Studierzimmer. Er sucht in seinen Büchern Wissen. Faust beginnt: „Geschrieben steht: Im Anfang war das Wort ..." So beginnt der 15 philosophische Wissenschaftler eine Serie von Reaktionen und neuen Versionen vom Bibeltext.

Für Faust ist „das Wort" zu passiv, also sagt er: „Im Anfang war der Sinn ..." Aber auch „der Sinn" ist Faust zu passiv, und so sagt er: „Im Anfang war die Kraft ..." Für Faust ist „die Kraft" besser, 20 aber die Kraft ist auch nicht aktiv genug. Dann sagt Faust: „Im Anfang war die Tat!" In diesem Moment denkt Faust: die Tat sagt mehr als das Wort.

Hier sind deutsche und englische Versionen von Fausts Reaktionen zum Johannes Evangelium: 25

Faust, Im Studierzimmer (aus *Faust I*):

Geschrieben steht: Im Anfang war das Wort!
Hier stock' ich schon! Wer hilft mir weiter fort?
Ich kann das Wort so hoch unmöglich schätzen,
Ich muss es anders übersetzen, 30
Wenn ich vom Geiste recht erleuchtet bin.
Geschrieben steht: Im Anfang war der Sinn.
Bedenke wohl die erste Zeile,
Dass deine Feder sich nicht übereile!

---

11 **erst** *first*
  Satz *(m.),* ¨-e *sentence, clause*
12 **Bibel** *(f.),* **-n** *Bible; Holy Scriptures*
  Szene *(f.),* **-n** *scene (theater play)*
13 **Zimmer** *(n.),* – *room*
  Goethe *Johann Wolfgang von Goethe (1749–1832)*
  Faust I *Goethe's first version of the Faust myth (published 1790)*
14 **Studierzimmer** *(n.),* – *study*
  suchen *to seek*
  Bücher *(pl.),* *books*
  Wissen *(n.)* *knowledge, learning*

15 **geschrieben steht** *(also:* **es steht geschrieben)** *it stands written; the words say* it is written
18 **für** *for*
19 **Sinn** *(m.)* *perception, thought*
20 **Kraft** *(f.),* ¨-e *power, strength*
21 **auch nicht aktiv genug** *not active enough either*
22 **Tat** *(f.),* **-en** *deed, act*
  denken *to think*
23 **mehr als** *more than*

35	Ist es der Sinn, der alles wirkt und schafft?
	Es sollte stehn: Im Anfang war die Kraft!
	Doch, auch indem ich dieses niederschreibe,
	Schon warnt mich was, dass ich dabei nicht bleibe.
	Mir hilft der Geist! Auf einmal seh' ich Rat
40	Und schreibe getrost: Im Anfang war die Tat!

Faust, Faust's Study

	'Tis written: "In the beginning was the Word!"
	Here now I'm balked! Who'll put me in accord?
	It is impossible, the Word so high to prize,
45	I must translate it otherwise
	If I am rightly by the Spirit taught.
	'Tis written: In the beginning was the Thought!
	Consider well that line, the first you see,
	That your pen may not write too hastily!
50	Is it then Thought that works, creative, hour by hour?
	Thus should it stand: In the beginning was the Power!
	Yet even while I write this word, I falter,
	For something warns me, this too I shall alter.
	The Spirit's helping me! I see now what I need
55	And write assured: In the beginning was the Deed!

KAPITEL 2

2.1 Case: Nominative and Accusative

Case is a grammatical phenomenon of which one need not be especially aware in order to read and understand a language such as English. German, however, has four distinct grammatical cases—nominative, accusative, dative, and genitive—which determine the function of the noun. We learn to differentiate among the cases and determine the function of the noun first of all by means of its definite article. The definite article, which also signals the gender and number of a German noun, indicates a noun's case by means of endings. The article assumes different forms in each of the cases and, thus, provides information that is key to understanding the noun's function and the overall meaning of the sentence. The forms of the definite article you learned in **Kapitel 1** were in the nominative case. We continue our declension below to include the accusative case.

		Singular		Plural
	Masculine	Feminine	Neuter	All genders
Nominative:	der	die	das	die
Accusative:	den	die	das	die

Since masculine articles exhibit a distinct change in the transition from nominative to accusative, they clearly indicate the masculine noun's function. Note, however, that feminine, neuter, and plural nouns have the same definite article in both nominative and accusative cases. Paying close attention to context will help you ascertain the case and function of plural nouns. See Appendix A for a complete overview of case endings (page 288).

A. Nominative

The nominative case indicates or names the subject and/or the predicate noun, also called the predicate nominative, in a sentence.

> **Der Mann** ist intelligent.
> *The man is intelligent.* (masculine subject)
> **Die Frau** arbeitet viel.
> *The woman works a lot.* (feminine subject)
> **Das Kind** singt und tanzt.
> *The child is singing and dancing.* (neuter subject)

Predicate nouns occur with the verbs **sein** *(to be)*, **werden** *(to become)*, and **heißen** *(to be called, be named)*. These verbs function like an equal sign indicating that the subject is equivalent to its predicate nominative.

> **Der Mann** ist **der Reporter.**
> *The man is the reporter.* (masculine subject and predicate)
> **Die Frau** wird **die** erste **Präsidentin.**
> *The woman is going to be the first president.* (feminine subject and predicate)
> **Der** erste **Präsident** heißt **der Vater** seines Landes.
> *The first president is called the father of his country.* (masculine subject and predicate)
> **Die Kinder** sind **die Zukunft.**
> *The children are the future.* (plural neuter subject and feminine predicate)

The nominative interrogative **wer** *(who)* is used for people and **was** *(what)* for things. The answer to the question will be the subject or the predicate noun.

> –**Wer** ist der Reporter? –**Der Mann** ist der Reporter.
> –**Was** sind die Kinder? –Die Kinder sind **die Zukunft.**

B. Accusative

In addition to a nominative subject, the following examples also have accusative direct objects. The direct object is the *target of the action* expressed in the verb.

> Der Student studiert **die Geschichte** von Berlin.
> *The student is studying the history of Berlin.*
> Das Buch beschreibt **die Situation** 1989 in Berlin.
> *The book describes the situation in Berlin in 1989.*
> Das Buch beschreibt auch **den Mauerfall.**
> *The book also describes the fall of the Wall.*
> **Den Mauerfall** versteht der Student, aber **die Situation** versteht er nicht. Der Student fragt **den Lehrer.**
> *The student understands the fall of the Wall, but he does not understand the situation. The student asks the teacher.*
> Der Lehrer erklärt **die Situation, die Mauer** und **den Mauerfall.**
> *The teacher explains the situation, the Wall, and the fall of the Wall.*

[handwritten margin note: word order not like English— endings help (if masculine)]

Context and grammatical endings help us identify subjects and direct objects. If a masculine singular noun is one of the actors in a sentence, grammatical endings identify the subject (**der** in the nominative) and the object (**den** in the accusative). Note how the inverted word order in the fourth example on the previous page—the direct object in the first position, followed by the verb in second position, followed immediately by the subject—emphasizes what it is that the student does and does not understand. Case signifiers plus context clarify the meaning of the sentence.

Context plays a more critical role in sentences where grammatical cues are ambiguous. For example: **Die Kinder lieben die Eltern** can mean: "The children love the parents," or "The parents love the children," as in "It's the children whom the parents love." Inversions (objects first followed by verb, then subject) are frequent and logical responses to German accusative interrogatives **wen** *(whom)* and **was** *(what)*.

> –Wen kennt die Studentin? –Den Lehrer kennt die Studentin.
> –Wen kennt der Lehrer nicht? –Die Studentin kennt der Lehrer nicht.
> –Was erklärt der Lehrer? –Den Mauerfall erklärt der Lehrer.
> –Wen lieben die Eltern? –Die Kinder lieben die Eltern.

2.2 Infinitive

Vocabularies and dictionaries normally list only the infinitive form of the verb, e.g., **gehen** *(to go)*, **kennen** *(to know)*, **sagen** *(to say)*, **liefern** *(to supply, deliver)*, **handeln** *(to act)*. These forms consist of a stem plus the ending **-en** or **-n**: geh + en, kenn + en, sag + en, liefer + n, handel + n.

Due to the close relationship of German and English, there are a large number of German and English infinitives that are nearly identical cognates (subtract the **-en** in German). You should recognize the following verbs readily.

beginnen	helfen	scheinen	springen
bringen	hören	schwimmen	starten
enden	kommen	senden	stinken
fallen	kosten	setzen	stoppen
finden	landen	singen	trinken
geben	lernen	sinken	wandern
gewinnen	salzen	sitzen	waschen
hängen			

Many German verbs ending in **-ieren** are cognates of English verbs with (nearly) identical stems. For example:

analysieren	funktionieren	protestieren
argumentieren	informieren	qualifizieren
debattieren	investieren	quantifizieren
demonstrieren	kombinieren	rationalisieren
dokumentieren	kommentieren	reparieren
dominieren	komplimentieren	rehabilitieren
evakuieren	komplizieren	studieren
evaluieren	nominieren	trainieren
fotografieren		

For a list of more cognates, see pages 6–7.

2.3 Present Tense of Regular Verbs

sagen   *to say*
ich sage   *I say, am saying, do say*
du sagst   *you say, are saying, do say*
er/sie/es sagt   *he/she/it says, is saying, does say*
wir sagen   *we say, are saying, do say*
ihr sagt   *you say, are saying, do say*
sie sagen   *they say, are saying, do say*
Sie sagen   *you say, are saying, do say*

antworten   *to answer*

ich antworte   *I answer, am answering, do answer*
du antwortest   *you answer, are answering, do answer*
er/sie/es antwortet   *he/she/it answers, is answering, does answer*
wir antworten   *we answer, are answering, do answer*
ihr antwortet   *you answer, are answering, do answer*
sie antworten   *they answer, are answering, do answer*
Sie antworten   *you answer, are answering, do answer*

A. Meanings

Note the three English meanings that equate to the German. When translating verbs, use the form that seems most appropriate to the context. Depending on the context, **Ich sage ...** may translate to *I say . . .* (general statement), *I do say . . .* (*yes/no* question), and/or *I'm saying . . .* (reaffirmation).

B. Endings

The present tense is formed from the stem of the infinitive. The infinitive ending is dropped and the personal endings are added. To find the meaning of a verb in the dictionary, look up the infinitive (verb stem plus **-en** or **-n**).

Verbs whose infinitive stems end in **-d-**, **-t-**, or in certain consonant clusters (**öffnen**, **regnen**) are conjugated like the verb **antworten**. An **-e-** precedes the endings **-st** and **-t**.

> Du antwort**est** auf Frage Nummer eins, und er antwort**et** auf Nummer zwei.
> *You answer question number one, and he answers number two.*
> Das Institut eröffn**et** im Sommer 2012 das neue Museum.
> *The institute will open the new museum in the summer of 2012.*
> (**Note**: present tense + future time implies future, i.e., *will . . .*)
> –Was machst du? –Ich öffn**e** das Buch.
> *–What are you doing? –I'm opening the book.*
> Es regn**et** viel im Frühjahr.
> *It rains a lot in spring.*
> Es regn**et** nie im Süden von Kalifornien.
> *It never rains in southern California.*

Verbs whose infinitive stem ends in **-s-**, **-ß-**, **-tz-**, or **-z-** drop the **-s** of the **-st** ending, so that the second- and third-person forms are identical in appearance.

> **heißen** *(to be called, named):* ich heiße, du heißt, er/sie/es heißt
> **sitzen** *(to sit):* ich sitze, du sitzt, er/sie/es sitzt

When the stem of the infinitive ends in **-el-** or **-er-**, e.g., **behandeln**, **liefern**, the first-person singular usually drops the **-e-** of the stem, and the first- and third-person plural endings of the verb are **-n**.

> **behandeln**   *to handle, treat*
>
> | | |
> |---|---|
> | ich behandle | wir behandeln |
> | du behandelst | ihr behandelt |
> | er/sie/es behandelt | sie/Sie behandeln |
>
> **liefern**   *to supply, deliver*
>
> | | |
> |---|---|
> | ich liefere | wir liefern |
> | du lieferst | ihr liefert |
> | er/sie/es liefert | sie/Sie liefern |

Das Theaterstück behandelt die Tragödie von Hamlet aus Ophe-
lias Perspektive.
The play treats Hamlet's tragedy from Ophelia's perspective.
Ich behandle in meinem Essay das Thema Hunger in Afrika.
In my essay I deal with the topic of hunger in Africa.
Die Firma liefert neue Medikamente.
The firm is delivering new medications.
Die NATO-Truppen liefern Essen und Waren an die Menschen
im Süden.
*The NATO troops are delivering food and supplies to the people
in the south.*

2.4 Present Tense of the Verb *haben* (to have)

haben

ich habe	wir haben
du hast	ihr habt
er/sie/es hat	sie/Sie haben

irregular { du hast / er/sie/es hat }

–Hast du eine große Familie, Johannes? –Ja, ich habe sieben
Geschwister. (Die Familie Bach hat acht Kinder.)
*–Do you have a large family, Johannes? –Yes, I have seven sib-
lings. (The Bach family has eight children.)*

2.5 Cardinal Numbers

0	null	10	zehn	20	zwanzig
1	ein(s)	11	elf	21	einundzwanzig
2	zwei	12	zwölf	30	dreißig
3	drei	13	dreizehn	40	vierzig
4	vier	14	vierzehn	50	fünfzig
5	fünf	15	fünfzehn	60	sechzig
6	sechs	16	sechzehn	70	siebzig
7	sieben	17	siebzehn	80	achtzig
8	acht	18	achtzehn	90	neunzig
9	neun	19	neunzehn	100	hundert

21 einundzwanzig | and 20

1 000	tausend
1 000 000	eine Million
1 000 000 000	eine Milliarde *(billion)*
1 000 000 000 000	eine Billion *(trillion)*

Grundwortschatz

all-	all, every		**Licht** (n.)	light
Arbeit (f.)	work		**machen**	to do, make, cause
arbeiten	to work		**Mann** (m.)	man, husband
behandeln	to handle, treat, deal with		**meist**	most
			Mensch (m.)	mankind, human being, person
bei	at			
Beispiel (n.)	example		**Monat** (m.)	month
betrachten	to observe		**nein**	no
Blut (n.)	blood		**neu**	new
Buch (n.)	book		**öffnen**	to open
denken	to think		**Pflanze** (f.)	plant
europäisch	European		**regnen**	to rain
Familie (f.)	family		**sterben (stirbt, starb)**	to die (dies, died)
fast	about, almost			
gebrauchen	to use, employ		**Tier** (n.)	animal
Geld (n.)	money		**ungefähr**	approximately
gesund	healthy		**untersuchen**	to examine, investigate
heißen	to be called, be named			
			versichern	to insure
heute	today		**viel**	much
jetzt	now		**viele**	many
kalt	cold		**Welt** (f.)	world
kennen	to know, be acquainted with		**wenig**	little, few
			wichtig	important
Kind (n.), **-er**	child		**Woche** (f.)	week
Kindheit (f.)	childhood		**z.B. (zum Beispiel)**	e.g. (for example)
leben	to live			
Leben (n.)	life			

 Lösungen zu Übungssätzen auf **academic.cengage.com/german/korb**

Übungssätze

1. Ein Jahr hat zwölf Monate, zweiundfünfzig Wochen und 365 Tage.
2. —Wie viel Geld hast du, Hans? —Ich habe wenig Geld, aber ich arbeite sehr viel. Wir alle arbeiten viel.
3. Man sagt: „Arbeit macht das Leben süß.“
4. Deutschland hat viele gute Universitäten. Ich denke z.B. an die Freie Universität Berlin oder an die Technische Hochschule in Darmstadt.

3. **süß** *sweet*   4. **denken an** *to think about*

5. Einige Studenten studieren Deutsch. Hanna studiert Spanisch, und sie lernt sehr schnell. Was studiert ihr? Studiert ihr Englisch, Spanisch oder Deutsch?

6. Ich studiere Wirtschaft und Geographie. Ich finde Geld und die Erde interessant und auch wichtig.

7. Gold und Silber haben heute einen hohen Wert.

8. Der Äquator hat eine Länge von 40 070 Kilometern. Ecuador liegt direkt am Äquator in Südamerika.

9. Kanada hat viele hohe Berge und schöne Seen. Das Wasser in den Seen ist kalt und klar.

10. Wir betrachten jetzt ein konkretes Beispiel. Öffnen Sie das Buch!

11. –Kennen Sie das Buch? –Nein, ich kenne das Buch nicht.

12. –Karl, kennst du den Mann? –Ja, ich kenne den Mann, er heißt Klaus Schumann.

13. –Wie heißen Sie? –Ich heiße auch Schumann, Marlena Schumann. Wer sind Sie?

14. Der Historiker untersucht jetzt eine wichtige Quelle. Er sucht neue Informationen.

15. Der Mensch verändert die Umwelt, und die Umwelt verändert den Menschen.

16. Die Schwedische Akademie in Stockholm wählt die Nobelpreisträger.

17. Die Nobelpreisträgerin für Medizin und Physiologie war 1995 die deutsche Professorin Christiane Nüsslein-Volhard.

18. Nüsslein-Volhard ist Direktorin am Max-Planck-Institut für Entwicklungsbiologie in Tübingen.

19. Alle europäischen Staaten gebrauchen das metrische System.

20. Die Amerikaner gebrauchen das metrische System viel weniger als die Europäer. Viele Amerikaner kennen das System überhaupt nicht.

---

6. **Wirtschaft** (*f.*) *economics*
7. **Wert** (*m.*) *value, price*
8. **Länge** (*f.*) *length*
9. **Berg** (*m.*), **-e** *mountain*
   See (*m.*), **-n** *lake*
10. **Öffnen Sie!** (*imperative form*) *Open!*
14. **Historiker** (*m.*) *historian*
    Quelle (*f.*) *source*

15. **verändern** *to change, alter*
   borrowed – from Yiddish **Mensch** (*m.*) *mankind* (**-en** *ending denotes accusative case*)
15. **Umwelt** (*f.*) *environment*
16. **wählen** *to choose, select*
    Nobelpreisträger (*pl.*) *Nobel Prize recipients*
18. **Entwicklungsbiologie** (*f.*) *developmental biology*
20. **überhaupt** *generally; at all*

JOHANN SEBASTIAN BACH: SEINE MUSIK UND SEINE FAMILIE

Johann Sebastian Bach ist besonders bekannt für seine Fugen und Kantaten. Der Musiker und Komponist wurde 1685 in Eisenach in Thüringen geboren. Sein Vater, Ambrosius Bach, war Hofmusiker. Ambrosius Bach und seine Frau Elisabeth hatten eine große Familie. Johann war das achte Kind. 5

Bachs Kindheit war hart: 1695 stirbt seine Mutter. Sechs Monate später stirbt auch sein Vater. Johann Sebastian lebt mit seinem Bruder Christoph. Christoph spielt Orgel in einer Kirche. Johann Sebastian besucht fünf Jahre die Lateinschule und lernt alte Sprachen, Logik, Mathematik, Rhetorik, Theologie und Musik. Im Jahr 1700 10 geht Bach dreihundert Kilometer zu Fuß nach Lüneburg und arbeitet zwei Jahre als Chorsänger. 1702 hat er seine erste Stelle als Organist.

Im Oktober 1707 heiratet Bach seine Cousine Maria Barbara. Bach wird Kapellmeister am Hof des Herzogs von Sachsen Weimar. 15 In Weimar schreibt der junge Komponist Orgelmusik und Kantaten. Zehn Jahre später wird Bach Konzertmeister am Hof des Fürsten

1 **besonders bekannt für** *especially known for/as*
 Fuge *(f.)*, **-n** *fugue*
2 **Kantate** *(f.)*, **-n** *cantata*
3 **Eisenach in Thüringen** *(town of) Eisenach in (eastern German principality of) Thuringia*
 geboren *(past participle) born*
4 **Hofmusiker** *(m.) court musician*
7 **später** *later*
 leben mit *lives with*
8 **Orgel** *(f.)*, **-n** *organ (mus.)*
 Kirche *(f.)*, **-n** *church*
9 **die Schule besuchen** *to visit/ attend school*
10 **im Jahr** *in the year*
11 **zu Fuß gehen** *to travel by foot*
 nach Lüneburg *to (the northwestern German town of) Lüneburg*

12 **Chorsänger** *(m.) singer in a choir*
14 **heiraten** *to marry*
15 **Kapellmeister** *(m.) music director, choral director*
 am Hof des Herzogs *at the court of the duke*
 Sachsen Weimar *(eastern German principality of) Saxe-Weimar*
16 **schreiben** *to write*
17 **werden (wird)** *to become (becomes)*
 Konzertmeister *(m.) concertmaster*
 am Hof des Fürsten *at the court of the prince*

von Anhalt-Köthen. In Köthen komponiert er die Brandenbur-
gischen Konzerte und das Orgelbüchlein.

20   Maria Barbara Bach stirbt im Sommer 1720. Ein Jahr später,
im Dezember 1721, heiratet Johann eine junge Sängerin, Anna
Magdalena Wilcken. Bach und seine zweite Frau hatten dreizehn
Kinder. Leider sterben sechs von den Kindern früh. Vier von Bachs
Söhnen werden später Musiker und Komponisten.

25   Im Jahr 1723 wird Bach in Leipzig Kantor. Hier komponiert er
die großen religiösen Werke: die Johannes- und die Matthäuspas-
sion, das Weihnachts- und das Osteroratorium. In Leipzig schreibt
Bach auch die große h-moll-Messe und fast dreihundert Kantaten.
Im Alter von fünfundsechzig Jahren starb Bach am 28. Juli 1750.

30 Heute spielt man Bachs Musik in Konzerthallen in der ganzen Welt.

18 **Anhalt-Köthen** *(eastern German principality of) Anhalt-Köthen*
19 **Orgelbüchlein** *(n.)* *Little Organ Book*
23 **leider** *unfortunately*
   früh sterben *to die young*
25 **Leipzig** *(eastern German city of) Leipzig*
   Kantor *(m.)*, **-en** *choirmaster*

26 **Werk** *(n.)*, **-e** *work*
27 **Weihnachts- und Osteroratorium** *(n.)* *Christmas Oratorium and Easter Oratorium*
28 **h-moll-Messe** *mass in B minor*
29 **im Alter (von)** *at the age (of)*

KAPITEL 3

3.1 Dative

Dative-case nouns function as indirect objects or as objects of so-called dative verbs, adjectives, or prepositions. The function of the dative noun is to indicate to whom or for whom something is done. The definite articles of singular dative nouns are **dem** for masculine, **der** for feminine, and **dem** for neuter. Plural dative-case nouns take the definite article **den** plus an **-(e)n** ending where possible. The dative interrogative **wem** means *to whom* or *for whom*.

	Singular			Plural
	Masculine	**Feminine**	**Neuter**	**All genders**
Nominative:	der	die	das	die
Accusative:	den	die	das	die
Dative:	dem	der	dem	den (+ **n**)

For a more complete overview of the German case system, see Appendix A, page 288.

A. Indirect object

The dative articles and nouns printed in boldface in the following sentences are examples of indirect objects. For assistance in identifying the gender and case of any of the other nouns, refer to the outline above.

> Der Professor gibt **der Studentin** den Artikel über die Ökologie.
> *The professor gives the article about ecology **to the student**.* or:
> *The professor gives **the student** the article about ecology.*
> Die Sonne gibt **der Erde** Wärme.
> *The sun gives **the earth** warmth.*
> Der Regisseur erklärt **dem Schauspieler** den Text. **Wem? Dem Schauspieler**.
> *The director explains the text **to the actor**. **To whom**? **To the actor**.*
> Wir zeigen **den Besuchern** das Parlament.
> *We are showing the parliament **to the visitors**.* or: *We are showing **the visitors** the parliament.*

Indirect-object nouns (dative nouns) precede direct-object nouns (accusative nouns) in German sentence structure. This may or may not be the case in the English translation where the regular German word order *(nominative subject noun + verb + dative indirect-object noun + accusative direct-object noun)* is translated with a prepositional phrase to indicate to whom or for whom the action is done. Pronouns can alter the sequential pattern. See **Kapitel 5** (pages 47–49) for details.

Some verbs occur with both an indirect (dative) and a direct (accusative) object. Common examples are **erklären** *(to explain)*, **geben** *(to give)*, **kaufen** *(to buy)*, **schenken** *(to present)*, **schicken** *(to send)*, **zeigen** *(to show)*.

In the following examples, ask yourself who is doing what to/for whom.

> Der Architekt zeigt dem Ingenieur die Pläne für das neue Haus.
> *The architect is showing the engineer the plans for the new house.* or: *The architect is showing the plans for the new house to the engineer.*
> Der Großindustrielle schenkt dem Staat das Grundstück.
> *The industrialist is giving the land to the government.*
> —Wem schicken Sie die Rechnung? —Ich schicke dem Industriellen die Rechnung.
> *—To whom are you sending the bill? —I'm sending the bill to the industrialist.*
> Die Kindergärtnerin kauft den Kindern die Eintrittskarten fürs Museum.
> *The preschool teacher buys tickets to the museum for the children.*

B. Dative verbs

German also has a number of *dative verbs* in which the act of giving something is implicit or the preposition *to* is understood. These situations result in a dative object.

> Ich helfe **dem Regisseur**.   *I help the director.*
> (= *I give help to the director.*)
> Wir danken **der Professorin**.   *We thank the professor.*
> (= *We give [our] thanks to the professor.*)
> Wir glauben **den Berichten**.   *We believe the reports.*
> (= *We put our belief in the reports.*)
> Die Bücher gehören **der Universität**.
> *The books belong to the university.*

Common verbs with dative objects are **antworten** *(to answer)*, **danken** *(to thank)*, **gefallen** *(to be pleasing to)*, **gehören** *(to belong to)*, **glauben** *(to believe)*, **helfen** *(to help)*, **schmecken** *(to taste)*, **zuhören** *(to listen to)*.

3.2 Genitive

The genitive case primarily denotes possession. Relations between possessed and possessor are indicated largely by genitive articles. The genitive article in German for masculine and neuter nouns is **des** and is accompanied most often by an **-(e)s** attached to the masculine or neuter noun. The genitive article for all feminine and plural nouns is **der**. Feminine and plural nouns have no special genitive ending. Schematically, the definite articles in the genitive case in German are as follows.

	Singular			Plural
	Masculine	**Feminine**	**Neuter**	**All genders**
Genitive:	des (+ **s**)	der	des (+ **s**)	der

See Appendix A, page 288 for an overview of the German case system.

The genitive articles **des**, **der**, **des**, **der** can be translated roughly as *of the*.

der Name **des** Künstlers   *the artist's name; the name of the artist*
das Werkzeug **des** Arbeiters   *the worker's tool*
die Bewegung **der** Erde   *the movement of the earth*
das Jahr **der** Frau   *the Year of the Woman*
die Farbe **des** Hauses   *the color of the house*
die Macht **der** Kirchen   *the power of the churches*
der Einfluss **der** Kirche   *the influence of the church*
die Meinung **der** Leute   *the people's opinion; the opinion of the people*
die Stimme **des** Volkes   *the voice of the populace (people)*

Articles and noun endings are essential keys to deciphering relationships between nouns in a German sentence. Once the reader recognizes the pattern *article + noun + article + noun,* it is a simple procedure to ascertain whether the pattern indicates possession (Hier ist **das Geld des Mannes**: the second article and noun are genitive) or an indirect/direct-object relationship (Ich gebe **dem Mann das Geld**: dative followed by accusative).

In dem Theaterstück schreibt der Autor über die Meinung **des Volkes** und die Macht **der Kirche**. (possession)
In the play the author writes about the opinion of the people and the power of the church.

Das Volk gibt **der Kirche das Geld**. (indirect/direct object)
The people give the money to the church.

Die Professorin fragt: „Wie heißt der Titel **des Stückes**?"
(possession)
The professor asks: "What is the title of the play?"

Der Student sagt **der Professorin den Titel**. (indirect/direct object)
The student tells the professor the title.

Das Stück heißt: „**Das Leben des Galilei**." (possession)
The book is called "The Life of Galileo."

Possession or a possessive relationship between German nouns (English *of the* or *'s*) is almost always expressed in the genitive case. Please note that the -**(e)s** ending may at first lead you to misidentify singular masculine or neuter nouns as plurals (because of the great frequency of the plural -*s* ending in English). The -**s** ending in German is rare as a plural ending. Be careful of this misconception when translating into English; do not mistake these singular genitive forms for plurals!

3.3 Plural of Nouns

Plural noun endings exhibit a much greater variety in German than is the case in English. Plural endings are best learned along with the gender and meaning of nouns when you first encounter them in your reading. It is not necessary, however, to memorize the plural ending of every noun in order to recognize the plural mode in most situations. In **Kapitel 1** you already encountered the most important rule for determining if the subject is singular or plural: *Subject and verb always agree in number*. Whenever you see a verb ending in -**en** or -**n** or the form **sind**, you know immediately that the subject is plural, with the exception of the formal, singular **Sie**.

It is also easy to recognize a plural noun in a dative situation because of the *double -n configuration*: The article ends in -**n** and the noun also ends (wherever possible) in -**n**. Plural genitive nouns have no ending.

Context is of key importance in recognizing whether accusative nouns are singular or plural.

In vocabularies and dictionaries you will generally find plurals indicated with the symbols given below in the right-hand column. Study the various plural endings and the symbols used to indicate them. Noting the plural form of nouns will assist you in becoming a more accurate reader and/or a more efficient translator.

Singular	Plural	Change	Dictionary symbol *KNOW THESE*
der Verfasser *author*	die Verfasser	no change	–
der Mantel *coat*	die Mäntel	umlaut added	¨
der Versuch *experiment*	die Versuche	**e** added	**-e**
der Sohn *son*	die Söhne	umlaut plus **e**	**¨e**
der Mann *man*	die Männer	umlaut plus **er**	**¨er**
das Bild *picture*	die Bilder	**er** added	**-er**
die Lehre *doctrine*	die Lehren	**n** added	**-n**
das Auto *auto*	die Autos	**s** added	**-s** *not common — used for borrowed nouns*
die Frau *woman*	die Frauen	**en** added	**-en**

3.4 *N*-nouns

Masculine nouns that take an **-(e)n** ending in the plural as well as in the singular in all cases but the nominative are often referred to as *n-nouns*. The positive, uninflected form of the *n-noun* occurs only as a subject or predicate nominative.

> Der Student ist ein guter Mensch. *Nominative, singular subject and predicate, **no** endings.*
> Die Studen**ten** sind gute Mensch**en**. *Nominative, plural subject and predicate, **with -en** ending.*

Wir suchen einen guten Menschen. *Accusative singular **with** -en ending.*

Wir suchen gute Studenten. *Accusative plural **with** -en ending.*

Wir helfen dem guten Menschen. *Dative singular, **with** -en ending.*

Wir helfen den Studenten. *Dative plural, **with** -en ending.*

Was ist der Name dieses Menschen? *Genitive singular, **with** -en ending.*

Was sind die Namen dieser Studenten? *Genitive plural, **with** -en ending.*

The inflected n-noun may look plural, so it is important to pay attention to its inflected article and function in the sentence. To help you be aware of this phenomenon, the vocabulary lists in this book indicate n-nouns.

Mensch (*m., n-noun*), **-en**   *human being; man, mankind*
Student (*m., n-noun*), **-en**   *student*

Most dictionaries list a masculine noun like **Mensch** as follows:

Mensch (*m.*), **-en**, **-en**   *human being; man, mankind*

Other common n-nouns include the following:

Advokat (*m., n-noun*), **-en**   *lawyer*
Affe (*m., n-noun*), **-n**   *ape*
Bär (*m., n-noun*), **-en**   *bear*
Bauer (*m., n-noun*), **-n**   *farmer*
Elefant (*m., n-noun*), **-en**   *elephant*
Fürst (*m., n-noun*), **-en**   *prince, ruler*
Hase (*m., n-noun*), **-n**   *hare*
Herr (*m., n-noun*), **-en**   *gentleman, lord*
Intendant (*m., n-noun*), **-en**   *theater director*
Komponist (*m., n-noun*), **-en**   *composer*
Löwe (*m., n-noun*), **-n**   *lion*
Nachbar (*m., n-noun*), **-n**   *neighbor*
Philosoph (*m., n-noun*), **-en**   *philosopher*
Präsident (*m., n-noun*), **-en**   *president*
Prinz (*m., n-noun*), **-en**   *prince*
Repräsentant (*m., n-noun*), **-en**   *representative*

3.5 Past Tense of Weak Verbs and of *haben*

literary past – *more common in written German* **spielen** *to play*	**antworten** *to answer*	**haben** *to have*
ich spielte	antwortete	hatte
du spieltest	antwortetest	hattest
er/sie/es spielte	antwortete	hatte
wir spielten	antworteten	hatten
ihr spieltet	antwortetet	hattet
sie/Sie spielten	antworteten	hatten

Weak verbs are verbs whose stem vowels do not change in the past tense, like the English verbs that take an *-ed* ending in the simple past: *to play—played; to answer—answered.* Strong verbs experience stem vowel changes in the past tense: *to sing—sang.*

The characteristic ending of the past tense of German weak verbs, such as **spielen**, is **-te**. Verbs whose stems end in **-d** or **-t** (e.g., **enden**, **antworten**) or in certain consonant clusters (e.g., **öffnen**, **regnen**) add an **-e-** in front of the past-tense ending.

Present
er spielt   wir öffnen   ihr antwortet   er hat   ich habe

Past
er spielte   wir öffneten   ihr antwortetet   er hatte   ich hatte

3.6 Meanings of the Past Tense

Just as in the present tense, German past tense may also have three English meanings. Use the one that best fits the context.

> Er spielte die Rolle von Galilei.
> *He played the role of Galileo.*
> *He was playing the role of Galileo.*
> Spielte er die Rolle gut?
> *Did he play the role well?*

antworten	to answer	**Luft** (f.), **⸚e**	air
bauen	to build	**Ökologie** (f.)	ecology
beantworten	to answer,	**Regisseur** (m.), **-e;**	director
	reply to	**Regisseurin**	(movie,
bedeuten	to mean, signify	(f.), **-nen**	theater)
Bedeutung (f.),	meaning,	**Römer** (m.), **–;**	Roman
-en	significance	**Römerin** (f.), **-nen**	
bekannt	(well-) known	**sagen**	to say
bezahlen	to pay	**Schauspieler** (m.),	actor/actress
danken	to thank	**–; Schauspielerin**	
dann	then	(f.), **-nen**	
dienen	to serve, be used	**Staat** (m.)	state, country,
	for		nation
einkaufen	to shop (for)	**Teil** (m.), **-e**	part
entdecken	to discover	**Teil** (n.), **-e**	piece
Entdeckung (f.), **-en**	discovery	**Versuch** (m.), **-e**	experiment,
erfinden	to invent		attempt
Erfindung (f.), **-en**	invention	**was für (ein)**	what kind of
erst	first, only	**Weltkrieg** (m.), **-e**	world war
Farbe (f.), **-n**	color	**wirtschaftlich**	economic,
Flüssigkeit (f.), **-en**	liquid		industrial
Forscher (m.), **–;**	researcher	**Wissenschaftler**	scholar,
Forscherin (f.),		(m.), **–;**	scientist
-nen		**Wissenschaftlerin**	
fragen	to ask	(f.), **-nen**	
gehören	to belong to	**wissenschaftlich**	scientific,
gestern	yesterday		scholarly
Idee (f.), **-n**	idea	**zählen**	to count
Jahrhundert (n.), **-e**	century	**die Zahl** (f.), **-en**	number
kaufen	to buy	**zahlen**	to pay
Lehre (f.), **-n**	teaching, theory	**zeigen**	to show

 Lösungen zu Übungssätzen auf **academic.cengage.com/german/korb**

Übungssätze

1. Wir leben in dem 21. Jahrhundert. Ein Jahrhundert ist ein Zeitraum von einhundert Jahren.
2. Die Länge eines Schaltjahres ist 366 Tage.
3. –Warum beantworteten Sie die Frage nicht? –Ich hatte keine Zeit und keine gute Antwort.

2. **Schaltjahr** (n.), **-e** *leap year*

4. Brecht erklärte den bekannten V-Effekt im Jahre 1929. „V" bedeutet „Verfremdung."

5. Brechts Lehre sagte: Der Schauspieler spielt eine Rolle, aber er identifiziert sich nicht mit der Rolle.

6. Der V-Effekt dient der Verfremdung des Zuschauers.

7. Brechts „episches Theater" revolutionierte die deutsche Bühne.

8. Der Volkswagen beeinflusste die Geschichte des 20. Jahrhunderts.

9. Das wirtschaftliche Ausmaß der Erfindung war bedeutend.

10. Ein Amerikaner bestätigte die Spaltung des Plutoniums. Er sagte: „Die Spaltung des Plutoniums verdanken wir den Forschern des Instituts."

11. Der Versuch machte den Forschern große Schwierigkeiten.

12. Friedrich der Große sagte: „Der Fürst ist der erste Diener des Staates."

13. Der Fürst lebte in Zeiten der Unruhe.

14. Der erste Teil des Buches behandelt den Ersten Weltkrieg.

15. Der Erste Weltkrieg dauerte ungefähr vier Jahre.

16. Die Römer besetzten viele Teile Europas. Den Einfluss der Römer findet man überall.

17. Die moderne Kunst ist den meisten Menschen unverständlich.

18. Was ist die Hauptrolle der Dozenten in einem Museum? Sie helfen dem Publikum.

19. Die Ideen Platons beeinflussten viele Philosophen der folgenden Jahrhunderte.

20. Die Parteien in einer parlamentarischen Monarchie treffen die Entscheidungen in allen Staatsgeschäften, und der Monarch ist der Repräsentant des Staates.

21. Ein Verkäufer in einer Buchhandlung verkauft Bücher.

22. –Was für Bücher verkaufen Sie? –Ich verkaufe Bücher über Kunstgeschichte und Theaterwissenschaft.

23. –Wie viel kostet das Buch? –Es ist billig, es kostet nur zehn Euro.

4. **Verfremdung** (f.), *alienation*
7. **Bühne** (f.), **-n** *stage*
8. **beeinflussen** *to influence*
9. **Ausmaß** (n.), **-e** *extent, impact*
10. **bestätigen** *to confirm*
    Spaltung (f.) *splitting*
11. **Schwierigkeit** (f.), **-en** *difficulty*
12. **Fürst** (m., *n-noun*), **-en** *prince, ruler*
    Diener (m.), **–** *servant*
13. **Unruhe** (f.), **-n** *unrest, upheaval*
15. **dauern** *to last*
16. **besetzen** *to occupy*
17. **unverständlich** *unintelligible*
18. **Hauptrolle** (f.), **-n** *main function*
    Dozent (m., *n-noun*), **-en** *docent*
20. **Partei** (f.), **-en** *political party*
    Entscheidungen treffen *to make decisions*
    Staatsgeschäft (n.), **-e** *government business or matter*
21. **Buchhandlung** (f.), **-en** *bookstore*
23. **kosten** *to cost*

Leben des Galilei: Ein Theaterstück in fünfzehn Bildern von Bertolt Brecht

Bild eins: Galileo Galilei, Lehrer der Mathematik zu Padua, will das neue kopernikanische Weltsystem beweisen.

Bild zwei: Galilei überreicht der Republik Venedig eine neue Erfindung.

5 Bild drei: *10. Januar 1610:* Vermittels des Fernrohrs entdeckt Galilei am Himmel Erscheinungen, welche das kopernikanische System beweisen. Von seinem Freund vor den möglichen Folgen seiner Forschungen gewarnt, bezeugt Galilei seinen Glauben an die menschliche Vernunft.

10 Bild vier: Galilei hat die Republik Venedig mit dem Florentiner Hof vertauscht. Seine Entdeckungen durch das Fernrohr stoßen in der dortigen Gelehrtenwelt auf Unglauben.

Bild fünf: Uneingeschüchtert auch durch die Pest setzt Galilei seine Forschungen fort.

15 Bild sechs: *1616:* Das Collegium Romanum, Forschungsinstitut des Vatikans, bestätigt Galileis Entdeckungen.

1 **Bild** (*n.*), **-er** *picture, scene*
Galileo Galilei *Italian mathematician, physicist, and astronomer (1564–1642)*
Padua *(Italian city of) Padua*
2 **will beweisen** *wants to prove*
3 **überreichen + *dativ*** *to hand over to*
5 **vermittels + *genitiv*** *by means of*
Fernrohr (*n.*) *telescope*
6 **am Himmel** *in the heavens/skies*
7 **Erscheinungen, welche ... beweisen** *occurrences which prove*
möglich *possible*
Folge (*f.*), **-n** *consequence*
8 **gewarnt von + *dativ*** *warned by*
gewarnt vor + *dativ* *warned about*

9 **seinen Glauben an die menschliche Vernunft bezeugen** *to declare his belief in human reason*
11 **hat x mit y vertauscht** *traded x for y*
Hof (*m.*), **¨e** *court*
durch + *akkusativ* *through*
12 **auf Unglauben stoßen** *run into disbelief*
in der dortigen Gelehrtenwelt *in the learned circles there*
13 **auch durch die Pest uneingeschüchtert** *not even scared off by the plague*
14 **setzt ... fort** *continues, carries on*
16 **bestätigen** *to confirm*

[handwritten margin note: mostly literative use]

Bild sieben: Aber die Inquisition setzt die kopernikanische Lehre auf den Index (5. März 1616).

Bild acht: Ein Gespräch.

Bild neun: Nach achtjährigem Schweigen wird Galilei durch die Thronbesteigung eines neuen Papstes, der selbst Wissenschaftler ist, ermutigt, seine Forschungen auf dem verbotenen Feld wieder aufzunehmen. Die Sonnenflecken.

Bild zehn: Im folgenden Jahrzehnt findet Galileis Lehre beim Volk Verbreitung.

Bild elf: *1633*: Die Inquisition beordert den weltbekannten Forscher nach Rom.

Bild zwölf: Der Papst.

Bild dreizehn: Galileo Galilei widerruft vor der Inquisition am 22. Juni 1633 seine Lehre von der Bewegung der Erde.

Bild vierzehn: *1633–1642:* Galileo Galilei lebt in einem Land-haus in der Nähe von Florenz, bis zu seinem Tod ein Gefangener der Inquisition. Die „Discorsi".

Bild fünfzehn: *1637.* Galileis Buch „Discorsi" überschreitet die italienische Grenze.

18 **auf den Index setzen** *to place on the Church's forbidden list*
19 **Gespräch** *(n.)*, -e *conversation*
20 **nach achtjährigem Schweigen** *after eight years of silence*
21 **durch die Thronbesteigung** *as a result of / through the crowning*
22 **wird ermutigt wieder auf dem verbotenen Feld** *in the forbidden field/area*
23 **aufzunehmen** is encouraged to take up again
23 **Sonnenflecken** *(pl.)* *sun spots*
25 **beim Volk Verbreitung finden** *to find acceptance among the people*
26 **beordern** *to order*
27 **nach Rom** *to Rome*
29 **widerrufen** *to recant*
30 **Bewegung** *(f.)* -en *movement*
32 **Gefangener** *(m.)* *prisoner, captive*
34 **überschreiten** *to cross over*
35 **Grenze** *(f.)*, -n *boundary, border*

KAPITEL 4

4.1 Indefinite Articles

The indefinite article **ein** (plus endings) corresponds in English to *a, an,* or *one.* In order to indicate case, **ein** takes the same case endings as the definite article (**den—einen, dem—einem, des—eines; die—eine, der—einer**) in all but the three forms boldfaced in the table below. Compare Appendix A on page 288.

	Singular		
	Masculine	**Feminine**	**Neuter**
Nominative:	**ein**	eine	**ein**
Accusative:	einen	eine	**ein**
Dative:	einem	einer	einem
Genitive:	eines (+ **s**)	einer	eines (+ **s**)

As with the definite articles, indefinite article endings provide key information regarding function and meaning of the noun. Note that, just like English, there is no plural. This means that indefinite plurals occur without an article.

4.2 *Kein* and Other *ein*-Words

Ein-words are limiting adjectives and are declined like **ein**. The other **ein**-words are the negative forms of the indefinite article **kein** (*no, not a*) and the possessive pronouns. These **ein**-words have singular and plural forms.

	Singular			Plural
	Masculine	**Feminine**	**Neuter**	**All genders**
Nominative:	**kein**	keine	**kein**	keine
Accusative:	keinen	keine	**kein**	keine
Dative:	keinem	keiner	keinem	keinen (+ **n**)
Genitive:	keines (+ **s**)	keiner	keines (+ **s**)	keiner

The primary forms of the possessive pronouns, listed on the next page according to singular and plural, identify the possessor. Like other limiting adjectives, their endings, which are identical to those for **kein**, identify the gender and function of the noun that is possessed.

Singular		Plural	
mein-	*my*	unser-	*our*
dein-	*your*	euer-	*your*
sein-	*his, its*	ihr-	*their*
ihr-	*her, its*	Ihr-	*your*

In addition to **kein** and the possessive pronouns, frequently occurring limiting adjectives are:

andere *(plural)   other, different*
Andere Länder, andere Sitten!
   Different countries, different customs!

einige *(plural)   some*
Einige Länder haben kostenlose Universitäten.
   Some countries have free universities.

mehrere *(plural)   several*
Mehrere Universitäten hier haben zu viele Studenten.
   Several universities here have too many students.

solch ein   *such a*
Solch ein Problem!
   Such a problem!

viele *(plural)   many*
Viele Studenten haben keine Wohnung.
   Many students have no place to live.

was für ein   *what kind of a*
Was für eine Universität suchen sie?
   What kind of a university are they looking for?

welch ein   *what a*
Welch ein Dilemma!
   What a dilemma!

wenige *(plural)   (a) few*
Wenige Leute haben eine gute Lösung.
   Few people have a good solution.

4.3 Irregular Forms in the Present Tense of Strong Verbs

	sehen	geben	laufen	fahren
	to see	*to give*	*to run*	*to drive, ride*
ich	sehe	gebe	laufe	fahre
du	**siehst**	**gibst**	**läufst**	**fährst**
er/sie/es	**sieht**	**gibt**	**läuft**	**fährt**
wir	sehen	geben	laufen	fahren
ihr	seht	gebt	lauft	fahrt
sie/Sie	sehen	geben	laufen	fahren

Vowel in stem changes (handwritten annotation)

Vowel changes occur in the second and third persons singular of some verbs. The most common vowel changes and the verbs that undergo these changes in the second and third persons singular of the present tense are the following ones.

Infinitive	English	du	er/sie/es
Vowel change: e to ie or i			
befehlen	*to order*	befiehlst	befiehlt
brechen	*to break*	brichst	bricht
empfehlen	*to recommend*	empfiehlst	empfiehlt
erschrecken	*to frighten*	erschrickst	erschrickt
essen	*to eat*	isst	isst
fressen	*to devour*	frisst	frisst
geben	*to give*	gibst	gibt
geschehen	*to happen*	–	geschieht
helfen	*to help*	hilfst	hilft
lesen	*to read*	liest	liest
messen	*to measure*	misst	misst
nehmen	*to take*	nimmst	nimmt
sehen	*to see*	siehst	sieht
sprechen	*to speak*	sprichst	spricht
stehlen	*to steal*	stiehlst	stiehlt
sterben	*to die*	stirbst	stirbt
treffen	*to meet, hit*	triffst	trifft
treten	*to tread, step*	trittst	tritt
verbergen	*to hide*	verbirgst	verbirgt
vergessen	*to forget*	vergisst	vergisst
werden	*to become*	wirst	wird
werfen	*to throw*	wirfst	wirft

exception to the exception: consonant of stem changes too (handwritten annotation pointing to nehmen)

Infinitive	English	du	er/sie/es
Vowel change: a to ä			
backen	*to bake*	bäckst	bäckt
empfangen	*to receive*	empfängst	empfängt
fallen	*to fall*	fällst	fällt
fahren	*to drive, ride*	fährst	fährt
fangen	*to catch*	fängst	fängt
halten	*to hold*	hältst	hält
laden	*to load*	lädst	lädt
lassen	*to allow, let*	lässt	lässt
raten	*to advise*	rätst	rät
schlafen	*to sleep*	schläfst	schläft
schlagen	*to hit*	schlägst	schlägt
tragen	*to carry, bear*	trägst	trägt
wachsen	*to grow*	wäch(se)st	wächst
waschen	*to wash*	wäsch(e)st	wäscht
Vowel change: au to äu ~ oi			
laufen	*to run*	läufst	läuft
saufen	*to drink, guzzle*	säufst	säuft
Vowel change: o to ö			
stoßen	*to push*	stößt	stößt

watch out for these (handwritten annotation pointing to wachsen/waschen)

Note that some dictionaries list strong and irregular forms only in an appended "Irregular Verb List," like the list in Appendix B on pages 292–295 of this book. Thus, if you do not recall that **spricht** means *speaks* and do not find the verb form in the alphabetical listing of your dictionary, check the irregular verb list for a verb beginning with **spr-**. In the column marked present indicative, you will find **spricht**. The infinitive is **sprechen**, which you will find listed in the dictionary proper.

4.4 Es gibt *there is, there are*

The expression **es gibt** means *there is* when it has a singular object or *there are* when the object is plural even though the subject **es** and the verb **gibt** always remain singular in form.

> Es gibt eine gute Universität in der Stadt.
> **There is** *a good university in the city. (singular object)*
> Es gibt einige Universitäten in der Stadt.
> **There are** *several universities in the city. (plural object)*

In questions or inverted word order, the subject **es** follows the verb:

> –**Gibt es** eine Hochschule in deiner Stadt? —Ja, in unserer Stadt
> **gibt es** mehrere guten Universitäten.
> *–Is there a university in your city? —Yes, there are several good*
> *universities in our city.*

For more examples and further information about the expression **es gibt** in other verb tenses see **Kapitel 26** and **30**.

4.5 Compound Nouns

One of the most salient features of German is its compound nouns, those "big long words" that you will quickly note when reading German. Here is a sampling taken from a **Studiumzulassungsantrag** (*application for permission to study*).

> das Wintersemester   *winter semester*
> die Hochschule   *university, institute of higher education*
> das Merkblatt   *leaflet, information sheet*
> Deutschkenntnisse   *knowledge of German*
> das Staatsexamen   *civil service examination*
> der Studiengang   *course of study*
> der Studienabschluss   *academic degree*
> der Geburtsort   *place of birth*
> das Geburtsdatum   *date of birth*
> die Staatsangehörigkeit   *citizenship*
> die Bundesrepublik   *Federal Republic*

Compound nouns are common in German because it is possible to form an almost unlimited number of word combinations. The combinations may consist of several nouns (occasionally with an **-s-** inserted between two nouns in the compound, as in **Staat-s-angehörigkeit**) or of nouns plus other modifying words (e.g., **Hochschule**). The key part of the compound is the final element, with the preceding elements usually functioning as modifiers.

As a rule of thumb for translating, follow these suggestions.

1. The final component of the compound noun becomes the first word in a literal English translation if both words are nouns: e.g., **die Korrespondenzadresse** = *address for correspondence (mailing address);* **die Postleitzahl** = *number that directs the mail (zip code).*

If the first component is an adjective, translate from left to right: e.g., **der Lieblingsprofessor** = *favorite professor;* **das Hauptfach** = *major field.*

2. If you need to look up the word and do not find it in the dictionary, look up each component and then create a logical meaning: don't be too literal!

3. The final component always determines the gender and plural ending of the compound.

Staat *(m.),* -en   *state, country*
Angehörigkeit *(f.),* -en   *status of belonging*
Staatsangehörigkeit *(f.),* -en   *citizenship*

Arbeit *(f.),* -en   *work*
Platz *(m.),* ⁼e   *place*
Arbeitsplatz *(m.),* ⁼e   *workplace*

When two or more compound nouns share an identical component—this can occur in the initial parts or in the final parts of the compounds—German uses a hyphen to avoid repetition.

Auf dem Studiumzulassungsantrag sind Fragen über **Geburtsort** und **-datum**.
On the application for admission to study there are questions about date and place of birth.

Ich studiere im **Winter-** und **Sommersemester** in der Bundesrepublik.
I am studying in both the winter and summer semesters in the Federal Republic.

Ich habe Fragen über mein **Haupt-** und **Nebenfach**.
I have questions about my major and my minor (courses of study).

4.6 Ordinal Numbers

German ordinals are indicated by the number followed by a period. Written out, the ordinals from **2.** *(second)* to **19.** *(nineteenth)* are formed by adding **-t** + *adjective ending* to cardinal numbers. From **20.** *(twentieth)* on, **-st** + *adjective ending* are added.

1. der/die/das   erste   *the first*
2.   zweite   *the second*
3.   dritte   *the third*

4.	vierte	*the fourth*
7.	siebte	*the seventh*
12.	zwölfte	*the twelfth*
19.	neunzehnte	*the nineteenth*
20.	zwanzigste	*the twentieth*
25.	fünfundzwanzigste	*the twenty-fifth*
30.	dreißigste	*the thirtieth*
100.	hundertste	*the hundredth*
101.	hunderterste	*the hundred-and-first*

Note that ordinal numbers in dates are usually indicated with numerals (using the number followed by a period), as in **der 3. Oktober 2008**, also commonly expressed as der **03.10.2008**. In German dates, the day appears first, followed by the month. In English, it is the opposite: first the month, then the day.

Grundwortschatz

also	*thus, therefore*	**Ihr**	*your*
ander-	*other, different*	**kurz**	*short*
Anfang *(m.),* **⁻e**	*beginning, origin*	**mein**	*my, mine*
aus	*out of, from*	**Mitarbeiter** *(m.),* **–;**	*coworker*
beschreiben	*to describe*	**Mitarbeiterin** *(f.),*	
betragen (beträgt)	*to amount to,*	**-nen**	
	come to, be	**nach**	*after, to*
bis	*until*	**Nebenfach** *(n.),*	*minor field*
Brief *(m.),* **-e**	*letter*	**⁻er**	*(of study)*
dein	*yours, your*	**nur**	*only*
dritt-	*third*	**schreiben**	*to write*
durch	*through, by*	**sehen (sieht)**	*to see*
enthalten (enthält)	*to contain,*	**sein**	*his, its (as*
	include		*pronoun, not*
essen (isst)	*to eat*		*verb)*
fallen (fällt)	*to fall*	**sondern**	*but (rather)*
Form *(f.),* **-en**	*form, shape, type*	**Sonne** *(f.),* **-n**	*sun*
frei	*free, unconnected*	**Stamm** *(m.),* **⁻e**	*tribe, stem*
für	*for, in favor of*	**Studium** *(n.),*	*studies at*
geben (gibt)	*to give*	**Studien**	*university*
es gibt	*there is,*	**über**	*over, about*
	there are	**Umwelt** *(f.)*	*environment*
Hauptfach *(n.),* **⁻er**	*major field (of*	**unser**	*our*
	study)	**verändern**	*to change*
heutig	*present*	**Volk** *(n.),* **⁻er**	*people, nation*
ihr	*her, its, their*		

Übungssätze

1. „Ein Gradmesser der Zivilisation eines Volkes ist die soziale Stellung der Frau." (Domingo F. Sarmiento 1811–1888, Argentinien)
2. Das Universalstimmrecht für Frauen in den USA hatte seinen Anfang mit dem neunzehnten Abänderungsantrag (1920). — *very specific honor for US gov. amendments*
3. Der dritte Paragraph enthält einen offensichtlichen Widerspruch. Da steht: „Der Mensch sieht seine eigenen Fehler nicht, nur die Fehler anderer Menschen."
4. „Der Mensch ist, was er isst", sagte Ludwig Feuerbach, ein deutscher Materialist des neunzehnten Jahrhunderts.
5. Mein Artikel beschreibt unsere neuen Versuchsergebnisse und ihre Bedeutung für die AIDS-Forschung.
6. Dein Mitarbeiter im Forschungszentrum bestätigte meine Resultate.
7. Er und seine Mitarbeiter untersuchten die Reaktion der T-Zellen.
8. Der Talmud enthält die Lehren und Gesetze für den jüdischen Gottesdienst, Vorschriften für die Lebensführung des jüdischen Volkes und geschichtliche, geographische und mathematische Lehren.
9. –Frau Doktor, wann beginnt Ihre Vorlesung? –Ich halte heute keine Vorlesung.
10. Heute schreibe ich meinem Vater und meiner Mutter einen langen Brief und beschreibe meine Afrikareise.
11. Im heutigen Afrika gibt es viele relativ neue Staaten, z.B. Simbabwe, Namibia oder Botswana.
12. Das Buch enthält eine kurze Geschichte der afrikanischen Stämme.
13. Wir verändern unsere Umwelt nicht nur durch unsere Tätigkeit, sondern auch durch unsere Untätigkeit.

1. **Gradmesser** *(m.)*, – *indicator* *(of the degree)*
   Stellung *(f.)*, **-en** *position*
2. **Universalstimmrecht** *(n.)*, **-e** *universal right to vote*
   Abänderungsantrag *(m.)*, **¨e** *amendment*
3. **offensichtlich** *obvious(ly)*
   Widerspruch *(m.)*, **¨e** *contradiction*
   eigen *own*
   Fehler *(m.)*, – *mistake, error*
5. **Versuchsergebnis** *(n.)*, **-se** *experimental result*

8. **Gesetz** *(n.)*, **-e** *law*
   jüdisch *Jewish*
   Gottesdienst *(m.)*, **-e** *religious service*
   Vorschrift *(f.)*, **-en** *rule*
   Lebensführung *(f.)*, **-en** *lifestyle*
9. **Vorlesung** *(f.)*, **-en** *lecture*
   halten (**hält**) *to hold*
13. **Tätigkeit** *(f.)*, **-en** *activity*
   Untätigkeit *(f.)*, **-en** *inactivity*

14. Die Niederschlagsmenge in den Bergen beträgt über tausend Millimeter. Dort fällt der erste Schnee des Winters.

15. Seine Arbeit beschreibt die Forschung eines Biologen über den Kuckuck in Mecklenburg-Vorpommern. Der junge Kuckuck wirft die Eier seiner Pflegeeltern aus ihrem Nest. Sie füttern ihr Adoptivkind, bis es aus dem Nest fliegt.

16. Deutschland hatte nach dem Ersten Weltkrieg über dreißig politische Parteien.

17. In totalitären Ländern gibt es keine Redefreiheit, in Demokratien ist die Redefreiheit die erste Freiheit.

18. Der Zweite Weltkrieg hatte seinen Anfang mit dem Einmarsch deutscher Truppen in Polen am 1. September 1939.

14. **Niederschlagsmenge** (*f.*), **-n** *amount of precipitation*
    Schnee (*m.*) *snow*
15. **Kuckuck** (*m.*), **-e** *cuckoo*
    werfen (wirft) *to throw*
    Ei (*n.*), **-er** *egg*
    Pflegeeltern (*pl.*) *foster parents*
    füttern *to feed*

15 **Adoptivkind** (*n.*), **-er** *adopted child*
17. **Redefreiheit** (*f.*), **-en** *freedom of speech*
18. **mit dem Einmarsch . . . in** *with the invasion . . . of*
    Truppe (*f.*), **-n** *troops*

 Leitfragen zum Lesetext auf **academic.cengage.com/german/korb**

KURZE GESCHICHTE DER DEUTSCHEN HOCHSCHULEN

Einige deutsche Universitäten sind sehr alt. Kaiser Karl IV. gründete die erste deutsche Universität im Jahre 1348 in Prag. Prag ist heute natürlich nicht in Deutschland, sondern in Tschechien. Die zweitälteste deutsche Universität ist in Wien
5 (1365), also auch nicht im heutigen Deutschland. Die älteste Hochschule Deutschlands ist die Universität Heidelberg (1386). Fast so alt ist die Universität Köln (1388). Mehrere andere

Title **Hochschule** (*f.*), **-n** *university, college (not: high school)*
2 **gründen** *to found*
4 **Tschechien** *Czech Republic*

4 **zweitältest** *second-oldest*
  Wien *Vienna*
7 **fast so alt** *nearly as old*

Universitäten nähern sich ihrer Sechshundertjahrfeier, zum Beispiel die Universitäten Leipzig (1409) und Rostock (1419). Es gibt auch einige ziemlich junge Universitäten, über 20 hatten ihren Anfang nach 1960. Die Otto-von-Guericke-Universität Magdeburg, im Jahre 1993 gegründet, gehört zu den jüngsten Universitäten Deutschlands.

Die Bundesrepublik hat heute über 2 Millionen Studenten und Studentinnen an mehr als 350 Universitäten, Gesamthochschulen, technischen Hochschulen und anderen Fachhochschulen, wie z.B., Musikhochschulen und pädagogischen Akademien. Das Gesicht von den Studierenden ist heute anders als in den ersten Jahren der Bundesrepublik. Einige Beispiele: Im Wintersemester 1952/53 kamen vier Prozent der Studienanfänger aus Arbeiterfamilien, im Jahre 2007 waren es rund 19 Prozent. Am Anfang der 50er Jahre waren ein Fünftel der Studenten Frauen. Am Anfang des 21. Jahrhunderts zählen die Studentinnen 50 Prozent. Das Gesicht ist heute auch internationaler: Im Jahre 2007 gab es 250 000 ausländische Studenten an deutschen Hochschulen.

8   **sich nähern**   *to approach*
    Sechshundertjahrfeier *(f.)*
    celebration commemorating six
    hundred years
10 **ziemlich**   *fairly, rather*
12 **gehört zu**   *belongs to*
14 **Bundesrepublik** *(f.)*   *Federal*
    Republic
15 **Gesamthochschule** *(f.)*, **-n**
    polytechnic university
16 **Fachhochschule** *(f.)*, **-n**   *advanced*
    technical college

17 **pädagogische Akademien**
    (pl.)   teachers' colleges
    Gesicht *(n.)*, **-er**   *face, look*
18 **von den Studierenden**   *of the*
    student body
20 **kommen (kamen)**   *to come (came)*
    Studienanfänger *(m.)*, **–**   *first-year*
    student
21 **rund**   *around, approximately*
22 **Fünftel** *(m.)*   *one fifth*
25 **ausländisch**   *foreign-born*

KAPITEL 5

5.1 *Der-* words

In addition to the definite articles that you learned in **Kapitel 1–3**, there are a number of pronouns that take the same case endings and, for that reason, are called **der-** words. These are the most frequently occurring **der-** words.

alle *(pl.)* *all*
beide *(pl.)* *both*
dieser *this, that, the latter*
jeder *each, every*
jener *that, the former*

mancher *many a*
manche *(pl.)* *some, several*
solcher *such*
welcher *which*

Case endings for the **der-** words follow this pattern.

	Singular			**Plural**
	Masculine	**Feminine**	**Neuter**	**All genders**
Nominative:	dieser	diese	dies(es)	diese
Accusative:	diesen	diese	dies(es)	diese
Dative:	diesem	dieser	diesem	diesen (**+ n**)
Genitive:	dieses (**+ s**)	dieser	dieses (**+ s**)	dieser

Alle, **beide**, and **manche** occur in combination with plural nouns.

When **jener** and **dieser** occur in the same sentence or sequence, they frequently mean *the former* and *the latter*.

> Washington und Lincoln waren amerikanische Präsidenten.
> **Jener** war der erste, **dieser** war der sechzehnte Präsident. Ihre
> Frauen hießen Martha Daindridge Washington und Mary
> Todd Lincoln. **Diese** lebte mit ihrem Mann im Weißen Haus
> zur Zeit des amerikanischen Bürgerkrieges (1860–1865), aber
> **jene** lebte nicht im Weißen Haus. Abigail Smith Adams, die
> Frau des zweiten Präsidenten, John Adams, wurde die erste
> Präsidentenfrau im Weißen Haus.
>
> *Washington and Lincoln were American presidents. The **former**
> was the first, the **latter** was the sixteenth president. Their wives'
> names were Martha Daindridge Washington and Mary Todd
> Lincoln. The **latter** lived with her husband in the White House
> at the time of the American Civil War (1860–1865), but the*

former did not live in the White House. Abigail Smith Adams, wife of the second president, John Adams, became the first presidential wife living in the White House.

5.2 Simple Past Tense of Strong Verbs

The preceding passage is written in the simple past tense and includes examples of both weak and strong verbs. The simple past consists of a verb stem plus endings. Note below the different endings on weak and strong verbs in the simple past.

	Weak	Strong		
	leben	**kommen**	**heißen**	**fahren**
	to live	*to come*	*to be called*	*to drive, ride*
ich	lebte	kam	hieß	fuhr
du	lebtest	kamst	hießt	fuhrst
er/sie/es	lebte	kam	hieß	fuhr
wir	lebten	kamen	hießen	fuhren
ihr	lebtet	kamt	hießt	fuhrt
sie/Sie	lebten	kamen	hießen	fuhren

Strong verbs have no ending in the first and thirdpersons singular. A stem-vowel change is characteristic of strong verbs in the simple past. Many types of vowel changes occur in the strong verb stems, but not all of these forms are listed as separate entries in a dictionary. Information about the strong verbs can be found in the strong and irregular verb list. If you cannot find a verb form in your vocabulary, check the list of irregular verbs in Appendix B (pages 292–295) to determine the infinitive that you will find in the vocabulary and dictionary.

The vocabulary at the back of this book indicates vowel changes for each strong verb listed. In **sehen (sah, gesehen; sieht)**, **sehen** is the infinitive, **sah** is the simple past, and **gesehen** is the past participle[1]; **sieht** is the third-person present-tense form resulting from a vowel change. Note the important variation in this listing: **finden (fand, gefunden)**. Here you are told that **finden** is the infinitive, **fand** the simple past, **gefunden** the past participle; however, there is no vowel change in the third-person present tense.

When no vowel changes are indicated, it means that the verb is weak and takes the simple past endings you learned in **Kapitel 3**.

---

1. See **Kapitel 9** regarding the past participle used to express the perfect tenses.

5.3 Irregular Weak Verbs

A small number of weak verbs are irregular. Like strong verbs, such irregular weak verbs have a vowel change in the simple past (as well as in the past participle that you will learn about beginning in **Kapitel 9**). Unlike strong verbs, irregular weak verbs take the same endings in the simple past as regular weak verbs.

The most common irregular weak verbs are listed below with their singular and plural endings in the simple past tense.

bringen *to bring*	ich brachte	er brachte	wir brachten
denken *to think*	ich dachte	er dachte	wir dachten
brennen *to burn*	ich brannte	er brannte	wir brannten
kennen *to know (a person)*	ich kannte	er kannte	wir kannten
nennen *to name*	ich nannte	er nannte	wir nannten
rennen *to run*	ich rannte	er rannte	wir rannten
wissen *to know (a fact)*	ich wusste	er wusste	wir wussten

5.4 Present and Simple Past Tense of *werden* (to become)

	Present	Simple past
ich	werde	wurde/ward
du	wirst	wurdest/wardst
er/sie/es	wird	wurde/ward
wir	werden	wurden
ihr	werdet	wurdet
sie/Sie	werden	wurden

(handwritten annotations: Contemporary; archaic — found in Bible; archaic but found in a bit!)

The form **ward** is archaic, but it still may be found occasionally, for example in a biblical passage.

Und Gott sprach: Es werde Licht! Und es ward Licht.
And God said, let there be light! And there was light.

Contemporary past-tense forms of **werden** are frequently used.

> Abigail Smith Adams wurde die erste Präsidentenfrau im Weißen Haus.
> *Abigail Smith Adams became the first presidential wife in the White House.*
> 200 Jahre später wurde die Geschichte der Präsidentenfrauen zu einem Lieblingsthema von Hillary Rodham Clinton.
> *Two hundred years later, the history of the First Ladies turned into a favorite topic of Hillary Rodham Clinton's.*
> Am Nachmittag wurde das Wetter kalt, und der Regen wurde zu Schnee. Die Straßen wurden zu einem Chaos.
> *In the afternoon it got cold, and the rain turned to snow. The streets turned into chaos.*

Note that the combination of **werden + zu** is best translated *to turn (in)to*.

5.5 Word Order

A. Position of verb

In a German statement the conjugated verb is always in the second position. The main verb always agrees in number with its subject.

In addition to the second position in a German statement—the conjugated (main) verb—the most important position in the German sentence is the final position. Always read the German sentence to the end before translating. Important elements commonly found in the final position include:

a. Negation (**Kapitel 6**)
b. Predicate adjectives (see **Kapitel 7**)
c. Verb prefixes (see **Kapitel 8**)
d. Compound verb components (see **Kapitel 9, 12–14, 16**)
e. Conjugated verbs in subordinate clauses (see **Kapitel 18** and C3 below)

B. Word order formula

Because of the set positions for German verbs and the gender/case indicators on all German nouns, German word order is often very different from English word order.

Reduced to a simplified formula, the word order in a German sentence may be stated as follows:

Sentence Formula: <u>X V1 s do io S Adverbs IO DO V2</u>
time/manner/place

Where:

X = one of the lexical items placed in the first position to emphasize it
V1 = conjugated (main) **V**erb
lower case **s** = pronouns functioning as **s**ubject
lower case **do** = pronouns functioning as **d**irect **o**bject
lower case **io** pronouns functioning as **i**ndirect **o**bject
upper case **S** = nouns functioning as **S**ubject

Adverbs generally occur in the sequence **time** / **manner** / **place** and are often prepositional phrases

upper case **IO** = nouns functioning as **I**ndirect **O**bject
upper case **DO** = nouns functioning as **D**irect **O**bject
V2 = **V**erb component completing the conjugated V1

Please note: Not every lexical item occurs in every sentence; adverbs of negation and particles are not taken into consideration in this simplified formula.

C. Word order types

There are three basic variations of this word order formula: normal, inverted, and dependent.

1. *Normal word order* means that the subject and its modifiers are in the first position. The conjugated verb follows in second position followed by its modifiers:

   1) S V1 Adverb DO
      Präsident Roosevelt verkündete im Jahre 1941 die vier Freiheiten.
      President Roosevelt proclaimed the Four Freedoms in 1941.

   2) s V1 do Adverb IO V2
      Er hat sie in einer Radiorede dem amerikanischen Publikum vorgestellt.
      He presented them to the American public in a radio speech.

2. *Inverted word order* occurs when the conjugated verb in second position precedes the subject. Any other element (except the subject or a conjunction) holds the first position and precedes the verb:

   1) Adverb V1 S DO
      Im Jahre 1941 verkündete Präsident Roosevelt die vier Frei-heiten.
      In 1941, President Roosevelt proclaimed the Four Freedoms.

   2) DO V1 S Adverb
      Die vier Freiheiten verkündete Präsident Roosevelt im Jahre 1941.
      President Roosevelt proclaimed the Four Freedoms in 1941.
      (also: *The Four Freedoms were proclaimed by President Roosevelt in 1941.*)

   3) IO V1 s do Adverb V2
      Dem amerikanischen Publikum hat er sie in einer Radiorede vorgestellt.
      He presented them to the American public *in a radio speech.*
      (Note emphasis: *To the* American public, *he presented them in a radio speech.*)

3. *Dependent word order* (see **Kapitel 18**) looks very different. Commas set off a dependent clause from the main clause, and the conjugated verb in the clause is in the *final* position. The dependent clause is introduced by a subordinating conjunction, followed by the subject and its modifiers, and closed by the conjugated verb in the final position of the dependent clause:

   1) s V1 Adverb // Subordinating Conjunction S Adverb DO V1
      Wir lernen in diesem Buch, dass Präsident Roosevelt im Jahre 1941 die vier Freiheiten verkündete.
      In this book we learn that President Roosevelt proclaimed the Four Freedoms in 1941.

   2) Adverb V1 io S // Subordinating Conjunction S do io Adverb V2 V1
      In seinem Buch erklärt uns der Autor, warum Roosevelt sie uns in einer Radiorede vorgestellt hat.
      In his book the author explains to us why Roosevelt presented them to us in a radio speech.

D. Translation hints

When a German sentence has normal word order, read the entire sentence, then translate the subject first followed by the verb (see example C1).

When a German sentence begins with an adverb or adverbial phrase, translate the adverb or phrase first, then the subject and verb (see example C2).

When a direct object begins a German sentence, translate the subject first followed by the verb. Alternatively, you may begin with the object and follow with a passive construction (example C2).

Should an indirect object be the initial element, it is best to begin with the subject (example C2).

Note that in spite of the variable word order in the German sentence, the main verb always remains in position two. The word order does not greatly alter the English translation (compare examples in C1, C2, and in the subordinate clause in C3).

Grundwortschatz

alle	*all*	**leben**	*to live*
als	*as, when, than*	**letzt**	*last*
auf	*on, upon*	**Lösung** *(f.)*, **-en**	*solution*
beginnen (begann)	*to begin*	**manch**	*some, many a*
beide	*both*	**mehr**	*more*
bringen (brachte)	*to bring*	**mit**	*with*
dieser	*this, the latter*	**nun**	*now*
Entwicklung *(f.)*, **-en**	*development*	**schaffen (schuf)**	*to create*
Ergebnis *(n.)*, **-se**	*result*	**schnell**	*rapid, fast*
erklären	*to explain*	**so**	*so, such*
etwa	*about, perhaps*	**solch**	*such*
Fluss *(m.)*, **Flüsse**	*river*	**Stadt** *(f.)*, **ᵂe**	*city*
Gebiet *(n.)*, **-e**	*area, region, field*	**stark**	*strong*
Gegend *(f.)*, **-en**	*region, district*	**steigen (stieg)**	*to rise, climb*
Jahrzehnt *(n.)*, **-e**	*decade*	**verschieden**	*various, different*
jeder	*each, every*	**von**	*of, from*
jener	*that, the former, the one*	**vor**	*before, ago*
		werden	
Kirche *(f.)*, **-n**	*church*	(**wurde; wird**)	*to become*
kommen (kam)	*to come*	**ziehen (zog)**	*to move, pull*
Krieg *(m.)*, **-e**	*war*	**zwischen**	*between*

Übungssätze

1. Das erste Buch Moses beginnt: „Am Anfang schuf Gott Himmel und Erde. Und die Erde war wüst und leer, und es war finster auf der Tiefe; und der Geist Gottes schwebte auf dem Wasser. Und Gott sprach: Es werde Licht! Und es ward Licht. Und Gott sah, dass das Licht gut war. Da schied Gott das Licht von der Finsternis und nannte das Licht Tag und die Finsternis Nacht. Da ward aus Abend und Morgen der erste Tag."

2. Die zwei Städte—Magdeburg und Halle—waren im Mittelalter wichtige Zentren. Diese war eine Salzstadt, jene war eine Kaiser- und Bischofsstadt. Beide Städte spielen auch heute eine große Rolle im politischen Leben der Gegend.

3. 1990 wurde Magdeburg die Landeshauptstadt von Sachsen-Anhalt. Vor der Wende war Halle die Hauptstadt dieses Landes im Osten.

4. In der Nachbarstadt Eisleben lebte und starb Martin Luther (1483–1546). Seine 95 Thesen schlug er im Jahre 1517 an die Tür der Schlosskirche zu Wittenberg.

5. In Wittenberg arbeitete im 16. Jahrhundert auch die berühmte Malerfamilie Cranach. Der Vater schuf religiöse Bilder wie z.B. „Ruhe auf der Flucht nach Ägypten" (1504).

1. **Himmel und Erde** *heaven and earth*
   wüst *barren*
   leer *empty*
   finster *dark*
   auf der Tiefe *in the deep*
   Geist (*m.*), **-er** *spirit*
   schweben *to hover*
   scheiden (schied) *to separate, divide*
   Finsternis (*f.*), **-se** *darkness*
2. **Mittelalter** (*n.*) *middle ages*
   Zentrum (*n.*), **Zentren** *center*
   Salzstadt (*f.*) *city that produced salt*
   Kaiser- und Bischofsstadt (*f.*), **¨e** *imperial and ecclesiastical city*
   eine große Rolle spielen *to play a big role*
3. **Landeshauptstadt** (*f.*), **¨e** *state capital*
   Sachsen-Anhalt (*Eastern German state of*) *Saxony-Anhalt*

3. **Wende** (*f.*), **-n** (*turning point*) *the fall of the Berlin Wall, 1989*
   im Osten (*m.*) *in the East*
4. **Nachbarstadt** (*f.*), **¨e** *neighboring city*
   Eisleben (*Eastern German city of*) *Eisleben*
   schlagen (schlug; schlägt) *to fasten to, nail to, hit*
   Tür (*f.*), **-en** *door*
   Schlosskirche *Castle Church* (*built in 1490–1511 in Wittenberg*)
5. **berühmt** *famous*
   Maler (*m.*), **–** *painter*
   Cranach (Lucas, Sr.) *Cranach* (*1472–1553*)
   Bild (*n.*), **-er** *picture*

6. In der Kunst der Renaissance trat die Darstellung des Menschen und seiner Umwelt in den Vordergrund. Die Schönheit des menschlichen Körpers wurde wichtig.
7. Die Arbeiten von Aerodynamikern in den letzten Jahrzehnten des zwanzigsten Jahrhunderts bestätigten manche alten Theorien, aber viele überstanden diesen Test nicht.
8. Die Zahl der Einwohner in Kalifornien stieg in den letzten Jahrzehnten sehr schnell an. Solch ein Zuwachs brachte manche komplizierte, soziale Entwicklungen.
9. Die Lösung dieses Problems ist schwierig aber nicht unmöglich.
10. Mancher Politiker sprach von „einer Umwertung aller Werte". Es klang wie Nietzsche.
11. Friedrich Nietzsche empfand den Niedergang des Menschen und forderte ein neues, kräftiges und starkes Menschengeschlecht, den „Übermenschen". Er sprach auch von der Umwertung aller Werte.
12. Nach dem Regen wurde das Wasser des Flusses trüb.
13. Die Überflutungen in manchen Gegenden zerstörten Häuser. Getreide- und Maisfelder standen unter Wasser.
14. Der Präsident verkündete in den Überflutungsgebieten den Notzustand.
15. Nach jedem Versuch schrieb der Forscher die Ergebnisse in sein Notizbuch.
16. Den Studenten erklärte Einstein nicht alle Einzelheiten seiner Theorie. Solche Details waren einfach zu kompliziert.

6. **Darstellung** (f.), **-en** *portrayal*
   Vordergrund (m.), **-̈e** *foreground*
7. **bestätigen** *to confirm*
   überstehen (überstand) *to withstand*
8. **Zuwachs** (m.) *growth*
9. **schwierig** *difficult*
   unmöglich *impossible*
10. **„Umwertung aller Werte"** *"reevaluation of all values"*
   klingen (klang) *to sound*
11. **empfinden (empfand)** *to feel, sense*
   Niedergang (m.) *decline*
   fordern *to demand, advocate*
   kräftig *powerful, vigorous*

11. **Geschlecht** (n.), **-er** *race*
   Übermensch (m., n-noun), **-en** *superman*
12. **Regen** (m.), **–** *rain*
   trüb *muddy, cloudy*
13. **Überflutung** (f.), **-en** *flood*
   zerstören *to destroy*
   Getreide- und Maisfelder *grain and corn fields*
14. **verkünden** *to declare*
   Notzustand (m.), **-̈e** *state of emergency*
15. **Notizbuch** (n.), **-̈er** *notebook*
16. **Einzelheit** (f.), **-en** *detail*
   einfach *simple, simply*
   kompliziert *complicated, complex*

17. Der Dreißigjährige Krieg (1618–1648) begann als Religionskrieg zwischen Protestanten und Katholiken, wurde aber später mehr und mehr zum Krieg um Macht- und Ländergewinn.
18. Der Physiker Otto von Guericke war Bürgermeister in Magdeburg und demonstrierte 1663 mit seinen „Magdeburger Halbkugeln" die Wirkung des Luftdrucks.

17. **später** *later*
um Macht- und Ländergewinn
for the gain of power and territories

18. **Halbkugel** *(f.)*, **-n** *hemispheric pump mechanism*
Wirkung *(f.)*, **-en** *effect*
Luftdruck *(m.)*, **⸚e** *air pressure*

 Leitfragen zum Lesetext auf **academic.cengage.com/german/korb**

ERZBISTUMSSTADT MAGDEBURG

Im Jahre 937 gründete Kaiser Otto I. (936–973) in Magdeburg eine Benediktinerabtei. Schon 968 wurde die Stadt zum Erzbistumssitz, und der Erzbischof von Magdeburg übersah fünf katholische Bistümer. Magdeburg war auch Ottos Lieblingsresidenz und „Otto der Große"—Begründer des Heiligen Römischen Reiches—liegt im Magdeburger Dom begraben. 5

Im Jahre 1207 brannte die ursprüngliche ottonische Kirche. Zwischen 1209 und 1363 baute man an dem neuen Dom—dem ersten gotischen Sakralbau auf deutschem Boden—und vollendete die Türme 1520. 10

Im Laufe der Zeit bekam das Erzbistum Magdeburg immer mehr kleinere Territorien und im späten Mittelalter wurde es ein relativ großer geistlicher Staat. 1513 wurde der Hohenzollern Albrecht

Title **Erzbistum** *(n.)*, **⸚er** *archbishopric*
1 **Kaiser** *(m.)*, **–** *emperor*
2 **Abtei** *(f.)*, **-en** *abbey*
schon 968 *already in (the year) 968*
3 **Erzbischof** *(m.)*, **⸚e** *archbishop*
übersehen (übersah, übersieht) *to oversee*
4 **Lieblingsresidenz** *(f.)*, **-en** *favorite residence*
6 **Heiliges Römisches Reich** *Holy Roman Empire*
Dom *(m.)* *cathedral*
begraben *buried*
7 **brennen (brannte)** *to burn*

7 **ursprünglich** *original*
8 **bauen an** + ***dative*** *to build on*
9 **Sakralbau** *(m.)* *religious building*
Boden *(m.)* *ground, territory*
vollenden *to complete*
10 **Turm** *(m.)*, **⸚e** *tower, steeple*
11 **im Laufe der Zeit** *in the course of time*
bekommen (bekam) *to get, obtain*
immer mehr *more and more*
12 **Mittelalter** *(n.)* *Middle Ages*
13 **geistlicher Staat** *ecclesiastical principality*
Hohenzollern *(German royal family, 1415–1918)*

von Brandenburg zum Erzbischof von Magdeburg. Sein Hof in der
Nachbarstadt Halle war sehr aufwendig und bald erlebte der
neue Erzbischof Geldnöte. Albrecht verkaufte in Deutschland
Ablassbriefe für den Papst. Die Kritik an dieser Praxis führte zur
Reformation.

In der Zeit der Reformation gab es viele soziale und religiöse
Kämpfe. Besonders brutal war der Bauernkrieg (1525). Im Jahre
1541 verließ Albrecht Halle und Magdeburg. Der Magdeburger
Dom wurde 1561 evangelisch. So endete die lange Entwicklung der
geistlichen Fürstentümer in der Gegend. Das war aber nicht das
Ende von religiösen Kämpfen in Magdeburg.

Der Dreißigjährige Krieg (1618–1648) brachte Magdeburg großes
Chaos und unzählige Tote. Am 20. Mai 1631 besetzten General
Tilly und seine kaiserlichen Truppen Magdeburg und verbrannten
die Stadt. 20 000 Menschen starben. Das „weinende Magdeburg"
wurde zu einem Symbol des Leidens im Dreißigjährigen Krieg.

14	**Hof** *(m.)*, **⁼e**	*court*
15	**aufwendig**	*expensive*
	erleben	*to experience*
16	**Geldnöte** *(pl.)*	*money shortages*
	verkaufen	*to sell*
17	**Ablassbrief** *(m.)*, **-e**	*letter of indulgence*
	Papst *(m.)* **⁼e**	*pope*
	führen zu	*to lead to*
19	**in der Zeit**	*in the time period*
	es gab	*there was/were*
20	**Kampf** *(m.)*, **⁼e**	*battle, struggle*
	besonders	*especially*
20	**Bauernkrieg** *(m.)*	*Peasants' War (1524/25)*
21	**verlassen (verließ; verlässt)**	*to leave*
23	**geistlich**	*religious, church*
	Fürstentum *(m.)*, **⁼er**	*principality*
26	**unzählig**	*innumerable*
	Tote *(m., f.)*	*dead person*
	besetzen	*to occupy (military)*
27	**kaiserlich**	*imperial*
	verbrennen (verbrannte)	*to burn*
28	**weinend**	*crying, wailing*
29	**Leiden** *(n.)*, **–**	*suffering*

WIEDERHOLUNG 1

DEUTSCHLAND

Die Bundesrepublik Deutschland liegt im Herzen Europas. Sie ist umgeben von neun Nachbarstaaten: Dänemark im Norden, den Niederlanden, Belgien, Luxemburg und Frankreich im Westen, der Schweiz und Österreich im Süden und von Tschechien und Polen im Osten.

Das Staatsgebiet der Bundesrepublik Deutschland ist rund 357 000 km² groß. Die Grenzen der Bundesrepublik haben eine Länge von insgesamt 3 758 km. Deutschland zählt rund 81 Millionen Einwohner. Italien hat 58, Großbritannien 57 und Frankreich 56 Millionen Menschen. Flächenmäßig ist Deutschland kleiner als Frankreich mit 544 000 und Spanien mit 505 000 Quadratkilometern.

1 **liegen (lag)** *to lie, be located*
im Herzen *in the heart, in the center*
2 **umgeben von (umgab; umgibt)** *surrounded by*
Nachbarstaat *(m.)*, **-en** *neighboring country*

6 **Staatsgebiet** *(n.)*, **-e** *state territory*
7 **Grenze** *(f.)*, **-n** *boundary, border*
8 **von insgesamt** *totaling*
9 **Einwohner** *(m.)*, **–** *inhabitant*
10 **flächenmäßig** *according to surface measure*
kleiner als *smaller than*

DIE LANDSCHAFTEN

Deutschland hat drei große Landschaftszonen: das norddeutsche Tiefland, das deutsche Mittelgebirge und das Alpengebiet. Das norddeutsche Tiefland ist die Fortsetzung des nordfranzösischen Tieflandes. Im Osten des norddeutschen Tieflandes ist das osteuropäische Tiefland. Die höchsten Erhebungen erreichen eine Höhe von 200 bis 300 m. Im norddeutschen

Title **Landschaft** *(f.)*, **-en** *landscape*
1 **Landschaftszone** *(f.)*, **-n** *geographic region*
2 **Tiefland** *(n.)*, **⁻er** *lowland*
Mittelgebirge *(n.)*, **–** *central chain of mountains*

3 **Alpengebiet** *(n.)*, **-e** *Alpine region*
Fortsetzung *(f.)*, **-en** *continuation*
5 **höchst-** *highest*
6 **Erhebung** *(f.)*, **-en** *elevation*
erreichen *to attain*
Höhe *(f.)*, **-n** *height*

Flachland gibt es viele Seen und Moore, Sand- und Schotter-
flächen.

Die deutschen Mittelgebirgslandschaften sind sehr mannigfaltig.
10 In diesem Teil Deutschlands finden wir viele Wälder und niedere
Berge. Die höchsten Erhebungen erreichen eine Höhe von 1600 m.

Die Alpen sind im Süden des Landes. Der höchste Berg ist die
Zugspitze (2968 m). In diesem Gebiet sind zahlreiche Gebirgsseen,
Flüsse und Wälder. Viele Touristen besuchen das Alpengebiet.

---

7 **Flachland** (*n.*), **⸚er** *lowland,*
flatland
See (*m.*), **-n** *lake*
Moor (*n.*), **-e** *swamp, moor*
Schotter (*m.*), **–** *stone, slag, rock*
8 **Fläche** (*f.*), **-n** *area, surface*

9 **mannigfaltig** *varied, manifold*
10 **Wald** (*m.*), **⸚er** *forest, woods*
nieder *low*
13 **zahlreich** *numerous*
14 **besuchen** *to visit*

DIE GESCHICHTE

Die Sprache der Bewohner Deutschlands gehört zum germanischen Zweig der indogermanischen Sprachfamilie. Um
Christi Geburt besetzten die Römer Teile des Landes. Die
Bayern, Alemannen, Sachsen und Friesen kamen während der
5 Völkerwanderung des dritten bis fünften Jahrhunderts in ihre heutigen Gebiete. Die Franken zogen weiter nach Westen.

Wir finden den Anfang des „deutschen" Staates im groß-
fränkischen Reich Karls des Großen (768–814). Im Jahre 800   *Charlemagne*
krönte der Papst Karl den Großen in Rom zum Kaiser. Die   *emperor*
10 Blütezeit des mittelalterlichen Deutschlands fällt in die Epoche

---

1 **Bewohner** (*m.*), **–** *inhabitant,*
resident
zum *to the*
2 **Zweig** (*m.*), **-e** *branch*
indogermanisch *Indo-European*
Sprachfamilie (*f.*), **-n** *family of*
languages
um *around, about*
3 **Geburt** (*f.*), **-en** *birth*
besetzen *to occupy*
4 **Bayer** (*m.*), **-n** *Bavarian (person)*
Alemanne (*m., n-noun*), **-n**
Alemannian

4 **Sachse** (*m., n-noun*), **-n** *Saxon*
Friese (*m., n-noun*), **-n** *Frisian*
während *during, in the course of*
5 **Völkerwanderung** (*f.*), **-en** *great*
migration
6 **Franke** (*m., n-noun*), **-n**
Franconian
weiter *farther, further*
8 **Reich** (*n.*), **-e** *empire*
9 **krönen** *to crown*
Papst (*m.*), **⸚e** *pope*
10 **Blütezeit** (*f.*), **-en** *golden age*
mittelalterlich *medieval*

zwischen 900 und 1250. Von 1438 bis 1806 regierten die Habsburger als Kaiser des „Heiligen Römischen Reiches Deutscher Nation".

Im 18. Jahrhundert begann Preußens Aufstieg, und in dieses Jahrhundert fällt auch die Blütezeit der klassischen deutschen Dichtung. Nach dem siegreichen Krieg gegen Frankreich wurde der preußische König, Wilhelm I., der erste Kaiser des Deutschen Reiches (1871). Dieses Reich war ein Bundesstaat. Nun folgte ein bedeutender politischer und wirtschaftlicher Aufstieg, besonders in der Industrie. Großstädte entstanden, und Berlin wurde zu einer Weltstadt. Der Lebensstandard des deutschen Volkes stieg. Die deutschen wissenschaftlichen, technischen und kulturellen Leistungen wurden in der ganzen Welt bekannt.

Die erste Hälfte des 20. Jahrhunderts repräsentiert eine besonders dunkle Zeit für Deutschland. Nach dem Ersten Weltkrieg (1914 bis 1918) gab es eine Periode von blutigen Revolutionen. Deutschland wurde 1919 eine Republik. Die wirtschaftliche Depression und die innere Schwäche der Weimarer Republik, mit über dreißig politischen Parteien, verhalfen Adolf Hitler 1933 zur Macht. Hitlers nationalsozialistische Politik führte schließlich zum Zweiten Weltkrieg (1939 bis 1945) und zum Holocaust. Die Rassenpolitik der Nationalsozialisten führte zu einem tödlichen System von Konzentrations- und Vernichtungslagern. In Lagern wie Auschwitz, Sachsenhausen und Buchenwald starben Millionen von Juden, Polen, Roma und Sinti, Homosexuellen und politischen Gegnern. 1945

11 **regieren** *to rule*
12 **heilig** *holy*
13 **Preußen** *Prussia*
   Aufstieg (*m.*), -e *rise*
15 **Dichtung** (*f.*), -en *literature*
   siegreich *victorious*
   gegen *against*
17 **Bundesstaat** (*m.*), -en *federal state*
   folgen *to follow*
18 **bedeutend** *significant*
   Aufstieg (*m.*) *rise*
   besonders *especially*
19 **entstehen (entstand)** *to emerge, come into being*
20 **Weltstadt** (*f.*), ¨-e *metropolis*
22 **Leistung** (*f.*), -en *achievement*
24 **dunkel** *dark*
25 **blutig** *bloody*
27 **Schwäche** (*f.*), -n *weakness*
28 **Partei** (*f.*), -en *party (political)*
   verhelfen (verhalf; verhilft) *to aid, help*
   Macht (*f.*), ¨-e *power*
29 **führen** *to lead*
   schließlich *finally, eventually*
30 **Rassenpolitik** (*f.*) *racial policy*
31 **tödlich** *lethal*
32 **Konzentrations- und Vernichtungslager** (*pl.*), – *concentration and death camps*
   Lager (*n.*), – *camp*
34 **Roma und Sinti** *gypsies*
   Gegner (*m.*), – *opponent*

35 erlebte Deutschland eine totale Niederlage. Das Land war in Trüm-
mern. Mehr als 20 Millionen Menschen waren von der Zerstörung
ihres Wohnraums betroffen.

Über vierzig Jahre lang existierten zwei deutsche Länder mit
zwei Hauptstädten: Im Osten war Ost-Berlin die Hauptstadt der
40 Deutschen Demokratischen Republik (DDR), und im Westen war
Bonn die Hauptstadt der Bundesrepublik Deutschland (BRD). Im
Jahre 1990 unterzeichneten Politiker aus dem Osten und Westen
einen „Einigungsvertrag", und am 3. Oktober 1990 feierten die
Deutschen die Vereinigung. Kurz nach der Wiedervereinigung
45 wurde Berlin wieder die Hauptstadt von Deutschland. Seit dem 1.
September 1999 haben der Deutsche Bundestag und die Bundesregierung ihren Sitz in der Bundeshauptstadt Berlin.

35	**erleben** _to experience_	43	**Einigungsvertrag** _(m.)_ _unification agreement_
	Niederlage _(f.),_ **-n** _defeat_		**feiern** _to celebrate_
36	**Trümmer** _(pl.)_ _ruins_	44	**Vereinigung** _(f.)_ _unification_
	mehr als _more than_	45	**seit** _since_
	Zerstörung _(f.),_ _destruction_	46	**Bundestag** _(m.)_ _parliament_
37	**Wohnraum** _(m.)_ _living quarters_	47	**Bundesregierung** _(f.)_ _federal government_
	betroffen von _affected by, hit by_		**Sitz** _(m.)_ _seat_
39	**Hauptstadt** _(f.),_ **-̈e** _capital city_		
42	**unterzeichnen** _to sign_		

KAPITEL 6

6.1 Prepositions

Recognizing that German prepositions are grouped into four grammatical categories can sometimes assist you in clarifying or establishing connections among words in a sentence. It is, first of all, important to recognize a noun or pronoun that is the object of a preposition. Objects of prepositions are *never* in the nominative. Object nouns and pronouns may be in the accusative, dative, or genitive.

A. Accusative prepositions

These prepositions (listed here with their basic meanings) always take the accusative case.

bis	*until, up to, as far as*	gegen	*against, toward*
durch	*through, by, by means of*	ohne	*without*
entlang	*along*	um	*around, about, at (+ time)*
für	*for*	wider	*against*

B. Dative prepositions

These prepositions always take the dative case.

aus	*out of, of, from*	mit	*with*
außer	*besides, except*	nach	*after, to, according to*
bei	*with, near*	seit	*since, for*
entgegen	*toward*	von	*from, by, of*
gegenüber	*opposite*	zu	*to, at*
gemäß	*in accordance with*		

C. Genitive prepositions

These prepositions always take the genitive case.

(an)statt	*instead of*	infolge	*as a result of, due to*
außerhalb	*outside of*	inmitten	*in the midst of*
innerhalb	*inside of, within*	mittels	*by means of*
oberhalb	*above*	trotz	*in spite of*
unterhalb	*below*	um ... willen	*for the sake of*
diesseits	*on this side of*	während	*in the course of, during*
jenseits	*on that side of*		
halber	*for the sake of*	wegen	*on account of, because of*

D. Dative and accusative prepositions

These prepositions take dative objects if the prepositional phrase expresses time or location; they take accusative objects if a direction is indicated.

an	*at, to, on (vertically)*	über	*over, above, about,*
auf	*on (horizontally), in, to*		*concerning, via*
hinter	*behind*	unter	*under, between, among*
in	*in, into*	vor	*in front of, before, prior, ago*
neben	*next to, beside*	zwischen	*between, among*

6.2 Idiomatic and Special Meanings

Prepositions indicate relations such as time, position, direction, and cause and effect between their noun or pronoun object and other items in a sentence. Establishing meanings of prepositions is complicated by the fact that most prepositions have a variety of applications and meanings. There is not always a simple correlation between German and English when dealing with usage or meaning of prepositions. Context plays a crucial role. Dictionary listings and verb-and-idiom lists help establish the most accurate meaning. Check dictionary entries for nouns or verbs with special or idiomatic meanings in connection with specific prepositions. In the dictionary, you will also find examples and idiomatic expressions listed under the prepositions themselves. Here is part of the definition for the preposition **nach** as it appears in *Collins German Unabridged Dictionary*.

---

nach [na:x] **PREP** +*dat* **a** (*örtlich*) to; **ich nahm den Zug ~ Mailand** (= *bis*) I took the train to Milan; (= *in Richtung*) I took the Milan train, I took the train for Milan; **das Schiff/der Zug fährt ~ Kiel** the boat/train is bound for Kiel, the boat/train is going to Kiel; **er ist schon ~ London abgefahren** he has already left for London; **~ Osten** eastward(s), to the east; **~ Westen** westward(s), to the west; **von Osten ~ Westen** from (the) east to (the) west; **~ links/rechts** (to the) left/right; **von links ~ rechts** from (the) left to (the) right; **~ jeder Richtung, ~ allen Richtungen** (*lit*) in all directions; (*fig*) on all sides; **~ hinten/vorn** to the back/front; (*in Wagen/Zug etc auch*) to the rear/front; **~ ... zu** towards ... (*Brit*), toward ... (*US*); **~ Norden zu** or **hin** to(wards) the north **b** (*in Verbindung mit vb siehe auch dort*) **~ jdm/etw suchen** to look for sb/sth; **sich ~ etw sehnen** to long for sth; **~ etw schmecken/riechen** to taste/smell of sth **c** (*zeitlich*) after; **fünf (Minuten) ~ drei** five (minutes) past or after (*US*) three; **~ Christi Geburt, ~ unserer Zeitrechnung** AD, anno Domini (*form*); **sie kam ~ zehn Minuten** she came ten minutes later, she came after ten minutes; **~ zehn Minuten war sie wieder da** she was back in ten minutes, she was back ten minutes later; **~ zehn Minuten wurde ich schon unruhig** after ten minutes I was getting worried; **was wird man ~ zehn Jahren über ihn sagen?** what will people be saying about him in ten years or in ten years' time?; **~ Empfang** or **Erhalt** or **Eingang** on receipt; **drei Tage ~ Empfang** three days after receipt; **~ allem, was geschehen ist** after all that has happened **d** (*Reihenfolge*) after; **eine(r, s) ~ dem/der anderen** one after another or the other; **die dritte Straße ~ dem Rathaus** the third road after or past the town hall; **ich komme ~ Ihnen!** I'm or I come after you; **(bitte) ~ Ihnen!** after you!; **der Leutnant kommt ~ dem Major** (*inf*) a lieutenant comes after a major; **~ „mit" steht der Dativ** "mit" is followed by or takes the dative **e** (= *laut, entsprechend*) according to; (= *im Einklang mit*) in accordance with; **~ dem Gesetz, dem Gesetz ~** according to the law; **~ römischem Gesetz** according to or under Roman law; **~ Artikel 142c** under article 142c; **manche Arbeiter werden ~ Zeit, andere ~ Leistung bezahlt** some workers are paid by the hour, others according to productivity; **etw ~ Gewicht kaufen** to buy sth by weight; **~ Verfassern/Gedichtanfängen** in order of or according to authors/first lines; **die Uhr ~ dem Radio stel-**

It is important to note the basic as well as some of the most common idiomatic meanings of the prepositions. For example:

Preposition	Basic Meaning(s)	Common Idiomatic Applications	English Translation
an	*on, at, to*	am (an dem) Tage; am 17. Juni	*during the day; on June 17*
		Russland ist reich an Mineralien.	*Russia is rich in minerals.*
auf	*on, upon*	Wir warten auf den Frühling.	*We're waiting for spring.*
		Die Lebensbedingungen auf dem Land sind anders.	*Living conditions in the country are different.*
		Auf diesem Gebiet habe ich keine Erfahrung.	*In this field I have no experience.*
aus	*out of, of, from*	aus diesem Grund(e)	*for this reason*
		aus Liebe zu einem Freund	*out of love for a friend*
bei	*at, with, near; in the process of*	bei indogermanischen Sprachen	*in the case of Indogermanic languages*
		beim Lesen	*in (the process of) reading*
		Bei uns findet man alles.	*At our place (at our house) one finds everything.*
durch	*through, by, by means of*	Durch diesen Versuch bewies er seine Theorie.	*With this experiment he proved his theory.*
für	*for*	Ich interessiere mich für die gotische Baukunst.	*I'm interested in Gothic architecture.*
		Er hält mich für wichtig.	*He thinks I'm important.*
in	*in, into*	Die Forscher arbeiteten in der Nacht.	*The researchers worked at night.*
		im Land/auf dem Lande	*here at home; in the country*

Preposition	Basic Meaning(s)	Common Idiomatic Applications	English Translation
nach	*after, to, according to*	dem Buch nach; meiner Meinung nach	*according to the book; in my opinion*
		Nach der Schule gingen die Kinder nach Hause.	*After school the children went home.*
über	*above; about*	Das Buch über den Aufstand	*The book about the revolt*
um	*at, around*	Die Zahl ist um 30% gestiegen.	*The number has increased by 30%.*
		Die Vorlesung beginnt um acht Uhr.	*The lecture begins at eight o'clock.*
von	*from, by, of*	Das Buch handelt von der Revolution.	*The book deals with the revolution.*
		Diese Tiere leben von Pflanzen.	*These animals live on plants.*
vor	*in front of; before; ago*	Vor fünfzig Jahren war der Aufstand.	*The revolt was 50 years ago.*
zu	*to, at*	Was gibt es zum Essen?	*What's for dinner?*
		Zu der Zeit ...	*At that time . . .*
		Wir bleiben heute abend zu Hause.	*We'll stay at home tonight*

6.3 Contraction of Prepositions

Prepositions are often contracted with certain definite articles. These contractions are common, and except in the case of idiomatic meanings, the two variations are identical in meaning.

am	=	an dem	ins	=	in das
aufs	=	auf das	ums	=	um das
beim	=	bei dem	vom	=	von dem
durchs	=	durch das	zum	=	zu dem
fürs	=	für das	zur	=	zu der
im	=	in dem			

6.4 Prepositions Following Nouns or Pronouns

Some prepositions follow the noun or pronoun object.

den Vorschriften **gemäß**   *according to the regulations*
deswegen   *because of this, for this reason*

meiner Meinung **nach**   *in (according to) my opinion*
dem Gesetz **gegenüber**   *compared to, with respect to the law*
demnach   *according to this*
demgegenüber   *compared to that*
der Genauigkeit **halber**   *for the sake of accuracy*

entlang ⟶ *along*

A number of prepositions are used frequently in academic texts to mean *according to*. All four of the German expressions **diesem Buch gemäß, laut diesem Buch, diesem Buch nach,** and **diesem Buch zufolge** mean *according to this book*. The prepositions **gemäß** and **nach** may occur before or after the object.

6.5 Indefinite Pronouns: *man, jemand, niemand*

Man is an indefinite pronoun meaning *one, they, people, we* (and also *you, a person, someone, somebody*). **Man** is always the subject of the clause. **Man** is sometimes best expressed by an English passive construction. Thus, the frequently used expression. **man sagt** equates in English to *it is said, one says, people say, we say*.

> Man strebt, solange man lebt.
> *One strives as long as one lives.*
> Wenn man bei einem Wort Hilfe braucht, verwendet man ein Wörterbuch.
> *When you need help with a word, you use a dictionary.*

There is no connection to, but occasionally confusion with, the noun **der Mann**, meaning *man*.

Jemand *(somebody, anybody)* and **niemand** *(nobody)* may or may not be declined.

> Die Polizei sucht jemanden. = Die Polizei sucht jemand.
> *The police are looking for somebody.*
> Ist jemand zu Hause? Nein, niemand ist da.
> *Is anybody home? No, nobody is there.*

6.6 Using the Dictionary

Basic vocabulary lists and glosses are first steps in learning to read German. Attending to context, recognizing a word's function in a sentence, and knowledge of a topic can also help you deduce meaning. These "smart-guessing" strategies help you get a basic understanding. Often, as you read on, you find further cues that confirm or unseat your guess.

Likewise, a good dictionary is a must. In future chapters of this book, vocabulary and glosses will focus on text-specific and idiomatic definitions. Use your dictionary to find common expressions and build a personal vocabulary list. Refer to Appendix C (pages 296–298) for help in choosing the right dictionary and using it effectively.

Grundwortschatz

allein	alone, only, but	**meinen**	to opine, state an opinion, to think
Aufstand (m.)	revolt		
Bauer	farmer,	**Meinung** (f.), **-en**	opinion
(m., n-noun), **-n**	peasant	**menschlich**	human, humane
bestehen aus	to consist of	**möglich**	possible
(bestand)		**Möglichkeit** (f.), **-en**	possibility
bestimmt	certain, definite	**nennen (nannte)**	to name
brauchen	to need, require	**niemand**	nobody
bzw.		**ohne**	without
(beziehungsweise)	or, respectively	**Regierung** (f.), **-en**	government
damals	at that time, in those days	**Reich** (n.), **-e**	empire, state, realm
denken (dachte)	to think	**seit**	since
denken an	to think about	**sowohl ... wie**	not only . . . but also
eng	narrow		
Erklärung (f.), **-en**	explanation, declaration	**um**	around, about, at (+ time)
folgen	to follow	**unterstützen**	to support
geben (gab; gibt)	to give	**Unterstützung** (f.), **-en**	support
gegen	against, toward		
gemäß	according to	**Untersuchung** (f.), **-en**	investigation, examination
glauben	to believe		
immer	always, ever	**verstehen (verstand)**	to understand
war schon immer	has always been	**während**	in the course of, during
jemand	somebody, anybody	**wegen**	because of
kaum	hardly	**Werk** (n.), **-e**	work, plant
Lage (f.), **-n**	position, situation	**Zeit** (f.), **-en**	time

Übungssätze

1. Lange Zeit gab es ein Deutsches Reich nur dem Namen nach.
2. Das Oberhaupt eines Königreiches nennt man einen König. Ludwig XIV. von Frankreich nannte man „den Sonnenkönig".
3. Die Erde bewegt sich in einem Jahr um die Sonne. Vor dreieinhalb Jahrhunderten wurde Galileo Galilei in den Augen der Kirche zum Ketzer, denn er erklärte, die Erde bewegte sich um die Sonne, nicht die Sonne um die Erde, wie man damals glaubte.
4. In der Zeitung vom 17. Juni 2003 stand: „Vor fünfzig Jahren begann der erste Volksaufstand in der DDR. Damals gab es 100 000 Menschen in Berlin auf der Straße. Heute spricht man nicht oft von diesem Aufstand."
5. Der Aufstand begann wegen der Situation mit der Produktion und wegen des langen Arbeitstags in der DDR. Bauarbeiter protestierten gegen „Mehr Arbeit für gleichen Lohn."
6. In den Untersuchungen damals stellte niemand Fragen über die Lage oder die Meinung der Arbeiter in der Stadt oder der Bauern auf dem Land.
7. Eine ausführliche Erklärung ist innerhalb des engen Bereiches der Untersuchung nicht möglich.
8. Da steht jemand an der Ecke neben der Kirche und protestiert gegen die Regierung. Weiß jemand, wer das ist?—Nein, niemand weiß es.

1. **nur dem Namen nach** *in name only*
2. **Oberhaupt** *(n.),* **ⁱer** *head, ruler*
   Königreich *(n.),* **-e** *kingdom*
3. **sich bewegen um** *to orbit*
   dreieinhalb *three and a half*
   Auge *(n.),* **-n** *eye*
   Ketzer *(m.),* **–** *heretic*
4. **Volksaufstand** *(m.)* *popular uprising, revolt*

4. **DDR = Deutsche Demokratische Republik** *GDR = German Democratic Repubic*
5. **Bau-** *construction*
   Lohn *(m.),* **ⁱe** *salary*
6. **Fragen stellen** *to ask questions*
7. **ausführlich** *detailed*
   Bereich *(m.),* **-e** *range, scope, realm*
8. **wissen (wusste, weiß)** *to know*

9. Einem neuen Bericht nach zeigt die Bundesrepublik heute ein starkes Interesse für die Medizinforschung. Aus diesem Grund kämpft die Regierung für die Finanzierung eines neuen Forschungszentrums. Jemand von der Regierung sagte, „Das war schon immer wichtig."

10. Einem berühmten französischen Komponisten nach braucht man heute in der Musikwelt sowohl Ausdauer als auch Talent. Für jemanden ohne Ausdauer ist Talent kaum genug.

11. Junge Musiker denken oft zu viel an Genie und Talent. Für einen talentierten Musiker gibt es immer Möglichkeiten, aber wie man sagt: „Übung macht den Meister."

12. Die wirtschaftliche und politische Lage im Lande ist hoffnungslos. Deswegen ist meiner Meinung nach eine Revolution unvermeidlich.

13. Nach einem solchen totalen Krieg braucht man für den Wiederaufbau der Wirtschaft sowohl den guten Willen des Siegers wie auch sehr viel Kapital.

14. Bei solchen sozioökonomischen Prozessen betragen allein die Kosten zum Wiederaufbau von Wohnungen unzählige Millionen Dollar.

15. Den Vorschriften gemäß unterstützen die Hilfsorganisationen nicht nur Kindergärten, sondern auch Institutionen für Behinderte.

16. Nicht nur für die Deutschen, sondern auch für die Österreicher bedeutete der Marshall-Plan einen neuen Anfang.

17. Damals nannte man Amerika „das Land der unbegrenzten Möglichkeiten."

18. Seiner Lage wegen war Österreich schon immer ein strategisch wichtiges Land.

9. **Bericht** *(m.)*, **-e** *report*
   zeigen *to show, demonstrate*
   wichtig *important*
10. **berühmt** *famous*
   Ausdauer *(f.)* *perseverance*
12. **hoffnungslos** *hopeless*
   unvermeidlich *unavoidable*
13. **Wiederaufbau** *(m.)* *rebuilding, reconstruction*

13. **Wille** *(m.)*, **-n** *will*
   Sieger *(m.)*, **–** *winner, conqueror*
14. **unzählige** *countless*
15. **Vorschrift** *(f.)*, **-en** *rule, regulation*
   Behinderte *(pl.)* *disabled individuals*
17. **unbegrenzt** *unlimited*

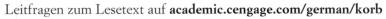

DER 17. JUNI 1953

Vom 16. bis 21. Juni 1953 gab es in fast 700 Orten der DDR Demonstrationen und Streiks. Über eine Million demonstrierten bzw. streikten in den ersten und (bis 1989) letzten Massenprotesten der DDR. Mit der Unterstützung von sowjetischen Panzern endete die DDR Regierung den Volksaufstand. 5
Mehr als 100 Menschen starben. Tausende DDR Bürger landeten wegen des Aufstands im Gefängnis. Die Bundesrepublik feierte bis 1990 den 17. Juni als „Tag der Deutschen Einheit".

In Stefan Heyms Roman *5 Tage im Juni* begann am 16. Juni die Streikaktion im „VEB Merkur" mit dem folgenden Dialog 10
zwischen unruhigen Arbeitern und ihrem parteitreuen Kollegen Teterow:

Kallmann sagte: „Niemand hier ist gegen die Regierung, Kollege Teterow, oder gegen die Partei. Aber die Kollegen verstehen nicht, warum sie diese Normerhöhung hinnehmen sollen. [...] 15
Jeder Kartoffelbauer kriegt Geschenke von der Arbeiterregierung, bloß nicht der Arbeiter." [...]

„Früher", sagte Bartel, „durfte man eine Delegation schicken und heute nicht? Was ist das für ein Arbeiterstaat?"

„Aber Vorsicht!" warnte Wiesener. „Vorsicht, Kollegen! Viel- 20
leicht weiß der Kollege Teterow sehr gut, warum er nicht für uns mit der Betriebsleitung sprechen will. Wenn die nun die Staatssicherheit holen und wir unseren Delegierten nie wieder sehen—was dann?"

1 **Ort** *(m.)*, **-e** *place, local*
7 **Gefängnis** *(n.)*, **-se** *prison*
9 **Roman** *(m.)*, **-e** *novel*
10 **VEB Merkur (volkseigener Betrieb)** *(GDR) state-owned factory "Merkur"*
11 **unruhig** *discontent*
   parteitreu *true to the (communist SED) party*
   Kollege *(m., n-noun)*, **-n** *coworker, colleague*
15 **Normerhöhung** *(f.)*, **-en** *increase in production norms*
   hinnehmen sollen *ought to accept, put up with*
16 **Kartoffelbauer** *(m., n-noun)*, **-n** *potato farmer*
   kriegen *to get*

Geschenk *(n.)*, **-e** *present, gift*
17 **bloß nicht** *the only one who doesn't (is); so why not*
18 **durfte ... schicken** *was allowed to send*
20 **Vorsicht!** *Be careful! Caution!*
21 **vielleicht** *maybe, perhaps*
   wissen (wusste; weiß) *to know*
22 **Betriebsleitung** *(f.)* *company/plant management*
   nicht sprechen will *doesn't want to speak*
   wenn die *if they*
   Staatssicherheit *(f.)* *(GDR) state police*
23 **Delegierte** *(f. or m.)*, **-n** *delegate*
   nie wieder *never again*

„Dann eben—Streik!"

25 „Alle Räder stehen still", deklamierte Bartel, „wenn dein starker [Arm es will] ..."

Teterow war auf einmal hilflos. Streik, dachte er, und ich bin schuld, ich hab angefangen davon, ich hab sie warnen wollen davor und jetzt kehrt es sich gegen mich, gegen uns, gegen sie selber.

30 „Kollegen", sagte er, „das ist doch—"

„Kallmann!"

„Kallmann unser Delegierter!"

Kallmann hob abwehrend die Hände, aber er lächelte.

„Streik ist die Waffe der Arbeiter gegen ihre Unterdrücker", sagte

35 Teterow heiser. „Wir haben die Unterdrücker abgeschafft."

„Kallmann ist gewählt!"

Ein Zug bildete sich. An der Spitze marschierte Wiesener und rief im Takt: „Nieder mit der Norm mit der Norm mit der Norm, nieder mit der Norm, mit der Norm mit der Norm."

40 Dann waren sie verschwunden, hinaus aus der Werkhalle, das Echo verstummte. [...]

(Auszug leicht geändert aus: Stefan Heym *5 Tage im Juni: Roman*, Kapitel 25 „Dienstag, 16. Juni 1953, 6.45 Uhr". © Bertelsmann Verlag, München 1974. Seite 168–186.)

25 **Rad** (*n.*), ⸚**er** *wheel*	35 **heiser** *hoarsely*
26 **wenn ... will** *if your strong arm wants it (to happen)*	**wir haben ... abgeschafft** *we've abolished/done away with*
27 **auf einmal** *suddenly*	36 **gewählt** *elected*
hilflos *helpless*	37 **ein Zug bildete sich** *a procession took shape*
28 **schuld** *guilty*	**an der Spitze** *at the front*
ich hab angefangen davon *I started with that*	**rufen (rief)** *to shout, call out*
ich hab sie warnen wollen davor *I wanted to warn them about that*	38 **im Takt** *(rythmically) in time*
	nieder *down*
29 **jetzt kehrt es sich** *now it turns*	40 **war verschwunden** *was gone; had disappeared*
33 **heben (hob)** *to raise*	**hinaus** *away, outside*
abwehrend *in defense*	**Werkhalle** (*f.*), **-n** *factory building*
lächeln *to smile*	41 **verstummen** *to fall silent*
34 **Waffe** (*f.*), **-n** *weapon*	42 **Auszug leicht geändert** *slightly altered excerpt*
Unterdrücker (*m.*), **–** *oppressor*	

KAPITEL 7

7.1 Adjective Endings

From the very beginning of this book you have been reading and translating a considerable number of adjectives without great difficulty, for the most part paying little or no attention to adjective endings. In this chapter you will begin to be aware of the extent to which adjective endings supply essential information and help you read and translate accurately.

A. Adjectives without endings

> Aller Anfang ist **schwer**.
> *Every beginning is **difficult**.*
> Die Aufgaben wurden **interessant** aber **schwierig**.
> *The exercises became **interesting** but **difficult**.*
> Die Lebensbedingungen bleiben **gut**.
> *Living conditions remain **good**.*

Predicate adjectives, following the verbs **sein**, **werden**, and **bleiben**, do not have adjective endings.

Note that uninflected adjectives and some adverbs are identical in appearance, though they function entirely differently:

schnell as adjective: Der Wagen ist schnell.   ein schneller, fahrender Wagen
The car is fast.   *a fast, moving car*

schnell as adverb: Der Wagen fährt schnell.   ein schnell fahrender Wagen
The car moves rapidly.   *a rapidly moving car*

While adjectives can occur both with and without endings, adverbs never have endings. See **Kapitel 8** and **Kapitel 11** for detailed information on adverbs.

B. Adjectives with endings

> politisch**es** Theater *political theater*
> das politisch**e** Theater *the political theater*
> ein groß**er** Dichter des politisch**en** Theaters
> *a great poet of the political theater*

Attributive adjectives precede a noun and have endings determined by the gender, number, and case of the noun that they modify. When looking up an adjective in the dictionary, you will find the form without endings.

Unlike English, proper noun adjectives are not capitalized in German.

> deutsches Theater *German theater*
> der amerikanische Kritiker *the American critic*

Descriptive adjectives derived from city names, however, are capitalized and have an **-er** ending in all cases and genders, singular and plural.

> ein neues Berliner Theater *a new Berlin theater*
> der bekannte New Yorker Kritiker *the well-known New York critic*

7.2 Information from Adjective Endings

A. Adjectives not preceded by a *der-* or *ein*-word

Attributive adjectives that are not preceded by an article or **der**-word assume the endings that the article would have and thus signify information regarding gender, number, and function of the modified noun.

	Singular Masculine	Singular Feminine
Nominative:	warmer Regen	warme Luft
Accusative:	warmen Regen	warme Luft
Dative:	warmem Regen	warmer Luft
Genitive:	warmen Regens	warmer Luft

	Singular Neuter	Plural All Genders
Nominative:	warmes Wasser	warme Temperaturen
Accusative:	warmes Wasser	warme Temperaturen
Dative:	warmem Wasser	warmen Temperaturen
Genitive:	warmen Wassers	warmer Temperaturen

These adjective endings and the **der**-word endings are identical, except for the masculine and neuter genitive singular. Adjectives not preceded by an article are very common in the plural, and when singular and plural forms are identical, detecting these endings becomes key to understanding. Note the difference:

Sehr geehrt**er** Lehrer! *vs.* Sehr geehrt**e** Lehrer!
schön**es** Mädchen *vs.* schön**e** Mädchen
Gut**er** Berliner und Gut**e** Berlinerin! *vs.* Gut**e** Berliner und Berlinerinnen!

In singular, adjectives not preceded by an article occur largely with noncountable nouns, as seen in the table on page 70. For example:

Das Kilogramm ist das Gewicht eines Liters destillier**ten** Wassers bei 4 Grad Celsius.
The kilogram is the weight of a liter of distilled water at a temperature of 4 degrees Celsius.

B. Adjectives preceded by a *der*-word or an *ein*-word

The definite article already provides the essential information about a noun's gender, number, and case. The beginning reader may find it useful to note that the combination **die + -en** is an immediate tip-off that the noun is plural (and may be either nominative or accusative).

	Nominative	Accusative
Masculine:	der alte Lehrer	den alten Lehrer
Feminine:	die alte Mutter	die alte Mutter
Neuter:	das junge Mädchen	das junge Mädchen
Plural:	**die** al**ten** Lehrer	**die** al**ten** Lehrer
	die al**ten** Mütter	**die** al**ten** Mütter
	die jun**gen** Mädchen	**die** jun**gen** Mädchen

The similarity of the indefinite article **ein** for both masculine and neuter nouns in the nominative provides one additional important indicator: the masculine nominative combination **ein + -er** has to be a subject or predicate. Any other **ein**-word ending in **-e + -en** once again indicates a plural noun.

	Nominative	Accusative
Masculine:	**ein** alt**er** Lehrer	ein**en** alt**en** Lehrer
Feminine:	ein**e** alt**e** Mutter	ein**e** alt**e** Mutter
Neuter:	ein jung**es** Mädchen	ein jung**es** Mädchen
Plural:	mein**e** alt**en** Lehrer	dein**e** alt**en** Lehrer
	eur**e** alt**en** Mütter	unser**e** alt**en** Mütter
	kein**e** jung**en** Mädchen	ihr**e** jung**en** Mädchen

For a complete overview of adjective endings following **der-** and **ein-** words see Appendix A on page 288.

7.3 Adjectives Used as Nouns

All adjectives can be used as nouns in German. These adjectival nouns are much more common than in English where the use is generally restricted to plural expressions such as the old, the rich, the Swiss, etc. German adjectival nouns, as can be seen in the table below, can refer both to people—in which case they are masculine or feminine as in **der Alte** (*the old man*), **die Reiche** (*the rich woman*), **die Deutschen** (*the Germans*)—and to abstract concepts, in which case they tend to be neuter: **das Gute und das Böse** (*the good and the evil*), **das Schöne** (*that which is beautiful*).

Singular			Plural
Masculine	**Feminine**	**Neuter**	**All genders**
der Alte	die Alte	das Alte	die Alten
ein Alter	eine Alte		Alte
der Deutsche	die Deutsche	das Deutsche	die Deutschen
ein Deutscher	eine Deutsche		Deutsche
der Schöne	die Schöne	das Schöne	die Schönen
ein Schöner	eine Schöne		Schöne

Adjectival nouns are inflected like adjectives preceding a noun.

der Deutsche	ein Deutscher
den Deutschen	einen Deutschen
dem Deutschen	einem Deutschen
des Deutschen	eines Deutschen

Unpreceded plural forms are quite common.

> Hier ist das Institut für **Behinderte**.
> *Here is the institute for disabled individuals.*
> **Alte** und **Junge** suchen hier Hilfe.
> *Old and young (people) seek help here.*

Neuter adjectival nouns often occur in combination with indefinite pronouns.

> **nichts Schwieriges**   *nothing difficult*
> **viel Interessantes**   *much that is interesting*
> **wenig Wesentliches**   *little of consequence*
> **etwas Wichtiges**   *something important*

When a literal translation results in stilted or incorrect English, find an idiomatic equivalent to suit the context.

Grundwortschatz

ähnlich	similar	**Grieche** (m.), **-n;**	Greek
arm	poor	**Griechin** (f.),	
ausführlich	detailed	**-nen**	
außer	besides,	**Hälfte** (f.), **-n**	half
	except for	**Interesse** (n.), **-n**	interest
beeinflussen	to influence	**Körper** (m.), **–**	body
Bereich (m.), **-e**	realm, sphere	**krank**	sick, ill
besuchen	to visit	**Mittelalter** (n.)	Middle Ages
bewegen	to move	**Nacht** (f.), **-̈e**	night
Blütezeit (f.), **-en**	golden age	**nichts**	nothing
Einfluss (m.),	influence	**noch**	still, even
Einflüsse		**noch nicht**	not yet
einzig	only, single	**politisch**	political
entwickeln	to develop	**Roman** (m.), **-e**	novel
etwas	something, some,	**schon**	already
	somewhat	**wir wissen es**	we have known
finden (fand)	to find	**schon lange**	it for a long time
Flugzeug (n.), **-e**	airplane	**schwierig**	difficult
früh	early	**Stil** (m.), **-e**	style
führen	to lead	**tot**	dead
führen zu	to lead to	**tragen**	to carry, bear,
geistig	intellectual,	**(trug; trägt)**	wear
	spiritual, mental	**wesentlich**	essential,
gelten (galt; gilt)	to be valid, to be		important,
	true, to apply		considerable
gleich	same, equal	**wissen**	to know (facts)
glücklich	happy, fortunate	**(wusste; weiß)**	

Übungssätze

1. Während der Wirtschaftskrise von 1930 hatte Deutschland über sieben Millionen Arbeitslose.
2. Viele Verwandte und Bekannte besuchten die Kranke im Krankenhaus. Niemand wusste aber, wie krank sie war.
3. Die neue Untersuchung ergab nichts Wesentliches.
4. In dem neuen Buch fragt man: Verteilte Tolstoi sein großes Vermögen an die Armen aus christlicher Nächstenliebe oder nicht?
5. Das Gute an dem Buch ist nicht neu, und das Neue ist nicht gut.
6. Das Gleiche gilt auch für viele andere Bücher.
7. Nach dem Flugzeugunfall im brasilianischen Dschungel fand man nur Tote und Schwerverletzte. Die Namen der Verletzten standen in der heutigen Zeitung.
8. Vor 200 Jahren wurde der Franzose Louise Braille geboren. Im Alter von drei Jahren wurde Braille blind und 1825 entwickelte der Sechzehnjährige seine Schrift für die Blinden.
9. Im frühen Mittelalter zogen einige germanische Stämme nach Österreich.
10. Eine Urkunde mit dem Landesnamen „Ostarrîchi" gab es erstmals im Jahre 996; aus dieser mittelalterlichen Version entwickelte sich die heutige Schreibweise Österreich.
11. Jedes Schulkind weiß, farbloses Licht ist ein Gemisch von Lichtwellen verschiedener Längen. Man lernt diese Tatsache aus einem wissenschaftlichen Lehrbuch.
12. In den Untersuchungen mit Kupfer fand man etwas Wichtiges: Kupfer ist, außer Gold, das einzige farbige Metall und außer Silber der beste Leiter für Wärme und Elektrizität.

1. **Wirtschaftskrise** (*f.*), **-n**   *economic crisis, depression*
   Arbeitslose (*f. or m.*), **-n**   *unemployed person*
2. **Verwandte** (*f. or m.*), **-n**   *relative*
   Bekannte (*f. or m.*), **-n**   *acquaintance*
3. **ergeben** (**ergab; ergibt**)   *to yield, give, show*
4. **verteilen**   *to distribute*
   Vermögen (*n.*), **–**   *wealth*
4. **Nächstenliebe** (*f.*)   *love for one's fellow man, charity*

7. **Unfall** (*m.*), **⸚e**   *accident*
   Dschungel (*m.*), **–**   *jungle*
   schwerverletzt   *seriously injured*
8. **Schrift** (*f.*), **-en**   *script, form of writing*
10. **Urkunde** (*f.*), **-n**   *document*
11. **farblos**   *colorless*
    Gemisch (*n.*), **-e**   *mixture*
    Welle (*f.*), **-n**   *wave*
    Tatsache (*f.*), **-n**   *fact*
12. **Kupfer** (*n.*)   *copper*
    farbig   *colored*
    Leiter (*m.*), **–**   *conductor*

13. Das ist natürlich nichts Neues, wir wissen es schon lange.

14. Etwas Ähnliches wussten schon in der Antike die alten Griechen.

15. Laut dem Protagonisten des Romanes unterscheiden sich das Wahrscheinliche und das Unwahrscheinliche nur der Häufigkeit nach.

16. Edmund Burke, der große englische Staatsmann und Redner, hatte zwei Gesichter: Der eine Burke war der Bewahrer des Alten, der andere war der Reformer, der Liberale.

17. Die wirtschaftliche Entwicklung des letzten Jahrzehnts war fast unglaublich. Das Berliner Stadtbild ist heute als Resultat dieser Entwicklung wesentlich anders.

18. In seinem ersten Buch über die deutsche Literaturgeschichte gibt es ausführliche Einblicke sowohl in die Berliner als auch in die Jenaer Romantik.

19. Die Romantik beeinflusste in der ersten Hälfte des 19. Jahrhunderts fast alle Bereiche des kulturellen und geistigen Lebens in Deutschland.

20. Die literarische Form des Briefes hatte besonders in der Zeit der Romantik ihre Blütezeit.

14. **Antike** *(f.)* *antiquity*
15. **laut dem Protagonisten** *according to the protagonist*
    sich unterscheiden *to differ*
    wahrscheinlich *probable*
    Häufigkeit *(f.),* **-en** *frequency*
16. **Redner** *(m.),* **–** *orator, speaker*
    Gesicht *(n.),* **-er** *face*

16. **Bewahrer** *(m.),* **–** *preserver*
17. **unglaublich** *unbelievable*
    Stadtbild *(n.),* **-er** *general character of a town/city*
18. **Einblick** *(m.),* **-e** *insight*
    Jena *(Eastern German city of) Jena (center of early romanticism ca. 1798–1802)*

 Leitfragen zum Lesetext auf **academic.cengage.com/german/korb**

DIE ROMANTIK

D ie Romantik war eine ästhetisch-literarische Epoche in der Literatur verschiedener europäischer Länder. In Deutschland dauerte sie von ungefähr 1790 bis 1840. Sie ist gekennzeichnet durch einen Abfall vom verstandesmäßigen Denken und von aller Nüchternheit. Gefühl, Fantasie, Stimmung und Sehnsucht

4 **gekennzeichnet** *characterized*
  Abfall *(m.)* **von** *revolt against*

5 **aller Nüchternheit** *(f.)* *all types of sobriety*
  Stimmung *(f.),* **-en** *emotion*

bewegten die Romantiker. Ihre Sehnsucht trug sie aus der
Wirklichkeit in eine glückliche Vergangenheit und in ferne Länder.
  Die Romantiker „entdeckten" das Mittelalter wieder und
schätzten an ihm die Einheit von Leben und christlichem Glauben.
10 Dieses Interesse an die Vergangenheit führte zur Sammlung von
Volksliedern, Sagen und Märchen (Brüder Grimm). In Märchen und
Erzählungen mischen sich Fantasie, Spuk und Wirklichkeit. Das
Geheimnisvolle und Unergründliche, der Traum und die Nacht
faszinierten das Denken der Romantiker.
15   Die Romantik hatte einen starken Einfluss auf fast alle Bereiche
des kulturellen und geistigen Lebens. Sie beeinflusste die Kunst,
Musik, Philosophie und andere Gebiete. Bildende Künste, u.a. die
Malerei der Romantik, suchten in der Wiedererweckung der mittel-
alterlichen Welt eine ideale, harmonische Welt zu finden und stellten
20 in Landschaftsbildern die Schönheit und Großartigkeit der Natur dar.
Mit der Musik schilderten die Romantiker Naturstimmungen oder
Gefühle. Bekannte Namen in der Musik sind Weber, Schubert und
Mendelssohn. Im Gesellschaftlichen führte der romantische Subjekti-
vismus zu neuen Alternativen der traditionellen sittlichen Bindungen.
25   Zum ersten Mal in der Romantik spielten Frauen auch eine große
Rolle im geistigen Leben der deutschen Geschichte. Vor allem aus
den Briefen solcher geistreichen Frauen wie Bettina von Arnim und
Caroline Schlegel-Schelling lernt man viel Interessantes über die
Romantik: sowohl private biographische Ereignisse wie Berichte
30 über die literarischen Salons.

8	**wieder** *again*	20	**stellte ... Großartigkeit der Natur**
9	**schätzen (an)** *to think highly (about), esteem*		**dar** *represented the grandeur of nature*
12	**sich mischen** *to combine, blend, be mixed together*	23	**im Gesellschaftlichen** *in the social realm*
13	**geheimnisvoll** *mysterious*	24	**sittlich** *moral, ethical*
	unergründlich *unfathomable*		**Bindung** *(f.)*, **-en** *bond, tie*
17	**bildende Künste** *(pl.)* *fine arts*	25	**zum ersten Mal** *for the first time*
	u.a. (unter anderem) *among other things*	26	**vor allem** *above all (else)*
18	**suchte ... zu finden** *sought to find . . .*	27	**geistreich** *ingenious, gifted*
	Wiedererweckung *(f.)*, **-en** *reawakening*		

Handwritten margin notes:
- *the Romantics* (next to line 7)
- *its* (next to line 8)
- *Romanticism* (next to line 14)

KAPITEL 8

8.1 Adverbs

Adverbs modify verbs, adjectives, or other adverbs.

A. Adverbs modify verbs

Dieser Baustil kam **ursprünglich** aus Preußen und schlug schnell ein.
This building style originally came from Prussia and caught on quickly.
Die Architekten überprüfen **regelmäßig** die Baupläne.
The architects check the blueprints regularly.

B. Adverbs modify adjectives

In einem **wahrhaft** alten Haus sind die Räumlichkeiten **bedeutend** kleiner als in den **relativ** neuen Häusern.
In a truly old house, the rooms are significantly smaller than in relatively new houses.
Es gibt **wirklich** unglaubliche Unterschiede.
There are truly unbelievable differences.

C. Adverbs modify other adverbs

Das neue Gebäude wächst **verhältnismäßig schnell**.
The new building is rising relatively rapidly.
Die neuen Einwohner ziehen in die Häuser **gleich schnell** ein.
The new residents move into the houses equally rapidly.

Unlike their often identical adjective forms, German adverbs used in the positive or comparative form never take an ending.

Adverb forms	Adjective forms
Er arbeitet gut.	Seine Arbeit ist gut.
He works well.	*His work is good.*
Das Auto fährt schneller.	Mein Auto ist schneller. Ich fahre das schnellere Auto.
The car drives (goes) faster.	*My car is faster. I drive the faster car.*
die unglaublich schöne Geschichte	die unglaubliche schöne Geschichte
the unbelievably beautiful story	*the unbelievable, beautiful story*

Translating tips:

Note that adverbs in a German sentence generally follow the main verb and precede direct-object nouns: **Die Architekten überprüfen regelmäßig die Baupläne**. The English equivalent follows a slightly different pattern: *The architects check the blueprints regularly.* Or: *The architects regularly check the blueprints.*

When a German sentence begins with an adverb or adverbial phrase, translate the adverb or phrase first, then the subject and verb (review **Kapitel 5**).

Most of the corresponding English adverbs end in *-ly*.

8.2 Verbs with Inseparable and Separable Prefixes

Simple German verbs often are used to form compound verbs. Separable or inseparable prefixes added to the simple verb change the overall meaning of the verb but do not affect the regular or irregular forms of the stem verb. Take for example the simple verb **kommen** and derivative verbs with inseparable or separable prefixes.[1]

kommen (kam; kommt)   *to come*

Inseparable prefixes
bekommen (bekam; bekommt)   *to receive*
entkommen (entkam; entkommt)   *to escape*
verkommen (verkam; verkommt)
  to decay, to come down in the world

Separable prefixes
ab/kommen (kam ... ab; kommt ... ab)   *to come away, deviate*
an/kommen (kam ... an; kommt ... an)   *to arrive*
auf/kommen (kam ... auf; kommt ... auf)   *to come up*
aus/kommen (kam ... aus; kommt ... aus)   *to get along (with), agree, get by*
ein/kommen (kam ... ein; kommt ... ein)   *to come in*
her/kommen (kam ... her; kommt ... her)   *to come from, originate*
hin/kommen (kam ... hin; kommt ... hin)   *to come to*

---

1. Infinitive forms of verbs with separable prefixes are indicated throughout the text with a slash (/) separating the prefix from the infinitive.

mit/kommen (kam ... mit; kommt ... mit)   *to accompany*
nach/kommen (kam ... nach; kommt ... nach)   *to follow*
um/kommen (kam ... um; kommt ... um)   *to perish, die*
vor/kommen (kam ... vor; kommt ... vor)   *to occur, happen*
zurück/kommen (kam ... zurück; kommt ... zurück)   *to return*
zusammen/kommen (kam ... zusammen; kommt ... zusammen)
   to come together

A. Inseparable prefixes

Some German verbs have unstressed prefixes that are never separated from any form of the verb, and in the perfect tenses these verbs do not take the participial prefix **ge-** (see **Kapitel 9**). The most common of these prefixes are **be-**, **emp-**, **ent-**, **er-**, **ge-**, **miss-**, **ver-**, and **zer-**.

While some prefixes imply certain types of actions and allow you to surmise a meaning based on the simple verb + prefix meaning, there are numerous exceptions. It is always best to check the meaning of compound verbs in your dictionary. Two prefixes, **ent-** and **zer-**, have fairly consistent meanings that may help you determine the meaning of the resulting verb with prefix.

ent-   *away from*
entdecken   *to discover* (**decken**   *to cover*)
entfernen   *to remove, take away from*
entwässern   *to drain, take water away from, dehydrate*
entziehen   *to withdraw, pull away from* (**ziehen**   *to pull*)

zer-   *to pieces*
zerbrechen   *to break into pieces* (**brechen**   *to break*)
zerreißen   *to rip into pieces* (**reißen**   *to rip*)
zerschlagen   *to beat up* (**schlagen**   *to beat*)
zerstören   *to destroy* (**stören**   *to disturb*)

B. Separable prefixes

Separable prefixes often cause confusion for beginning readers because (1) the prefixes are identical to prepositions or adverbs, (2) separable prefixes alter the meaning of the simple verb conjugated in the sentence, and (3) the prefix generally occurs in the final position of a clause separated from the conjugated verb. Consider the following examples:

> Die neuen Einwohner **zogen** gestern ohne ihre Möbel **ein**.
> (**ein/ziehen**   *to move in*)
> *The new residents moved in yesterday without their furniture.*
> Hoffentlich **kommen** ihre Möbel heute oder morgen **an**.
> (**an/kommen**   *to arrive*)
> *Hopefully, their furniture will arrive today or tomorrow.*
> Ich **lade** sie vielleicht heute Abend zum Essen **ein**.
> (**ein/laden**   *to invite*)
> *Maybe I'll invite them for dinner this evening.*

If you begin to translate from left to right, you are likely to fall into the trap of looking up the infinitives **ziehen**, **kommen**, and **laden**, which mean *to draw, to come,* and *to load.* Since, however, the separable prefix is located in the final position of the clause, it is always necessary to read each sentence to the end before translating.

Separable prefixes generally consist of short, simple words largely identical to prepositions or adverbs. The most common separable prefixes are: **ab-, an-, auf-, aus-, bei-, ein-, fort-, her-, hin-, mit-, nach-, vor-, weg-, zurück-, zusammen-**. The prefix **hin-** indicates a motion away from the speaker or action; the prefix **her-** indicates a motion toward the speaker or action. Both may occur in combination with other prefixes: **hinab-, heran-, hinauf-, herein-, hervor-**.

Separable prefixes are separated slightly differently from their verb stems in the perfect tenses (see **Kapitel 9**) and in infinitive phrases (**Kapitel 22**).

Translating tips:

Always read the entire sentence before attempting to translate. Pay close attention to the end of the clause. Frequently, the last word of the clause may be a separable prefix. Attach it to the stem of the simple verb and look up this combination in the dictionary.

If you need the assistance of the irregular verb list to help ascertain the infinitive, check the list for the infinitive of the simple verb, reattach the prefix, and then proceed to look up the compound verb.

8.3 Recognizing Singulars and Plurals of Nouns

By now you know that articles and adjectives preceding nouns provide important information for determining a noun's function and meaning in context. Here is a summary of indicators that may help you determine singulars and plurals of nouns.

A. Singular

- when preceded by **das, des,** or **dem:**
  das Buch des Mannes; auf dem Tisch
- when preceded by **ein-** words without endings or with the endings **-es** or **-em:**
  ein Freund meines Freundes; in unserem Haus
- subject noun, if verb does not have **-en** ending
- feminine nouns ending in **-ung, -heit, -keit, -schaft, -ie, -ik, -in, -ion, -tät, -ei** (plural forms end in **-en**)

B. Plural

- **die** with obviously masculine noun: **die Männer**
- **die** plus noun ending in **-en: die Klassen**
- **die** plus adjective ending in **-en: die gefährdeten Tiere** *(the endangered animals)*
- subject noun, if verb ends in **-en, -n,** or is **sind**
- frequently, noun without article (check context before deciding)
- frequently, noun with unpreceded adjective ending in **-e**

Note that an **-s** ending indicates a plural ending *in English* but generally *not in German*.

When these rules or the context still do not provide enough information to help you, consult the vocabulary list or look the word up in a dictionary.

Grundwortschatz

an/fangen (fing ... an; fängt ... an)	*to begin*	**kaum**	*hardly*
an/ziehen (zog ... an)	*to attract*	**Kraft** *(f.)*, **⸚e**	*power, force, strength*
Aufgabe *(f.)*, **-n**	*task, problem, duty*	**Reise** *(f.)*, **-n**	*trip*
aus/führen	*to carry out, execute*	**sofort**	*immediately*
aus/üben	*to exert*	**statt/finden** (fand ... statt)	*to take place, occur*
aus/wandern	*to emigrate*	**Umweltschutz** *(m.)*	*environmental protection*
Bau *(m.)*, **-ten**	*construction, building*	**um/ziehen** (zog ... um)	*to move*
besitzen (besaß)	*to possess, have*	**Ursprung** *(m.)*, **⸚e**	*origin, source*
Bruder *(m.)*, **⸚**	*brother*	**ursprünglich**	*original(ly)*
daher	*therefore, hence*	**Veränderung** *(f.)*, **-en**	*change*
dar/stellen	*to represent, depict*	**verhältnismäßig**	*relatively, comparatively*
Eigenschaft *(f.)*, **-en**	*property, quality*	**Vielfalt** *(f.)*	*diversity, variety, multiplicity*
einfach	*simple, simply*	**Voraussetzung** *(f.)*, **-en**	*assumption, hypothesis, prerequisite*
Einführung *(f.)*, **-en**	*introduction*		
ein/laden (lud ... ein; lädt ... ein)	*to invite*	**vor/ziehen** (zog ... vor)	*to prefer*
ein/nehmen (nahm ... ein; nimmt ... ein)	*to take up, occupy*	**wahrscheinlich**	*probably*
ein/teilen	*to divide, classify*	**weich**	*soft*
Erziehung *(f.)*	*education, upbringing*	**weiß**	*white*
gefährdet	*endangered*	**weiter**	*further*
grün	*green*	**Wort** *(n.)*, **-e; ⸚er**[2]	*word*
grundsätzlich	*fundamental(ly)*	**zurück/kehren**	*to return*
Grundzug *(m.)*, **⸚e**	*main feature, characteristic*	**z.B.** (zum Beispiel)	*e.g. (for example)*
Heimat *(f.)*	*home, homeland*		

---

2. German has two plural forms for **Wort**. The plural form **Wörter** refers to *unconnected words*. Otherwise, the plural is **Worte**.

Übungssätze

1. Das Bauhaus war ursprünglich eine Unterrichtsstätte in Weimar.
2. 1925 siedelte das Bauhaus nach Dessau um, und einige Jahre später zog die Schule für Kunst, Handwerk und Technik nach Berlin um.
3. Im Artikel 20a des Grundgesetzes erhob der Staat 1994 den Umweltschutz zum Staatszweck.
4. Der konsequente Schutz von Luft, Wasser und Boden ist natürlich eine zentrale Voraussetzung für eine gesunde wirtschaftliche Entwicklung.
5. Die globalen Umweltprobleme wie z.B. Klimaänderung, Abbau der Ozonschicht und der Rückgang der biologischen Vielfalt stellen eine besondere Aufgabe für den Staat dar.
6. Der Architekt Andreas Schlüter prägte fast eigenhändig den preußisch-berlinerischen Barockbaustil.
7. Der Große Kurfürst (1620–1688) forderte seinen Hofarchitekten auf, Berlin grundsätzlich umzugestalten.
8. Das Zeughaus illustriert das Wesentliche des preußisch-berlinerischen Stils: einen Sinn für Realität findet man hier zusammen mit verschnörkelten Dekorationen.

1. **Bauhaus** (*n.*) *Bauhaus (1919–1933 German school of design)*
   Unterrichtsstätte (*f.*), **-n** *pedagogical workshop*
2. **um/siedeln** *to shift to new quarters, relocate*
3. **Grundgesetz** (*n.*) *Basic Law of the Federal Republic of Germany*
   erheben (erhob) *to elevate*
   Staatszweck (*m.*), **-e** *civic goal, purpose*
4. **konsequent** *consistent, ongoing (not: consequent)*
5. **Abbau der Ozonschicht** *depletion of the ozone layer*
   Rückgang (*m.*), **⁻e** *decline*

6. **prägen** *to coin, give something a characteristic look*
   fast *nearly*
   eigenhändig *single-handedly*
7. **der Große Kurfürst** *the Great Elector*
   auf/fordern *to call upon, command, invite*
   Hofarchitekt (*m., n-noun*), **-en** *court architect*
   umzugestalten (um/gestalten + zu-construction) *to reconfigure*
8. **Zeughaus** (*n.*), **⁻er** *military storehouse*
   Sinn (*m.*), **-e** *sense*
   verschnörkelt *ornate*

9. In seinem Edikt von 1671 hob Friedrich das Verbot gegen die Ansiedlung von Juden auf. In dieser Zeit kamen viele jüdische Familien nach Berlin.
10. Einige Zeit später lud der Kurfürst verfolgte Calvinisten aus Frankreich nach Berlin ein.
11. Zwischen 1820 und 1920 wanderten über sechs Millionen Deutsche in die Neue Welt aus.
12. Hunderttausende kehrten aber auch in ihre deutsche Heimat zurück und verbrachten ihren Lebensabend in Deutschland.

discovered X-rays ←

13. 1895 gab Röntgen seine große Entdeckung bekannt. Die Bekanntgabe fand in seinem Labor in München statt.
14. Die Brüder Orville und Wilbur Wright führten im Jahre 1903 mit einem selbstgebauten Doppeldecker den ersten Motorflug aus.
15. 1912 stieß der englische Dampfer Titanic auf seiner ersten Reise nach New York mit einem Eisberg zusammen und ging mit 1500 Menschen unter.
16. In seiner Autobiographie beschrieb der Staatsmann die Einflüsse seiner Erziehung auf seine persönliche Entwicklung. Seine Beschreibung ist verhältnismäßig glaubwürdig.
17. Die alten Römer teilten das Jahr in nur zehn Monate ein. Sie fingen mit dem Kriegsgott Mars an, und am Ende zählten sie mit September bis Dezember den siebten bis zum zehnten Monat ab. Der zweite römische Kaiser fügte schließlich zwei weitere Monate hinzu: Januar und Februar.

9. **auf/heben (hob ... auf)** *to suspend, repeal*
Verbot gegen die Ansiedlung von Juden *prohibition of Jewish immigration*
10. **verfolgt** *persecuted*
12. **verbringen (verbrachte)** *to spend*
Lebensabend *(m.),* **-e** *last days of one's life*
13. **bekannt/geben (gab ... bekannt; gibt ... bekannt)** *to make known, make public*
Röntgen *(Wilhelm Konrad) Roentgen (1845–1923; discoverer of X-ray)*

14. **selbstgebaut** *homemade*
Flug *(m.),* **⁼e** *flight*
15. **zusammen/stoßen (stieß ... zusammen; stößt ... zusammen)** *to collide*
unter/gehen (ging ... unter) *to sink*
16. **glaubwürdig** *believable, worthy of believing*
17. **ab/zählen** *to count down*
hinzu/fügen *to add (to)*
schließlich *finally*

18. Die gut bekannten Werke von Karl Friedrich Schinkel schließen viele Bauten ein, wie z.B. Museen, Kirchen und Schlösser. Die vorliegende Einführung über den Architekten und Künstler stellt relativ unbekannte Werke dar.

18. **einschließen (schloss ... ein)** *to include*   **vorliegend** *present, currently under discussion*

 Leitfagen zum Lesetext auf **academic.cengage.com/german/korb**

Dioramenmaler: Der nicht so gut bekannte Schinkel

Der Name Karl Friedrich Schinkel ist eng mit der Baugeschichte Berlins verbunden. Seinen Namen assoziieren wir grundsätzlich mit dem klassischen Stil von Berliner Architektur. Die besten Beispiele seines architektonischen Handwerks stellen die Neue Wache (1816–1818), das Schauspielhaus am Gendarmenmarkt (1818–1821) und das Museum am Lustgarten (1824–1830) dar. In diesen Bauten brachte Schinkel Schönheit und Funktionalität zusammen, und in ihren neu renovierten aber im Wesentlichen erhaltenen Formen bieten sie dem heutigen Berlin-Besucher ein gutes Bild vom klassischen Berlin dar.   5

Weniger bekannt sind Schinkels Entwürfe und Ausführungen von Dioramen und Panoramen in der Zeit der französischen Besetzung von Berlin (1806–1808).   10

Ein Panorama baut man in einem dunkel beleuchteten Raum auf. Großformatige, runde Gemälde umgeben die Betrachter. Man   15

2 **eng verbunden mit** *closely connected to*
5 **Handwerk** (*n.*) *craft, trade*
 Neue Wache *New Guardhouse*
6 **Gendarmenmarkt** *(Berlin's) Gendarme Square*
 Lustgarten (*m.*) *Pleasure Garden*
8 **zusammen/bringen (brachte ... zusammen)** *to combine, bring together*
9 **im Wesentlichen erhalten** *essentially preserved*

10 **dar/bieten (bat ... dar)** *to offer, present (to)*
11 **Entwurf** (*m.*), ¨-e *sketch, draft*
 Ausführung (*f.*), -en *realization (of project)*
12 **Besetzung** (*f.*) *(military) occupation*
14 **auf/bauen** *to construct, set up*
 beleuchtet *lighted, lit*
15 **großformatig** *large-format*
 rund *round, circular*
 umgeben (umgab) *to surround*
 Betrachter (*m.*), – *viewer*

schaut die Gemälde von der Mitte des Raumes an. Zu einem
Diorama kommt zwischen dem Gemälde und dem Standort des
Betrachters ein Rahmen oder eine Kolonne hinzu. Das Resultat ist
eine perspektivisch-optische Illusion. Dreidimensionale Objekte
20 (z.B. bei Landschaftspanoramen Sand, Steine, Büsche usw.), effekt-
volle Beleuchtung und manchmal Musik steigern den Effekt der
perspektivisch-optischen Gemälde.

    Kaum fünfundzwanzig Jahre alt, fing Schinkel 1806 an, Panora-
men und Dioramen zu produzieren. 1807 stellte er seinen ersten
25 Zyklus von Dioramen aus: Große Bilder von Konstantinopel,
Jerusalem und Ägypten transportierten die Betrachter in eine Welt
der Illusion. In den nächsten acht Jahren führte der spätere „klassische Baumeister von Berlin" über 40 Dioramen aus, und zu den
berühmtesten Panoramen dieser Zeit zählt Schinkels 1808 gemaltes
30 Panorama von Palermo (5 m × 30 m). Als Friedrich Wilhelm III. aus
dem Exil nach Berlin zurückkehrte, führte ihm Schinkel seine
Dioramen stolz vor.

16 **an/schauen** *look at, view*
Mitte (*f.*) *middle, c*
17 **Standort** (*m.*), **-e** *position*
18 **Rahmen** (*m.*), **–** *frame, border*
Kolonne (*f.*), **–** *column*
hinzu/kommen (kam ... hinzu) *to
be added to*
19 **perspektivisch-optisch** *two- vs.
three-dimensional optical*

20 **usw. (= und so weiter)** *etc.*
(=et cetera)
21 **Beleuchtung** (*f.*) *lighting*
steigern *to increase*
28 **Baumeister** (*m.*), **–** *master builder*
(also: architect)
29 **berühmtest-** *most famous*
zählen zu *to rank among*
gemalt *painted*

KAPITEL 9

9.1 Perfect Tenses

In English, the perfect tenses consist of forms of the auxiliary verb *to have* plus the past participle of the main verb, e.g., *he has acted* and *she has seen* (present perfect forms of a regular and an irregular verb); *he had acted* and *she had seen* (past perfect forms). Much as in German, regular and irregular verbs are clearly differentiated by weak and strong endings, as well as by vowel changes in the strong forms. Unlike contemporary English, which uses the auxiliary verb *to have* for all perfect tense forms, the auxiliary verb in the perfect tenses in German may be **haben** or **sein**. Note, however, that this fact does not lead to two different translations. Both auxiliaries have the same translation in English.

Present perfect

Weak verbs

er/sie/es hat gesagt   *he/she/it said (has said)*
sie haben gesagt   *they said (have said)*
er/sie/es ist gereist   *he/she/it traveled (has traveled)*
sie sind gereist   *they traveled (have traveled)*

Strong verbs

er/sie/es hat gesehen   *he/she/it saw (has seen)*
sie haben gesehen   *they saw (have seen)*
er/sie/es ist gekommen   *he/she/it came (has come)*
sie sind gekommen   *they came (have come)*

Past perfect

Weak verbs

er/sie/es hatte gesagt   *he/she/it had said*
sie hatten gesagt   *they had said*
er/sie/es war gereist   *he/she/it had traveled*
sie waren gereist   *they had traveled*

Strong verbs

er/sie/es hatte gesehen   *he/she/it had seen*
sie hatten gesehen   *they had seen*
er/sie/es war gekommen   *he/she/it had come*
sie waren gekommen   *they had come*

Transitive verbs (verbs that take a direct object) always use **haben** as the auxiliary verb in the perfect tenses. *Intransitive verbs* (verbs that do not take direct objects), particularly when they indicate motion or state of being, usually use **sein**. Most German verbs use **haben**.

9.2 Meanings of the Perfect Tenses

The German present perfect is usually equivalent to the English past tense. Occasionally, however, the English present perfect may be better. This is true, for example, in the presence of the adverbs **gerade** (*just*) or **schon** (*already*).

> Der Neinsager hat „nein" gesagt.
> *The naysayer said "no."*
> Der Neinsager hat gerade „nein" gesagt.
> *The naysayer has just said "no."*
> Der Neinsager ist gekommen und gegangen.
> *The naysayer came and went.*
> Der Neinsager ist schon gekommen und gegangen.
> *The naysayer has already come and gone.*

Remember that the German differentiation between **haben** and **sein** has no influence on the English meaning.

> Er hatte (gerade) nein gesagt.
> *He had (just) said no.*
> Er war (schon) gekommen und gegangen.
> *He had (already) come and gone.*

The past perfect is used to differentiate between events in past time and events that had happened at an earlier time in the past. Whereas German expresses past events using either or both simple past and present perfect, the past perfect is always expressed by means of a compound tense utilizing **hatt-** or **war-** plus the past participle. In the past perfect, both **hatt-** and **war-** are equivalent to *had*.

9.3 *Seit* + Present Tense = *have been + -ing*

When answering questions about how long one has been doing something (which continues to be happening), German uses **seit** plus the present tense. The dative preposition **seit** often occurs with the adverb **schon** (*already*).

(schon) seit + amount of time = *(already) for +*
amount of time

(schon) seit + specific time = *(already) since + specific time*

Seit wann lernen Sie Deutsch?
How long have you been learning German?
Ich spreche schon seit drei Jahren Deutsch.
I have been speaking German already for three years.
Wir wohnen (schon) seit März 2007 in Berlin.
We've been living in Berlin (already) since March 2007.

9.4 Past Participles

As you begin to learn the past participle forms of German verbs, you will quickly recognize great similarities between the German and the English verb systems, not only with regard to endings on weak and strong verbs but also in the vowel changes in the many strong verbs that are alike in German and English.

Dictionaries do not always list past participles. You must, therefore, be able to derive the infinitive of a verb by analyzing the past participle.

A. Weak verbs

Past participles ending in **-t** generally equate to English past participle *-ed*. To derive the infinitive note the following patterns and variations that occur among them:

Past Participle	Components	Stem Type	Infinitive
gesagt	ge-sag-t	regular (weak) verb	sagen
gearbeitet	ge-arbeit-et	regular verb ending in **-t/-d**	arbeiten
fotografiert	fotografier-t	ending in **-ieren**	fotografieren
bezahlt	bezahl-t	inseparable prefix regular verb	bezahlen
verzeichnet	verzeichn-et	inseparable prefix, ending in consonant cluster	verzeichnen
ausgedrückt	aus-ge-drück-t	separable prefix	aus/drücken
aufgehört	auf-ge-hör-t	regular verb	auf/hören

(mixed verbs need to be added to this list) neunundachtzig ▼ 89

To determine the infinitive from the past participle of the majority of weak verbs, simply drop the prefix **ge-** and the ending **-(e)t**, and add **-en** to the stem. Infinitives of **-ieren** verbs and inseparable prefixes are even more readily identifiable.

Note that for verbs with separable prefixes (**ausgedrückt, aufgehört**), **ge-** stands between the separable prefix and the stem of the verb in the past participle.

B. Strong verbs

Past participles ending in **-en** generally correspond to English past participles likewise ending in *-(e)n*. Note also the parallels between many English and German strong verb parts. For example:

> **hat gesungen / singen** *has sung / to sing*
> **hat gegeben / geben** *has given / to give*
> **hat getrunken / trinken** *has drunk / to drink*

Participles of strong verbs have three basic stem types:

Past Participle	Components	Stem Type	Infinitive
(hat) gesungen	ge-sung-en	common strong stem	singen
(ist) gefahren	ge-fahr-en		fahren
(hat) genommen	ge-nomm-en		nehmen
(hat) bestanden	bestand-en	inseparable prefix	bestehen
(ist) verfallen	verfall-en		verfallen
(hat) vergessen	vergess-en		vergessen
(hat) angefangen	an-ge-fang-en	separable prefix	an/fangen
(ist) vorgefahren	vor-ge-fahr-en		vor/fahren
(hat) beigetragen	bei-ge-trag-en		bei/tragen

To determine the infinitive of a strong verb, identify the stem and then check the irregular verb list for the corresponding infinitive. Note that the vowel and the stem in some participles, for example **genommen / nehmen**, differ markedly from the infinitive, leaving little but the first letter of the stem as a clue to help find the verb in the list of irregular verbs.

On the other hand, past participles formed from some inseparable-prefix verbs (**verfallen, vergessen**) are identical with their infinitive. These participles also resemble the plural forms in the present tense.

Note the difference: Participles occur with a helping verb; present-tense plurals stand alone.

> Wir **vergessen** den Namen des Autors.
> *We forget the author's name.*
> Wir **haben** den Namen des Autors **vergessen**.
> *We forgot / have forgotten the author's name.*
> In diesem Stadtteil **verfallen** die Häuser.
> *The houses in this part of town are falling apart.*
> In diesem Stadtteil **sind** die Häuser **verfallen**.
> *The houses in this part of town have fallen apart.*

In past participles of verbs with separable prefixes (**angefangen**, **beigetragen**), **ge-** stands between the separable prefix and the stem. Find the infinitive of the stem in the irregular verb list, reattach the prefix, and then look up the verb.

Be aware of "look-alike" pairs of participles, for example **gelesen** und **gelassen** (from **lesen** and **lassen**) or **gegessen** and **gesessen** (from **essen** and **sitzen**). Intelligent guessing and memorizing the principal parts of common strong verbs are valuable skills for decoding participles. Memorization is the only way to recognize **gewesen**, the past participle of **sein** *(to be)*:

> Wer **ist** heute Bundeskanzler?
> *Who is the Federal Chancellor today?*
> Wer **ist** 1999 Bundeskanzler **gewesen?**
> *Who was the Chancellor in 1999?*
> Wer **war** vor 1999 Bundeskanzler gewesen?
> *Who had been the Chancellor before 1999?*

C. Principal parts of strong verbs

The vocabulary lists in this book indicate the principal parts of a verb when its forms vary from the infinitive. The principal parts of a verb are the infinitive (**fallen**; **beginnen**) plus the third-person singular forms of the verb's simple past (**fiel**; **begann**), past participle (**gefallen**; **begonnen**), and present (**fällt**; **beginnt**). Note the difference between the vocabulary listings for these two verbs.

> **fallen (fiel, ist gefallen; fällt)** *to fall*
> **beginnen (begann, begonnen)** *to begin*

Fallen is an example of how the lists note verbs that take the auxiliary verb **sein** and that have a vowel change in the present tense. **Beginnen** exemplifies verbs that take the auxiliary verb **haben** and that do not experience a vowel change in the present tense.

The vocabulary lists in this book do not make special note of the principal parts of regular verbs.

9.5 Word Order

German perfect tense verbs are compound verbs, meaning they have at least two components. For example:

> Viele deutsche Revolutionäre sind 1848 und 1849 nach Amerika gekommen.
> *Many German revolutionaries came to America in 1848 and 1849.*

The complete compound verb is **sind gekommen** (*came*). The past participle (**gekommen**) stands at the end of the main clause. The auxiliary (**sind**) stands in second position because it is the *finite* verb. Based on the sentence formula in **Kapitel 5**, an outline of the sentence is: S + V1 + Adverbs (time/place) + V2.

The finite verb (V1) is the *inflected or conjugated* form of the verb, indicating person, number of the subject, and tense. In simple tenses, V1 is the main verb itself. In compound tenses, the finite verb is the auxiliary for the participle (V2). Remember: When you come to a form of **haben** or **sein**, *check the end of the clause for a past participle to see whether the form of* haben *or* sein *is an auxiliary of the perfect tense.* If this is the case, translate the two-part verb as a single unit.

Translating Tip:

Use the following translating order: First translate the subject, then the compound verb as a unit. Proceed by translating verb complements (adverbs, objects, prepositional phrases in adverbial functions) in what may seem to be reverse order since the German sequence is often a mirror image of the English.

Viele deutsche Revolutionäre sind 1848 und 1849 nach Amerika gekommen.

1. Viele deutsche Revolutionäre   *Many German revolutionaries*
2. sind gekommen   *came*
3. nach Amerika   *to America*
4. 1848 und 1849   *in 1848 and 1849*

Grundwortschatz

bei/tragen (trug ... bei, beigetragen; trägt ... bei)	*to contribute*	**Grenze** *(f.)*, **-n**	*boundary, border*
		Hauptstadt *(f.)*, **̈e**	*capital city*
berichten	*to report*	**hören**	*to hear*
bestimmen	*to ascertain, define*	**kämpfen**	*to fight, battle*
		kennen lernen	*to get to know, become acquainted with*
bleiben (blieb, ist geblieben)	*to stay, remain*		
bürgerlich	*middle class, bourgeois; civic*	**lesen (las, gelesen liest)**	*to read*
deshalb	*therefore*	**nötig**	*necessary, needed*
Einwohner *(m.)*, **–; Einwohnerin** *(f.)*, **-nen**	*inhabitant*	**rein**	*pure, clean*
		spät	*late*
erhöhen	*to increase, raise*	**Sprache** *(f.)*, **-n**	*language*
ermöglichen	*to make possible*	**sprechen (sprach, gesprochen; spricht)**	*to speak*
erscheinen (erschien, ist erschienen)	*to appear; to be published*		
		steigern	*to increase, raise*
Gegenstand *(m.)*, **̈e**	*object*	**Teilnehmer** *(m.)*, **–; Teilnehmerin** *(f.)*, **-nen**	*participant*
Gelehrte *(f. or m.)*, **-n**	*scholar, scientist*	**Vereinigte Staaten** *(pl.)*	*United States*
geschehen (geschah, ist geschehen; geschieht)	*to happen, take place*	**Vernunft** *(f.)*	*reason*
		vor	*before, ago*
		vor zehn Jahren	*ten years ago*
Gesetz *(n.)*, **-e**	*law*	**vor/bereiten**	*to prepare*
Gesundheit *(f.)*	*health*		

Übungssätze

1. Sind Sie schon in Salzburg gewesen? Diese Stadt, die Hauptstadt des Bundeslandes Salzburg, hat in den letzten Jahren viel zur Förderung des Fremdenverkehrs beigetragen.
2. Die Salzburger Festspiele sind letztes Jahr ein großer Erfolg gewesen. Rund 500 000 Touristen haben die Stadt besucht.
3. Nach seiner achten Sinfonie hat Gustav Mahler „Das Lied von der Erde" komponiert. Es ist eine Sinfonie für Alt, Tenor und großes Orchester.
4. 1980 hat man AIDS (erworbenes Immundefekt-Syndrom) entdeckt. Die Medizinforschung der Neunziger hat die Lebenserwartung der Aidskranken wesentlich erhöht.
5. Eine wirksame Behandlungsmethode sucht man schon seit Jahren.
6. Am Anfang des neunzehnten Jahrhunderts hat man wieder ziemlich viel über den großen deutschen Mystiker Jakob Böhme gehört. Außer der Bibel hatte Böhme nur einige mystische Schriften theosophischen und alchimistischen Inhalts gelesen.
7. Mit seiner Bibelübersetzung hatte Luther der deutschen Sprache einen großen Dienst erwiesen.
8. Ein türkischer Student in Deutschland berichtet: „Das Wort des Familienoberhaupts ist in einer sehr frommen moslemischen Familie eine Art Gesetz. Die fremde Umgebung in der neuen Heimat, z.B. in Deutschland, hat dieses Gesetz nicht geändert.
9. Nach dem Fall der Mauer (1989) haben manche nicht zu Unrecht Marx und Engels „Wessis" genannt: Karl Marx hatte zuerst in Bonn studiert und „Das Kapital" in London vollendet. Engels war

1. **Förderung** (*f.*), **-en** *advancement*
   Fremdenverkehr (*m.*) *tourism*
2. **Erfolg** (*m.*), **-e** *success*
   rund *approximately, around*
3. **Lied** (*n.*), **-er** *song*
4. **Lebenserwartung** (*f.*) *life expectancy*
5. **wirksam** *effective*
   Behandlungsmethode (*f.*), **-n** *method of treatment*
6. **außer** *besides*
   Schrift (*f.*), **-en** *work, writing, script*
   Inhalt (*m.*), **-e** *content*

7. **Übersetzung** (*f.*), **-en** *translation*
   erweisen (erwies, erwiesen) *to render*
   Dienst (*m.*), **-e** *service*
8. **Oberhaupt** (*m.*), **-̈er** *head*
   fromm *devout*
   Art Gesetz *type / sort of law*
   fremd *foreign*
   Umgebung (*f.*), **-en** *surroundings*
9. **Mauer** (*f.*), **-n** *wall; Berlin Wall*
   nicht zu Unrecht *not totally without reason*
   „Wessis" *"westerners"*

in Wuppertal in eine Unternehmerfamilie geboren und hatte in Wuppertal und Manchester in der väterlichen Fabrik gearbeitet.

10. Zusammen haben Marx und Engels im Jahre 1848 „Das kommunistische Manifest" verfasst. Engels hatte schon 1844 in Paris den Gelehrten Marx kennen gelernt. *past perfect*

11. Nach der Revolution von 1848 sind viele deutsche Intellektuelle in die Vereinigten Staaten ausgewandert. Marx und Engels sind aber in London gelandet.

12. Der norwegische Polarforscher Roald Amundsen hat während der Suche nach Nobiles Luftschiff sein Leben für seinen italienischen Rivalen Nobile geopfert. Amundsen ist 1928 bei Spitzbergen verschollen.

13. Mit Nobile und Ellsworth war er selber 1926 über den Nordpol geflogen.

14. In seiner „Kritik der reinen Vernunft" hat Kant die Grenzen aller menschlichen Erkenntnis untersucht und bestimmt. Das Wissen selbst ist hier zum Gegenstand der Kritik geworden.

15. Seine wichtigsten philosophischen Arbeiten sind in dem vorletzten Jahrzehnt des achtzehnten Jahrhunderts erschienen.

16. James Watt hat im Jahre 1765 die erste brauchbare Dampfmaschine erfunden. Die Erfindung der ersten Dampfmaschine hat die Massenherstellung von industriellen Produkten ermöglicht.

17. Das Stadtbild der Stadt Augsburg ist u.a. von Renaissancebauten geprägt.

18. Die günstige Lage an der Handelsstraße nach Italien hat schon im fünfzehnten Jahrhundert Augsburg zu einem wichtigen Handelsplatz gemacht.

vollenden *to complete*
Unternehmer (*m.*), – *entrepreneur*
väterlich *paternal*
12. **Suche** (*f.*), **-n** *search*
Luftschiff (*n.*), **-e** *airship*
opfern *to sacrifice*
verschollen *disappeared,* ~~sunk~~ ~~into oblivious~~
14. **Erkenntnis** (*f.*), **-se** *knowledge*
15. **vorletzt** *next-to-last*
16. **brauchbar** *practical*
Herstellung (*f.*), **-en** *production*

17. **Stadtbild** (*n.*) *cityscape; city's general character*
u.a. (unter anderem) *among other things*
Renaissancebau (*m.*), **-ten** *building of the Renaissance period*
prägen *to coin, shape, mold, leave an impression upon*
18. **günstig** *favorable*
Handelsstraße (*f.*), **-n** *trade route*
Handelsplatz (*m.*), **⁻e** *place of trade, commercial center*

DIE ANFÄNGE BERTOLT BRECHTS

Augsburg ist u.a. die Geburts- und Heimatstadt von Bertolt Brecht. Der berühmte Schriftsteller und Regisseur ist am 10. Februar 1898 in dieser bayrischen Kleinstadt geboren und dort in einem bürgerlichen Milieu aufgewachsen. Sein Vater hat als
5 kaufmännischer Angestellter gearbeitet und ist 1914 Direktor einer Papierfabrik geworden. Ab 1908 hat der junge Brecht das Königliche Realgymnasium besucht. Besonders gut in der Schule war er nicht, aber schon mit 15 Jahren hat der Schüler Brecht angefangen, Gedichte zu schreiben. Seine ersten Gedichte sind in der Augsburger Schüler-
10 zeitschrift „Die Ernte" erschienen. In dieser Zeit hat er auch seinen ersten Ein-Akter geschrieben; er ist aber leider verschollen.

Auf Dauer ist Augsburg Brecht zu klein geworden, und er ist bald nach seinem Abitur nach München umgezogen. In der bayrischen Landeshauptstadt hat der junge Pazifist an der Universität
15 Medizin studiert und den Ersten Weltkrieg überstanden. Nach dem Tod seiner Mutter im Jahre 1920 hat Brecht langsam seine enge Verbindung zu Augsburg abgebrochen.

Im Jahre 1922 hat Brecht für seine Stücke „Baal", „Trommeln in der Nacht" und „Im Dickicht der Städte" den Kleist-Preis bekommen.
20 Im ersten Akt von „Baal" hat er den bürgerlichen Literatur-Salon ~~literary Salon~~ dargestellt und satirisiert. Baals Sprache ist durch das Gemeine und Brutale charakterisiert. Seine Verehrer sind komisch-grotesk. Frauen und Männer fallen ihm zu Füßen. So eine extreme Offenheit hat die

---

3 **bayrisch** *Bavarian*
4 **auf/wachsen (wuchs ... auf, ist aufgewachsen; wächst auf)** *to grow up*
5 **angestellt** *employed*
7 **Realgymnasium** *(n.), -gymnasien high school*
   besonders *especially*
8 **Gedichte zu schreiben** *to write poems*
10 **Ernte** *(f), -n harvest*
11 **verschollen** *missing, lost*

13 **Abitur** *(n.) high school diploma*
15 **überstehen (überstand, überstanden)** *to survive*
18 **Trommel** *(f.), -n drum*
19 **Dickicht** *(n.), -e jungle*
21 **gemein** *ordinary, vulgar*
22 **Verehrer** *(m.), – admirer*
23 **jemandem zu Füßen fallen (fiel, ist gefallen; fällt)** *to fall at someone's feet*
   Offenheit *(f.) openness, frankness*

kleinbürgerlichen Zuschauer und auch viele Kritiker in München schockiert. Der Berliner Kritiker Herbert Ihering hat aber Brechts Zeitkritik verteidigt und sein Lob gesungen. Mit diesem wichtigen Kontakt hat die Geschichte des größten deutschen Dramatikers des zwanzigsten Jahrhunderts ihren Anfang genommen.

26 **sein Lob singen (sang, gesungen)**
    to sing his praises

28 **Anfang nehmen (nahm, genommen; nimmt)** *to get a start*

KAPITEL 10

10.1 Present Participle

The present participle in German functions primarily as a modifier.

> der **sterbende** Wald   *the dying forest*
> das **fließende** Wasser   *the running water*
> der **entscheidende** Moment   *the deciding (decisive) moment*

The present participle is formed by adding **-d** to an infinitive: **sterben—sterbend, fließen—fließend, entscheiden—entscheidend**. Watch for words ending in **-end** (plus adjective ending). All German infinitives can be turned into a present participle, thus creating many forms that require a relative clause construction in English.

> eine **alleinstehende** Mutter
> *a mother who is living on her own (a single mother)*
> das **antwortende** Kind
> *the child who is answering*
> der im Wald **stehende** Bär
> *the bear that's standing in the woods*

The phenomenon of the "extended-adjective construction," which you see in the final example above, is discussed in detail in **Kapitel 23** and **24**.

10.2 Participles Used as Adjectives and Adverbs

A. Adjectives

Present and past participles will occur frequently as adjectives.

> das **bedrohte** Tier   *the threatened animal*
> **fließendes** Wasser   *running water*
> Das ist **verboten**.   *That is forbidden.*
> Die Antwort war **überraschend**.   *The answer was surprising.*

When used as attributive adjectives (preceding a noun), both past participles (**bedrohte**) and present participles (**fließendes**) have endings in accordance with the outline for adjective endings in **Kapitel 7**. As predicate adjectives (**verboten, überraschend**), they take no endings.

B. Adverbs

Present participles are often used as adverbs.

> **fließend** Deutsch sprechen   *to speak German fluently*
> **dringend** nötige Hilfe   *urgently needed help*
> **überraschend** hohe Preise   *surprisingly high prices*

Participles used as adverbs have no endings.

10.3 Meanings of Present and Past Participles

Remember: nouns modified by a *present* participle are *doing* something.

> das **schlafende** Kind
> *the sleeping child (the child who is sleeping)*
> die Bücher **schreibende** Frau
> *the woman who is writing books*
> die **blühende** Blume   *the blossoming flower*

When a noun is modified by a *past* participle, something *has been done* to the noun, or the past participle shows something that the noun *has done*.

> das **geschriebene** Wort
> *the written word (the word that was written)*
> der gerade **angekommene** Zug
> *the train that just arrived*
> die im Text **angeführten** Informationen
> *the information that was cited in the text*

10.4 Past Participle Used with *sein* to Express State of Being

You will remember from **Kapitel 9** that transitive verbs (verbs that take a direct object) normally use **haben** as an auxiliary to form the perfect tenses. When a form of **sein** is used with the past participle of a transitive verb, the past participle functions as a predicate adjective describing a state of being or status. You must learn to differentiate among the various uses of the past participle demonstrated in the following examples.

> In der Tabelle **haben** wir die Ergebnisse **wiedergegeben**.
> *We have shown the results in the table.*

Note that **haben wiedergegeben** is the present perfect tense.

> In der Tabelle **sind** die Ergebnisse **wiedergegeben**.
> *The results are shown in the table.*

In this sentence, **wiedergegeben** (following **sind**) functions as a predicate adjective defining the status of the results.

> Die Studenten **sind** in die Bibliothek **gegangen**.
> *The students went to the library.*

Sind gegangen is the present perfect tense. Like most intransitive verbs, **gehen** uses **sein** to form the perfect tenses.

Determine the functions and meanings of the past participles in the following sentences.

1. Der Schriftsteller hat drei Bücher geschrieben, und er recherchiert für ein viertes Buch. Sein viertes Buch ist noch nicht geschrieben.
2. Die Tür ist geschlossen. Das kleine Kind hat die Tür geschlossen und ist hinausgegangen.
3. Unsere Schule hat Rauchen und Trinken verboten. Rauchen und Trinken sind in unserer Schule verboten.

10.5 Participles Used as Nouns

Like all German adjectives, participles may also function as nouns, in which case they are capitalized and inflected like other adjectives used as nouns (**Kapitel 7**). Participial nouns may represent concepts or living beings:

> Das **Berichtete** hat alles bestätigt. *What was reported confirmed everything.*
> Das **Folgende** bestätigt das schon **Gesagte**. *The following confirms what has already been said.*
> der Verwundete *the injured, wounded man*
> die Schlafende *the sleeping woman*
> der Sterbende *the dying man*
> der Gestorbene *the man who has died*

Participles as adjectives can also be used elliptically, in which case an unstated noun is understood. Here the adjective is not capitalized.

> Im Text besprechen wir eine arbeitende Frau und dann eine nicht **arbeitende**.
> *In the text we discuss a woman who is working and then one who isn't working.*

Since many nouns derived from participles are not listed in the dictionary, their meaning must be determined from the infinitive.

10.6 Infinitives Used as Nouns

Infinitives used as nouns are always neuter. English often uses a gerund (*verb + -ing*) in place of the German infinitive used as a noun.

> In dieser Zeit blühte **das Denken** der Romantiker.
> *At this time, the romanticists' thinking blossomed.*
> **Das Singen** der Kinder war überraschend schön.
> *The children's singing was surprisingly beautiful.*
> **Das Rauchen** und **Trinken** sind verboten.
> *Smoking and drinking are forbidden.*

The frequent combination **zum** + infinitive translates to *for + verb + -ing*:

> Zum Lernen braucht man Bücher. Zum Verstehen braucht man Intelligenz.
> *For learning one needs books. For understanding one needs intelligence.*

Grundwortschatz

Abb. = Abbildung (f.), **-en**	*illustration*	**krönen**	*to crown*
an/führen	*to cite, state*	**von Erfolg gekrönt**	*to crown with success; to succeed*
Anwendung (f.), **-en**	*use, application*	**lehren**	*to teach*
auf/bauen	*to build up, synthesize*	**Leute** (pl.)	*people*
Bär (m., n-noun), **-en**	*bear*	**lösen**	*to solve, dissolve*
		oben	*above*
besprechen (besprach, besprochen; bespricht)	*to discuss*	**reifen**	*to ripen, mature*
		schnell	*rapid(ly)*
		Seite (f.), **-n**	*page*
bestätigen	*to confirm*	**Stoff** (m.), **-e**	*substance, material*
Bewegung (f.), **-en**	*movement*	**überraschen**	*to surprise*
blühen	*to bloom, blossom*	**unten**	*below*
da	*there, then, here*	**verbieten** (verbot, verboten)	*to forbid*
einzeln	*individual, single*		
Freiheit (f.), **-en**	*freedom*	**verlangen**	*to demand, ask, require*
ganz	*entire(ly)*	**wachsen** (wuchs, gewachsen; wächst)	*to grow*
Ganze (n.)	*whole, entirety*		
Hilfe (f.), **-n**	*help, aid*	**wie**	*as, like, how*
klein	*small*	**wiederholen**	*to repeat*
		Zelle (f.), **-n**	*cell*

Übungssätze

1. Das Museum ist weltweit für die Qualität und Vielfalt seiner ausgestellten Werke bekannt.
2. Die Sammlung des Museums ist von der ursprünglichen Schenkung von acht Drucken und einer Zeichnung schnell auf mehr als 10 000 Gemälde, Skulpturen, Zeichnungen, Drucke, Fotografien und Architekturmodelle und -pläne angewachsen.
3. Die ursprüngliche Aufgabe der Aktionsgruppe war die Rettung der gefährdeten und bedrohten Pandabären.
4. Ihre Arbeit ist nicht immer von Erfolg gekrönt.
5. Zum Gedeihen brauchen die Pflanzen außer Licht, Wärme, Luft und Wasser auch Nährstoffe.
6. Feste Stoffe dringen nur in gelöster Form in die Pflanze ein.
7. Die Pflanzen sind aus Zellen aufgebaut.
8. Schweden hat als erstes Land der Europäischen Union die Anwendung von DDT verboten. Heute ist sie in der ganzen EU verboten.
9. Das christliche „Alte Testament" ist zum großen Teil in hebräischer Sprache abgefasst. Es ist die Bibel der Juden. Die christliche Kirche hat es aufgenommen und mit den Schriften des Neuen Testaments zur christlichen Bibel vereinigt.
10. Der Kandidat wiederholte mehrfach seine Behauptung: „Das Lösen dieses ergreifenden Problems ermöglicht eine Steigerung des Lebensstandards."

1. **aus/stellen** *to exhibit*
2. **Sammlung** *(f.)*, **-en** *collection*
   Schenkung *(f.)*, **-en** *gift, donation*
   Druck *(m.)*, **-e** *print*
   auf mehr als *to more than*
3. **Rettung** *(f.)*, **-en** *rescue*
   gefährden *to endanger*
   bedrohen *to threaten*
5. **gedeihen** *to flourish*
   Nährstoff *(m.)*, **-e** *nutrient*

6. **ein/dringen (drang ... ein, ist eingedrungen)** *to penetrate*
9. **ab/fassen** *to write, compose*
   auf/nehmen (nahm ... auf, aufgenommen; nimmt ... auf) *to adopt, take up*
   vereinigen *to combine, unify*
10. **Behauptung** *(f.)*, **-en** *assertion, statement*
    ergreifend *gripping*

11. Das fast ununterbrochene nördliche Tageslicht in Alaska beschleunigt den Wachstumsrhythmus und drängt Blühen und Reifen auf wenige Monate zusammen.
12. Die oben angeführten Ergebnisse sind auf Seite 67 in Abb. 5 wiedergegeben.
13. Das Besprochene ist auch durch die unten beschriebenen Versuche bestätigt.
14. Das Aufrechterhalten des Friedens verlangt andauernde Übereinstimmung aller beteiligten Parteien.
15. „Zum Kriegführen sind dreierlei Dinge nötig: Geld, Geld, Geld", sagte Marschall Trivulzio zu Ludwig XII. von Frankreich.
16. In der englischsprechenden Welt wurde Beethovens Klavierkonzert Nummer fünf in Es-Dur als „Emperor"-Concerto populär. Das inspirierende Moment für das Werk war Beethovens Bewunderung Napoleons.
17. Wie die Universität als Ganzes, so genießt auch der einzelne Professor in Deutschland vollkommene Freiheit im Denken, Lehren und Handeln.
18. Nach den Unruhen im Winter und Frühjahr 1968 zeigte die deutsche Studentenbewegung eine überraschend schnelle Entwicklung.
19. Die Gaszellen des Zeppelins waren mit brennbarem Wasserstoff gefüllt. Das Füllen ging relativ schnell.
20. Das Luftschiff ist nach seinem Erfinder „Graf Zeppelin" benannt.

11. **ununterbrochen** *uninterrupted*
    beschleunigen *to accelerate*
    Wachstum *(n.)* *growth*
    zusammen/drängen *to compress*
12. **wieder/geben (gab ... wieder, wiedergegeben)** *to reproduce*
14. **aufrecht/erhalten (erhielt ... aufrecht, aufrechterhalten; erhält ... aufrecht)** *to maintain*
    Friede *(m., n-noun)*, **-n** *peace*
    an/dauern *to last, continue*
    Übereinstimmung *(f.)*, **-en** *agreement*
    beteiligt *involved*
15. **Kriegführen** *(n.)* *waging of war*
    dreierlei *three kinds of*
    Ding *(f.)*, **-e** *thing*
16. **Es-Dur** *E-flat major*
17. **genießen (genoss, genossen)** *to enjoy*
18. **Unruhen** *(pl.)* *disturbances*
19. **brennbar** *combustible*
    Wasserstoff *(m.)* *hydrogen*
    füllen *to fill*

DER BÄR: STADTSYMBOL UND NATURPHÄNOMEN

Im Wappen der Stadt Berlin sieht man einen stehenden Bär, und wie ein König ist er mit einer goldenen Krone gekrönt. Der Bär ist überhaupt das Symbol von der schnell wachsenden Hauptstadt von Deutschland. Lebende Berliner Bären gibt es heute leider
5 nur im Zoologischen Garten und im Tierpark. Als Naturphänomen sind Bären in Deutschland schon seit mehr als 150 Jahren ausgestorben. In vielen anderen Ländern stehen sie auf der Liste von bedrohten, gefährdeten oder schon ausgestorbenen Tieren. Aus diesem Grund sind Bären besonders faszinierend.
10 Hauptsächlich in der nördlichen Hemisphäre lebend, sind Bären massige, großköpfige Tiere (rund 1 bis 3 Meter groß) und gehören zur Raubtierfamilie. Bären sind Allesfresser (sie fressen alles) und Sohlengänger (beim Gehen treten sie mit der ganzen Fußsohle auf den Boden).
15 Die männlichen Tiere verbringen ihr Leben zum großen Teil allein. Das Familienleben eines Bären ist durch das väterliche Benehmen stark geprägt. Im Mai oder Juni paaren sich männliche und weibliche Bären. Nach der Paarung verschwinden die Bärenmänner. Getrennt verbringen die riesigen Raubtiere den Winter
20 dann meist mit Schlafen.

1 **im Wappen** *on the coat of arms*
3 **überhaupt** *altogether*
4 **leider nur** *unfortunately only*
5 **Zoologischer Garten** *(western Berlin) zoo*
   Tierpark *(eastern Berlin) zoo*
6 **aus/sterben (starb ... aus, ist ... ausgestorben; stirbt ... aus)** *to die out, become extinct*
8 **aus diesem Grund** *for this reason*
9 **besonders** *especially*
10 **hauptsächlich** *mainly, predominantly*
11 **gehören zu** *to belong to*
12 **Raubtier** *(n.)*, **-e** *predatory animal*
    Allesfresser *(m.)*, **–** *omnivore*
13 **Sohlengänger** *(m.)*, **–** *plantigrade animal*
15 **zum großen Teil** *for the most part, to a large extent*
17 **Benehmen** *(n.)* *behavior*
    geprägt *characterized*
    sich paaren *to mate*
18 **Paarung** *(f.)* *mating*
19 **verbringen (verbrachte, verbracht)** *to spend*

Im Februar werden Bärenbabys geboren. Die kleinen Bären—ein bis drei Säuglinge in einem Wurf—kommen blind in die Welt und wiegen rund 500 g. Drei Monate werden sie mit der Muttermilch gesäugt. Mama Bär (etwa 225 Kilo schwer, 2 bis 3 Meter groß) unterrichtet ihre Kinder drei Jahre lang im Fischen, Schwimmen, Klettern und Beeren-Pflücken. Die beschützende Mutter hält ständig Ausschau nach Männern. Als Einzelgänger sind Bärenmänner besonders gefährlich: sie töten ihre eigenen Kinder.

25

21	**werden geboren** *are born*	26	**beschützen** *to protect*
22	**Säugling** *(m.)*, **-e** *infant, suckling*	27	**ständig** *constantly*
	Wurf *(m.)*, **-e** *brood, litter*		**Ausschau** *(m.)* *watch out*
23	**werden gesäugt** *are suckled*		**Einzelgänger** *(m.)*, **–** *loner*

WIEDERHOLUNG 2

DIE BEWOHNER ÖSTERREICHS

Die Vielfältigkeit der österreichischen Bevölkerung heute hat eine interessante Geschichte. Wegen seiner geographischen Lage ist Österreich schon immer ein strategisch wichtiges Land gewesen, und viele Völker sind auf der Suche nach festen und guten Wohnsitzen durch das Land gezogen.

In den letzten Jahren der Eiszeit sind die Kelten vom Westen zu dem Alpengebiet gekommen, verdrängten die einheimischen Illyrer und gründeten das Königreich Noricum. Später sind dann die römischen Legionen von Süden durch die Alpenländer gezogen und sind bis an die Donau vorgedrungen. An der Donau haben die Römer Festungen gebaut. Diese sicherten die nordöstlichen Grenzen des Römischen Reiches gegen die Germanen am anderen Ufer der Donau.

Auf dem Weg nach dem Süden sind die Zimbern durch dieses Gebiet gezogen und sind mit den Römern in der Schlacht von Noreja (113) zusammengestoßen. Dieser Zusammenstoß war einer der ersten zwischen den germanischen Völkern und den Römern. Fünfzig Jahre später überquerten die Markomannen die Donau und sind bis nach Venetien vorgedrungen, aber der römische Kaiser Mark Aurel hat sie wieder über die Donau zurückgetrieben.

Title **Bewohner** *(m.), –* *inhabitant*
1 **Vielfältigkeit** *(f.), -en* *diversity*
4 **Suche** *(f.)* *search*
5 **Wohnsitz** *(m.), -e* *abode, domicile*
  ziehen durch *(zog, ist ... gezogen)* *to roam through*
7 **verdrängen** *to push out*
  einheimisch *native*
8 **später** *later*
10 **Donau** *(f.)* *Danube*
  vor/dringen *(drang ... vor, ist vorgedrungen)* *to advance, penetrate*
11 **sichern** *to secure*

12 **Ufer** *(n.), –* *bank*
13 **auf dem Weg** *(m.), -e* *on the way*
  Zimber *(m.), -n* *Cimbrian*
15 **zusammen/stoßen** *(stieß ... zusammen, ist zusammengestoßen; stößt ... zusammen)* *to clash*
  einer der ersten *one of the first*
17 **überqueren** *to cross*
  Markomanne *(m.), -n* *Germanic tribe*
18 **Venetien** *(n.)* *Venetia*
19 **zurück/treiben** *(trieb ... zurück, zurückgetrieben)* *to drive back*

Die römischen Donauprovinzen sind schließlich in der Völker-
wanderung gefallen. Germanische Stämme fielen in das Land ein und
zogen nach Westen und Süden. Die Westgoten drangen bis nach
Spanien vor, die Langobarden haben das nördliche Italien besetzt.
Auch die Hunnen unter ihrem großen König Atilla fielen in die
Donaugebiete und sogar in die Alpentäler ein.

20

25

Vom 10. bis zum 13. Jahrhundert hat wieder eine starke Einwanderung von Bayern und Franken die deutsche Besiedlung Österreichs
gefördert. Am Ende des 12. Jahrhunderts war Wien schon eine
bedeutende Stadt geworden und wurde später die Residenzstadt der
Habsburger. Die Habsburger regierten in Österreich von 1282 bis
1918. Vom Jahre 1438 bis 1806 haben die österreichischen Kaiser
auch die deutsche Kaiserkrone getragen.

30

Vor dem Zusammenbruch der österreich-ungarischen Monarchie
(1868–1918) im Jahre 1918 bestand die Bevölkerung dieses Reiches
aus Deutschen, Ungarn, Tschechen, Slowaken, Polen, Kroaten,
Rumänen, Slowenen und Italienern. Das heutige Österreich hat fast
dieselben Grenzen wie nach dem Ersten Weltkrieg.

35

Am 12. 3. 1938 marschierten deutsche Truppen in Österreich ein,
und einen Tag später kam die Vollziehung des Anschlusses mit dem
„Gesetz über die Wiedervereinigung Österreichs mit dem Deutschen
Reich". Nach dem Zweiten Weltkrieg teilten die Alliierten Österreich
in vier Besatzungszonen. Am 26. 10. 1955 wurde Österreich wieder
ein souveränes Land.

40

Wegen seiner zentralen Lage spielte Österreich eine wichtige
Rolle in der Politik des Kalten Krieges. Nach dem Zweiten Weltkrieg

45

---

20 **schließlich** *finally*
 Völkerwanderung *(f.),* **-en** *mass migration*
21 **ein/fallen (fiel ... ein, ist eingefallen; fällt ... ein)** *to invade*
22 **Gote** *(m., n-noun),* **-n** *Goth*
23 **Langobarde** *(m.),* **-n** *Lombard*
25 **sogar** *even*
 Alpental *(n.),* **⁼er** *Alpine valley*
27 **Besiedlung** *(f.),* **-en** *settlement*
28 **fördern** *to further, advance*
29 **bedeutend** *important*

32 **Kaiserkrone** *(f.),* **-n** *imperial crown*
33 **Zusammenbruch** *(m.),* **⁼e** *collapse*
34 **bestehen aus (bestand, bestanden)** *to be made up of*
36 **dieselben** *(pl.)* *the same*
39 **Vollziehung** *(f.)* *execution*
 Anschluss *(m.)* *annexation*
40 **Wiedervereinigung** *(f.)* *reunification*
42 **Besatzung** *(f.)* *occupation*

hat Österreich z.B. viele Flüchtlinge aus den kommunistischen Ländern aufgenommen. Es gehörte in dieser Zeit zu den sogenannten neutralen Nationen.

Heute zählt das Land ungefähr 8,3 Millionen Einwohner. Davon sprechen 98% Deutsch. Mehr als 814 000 Ausländer aus der ganzen Welt leben heute in Österreich. Die vielen Nationalitätsgruppen suchen politische Freiheit und auch kulturelle Autonomie. Das ist nicht immer unkompliziert. | 50

Die geographische Lage Österreichs und seine geschichtliche Entwicklung haben einen bedeutenden Einfluss auf die Zusammensetzung und Herkunft des österreichischen Volkes gehabt. Von allen Seiten sind verschiedene Völker in das Land eingezogen, und einige haben hier ihre Wohnsitze aufgeschlagen. Das kleine Land mit seiner langen interessanten Geschichte und seiner gemischten Bevölkerung ist sehr stolz auf seine Kultur und Traditionen, aber es gibt oft Spannungen in der Innen- und Außenpolitik des Landes. Im Frühjahr 2000 z.B. entstand ein großer Konflikt. Die ausländerfeindliche Politik einer konservativen Regierung isolierte das Land von seinen vielen Nachbarn. Viele Österreicher sehen eine große Chance in der Integration in Europa. | 55 | 60 | 65

Was wird aus Österreich im 21. Jahrhundert? Eine Antwort ist die Integration in Europa. Als Mitglied der Europäischen Union arbeitet Österreich mit seinen Nachbarn zusammen. Frieden, Freiheit und ökonomischer Fortschritt spielen eine große Rolle in dieser Zusammenarbeit. | 70

---

47 **auf/nehmen (nahm ... auf, aufgenommen; nimmt ... auf)** *to take in, absorb*
49 **davon** *of them*
55 **Zusammensetzung** *(f.)*, **-en** *composition*
56 **Herkunft** *(f.)*, **-̈e** *origins*
57 **ein/ziehen (zog ... ein, ist eingezogen)** *to enter, move in*
58 **einige** *some, a few*
auf/schlagen (schlug ... auf, aufgeschlagen; schlägt ... auf) *to set up, take up*

60 **stolz sein auf** *to be proud of*
61 **Spannung** *(f.)*, **-en** *tension*
Innen- und Außenpolitik *domestic and foreign policy*
62 **entstehen (entstand, entstanden)** *to develop, come about*
ausländerfeindlich *anti-foreigner*
64 **Nachbar** *(m, n-noun)*, **-n** *neighbor*
66 **was wird aus** *what'll become of*
68 **zusammen/arbeiten** *to cooperate*
Friede *(m., n-noun)*, **-n** *peace*
69 **Fortschritt** *(m.)*, **-e** *progress*

KAPITEL 11

11.1 Comparison of Adjectives and Adverbs

The three degrees of comparison are the positive (**lang**), comparative (**länger**), and superlative (**längst-**). Note the similarity to the corresponding English forms: *long, longer, longest*. Already in some of the very earliest and simplest German texts you may have encountered some of the following examples.

Positive	Comparative	Superlative	
lang	länger	längst-	*long*
schnell	schneller	schnellst-	*fast*
heiß	heißer	heißest-	*hot*
interessant	interessanter	interessantest-	*interesting*
groß	größer	größt-	*big, large*
kurz	kürzer	kürzest-	*short*

A. Comparative

The common element of the comparative degree is the **-er** ending, used in almost all cases to indicate comparison of German adjectives and adverbs no matter how many syllables the word has. For example, **interessant** becomes **interessanter**, which in English must be translated as ***more*** *interesting*. The umlaut added to **a**, **o**, or **u** in the comparative forms of short adjectives/adverbs is an additional aid to recognizing the comparative: **wärmer**, **größer**, **kürzer** (*warmer, greater, shorter*). Note that the comparative of **viel** (*much*) is **mehr** (*more*).

B. Superlative

The **-st** ending is characteristic of all superlatives; this is true no matter how long the word is. Here, too, most words of one syllable take an umlaut on the stem vowels **a**, **o**, or **u**. You will also see the ending **-est** on adjectives/adverbs ending in **s**, **ß**, **z**, **d**, or **t**, e.g., **heißest-**, **kürzest-**, but **größt-** (*hottest, shortest, greatest*).

Note that comparatives and superlatives that precede nouns have grammatical endings added to their characteristic endings of **-er** and **-st**.

> John F. Kennedy war der ält**ere** Bruder von Robert F. Kennedy.
> Robert F. Kennedy war ein jüng**erer** Bruder von dem Präsidenten.

Der jüngste Kennedy-Bruder heißt Edward.
Von den Kennedy-Brüdern war Joseph am ältesten.

The superlative construction **am -sten** has no equivalent English structure. The expression **am ältesten** translates simply as the *eldest*. The **am
-sten** construction also occurs as an adverb, for example:

die am wenigsten zahlreichen Länder
the least numerous nations

C. Umlauts

The umlaut added to **a**, **o**, or **u** makes it easier for the reader to recognize
the comparative and superlative. In addition to **alt**, **groß**, **jung**, **kurz**,
lang, and **warm** (seen in the examples above), the most common adjectives and adverbs which add an umlaut are listed below.

	Positive	Comparative	Superlative
poor	arm	ärmer	der/die/das ärmste; am ärmsten
healthy	gesund	gesünder	der/die/das gesündeste; am gesündesten
cold	kalt	kälter	der/die/das kälteste; am kältesten
sick, ill	krank	kränker	der/die/das kränkste; am kränksten
often	oft	öfter	am öftesten
sharp	scharf	schärfer	der/die/das schärfste; am schärfsten
slim, slender	schmal	schmäler	der/die/das schmälste; am schmälsten
weak	schwach	schwächer	der/die/das schwächste; am schwächsten
black	schwarz	schwärzer	der/die/das schwärzeste; am schwärzesten
strong	stark	stärker	der/die/das stärkste; am stärksten

11.2 Exceptional Comparisons

A. Stem changes

As in English, there are a few common adjectives and adverbs that experience changes to their stems in addition to adding the **-er** and **-(e)st** endings in the comparative and superlative.

	Positive	Comparative	Superlative
good; *well*	gut	besser	der/die/das beste; am besten
high	hoch, hoh-	höher	der/die/das höchste; am höchsten
near	nah(e)	näher	der/die/das nächste; am nächsten
much	viel	mehr	der/die/das meist-; am meisten
many	viele	mehr	die meisten *(pl.)*

B. Gern(e), lieber, am liebsten

(handwritten annotations above: like · prefer · most prefer)

Gern is a common adverb that has no direct equivalent in English and translates best as an indication of preference.

> Er liest **gern** Literatur.
> *He likes to read literature.*
> Ich lese **lieber** Geschichte.
> *I prefer to read history.*
> Unser Professor liest **am liebsten** Literaturgeschichte.
> *Our professor most prefers to read literary history.*

The adverb **gern** can only modify a verb. The combination of **gern haben** + a person or thing translates *to like the person or thing.*

> Der Patient hat die Medizin nicht gern.
> *The patient doesn't like the medicine.*
> Diese neue Medizin hat er lieber als die alte.
> *He likes the new medicine better than the old one.*
> *(He prefers the new one.)*

11.3 Recognition of Comparatives and Superlatives

Learning to recognize the characteristic endings of comparative and superlative forms of adjectives and adverbs will help avoid confusion in translating and reading.

A. Adjectives or adverbs ending in -er

There are three situations in which an adjective or adverb may end in **-er**.

1. The stem itself ends in **-er**:
   Die Arbeit ist schw**er**.
   The work is difficult.
   Die Medizin ist ungeheu**er** teu**er**.
   The medicine is tremendously expensive.

2. Comparatives are indicated with an **-er** ending:
   Ist diese Methode neu**er** oder ält**er** als jene?
   Is this method newer or older than that one?

3. Adjective endings in the following cases:

masculine nominative after **ein**-word	ein alt**er** Mann	*an old man*
masculine nominative, no article	arm**er** Krank**er**	*poor sick man*
feminine dative, no article	mit gut**er** Qualität	*with good quality*
feminine genitive, no article	der Preis effektiv**er** Medizin	*the price of effective medicine*
plural genitives, no article	die Resultate effektiv**er** Methoden	*the results of effective methods*

Pay close attention to adjectives or adverbs ending in **-er**. Ask yourself whether the final **-er** is part of the stem of the word, a comparative ending, or an ending on an adjective modifiying a noun (a highly common nominative masculine? an unpreceded dative or genitive feminine adjective? or perhaps a genitive plural?). The following examples include a variety of these situations. Learn to differentiate among them.

1. Diese Methode ist **schneller**. *comparative*
2. ein **schneller** Dampfer *adj. ending*
3. die **schnellere** Methode *comparative w/ adj. ending*
4. Dieser Generator ist **einfacher** gebaut.
5. ein **schwerer** Hammer *adj. ending*
6. ein **schwererer** Hammer *comparative w/ adj. ending*

7. Der Hammer ist **schwer**. adj.
8. eine sich **schneller** entwickelnde Situation
9. das Problem **höherer** Preise

Watch for **-er** before adjective endings. If **-er** is not part of the word, it is a comparative ending (as in Examples 3, 6, 9). The word **schwererer** (6) demonstrates a combination of all three **-er** permutations: the first **-er** is part of the word, the second **-er** indicates the comparative, and the final **-er** is the masculine nominative adjective ending after an **ein**-word. Example 8 may be translated as a *more rapidly developing situation* or *a situation (that is) developing more rapidly*. The adjective in Example 9 is comparative (note the umlaut and the **-er** before the adjective ending); the final **-er** in Example 9 is a genitive plural ending on an unpreceded adjective: *the problem of higher prices.*

B. Positives ending in *-el* or *-er*

Adjectives of more than one syllable ending in **-el** or **-er** drop the **-e-** in the comparative.

dunkel	dunkler	der/die/das dunkelste; am dunkelsten	*dark*
teuer	teurer	der/die/das teuerste; am teuersten	*expensive*

C. Characteristic *-st* ending

An **-st** preceding an adjective ending always indicates the superlative. The form consisting of **am** + the superlative ending with **-en** is always a predicate adjective or superlative adverb.

Die schnellsten Maschinen fahren über 200 km/h.
The most rapid machines travel over 200 km/hr.
Das schönste Bild im Museum ist von dem älteren Cranach.
The most beautiful picture in the museum is by the elder Cranach.
Der Stil dieses Hauses ist am interessantesten.
The style of this house is the most interesting.

Watch for **-st** preceding adjective endings; this combination almost always indicates a superlative.

D. Learn to differentiate

Remember that the verb forms for **du** also end in **-st** or **-est**.

> Du spiel**st** am besten.
> *You play the best.*
> Auch als kleinstes Kind spiel**test** du am liebsten Basketball.
> *Even as the smallest child you liked to play basketball the most.*

Do not let this similarity of endings confuse you.

11.4 Special Uses of the Comparative and Superlative

A. Comparative

1. Comparative followed by **als**

   A German comparative followed by the conjunction **als** (not necessarily immediately, but in the same sentence) is equivalent to an English comparative + *than*.

   > Der Mond ist **kleiner als** die Erde.
   > *The moon is smaller than the earth.*
   > Die Erde dreht sich viel **langsamer** um die Sonne **als** der Mond um die Erde.
   > *The earth revolves much more slowly around the sun than the moon around the earth.*
   > Bist du **älter als** ich?
   > *Are you older than I (am)?*

2. **Immer** + comparative

   immer besser   *better and better, increasingly better*
   immer reicher   *richer and richer, ever richer*
   immer ärmer   *poorer and poorer, continually poorer*

   Immer + comparative is best translated by repeating the comparative form in English.

   > Die Durchschnittstemperatur wird **immer höher**, der Treibhauseffekt **immer problematischer**.
   > *The average temperature gets higher and higher; the greenhouse effect more and more problematic.*
   > Solche Fälle kommen **immer häufiger** vor.
   > *Such cases occur more and more frequently.*

A similar translation is used to express the phrase **immer wieder** *(again and again),* although the expression is not a comparison.

> Dieser Kunsthistoriker erwähnt **immer wieder** die Werke von Lucas Cranach dem Älteren.
> *This art historian mentions the works of Lucas Cranach the Elder again and again.*

3. **Je** + comparative ... **desto/je/umso** + comparative

The two-part conjunction **je ... desto/je/umso** combines a comparative dependent clause with a comparative main clause. This construction indicates that the situation in the main clause increases or decreases at a similar level to the situation in the dependent clause. For example, **je mehr, desto besser** can be translated as *the more, the merrier.*

> **Je** höher die Zahl der Länder, **desto** mehr Repräsentanten gibt es im Parlament.
> *The higher the number of states, the more representatives there are in the parliament.*
> **Je** größer der Fleiß, **desto** höher der Lohn.
> *The greater the effort, the higher the reward.*
> Die jeweilige Lösung ist **umso** wertvoller, **je** weniger Probleme sie verursacht.
> *Any given solution is the more valuable, the fewer problems it causes.*

4. Comparison merely implied

Some adjectives of size and time may occur in the comparative in German but translate best using the positive.

> Eine größere Menge Rohstoffe wird exportiert.
> *A fairly (rather) large amount of raw materials is being exported.*
> Die Wachstumsrate nimmt seit längerer Zeit zu.
> *The growth rate has been increasing for a rather (fairly) long time.*
> Es ist uns schon länger bekannt, dass ...
> *It has been known (to us) for some time that . . .*

B. Superlative

Expressions in which no actual comparison is involved may use superlatives and have special meanings. Most dictionaries list these expressions, which occur frequently.

äußerst langsam   *very (extremely) slow*
höchstens   *at most, at best*
höchst lehrreich   *very (most) instructive*
in neuester Zeit   *most recently*
meistens   *usually, as a rule*
möglichst schnell   *as fast as possible*
wenigstens   *at least*

Die Forscher hatten eine **äußerst** schwierige Aufgabe mit dem Saurierschädel.
The researchers had an extremely difficult assignment involving the dinosaur skull.
Die alten Theorien waren **meistens** ohne wissenschaftliche Basis.
The old theories generally had no scholarly basis.

11.5 Comparatives and Superlatives Used as Nouns

As you already learned in **Kapitel 7**, all adjectives can be used as nouns in German. This also applies to comparative and superlative forms.

das Wichtigste   *the most important one (thing)*
der Größte   *the biggest one*
der Kleinere   *the smaller one*
das Wesentlichste   *the most essential one (thing)*
die Schönste   *the most beautiful one*

Note that the adjective is *not* capitalized when it represents a previously mentioned noun:

Welche Medizin ist besser? Die billigere oder die teuere?
Which medicine is better? The cheaper (one) or the more expensive (one)?

äußerst	very, extremely	**in erster Linie**	primarily, in the first place
besonders	(e)specially, particularly	**Meer** (n.), **-e**	ocean, sea
besser	better	**Nähe** (f.)	vicinity, nearness
dagegen	on the other hand, against it	**in der Nähe**	near
doch	however, indeed, yet	**niedrig**	low
		reich	rich, abundant
durchschnittlich	average, on the average	**rund**	approximately; round
erfolgreich	successful	**tief**	deep, low
Fall (m.), **⸚e**	case, situation	**u.a. (unter anderem, anderen)**	among other things, among others
auf jeden Fall	in any case	**um mehr als**	by more than
in diesem Fall(e)	in this case	**verbinden (verband, verbunden)**	to connect, combine, unite
geeignet	suited, suitable		
hart	hard		
Höhe (f.), **-n**	height, elevation		
immer	always	**vor/kommen (kam ... vor, ist vorgekommen)**	to occur, happen, seem
immer reicher	richer and richer		
immer wieder	again and again		
kennzeichnen	to characterize, to typify	**wachsen (wuchs, ist gewachsen; wächst)**	to grow, increase
lang	long		
drei Jahre lang	for three years		
langsam	slow	**Wachstum** (n.)	growth
Lauf (m.), **⸚e**	course	**zahlreich**	numerous
im Laufe	in the course (of)	**zu/nehmen (nahm ... zu, zugenommen; nimmt ... zu)**	to increase, grow
liegen (lag, gelegen)	to lie, be lying down		
Linie (f.), **-n**	line		

 Lösungen zu Übungssätzen auf **academic.cengage.com/german/korb**

1. In seinem berühmtesten Gemälde aus dem Jahr 1555, „Die niederländischen Sprichwörter", stellt Bruegel etwa hundert Sprichwörter und Redewendungen dar.

1. **Gemälde** (n.), **–**   *painting*
   Sprichwort (n.), **⸚er**   *saying, proverb*

   Redewendung (f.), **-en**   *figure of speech*
   dar/stellen   *to depict, represent*

2. Das bruegelsche Gemälde nannte man im späteren 16. Jh. meistens „Den blauen Mantel", aber im 17. Jh. war es unter dem Titel „Torheiten der Welt" viel besser bekannt.

3. Zwei der interessantesten Sprichwörter aus dem Werk heißen: „die größeren Fische fressen die kleineren" und „die Narren bekommen immer wieder die besten Karten."

4. Die Dampfmaschine spielte eine immer größere Rolle in der Weberei.

5. Je mehr die Webereien von Leinenstoffen auf Baumwolle umstiegen, desto wichtiger war Schlesiens Rolle auf dem Webergebiet.

6. Der Übergang zu Dampfantrieb und Großbetrieben kennzeichnet den Industrialisierungsprozess viel mehr als die meisten anderen Produktionselemente.

7. Die Hausindustriellen verloren immer mehr ihre Konkurrenzfähigkeit.

8. Die Auslesezüchtung war die älteste, einfachste und jahrhundertelang die einzige Form der Pflanzenzüchtung.

9. Zur Entwicklung hochwertiger Kulturpflanzen sind meistens Jahrhunderte nötig.

10. In diesem Fall ist das Wachstum bei Y am langsamsten und bei X am schnellsten.

11. Das Wichtigste an Röntgens Erfindung war: Röntgenstrahlen haben eine viel kürzere Wellenlänge als das Licht.

---

2. **das bruegelsche Gemälde** *the painting by Bruegel*
blau *blue*
Mantel (*m.*), ⸚ *coat*
Torheit (*f.*), **-en** *foolishness, stupidity*
3. **Narr** (*m., n-noun*), **-en** *fool*
4. **Weberei** (*f.*), **-en** *weaving mills*
5. **Leinenstoff** (*m.*), **-e** *linen*
Baumwolle (*f.*) *cotton*
um/steigen auf (stieg um, ist umgestiegen) *to switch over*
Schlesien (*n.*) *Silesia*
Weber (*m.*), **–** *weaver*
6. **Übergang** (*m.*), ⸚**e** *conversion*
Dampfantrieb (*m.*) *steam propulsion*
Großbetrieb (*m.*), **-e** *large-scale factory*

7. **Hausindustriellen** (*pl.*) *cottage industries*
Konkurrenzfähigkeit (*f.*) *ability to compete*
8. **Auslesezüchtung** (*f.*) *selective growing, breeding*
jahrhundertelang *for centuries, for hundreds of years*
9. **zur Entwicklung** *for the development*
hochwertig *high-grade*
Kulturpflanze (*f.*), **-n** *cultivated plant*
11. **Röntgen** *W. C. Roentgen (1845–1923, physicist)*
Röntgenstrahlen (*pl.*) *X-rays*
Wellenlänge (*f.*), **-n** *wavelength*

12. Die Grenzfrequenz ist umso höher, je kleiner die Partikeln sind und je stärker das Magnetfeld.
13. Im Laufe der letzten Jahrzehnte sind die reichen Länder reicher geworden und die armen verhältnismäßig ärmer.
14. In der Nähe der am dichtesten bevölkerten Nachbarschaften nehmen die Preise um mehr als € 20 je Quadratmeter Wohnplatz zu.
15. Die modernen Flugzeuge fliegen immer schneller und werden zur gleichen Zeit immer größer und teurer. Dieses äußerst komplexe Problem ist besonders kennzeichnend für die Flugindustrie.
16. Das Meer bedeckt einen größeren Teil der Erdoberfläche als die Landmassen.
17. Die Bevölkerung der Erde wird in neuester Zeit immer zahlreicher.
18. In den am wenigsten entwickelten Ländern ist die durchschnittliche Lebensdauer am kürzesten. Je mehr ein Land industrialisiert und entwickelt ist, desto höher ist meistens die Lebenserwartung.
19. Eine bessere Ernährungslage, besonders unter der ärmeren Bevölkerung, erhöht die Lebenserwartung des Menschen.
20. „Spieglein, Spieglein an der Wand, / Wer ist die Schönste im ganzen Land?"
    „Frau Königin, Ihr seid die Schönste hier, / Aber Schneewittchen über den Bergen / Bei den sieben Zwergen / Ist noch tausendmal schöner als Ihr."

12. **Grenzfrequenz** (f.), **-en** *boundary frequency*
    Partikel (f.), **-n** *particle*
14. **dicht** *dense*
    um mehr als *by more than*
    Wohnplatz (m.), **-̈e** *living space*
16. **bedecken** *to cover*
    Erdoberfläche (f.) *surface of the earth*
18. **Lebensdauer** (f.) *life span*
    Lebenserwartung (f.) *life expectancy*
19. **Ernährungslage** (f.) *food supply, state of nutrition*
    unter *among*
    erhöhen *to increase*
20. **Spiegel** (m.) – *mirror, looking glass*
    Spieglein (n.), – *(little) mirror*
    Wand (f.), **-̈e** *wall*
    Königin (f.), **-nen** *queen*
    Ihr *you*
    Zwerg (m.), **-e** *dwarf*

MENSCHEN MIT HIV UND AIDS

A m ersten Dezember 1981 hat man AIDS zum ersten Mal als eine Pandemie oder „Infektionskrankheit ohne Grenzen" gekennzeichnet. Am 20. Mai 1983 hat eine Arbeitsgruppe des französischen AIDS-Forschers Luc Montagnier zum allerersten Mal über die Isolierung der HI-Viren berichtet. Drei Jahrzehnte 5 später bleibt HIV-AIDS eine immer wachsende Globalepidemie und eins der tödlichsten Viren aller Zeiten.

Nach Zahlen aus einem 2007 Gesundheitsbericht vom Robert Koch Institut (http://www.rki.de/) sind zwischen 1982 und 2006 mindestens 13 349 Deutsche an AIDS gestorben. Dem Report nach 10 sind in der gleichen Zeit weltweit an der HIV-AIDS Krankheit 25 Millionen Menschen gestorben.

Zwischen 1995 und 2003 nahm auf dem Markt die Zahl der Medikamente zur Behandlung von AIDS um mehr als dreifach zu. Am wirksamsten bei AIDS-Patienten war eine Kombinationsthera- 15 pie mit AZT und ddl oder mit ddc. Leider bleiben die Kosten dieser Drogen höher als weniger wirksame Therapien und nur der geringste Prozentsatz der HIV-Infizierten kann sich die Kombinationstherapie leisten. Weniger als 4% der weltweit Infizierten oder ungefähr 1,2 Millionen erhalten diese lebenswichtige Therapie. 20

Es ist äußerst schwierig, exakte Daten zu bestimmen, aber die aktuellsten Informationen der Weltgesundheitsorganisation (WHO) machen immer wieder einen starken Eindruck: rund 42,5 Millionen Menschen leben im Jahre 2007 mit AIDS, davon sind 3,1 Millionen

7	**tödlich** *deadly*	17	**nur** *only*
10	**mindestens** *at least*	18	**gering** *small, minimal*
11	**gleich** *same*		**Prozentsatz** *(m.)* *percentage*
12	**sterben an (starb, ist gestorben;**		**infiziert** *infected*
	stirbt) to die of	19	**sich leisten können** *to be able to*
14	**Behandlung** *(f.)* *treatment*		*afford*
15	**wirksam** *effective*	20	**erhalten (erhielt, erhalten;**
16	**AZT, ddl, ddc** *medications used in*		**erhält)** *to receive, obtain*
	AIDS treatment	21	**zu bestimmen** *to ascertain*
	leider *unfortunately*	24	**davon** *of those*

Kinder. Die Anzahl der Kranken in GUS-Staaten und Asien nehmen seit 2000 äußerst zu. Man schätzt, 600 000 Menschen mit HIV oder AIDS leben in Westeuropa und 1,2 Millionen in Osteuropa und Zentralasien. In Deutschland leben 2007 rund 49 000 Menschen mit HIV— etwa 39 500 Männer, rund 9 500

30 Frauen und etwa 300 Kinder. Afrika hat immer noch die höchste Anzahl von neuen Infizierten. Auf der südlichen Hälfte des afrikanischen Kontinents leben fast 70% aller HIV-AIDS-Kranken. Vier Millionen Menschen haben sich dort im Jahre 2006 mit dem HI-Virus neu infiziert.

35 Und doch: zum ersten Mal seit dem Ausbruch der Epidemie in den achtziger Jahren ist das Wachstum der Krankheit niedriger. 2007 nahmen die Zahlen der Infizierten ab. Einem UNO-Bericht nach haben sich im Jahre 2007 4,1 Millionen Menschen mit HIV angesteckt. Das sind 7 000 weniger neu Angesteckte als im Jahre 2003.

25 **Anzahl** *(f.)* *number*
 GUS-Staaten *Eastern European nations (formerly in USSR)*
26 **man schätzt** *it's estimated*

35 **doch** *nevertheless, even so*
39 **sich anstecken mit** *to become infected by*

KAPITEL 12

12.1 Future Tense

A. *Werden* + infinitive

The verb **werden** as a main (finite) verb means *to become*. The future tense is a compound verb tense with **werden** as an auxiliary verb in second position of the main clause followed by an infinitive in final position of the clause. **Werden** + infinitive translates as *will* + infinitive.

Ich **werde** im Herbst ... studieren.	*I will study . . . in the fall.*
Du **wirst** das nächste Mal ... gewinnen.	*You'll win . . . next time*
Morgen **wird** sie/er ... reisen.	*S/he will travel . . . tomorrow.*
Zunächst **werden** wir ... lesen.	*First off we'll read . . .*
In der Zukunft **werdet** ihr ... feststellen.	*In the future you will ascertain . . .*
Sie **werden** nach zwei Jahren ... verkaufen und dann ... kaufen.	*You (They) will sell . . . after two years and then buy . . .*

Translating tips:

Identify the subject first, and then ask yourself whether **werden** stands alone *(= become/s)* or is an auxiliary *(= will)*. Locate the infinitive completing the future tense and translate it in conjunction with its auxiliary, then translate the objects and adverbs in reverse order. Repeat for multiple infinitives.

Beware of false cognates:

> German **will** = English *wants*
> German **wird** = English *will*

The third-person singular form of the German modal verb **wollen** (**Kapitel 16**) looks like the English future tense. However: **Er will arbeiten** means *he wants to work,* while **Er wird arbeiten** is the future tense, *he will work.* This is a frequent point of interference that you can avoid by remembering: The present tense of **werden** used with an infinitive is your clue for the future tense.

In the following you can see how both uses of **werden** as well as the false cognate **will** can coexist and require close attention:

Ein Lehrer macht Pläne: „Nach jeder Prüfung **werden** meine Schüler immer unruhig. Und dieses Jahr **ist** die Prüfung schwerer **geworden**, so **werden** die Schüler wahrscheinlich sehr unruhig **werden**. Ich **will** ein Experiment machen: Nach der Prüfung **werde** ich einen Assistenten im Zimmer haben, und wir **werden** die Schüler in zwei Gruppen teilen und ein Spiel spielen.“

B. Future-Time Expressions

In addition to the **werden** + infinitive construction, it is also quite common in German to imply the future by using the present tense plus an adverb which indicates future time. Some examples of future-time expressions are seen above with **werden**. The following examples demonstrate the use of present-tense verbs that translate into the future because of an adverb indicating future time:

> Die nächste Führung beginnt in zwanzig Minuten.
> *The next tour will begin in twenty minutes.*
> Ich gehe heute Nachmittag in die Austellung.
> *I'm going to go to the exhibit this afternoon.*

Note: **Ich studiere im Herbst** implies *I'm going to study in the fall,* whereas **Ich werde im Herbst studieren** indicates a definite intention, *I will (shall) study in the fall.*

12.2 Future Perfect Tense

The future perfect auxiliary **werden** can also occur with a past infinitive of a verb. The past infinitive consists of the past participle plus the infinitive of its appropriate auxiliary **haben** or **sein**.

> Bis zum Ende dieses Kapitels **werden** wir die neuen Verbenformen **gelernt haben.**
> *By the end of this chapter we will have learned the new verb forms.*
> In weniger als zwei Tagen **wird** er das Buch **gelesen haben.**
> *He will have read the book in less than two days.*
> Ein guter Student **wird** innerhalb von einer Stunde die Prüfung **beendet haben** und gleich nach Hause **gegangen sein.**
> *A good student will have completed the test within an hour and will have gone home immediately.*

Note: In each case this combination expresses actions that *will have happened* usually within a specifically stated time or circumstantial framework (**bis zum Ende der Woche / in weniger als zwei Tagen / innerhalb von einer Stunde / gleich**). Other commonly used expressions include:

auf die Dauer	*in the long run*
bis nächstes Jahr; **bis** sechs Uhr	*by next year; by six o'clock*
bis zum Ende des Monats	*by the end of the month*
in drei Wochen; **in** der Zukunft	*in three weeks (time); in the future*
gerade	*just*
immer wieder	*time and again; over and over*
mit (der) Zeit	*with time*
nach fünf Minuten	*after five minutes*
nach und nach	*after a while*
noch nicht	*not yet*
schon	*already*
um zwölf Uhr	*at twelve o'clock*
wenn es so weit ist,	*when the time comes*

Do not forget that participles may also be adjectives. In this case predicate adjectives always occur with **sein** to describe a state of being (review **Kapitel 10**). Learn to differentiate:

Wir **werden** den Versuch um zehn **beendet haben.**
We will have completed the experiment at ten o'clock.
Der Versuch **wird** um zehn Uhr **beendet sein.**
The experiment will be completed at ten o'clock.

12.3 Future Tenses Used to Express Probability

In German the future and the future perfect are used frequently to express probability. Used with an adverb like **wohl, (wohl) schon**, or **doch**, the future tense expresses probability or likelihood in reference to the present, while the future perfect + **wohl** expresses probability in reference to the past. For example:

Das wird wohl das Ende dieser Arbeit sein.
This is probably the end of this work.
Sie werden das Buch von Goethe schon kennen.
You probably (already) know Goethe's book.

Werther wird die Gefahr wohl nicht erkannt haben.

Werther probably did not recognize the danger.

Der Bräutigam wird wohl gestern angekommen sein und die
Situation gleich erfasst haben.

*The bridegroom probably arrived yesterday and figured out the
situation immediately.*

12.4 *Selbst, selber*

The pronouns **selbst** and **selber** are used to intensify or emphasize the
meaning of a noun or pronoun. When **selbst** or **selber** follows a noun or
personal pronoun, translate with *himself, herself, itself, themselves,* etc.

Der Professor selbst wusste es nicht.

The professor himself did not know it.

Haben Sie selber die Mitteilung der Forscher gelesen?

Did you yourself read the researchers' report?

Das wirst du selbst wohl nicht gelesen haben.

You yourself probably didn't read that.

However, when **selbst** precedes the noun or pronoun it is modifying,
the translation should be *even* + noun or pronoun.

Selbst die Ärzte standen vor einem Rätsel.

Even the doctors were mystified.

Selbst der Präsident wusste nicht, was das Problem war.

Even the president didn't know what the problem was.

Selbst Kinder werden diese Erklärung verstehen.

Even children will understand this explanation.

Grundwortschatz

ab/hängen von	*be dependent*	**Milliarde** *(f.),* **-n**	*billion*
(hing ... ab,	*upon*	**Mitteilung** *(f.),*	*report,*
abgehangen)		**-en**	*communication*
ab/nehmen	*to decrease,*	**nützlich**	*useful*
(nahm ... ab,	*take off*	**Papier** *(n.),* **-e**	*paper, document*
abgenommen;			*(not: newspaper,*
nimmt ... ab)			*term paper)*
an/kommen	*to arrive*	**Prüfung** *(f.),* **-en**	*test, examination*
(kam ... an, ist		**Quelle** *(f.),* **-n**	*source, spring*
angekommen)		**Regel** *(f.),* **-n**	*rule*
beenden	*to finish, complete*	**reisen**	*to travel*
Bevölkerung *(f.),*	*population;*	**selber**	*-self*
-en	*inhabitants (pl.)*	**er selber**	*he himself*
doppelt	*double, twice*	**selbst**	*-self; even*
Einwohnerzahl	*(total) population*	**sogar**	*even*
(f.)		**Stück** *(n.),* **-e**	*piece*
Entwicklungsland	*developing*	**studieren**	*to study (at the*
(n.), **-̈er**	*country*		*university)*
Erlebnis *(n.),* **-se**	*experience*	**usw. (und so**	*etc. (and so*
Ernährung *(f.)*	*feeding, food,*	**weiter)**	*forth)*
	nourishment	**wohl**	*well, perhaps,*
gewinnen	*to win, gain*		*probably, indeed,*
(gewann,			*no doubt*
gewonnen)		**Ziel** *(n.),* **-e**	*goal*
hauptsächlich	*main(ly), chief*	**Zuwachs** *(m.)*	*growth*
Kapitel *(n.),* **–**	*chapter*		
lernen	*to learn, to study*		
	(for a test)		

 Lösungen zu Übungssätzen auf **academic.cengage.com/german/korb**

Übungssätze

1. Die jüngere Generation wird immer gegen die Gesetze und Regeln der älteren protestieren.
2. In dieser Mitteilung werden wir die wichtigsten Ergebnisse unserer Untersuchungen angeben.
3. In diesem Kapitel werden wir voraussetzen, dass ...

2. **an/geben (gab ... an, angegeben; gibt ... an)** *to state, cite*

3. **voraus/setzen** *to assume, presuppose*

4. Wir werden in diesem Kapitel das Futur lernen. Ich lese das Kapitel am Wochenende. Bis Montag werde ich wohl diese neuen Verbformen gelernt haben.

5. Dieses Buch wird für jeden Erzieher nützlich sein, aber die genaue Anwendung der Methodik wird wohl sehr stark vom Ziel des Erziehers abhängen.

6. Die Konsequenzen deines Betragens wirst du wohl selbst vorhergesehen haben. Solch ein Betragen wird nicht ohne Folgen bleiben.

7. Selbst Edison wird dieses Prinzip wohl nicht gekannt haben. Die Erfindung des Phonographen hing aber glücklicherweise nicht von einem so unwichtigen Prinzip ab.

8. Es ist inzwischen 12.00 Uhr. Die Prüfung wird jetzt wohl schon beendet sein.

9. Durch das Experiment mit dem Glashaus werden wir wohl ungeheuer wichtige Erkenntnisse über Abfall-Recycling gewinnen.

10. Man wird mehr über den sauren Regen und das Ozonloch lernen.

11. Da sprach die Schlange zum Weib: „Ihr werdet sein wie Gott und werdet wissen, was gut und böse ist." (1. Moses 3, 5)

12. Durch anstrengende Arbeit werden die Muskeln eines jungen Menschen immer kräftiger.

13. Für viele Leser wird das Lesen dieses Buchs zu einem faszinierenden Erlebnis werden. Besonders interessant ist das letzte Kapitel.

14. Laut einem Bericht des Bundesverkehrsamts wird die Zahl der Unfälle demnächst zurückgehen, und die Autos werden sicherer werden.

15. Im Folgenden werden wir die steigende Weltbevölkerung besprechen.

4. **Futur** (n.) *future tense* (grammatical)
5. **Erzieher** (m.), – *educator, teacher*
   Anwendung (f.), **-en** *application*
6. **Betragen** (n.) *behavior*
   Folge (f.), **-n** *consequence*
8. **inzwischen** *in the meantime, meanwhile*
9. **Glashaus** (n.), **⁻er** *greenhouse*
   ungeheuer *huge, colossal, enormous*
   Abfall (m.), **⁻e** *garbage*
10. **saurer Regen** (m.) *acid rain*
   Loch (n.), **⁻er** *hole*

11. **Schlange** (f.), **-n** *snake*
   Weib (n.), **-er** *woman*
   böse *evil*
12. **anstrengend** *strenuous*
   Muskel (m.), **-n** *muscle*
13. **Leser** (m.), – *reader*
14. **Bundesverkehrsamt** (n.) *federal traffic department*
   Unfall (m.), **⁻e** *accident*
   demnächst *shortly, soon*
15. **im Folgenden** *in the following* (text)

16. Seit Anfang des 20. Jahrhunderts gibt es auf der Erde einen Zuwuchs von mehr als 4 Milliarden Menschen. 1927: 2 Milliarden, 1960: 3 Milliarden, 1974: 4 Milliarden, 1987: 5 Milliarden Menschen. 2007 leben 6,6 Milliarden Menschen auf der Erde.

17. Die Weltbevölkerungszahl wird jetzt wohl schon bei sieben Milliarden liegen.

18. Der größte Teil des Bevölkerungszuwachses wird in weniger entwickelten Ländern stattfinden. In einigen entwickelten Nationen nimmt die Bevölkerungszahl sogar ab.

19. Nach einer Prognose des Instituts der Deutschen Wirtschaft wird der schnell wachsende Großraum Berlin in den kommenden Jahren voraussichtlich vier bis fünf Millionen Menschen umfassen.

20. Steigende Bevölkerungszahlen werden in den kommenden Jahren einen enormen Druck auf das Ernährungssystem der Weltbevölkerung ausüben.

18. **statt/finden (fand ... statt, stattgefunden)** *to take place*
19. **Großraum** *(m.),* **⁻e** *metropolitan area*
    voraussichtlich *presumably, probably*

umfassen *to include, comprise*
20. **Druck** *(m.),* **⁻e** *pressure*
    aus/üben *to exert*

 Leitfragen zum Lesetext auf **academic.cengage.com/german/korb**

DIE WELTERNÄHRUNGSKRISE

Die immer zahlreicher werdende Bevölkerung der Erde wird zu immer größeren Problemen führen. Eines dieser Probleme wird natürlich die Ernährung der unglaublich schnell steigenden Weltbevölkerung sein. 1900 betrug sie etwa 1,5 Milliarden.
5 In den vergangenen 40 Jahren hat sich die Weltbevölkerung mehr als verdoppelt. Fast 7 Milliarden Menschen leben heute auf der Erde, in 40 Jahren werden es fast 10 Milliarden sein. Die entstehende Belastung für die Umwelt wird katastrophal sein. Schon heute wird die Ernährung der vielen Menschen, besonders in den unterent-
10 wickelten Ländern, immer schwieriger, denn diese Länder weisen das größte Bevölkerungswachstum auf.

1 **immer zahlreicher werdend** *continuously growing*
3 **unglaublich** *unbelievable*
8 **Belastung** *(f.),* **-en** *burden, stress*

9 **unterentwickelt** *underdeveloped*
10 **schwierig** *difficult*
   auf/weisen (wies ... auf, aufgewiesen) *to show, have*

In Studien zur Weltbevölkerung stellt man fest: Der „reiche"
Norden mit einem Fünftel der Weltbevölkerung verbraucht 70
Prozent der Weltenergie, 75 Prozent aller Metalle, 85 Prozent
des Holzes und konsumiert 60 Prozent der Nahrungsmittel. Die   15
Einwohnerzahl dieser „reichen" Teile der Welt wird bis zum Jahre
2025 auf 1,8 Milliarden steigen. Im ärmeren Süden wird es aber
6,8 Milliarden Menschen geben. Für diese Menschenmengen
werden nur 40 Prozent der Nahrungsmittel bleiben.

Die moderne Landwirtschaft hat in letzter Zeit in der Entwick-   20
lung der Bodenbearbeitung, Bewässerung, krankheitsresistenten
Züchtungen usw. Wunder vollbracht. Aber wird es möglich sein,
die moderne landwirtschaftliche Technologie, das notwendige
Transportsystem usw. in unterentwickelten Ländern und in Ent-
wicklungsländern in verhältnismäßig kurzer Zeit einzuführen? Dies   25
wird wohl notwendig werden, denn die Ausfuhr landwirtschaftlicher
Erzeugnisse der entwickelten Länder wird mit dem Anstieg in der
Weltbevölkerung kaum Schritt halten können.

12	**fest/stellen** *to determine; ascertain*	22	**vollbringen (vollbrachte,**
13	**verbrauchen** *to consume*		**vollbracht)** *to perform, accomplish*
15	**Holz** *(n.),* **⁻er** *wood, timber*	23	**notwendig** *necessary*
	Nahrungsmittel *(pl.)* *food*	25	**einzuführen** *to introduce . . .*
18	**Menge** *(f.),* **-n** *mass*	26	**Ausfuhr** *(f.),* **-en** *export*
21	**Bodenbearbeitung** *(f.),* **-en**	27	**Erzeugnis** *(n.),* **-se** *product*
	cultivation of the soil		**Anstieg** *(m.),* **-e** *rise*
	Bewässerung *(f.),* **-en** *irrigation*	28	**Schritt halten (hielt, gehalten; hält)**
	krankheitsresistent *disease-resistant*		*to keep pace*
22	**Züchtung** *(f.),* **-en** *strain of plants, growing*		**können (konnte, gekonnt; kann)** *to be able to*
	Wunder *(n.),* **–** *miracle, wonder*		

13.1 Passive Voice

The verb tenses that you have learned so far have all been in the active voice. A verb is in the active voice when its subject performs the action.

> Die Nobelpreisträgerin spielt die Geige.
> *The Nobel Prize recipient plays the violin.*

A verb is in the passive voice when its subject is the recipient of the action. The subject is acted upon in the passive voice.

> Die Geige wird von der Nobelpreisträgerin gespielt.
> *The violin is (being) played by the Nobel Prize recipient.*
> also: *The Nobel Prize recipient is playing the violin.*

The passive voice is common in written German; all verbs that can take objects (except reflexive verbs discussed in **Kapitel 15**) have a passive voice. If there is an agent identifying the source of the passive action (**von der Nobelpreisträgerin**), it is often more colloquial to translate the sentence actively. If the passive sentence does not indicate an agent and the English passive translation seems awkward, then convey the sentence actively using an unqualified subject such as *people* or *someone*.

> Im stillen Winkel der Kirche wird sanft gebetet.
> *In a quiet corner of the church someone is praying quietly.*

13.2 Present and Past Tenses of the Passive Voice

The German passive voice consists of the auxiliary **werden** + past participle of the verb. The tense of **werden** determines the tense of the passive voice.

Present
er/sie/es wird besucht *he/she/it is (being) visited*
sie werden besucht *they are (being) visited*

Past
er/sie/es wurde gebaut *it was (being) built*
sie wurden gebaut *they were (being) built*

Die byzantinische Kirche **wird** jedes Jahr von Touristen aus aller Welt **besucht.**
Tourists from all over the world visit the Byzantine church every year.
Das Hauptschiff der Kirche **wurde** schon um 600 n. Chr. **gebaut.**
The church's nave was built already around 600 A.D.

If the person or agent that causes the action is mentioned in a passive sentence, it follows the preposition **von** or **durch**, which are literally equivalent to English *by*.

Der Vertrag **wurde von** den Staatsmännern **unterzeichnet.**
The treaty was signed by the statesmen. Also: The statesman signed the treaty.
Der Friede **wird durch** Bombenanschläge ständig **gestört.**
The peace is constantly (being) disrupted by bombing attacks.

Note that in all of the passive situations above, an action is, in fact, taking place. Be careful not to confuse this type of passive that denotes action with states of being or "apparent passive" (see also **Kapitel 10**). Whereas a true passive combines **werden** + past participle and expresses an action, the statal passive combines **sein** + past participle (being used as an adjective) and expresses a condition which may be the result of an action in the passive voice.

Passive: Das Haus **wird** renoviert. *The house is being renovated.* (This action is in progress.)
State of Being: Das Haus **ist** renoviert. *The house is renovated.* (This is a completed result.)

13.3 Three Uses of *werden*

A. *Werden* = main verb

When **werden** = main verb, it is translated into English as *to become* (**Kapitel 5**).

Die deutsche Filmindustrie **wird** immer wichtiger.
The German film industry is becoming more and more important.

Remember that the best translation of **werden** + **zu** is *to turn into.*

Der unbekannte Schauspieler **wurde zu** einem großen Star.
The unknown actor turned into a big star.

B. *Werden* + *(wohl)* infinitive = future tense

When **werden** + **(wohl)** infinitive = future tense, it is translated into English as *(probably) will/going to* + infinitive (**Kapitel 12**).

Die deutsche Filmindustrie **wird** dieses Jahr (wohl) 100 bis 150 neue Spielfilme **herstellen**.
The German film industry probably will produce 100 to 150 new feature films this year.

C. *Werden* + past participle = passive voice

Werden + past participle = passive voice and is translated into English as *is (being)* + past participle.

Der neue Film **wird** von Detlev Buck **konzipiert**, **geschrieben** und **hergestellt**.
The new film is (being) conceived, written, and produced by Detlev Buck.

Determine the use and meaning of **werden** in the following statements.

1. Die Berliner Mauer wurde 1961 gebaut.
2. Sie wurde fast über Nacht von der SED-Regierung aufgestellt.
3. Sie wurde zum Symbol des Kalten Krieges.
4. In diesem Bericht werden wir über ihre Rolle in der Nachkriegs-politik diskutieren.
5. Das Land wurde geteilt, Familien wurden durch die Mauer getrennt.
6. Noch heute wird über die Verantwortung für den Mauerbau heftig debattiert.
7. Was wurde aus den Tausenden von russischen Soldaten in der ehemaligen DDR?
8. Heute werden sie wohl wieder in Russland leben.
9. Im Oktober 1989 wurde der 40. Jahrestag der DDR gefeiert.
10. Am 31. August 1990 wurde der Einigungsvertrag von Staatsmän-nern unterzeichnet.

13.4 Personal Pronouns

The personal pronouns in German (as in English) indicate number and case. They are declined as follows.

Nominative		Accusative		Dative		Genitive	
ich	*I*	mich	*me*	mir	*to me*	meiner	*of my*
du	*you*	dich	*you*	dir	*to you*	deiner	*of your*
er	*he/it*	ihn	*him/it*	ihm	*to him/to it*	seiner	*of his/its*
sie	*she/it*	sie	*her/it*	ihr	*to her/to it*	ihrer	*of hers/its*
es	*it*	es	*it*	ihm	*to it*	seiner	*of its*
wir	*we*	uns	*us*	uns	*to us*	unserer	*of ours*
ihr	*you*	euch	*you*	euch	*to you*	eurer	*of yours*
sie	*they*	sie	*them*	ihnen	*to them*	ihrer	*of theirs*
Sie	*you*	Sie	*you*	Ihnen	*to you*	Ihrer	*of yours*

13.5 Agreement of Pronoun and Antecedent

The third-person pronouns (**er**, **sie**, **es**; **sie**, and all their variants), agree with their antecedent (the nouns that they replace) in gender and number. Thus, when translating a pronoun, you must remember that in English, inanimate objects are all neuter, while in German they will be masculine, feminine, or neuter.

> Der Arbeiter erhitzt den Stein und legt **ihn** dann ins kalte Wasser.
> *The worker heats the stone and then lays **it** in cold water.*
> (not: . . . *and then lays him in cold water.*)
> Die Mauer wurde 1961 gebaut; **sie** wurde fast über Nacht aufgestellt.
> *The wall was built in 1961; **it** was put up almost overnight.*
> (not: . . . *she was put up almost overnight.*)
> Das Hauptschiff der Kirche wurde um 600 n. Chr. gebaut; **es** wird noch heute benutzt.
> *The church's nave was built around 600 A.D.; **it** is still used today.*

an/regen	to stimulate	**her/stellen**	to produce,
an/sehen	to regard,		make
(sah ... an,	look at	**jung**	young
angesehen;		**Krankheit** (f.), **-en**	illness, disease
sieht ... an)		**Leistung** (f.), **-en**	work, performance,
ausländisch	foreign		achievement
beliebt	popular	**Mal** (n.), **-e**	point of time, time,
Bericht (m.), **-e**	report		bout
dankbar	thankful, grateful	**Mauer** (f.), **-n**	wall
Dauer (f.)	duration	**nächst-**	next
Dichter (m.), **–;**	poet,	**Schicksal** (n.)	fate, destiny
Dichterin (f.),	creative writer	**Schriftsteller** (m.),	writer, author
-nen		**–; Schrift-**	
ein/führen	to introduce,	**stellerin** (f.),**-nen**	
	import	**schwer**	heavy, difficult,
einheimisch	native		severe
ein/richten	to organize, set up,	**Seele** (f.), **-n**	soul
	install	**sichtbar**	visible
erfinden (erfand,	to invent	**töten**	to kill
erfunden)		**Träger** (m.), **–;**	winner,
Erfolg (m.), **-e**	success	**Trägerin** (f.),	recipient
erwähnen	to mention	**-nen**	
Friede (m., n-noun)	peace	**zwar**	indeed, to be sure
Gefühl (n.), **-e**	feeling	**und zwar**	that is, they are;
genau	exact		namely

 Lösungen zu Übungssätzen auf **academic.cengage.com/german/korb**

1. Im Dezember 1770 wurde Ludwig van Beethoven in Bonn geboren. Er ist zu einem der beliebtesten Komponisten der Welt geworden. Sein Geburtshaus in Bonn wurde in den neunziger Jahren des 19. Jahrhunderts als Museum eingerichtet.

2. Jedes Jahr wird das Beethovenmuseum von Touristen aus der ganzen Welt besucht. 1999 wurde es komplett renoviert und mit einer Ausstellung der Werke des jungen Komponisten eingerichtet.

3. Beethovens Werke sind zum großen Teil Selbstbekenntnisse. Aus ihnen klingt das schwere Ringen der Menschenseele mit dem Schicksal.

4. Das Quecksilberthermometer wurde von Daniel Fahrenheit (1686–1736) erfunden. Dieses Thermometer wird noch heute in einigen Ländern gebraucht.

5. Die Viren sind Erreger von ansteckenden Krankheiten bei Menschen, Tieren und Pflanzen. Sie sind noch kleiner als Bakterien und im Lichtmikroskop nicht sichtbar.

6. Nach der spanischen Eroberung von Peru wurde die Kartoffel in Europa eingeführt. Sie wurde mit der Zeit sehr beliebt.

7. In meinem letzten Brief habe ich dich auf die Folgen deines unverantwortlichen Betragens aufmerksam gemacht. Du wirst mir eines Tages dankbar sein.

8. Hunderttausende neuer Arbeitsplätze wurden durch die Ansiedlung innovativer Industrien geschaffen.

9. Im nächsten Brief werde ich Ihnen einen genauen Bericht erstatten.

10. Petrus wurde wahrscheinlich im Jahre 67 in Rom gekreuzigt. Über dem vermuteten Grab des Apostels wurde die Peterskirche gebaut.

11. Die Bezeichnung „deutsch" wurde von der Sprache auf die Sprecher und schließlich auf ihr Wohngebiet („Deutschland") übertragen.

12. Panzerkampfwagen (Panzer) wurden zum ersten Mal im Ersten Weltkrieg, im November 1917, bei Cambrai eingesetzt.

13. 1867 wurde Alaska für 7,2 Millionen Dollar von Russland verkauft. Der Kauf wurde von vielen Amerikanern „Seward's folly" genannt.

3. **Selbstbekenntnis** *(n.)*, **-se** *self-revelation, personal confession*
klingen (klang, geklungen) *to resound*
ringen (rang, gerungen) *to struggle*
4. **Quecksilber** *(n.)* *mercury*
5. **Virus** *(n.)*, **Viren** *virus*
Erreger *(m.)*, **–** *cause, producer*
an/stecken *to infect*
Lichtmikroskop *(n.)* *optical microscope*
6. **Eroberung** *(f.)*, **-en** *conquest*
Kartoffel *(f.)*, **-n** *potato*
7. **Folge** *(f.)*, **-n** *consequence*
unverantwortlich *irresponsible*
Betragen *(n.)* *behavior*
aufmerksam machen auf *to call attention to*

8. **Ansiedlung** *(f.)*, **-en** *settlement, introduction into an area*
schaffen *to produce*
9. **erstatten** *to give, make*
10. **Petrus** *St. Peter*
kreuzigen *to crucify*
vermuten *to suppose, presume*
Grab *(n.)*, **⁻er** *grave*
11. **Bezeichnung** *(f.)*, **-en** *designation, term*
übertragen auf (übertrug, übertragen; überträgt) *to transfer to, convey upon*
12. **Panzer** *(m.)*, **–** *tank*
Cambrai *(French city) Cambrai*
ein/setzen *to employ*

14. Der Nobelpreis wurde 1901 von Alfred Nobel gestiftet. Bis 1969 wurden fünf Preise für hervorragende Leistungen verliehen, und zwar die Preise für Physik, Chemie, Medizin, Literatur und der Friedenspreis. Seit 1969 wird auch ein Preis für Ökonomische Wissenschaften verliehen. Die Nobelpreisträger für die fünf Wissenschaften werden von der Schwedischen Akademie in Stockholm ausgewählt. Die norwegische Volksvertretung bestimmt den Träger des Friedenspreises.

15. Diese Schriftsteller werden als Repräsentanten dieser Bewegung angesehen. Viele junge Dichter wurden von ihnen angeregt.

14. **stiften**   *to found, donate*
    hervorragend   *outstanding*
    verleihen (verlieh, verliehen)   *to grant, award*

14. **aus/wählen**   *to choose, select*
    Volksvertretung *(f.)*, **-en**   *parliament*

 Leitfragen zum Lesetext auf **academic.cengage.com/german/korb**

STURM UND DRANG

D er Sturm und Drang ist eine der beliebtesten Epochen der deutschen Literatur. Die Epoche dauerte eine verhältnismäßig kurze Zeit, von ungefähr Ende der 60er bis Anfang der 80er Jahre des 18. Jahrhunderts. Sie wurde von vielen einheimischen und

5   ausländischen Einflüssen angeregt. Von den letzteren werden wir nur Edward Young, einen englischen, und Jean-Jacques Rousseau, einen französischen Schriftsteller, erwähnen.

Die jungen Sturm-und-Drang-Dichter protestierten gegen die Herrschaft des abstrakten Verstandes und gegen zeitlos gültige Regeln

10 und Gesetze. Von ihnen wurden u.a. die schöpferische Kraft der leidenschaftlichen Gefühle, der Subjektivismus, das Individuelle und Irrationale verherrlicht.

1 **Sturm** *(m.)*, **⁻e**   *storm*
  Drang *(m.)*   *stress*
2 **verhältnismäßig**   *relatively*
9 **Herrschaft** *(f.)*, **-en**   *rule, dominance*
  Verstand *(m.)*   *understanding, intellect, reason*

9 **zeitlos**   *timeless, universal*
  gültig   *valid*
10 **schöpferisch**   *creative*
11 **leidenschaftlich**   *passionate, emotional*
12 **verherrlichen**   *to glorify*

Goethes „Goetz von Berlichingen" und Schillers „Die Räuber"
werden als repräsentative Werke dieser Periode angesehen. Die
Epoche verdankt ihren Namen Klingers Drama „Sturm und Drang".
Wohl den größten literarischen Erfolg der Zeit stellt aber Goethes
Briefroman „Die Leiden des jungen Werther" dar. *, play by Goethe*

In der Figur von Werther wurde der Typus des empfindsamen
bürgerlichen Intellektuellen verkörpert. In Werthers Briefen an
seinen Freund Wilhelm werden die überwältigenden Gefühle einer
gequälten Seele ausgeschüttet. Werthers religiöses Naturgefühl und
seine schwärmerische, bedingungslose Liebe für Lotte führen schließlich zum Selbstmord. Das Werk war sofort ein großer Erfolg. Goethe
wurde 1774 über Nacht zu einem weltbekannten Schriftsteller. Er
hatte mit dem „Werther" dem Lebensgefühl einer ganzen Generation
zu Wort verholfen.

15
20
25

13 **Räuber** (*m.*), – *robber*
15 **verdanken** *to owe, to be indebted to*
17 **Leiden** (*n.*), – *sorrow, suffering*
18 **empfindsam** *sentimental, sensitive*
19 **verkörpern** *to embody*
20 **überwältigen** *to overcome, overwhelm*
21 **quälen** *to torture*

21 **aus/schütten** *to pour out, empty out*
22 **schwärmerisch** *infatuated; enthusiastic*
   bedingungslos *unconditional, unqualified*
23 **Selbstmord** (*m.*), -e *suicide*
26 **zu Wort verhelfen** (**verhalf, verholfen; verhilft**) *to help express*

Tenses of the Passive Voice

___ you learned that all verbs with objects, except the reflexives, can be expressed in the passive voice and that the passive is formed with **werden** + past participle. You learned the present tense: **die Musik wird gespielt** *(the music is being played)* and the simple past: **die Musik wurde gespielt** *(the music was being played)*. As with all German verbs, the passive forms also have perfect tenses.

In the perfect tenses of the passive voice, the past participle of **werden** is **worden**. The past participle of **werden**, when it means *to become*, is **geworden** (e.g., **Es ist kalt geworden**).

Present perfect tense

er/sie/es ist behandelt worden   *he/she/it has been (was) treated*
sie sind behandelt worden   *they have been (were) treated*

Das Thema ist in ihrem neuen Buch eingehend **behandelt worden**.
   That topic has been treated thoroughly in her new book.

Past perfect tense

er/sie/es war behandelt worden   *he/she/it had been treated*
sie waren behandelt worden   *they had been treated*

In ihrem ersten Buch **war** es nicht so eingehend **behandelt worden**.
   It hadn't been treated so thoroughly in her first book.

Look over the following example sentences and determine the meaning of **werden** in the various situations.

1. Die Mauer ist 1961 gebaut worden.
2. Sie ist fast über Nacht von der SED-Regierung aufgestellt worden.
3. Sie ist zum Symbol des Kalten Krieges geworden.
4. Das Land ist geteilt worden.
5. Familien sind durch die Mauer getrennt worden.
6. Schon 1960 war von dem Bau einer Mauer gesprochen worden.
7. Die Grenze ist am 9. November 1989 geöffnet worden.
8. Im November 1989 war der 40. Jahrestag der DDR schon gefeiert worden.
9. Was ist wohl heute aus den russischen Soldaten geworden?

14.2 Infinitive of the Passive Voice

Just like active verbs, each of which has an infinitive that is conjugated into the various tenses to indicate temporal differences, passive verbs also have infinitives that are conjugated.

> **Present infinitive:**   gebaut werden   *to be built*
> **Past infinitive:**   gebaut worden sein   *to have been built*

The present passive infinitive consists of the past participle and **werden**. It is a common construction. For example, all but the third and the ninth of the exercise sentences on page 138 are conjugations of present passive infinitives: 1. **gebaut werden** *(to be built),* 2. **aufgestellt werden** *(to be put up),* 4. **geteilt werden** *(to be divided),* 5. **getrennt werden** *(to be separated),* 6. **gesprochen werden** *(to be spoken),* 7. **geöffnet werden** *(to be opened),* and 8. **gefeiert werden** *(to be celebrated).* Note that in the sixth and eighth sentences the present passive infinitive has been conjugated into the past perfect tense, indicating that the action *had been done.*

14.3 Future Tense of the Passive Voice

The passive infinitive also occurs in the future tense, which consists of the auxiliary **werden** + the passive infinitive.

> Die Preise **werden erhöht werden**.
> *The prices will be raised.*
> Die Soldaten **werden** nach Irak **geschickt werden**.
> *The soldiers will be sent to Iraq.*

When you encounter the first **werden**, check its use. In both cases above, you are dealing with **werden** + present passive infinitive = future tense of the passive voice.

14.4 Future Perfect of the Passive Voice

It is also possible in rare situations to find the future perfect passive, which consists of **werden** + past passive infinitive.

> Das Thema wird in einem älteren Buch **behandelt worden sein**.
> *That topic will have been treated in an older book.*

The most common use of this construction expresses probability in the past. In this case, the construction of **werden** + past passive infinitive is generally accompanied by **wohl** and should be translated as follows.

> Dieses Buch **wird wohl** schon **besprochen worden sein**.
> *This book has probably already been discussed.*

14.5 Suffix *-er*

A. Occupation

The **-er** suffix is masculine and frequently denotes an occupation.

der Ansager	*announcer*	der Chemiker	*chemist*
der Apotheker	*apothecary,*	der Dramatiker	*dramatist*
	druggist	der Künstler	*artist*
der Arbeiter	*worker*	der Lehrer	*teacher*
der Briefträger	*mail carrier,*	der Physiker	*physicist*
	mailman	der Schriftsteller	*writer*

The singular and plural forms of these nouns are identical. The plural article **die** is key to identifying their plural forms in the nominative or accusative cases. A plural subject also has a plural verb ending in **-n** or **-en**. The plural dative forms have an **-n** ending, and the genitive singular ends in **-s**. Do not confuse the genitive singular **-s** ending with the English plural form.

B. Origin

The suffix **-er** may also denote a male inhabitant (of a continent, state, city, etc.).

ein Amerikaner	ein New Yorker
ein Araber	ein Pariser
ein Berliner	ein Rheinländer
ein Hamburger	ein Schweizer
ein Japaner	ein Wiener

Here, again, the singular and plural forms are identical.

C. Action

With the infinitive stem of a verb, the **-er** suffix denotes a male person engaged in an activity indicated by the verb.

der Begründer	*founder*	der Leser	*reader*
der Denker	*thinker*	der Spieler	*player*
der Entdecker	*discoverer*	der Sprecher	*speaker*
der Erfinder	*inventor*	der Trinker	*drinker*
der Fahrer	*driver*		

Singular and plural forms are identical.

D. Instrument/Tool

Occasionally, the **-er** suffix denotes an instrument.

> der Bohrer   *drill*
> der Computer   *computer*
> der Hammer   *hammer*
> der Hörer   *receiver (telephone)*
> der Kugelschreiber   *ballpoint pen*
> der Schalter   *switch*
> der Zeiger   *pointer, hand (of a dial)*

The singular and plural forms are identical. Pay close attention to verb and/or case endings to differentiate between singular and plural.

14.6 Suffix *-in*

A. Occupation/Title

The **-in** suffix is feminine and frequently denotes an occupation or title.

> die Architektin   *architect*   die Ingenieurin   *engineer*
> die Ärztin   *physician*   die Köchin   *cook*
> die Autorin   *authoress*   die Königin   *queen*
> die Friseurin   *hairdresser*   die Prinzessin   *princess*
> die Fürstin   *ruler, princess*   die Sekretärin   *secretary*
> die Göttin   *goddess*

Plurals of these nouns add **-nen**. The resulting plural ending, **-innen**, is clearly identifiable and occurs in all cases. You can also recognize the plural subject by the plural verb ending, **-n** or **-en**.

B. Occupation/Origin/Action

Added to the masculine suffix **-er** indicating an occupation, an inhabitant, or a person engaged in an activity indicated by the verb stem, the suffix **-in** indicates a female person in that category.

> eine Amerikanerin   *an American*
> eine Berlinerin   *a Berliner*   die Physikerin   *physicist*
> die Leserin   *reader*   die Schriftstellerin   *writer*
> eine Mexikanerin   *a Mexican*   die Sprecherin   *speaker*
> die Nobelpreisträgerin   die Vertreterin   *representa-*
>   *Nobel Prize recipient*   *tive, saleswoman*

Here, again, the plural forms end in **-innen**.

Grundwortschatz

Arzt (m.), **¨e;** **Ärztin** (f.), **-nen**	*physician*	**Gymnasium** (n.)	*college preparatory high school*
Auflage (f.), **-n**	*edition*	**heiß**	*hot*
auf/nehmen (**nahm … auf,** **aufgenommen;** **nimmt … auf**)	*to take in, admit; to absorb; to record*	**Hochschule** (f.), **-n**	*university (not: high school)*
Autor (m., n-noun), **-en; Autorin** (f.), **-nen**	*author*	**landwirtschaftlich** **nah(e)** **nördlich**	*agricultural near northern, northerly*
Begründer (m.), **–;** **Begründerin** (f.), **-nen**	*founder*	**schaffen** (**schaffte,** **geschafft**)	*to make, accomplish*
Beitrag (m.), **¨e**	*contribution*	**schaffen** (**schuf,** **geschaffen**)	*to create, produce*
Beobachtung (f.), **-en**	*observation*	**Soldat** (m., n-noun), **-en; Soldatin** (f.), **-nen**	*soldier*
bereichern	*to enrich, enhance*		
Beruf (m.), **-e**	*occupation, job*	**Spiel** (n.), **-e**	*game*
berufstätig	*employed*	**um/arbeiten**	*to rewrite, revise*
berühmt	*famous*	**Unternehmer** (m.), **–; Unternehmerin** (f.), **-nen**	*contractor, entrepreneur*
Betrieb (m.), **-e**	*operation, plant, factory*		
Bildung (f.)	*education, training*	**vermerken**	*to annotate, note, remark*
eigen	*own, individual*	**vermutlich**	*presumable, possible*
eventuell	*possible, perhaps (not: eventually)*		
fremd	*foreign*	**Zukunft** (f.)	*future*
grundlegend	*basic*		

 Lösungen zu Übungssätzen auf **academic.cengage.com/german/korb**

Übungssätze

1. Das „königliche Spiel" Schach ist aus dem Orient vermutlich von den Arabern nach Europa gebracht worden.
2. Tocqueville wird als liberal-konservativer Denker angesehen.

1. **königlich** *royal*
   Schach (*n.*) *chess*

3. Anna Seghers (1900–1983) war eine der bekanntesten Schriftstellerinnen der ehemaligen DDR. Sie ist die Autorin von dem berühmten Roman „Der Aufstand der Fischer von St. Barbara".

4. Der Autor Somerset Maugham ist der unglücklichste Glückliche aller Zeiten genannt worden. Er hatte kein Talent fürs Glücklichsein.

5. Die erste Auflage seines Romans „Der Menschen Hörigkeit" erschien im Jahre 1917. Eine Filmversion wurde 1934 gedreht.

6. Die wesentlichen Grundlagen der heutigen Atomphysik waren schon von den alten Griechen geschaffen worden.

7. In der nahen Zukunft werden die meisten Unterseeboote mit Atomkraft ausgestattet sein.

8. In diesem neuen Buch wird die grundlegende Arbeit des Begründers des Schulsystems beschrieben.

9. Ein Gymnasium vermittelt Schülerinnen und Schülern eine allgemeine Grundbildung und bereitet sie fürs Studium an einer Hochschule oder Universität vor.

10. Die landwirtschaftliche Produktion ist durch einen Mechanisierungsprozess gesteigert worden. Neue Maschinen sind eingeführt worden.

11. Die Trennung von Staat und Kirche ist durch die Weimarer Verfassung von 1919 vollzogen worden. Historische Bindungen sind aber nicht ganz beseitigt worden.

12. Seit 1945 sind in Deutschland eine große Zahl Kirchen gebaut worden. Aus der Fülle der Bauten ragt die neue Kaiser-Wilhelm-Gedächtniskirche hervor. Die alte Kirche war im Kriege zerstört worden.

13. Im Mittelalter sind Operationen nicht von akademisch gebildeten Ärzten, sondern von Badern ausgeführt worden.

3. **ehemalig** *former*
DDR *GDR (=German Democratic Republic or "East Germany")*
4. **glücklich** *happy, fortunate*
5. **Hörigkeit** *(f.) bondage*
6. **Grundlage** *(f.), -n basis, foundation*
7. **aus/statten** *to equip*
9. **vermitteln** *to impart*
allgemein *general*
vor/bereiten *to prepare*
11. **Trennung** *(f.) -en separation*
Verfassung *(f.), -en constitution*

11. **vollziehen (vollzog, vollzogen)** *to accomplish, execute*
Bindung *(f.), -en tie, connection*
beseitigen *to eliminate, do away way*
12. **Fülle** *(f.) abundance, profusion*
Gedächtniskirche *(f.) (war ruin turned into a) memorial church in Berlin*
hervor/ragen *to stand out, be prominent*
13. **gebildet** *trained, educated*
Bader *(m.), – barber (obsolete usage)*

14. Die Chinesische Mauer war im 3. Jh. v. Chr. zur Abwehr der nördlich von China lebenden Nomadenvölker gebaut worden. Diese Mauer wird heute von Touristen aus aller Welt besucht.

15. Der Europarat ist 1949 gegründet worden und spielt heute eine wichtige Rolle für die neuen Demokratien Europas.

16. Seit 1990 wurden 23 Reformdemokratien aus Mittel- und Osteuropa in den Europarat aufgenommen.

17. Sein[1] politisch bedeutender Beitrag zur demokratischen Neuordnung im mittleren und östlichen Europa wurde auf dem ersten Gipfeltreffen der Staats- und Regierungschefs seiner Mitgliedsstaaten im Oktober 1993 in Wien unterstrichen.

18. Viele dieser Ideen werden von anderen Autoren und Autorinnen aufgenommen, durch neue Beobachtungen ergänzt und bereichert werden.[2]

19. In der neuen Auflage ihres Buches schreibt die Autorin über das Schicksal der Soldaten und Soldatinnen in dem Irakkrieg.

14. **Abwehr** (*f.*)   *protection (against), warding off*
15. **Europarat** (*m.*), ⁼e   *Council of Europe*
17. **Gipfeltreffen** (*n.*), –   *summit meeting*

17. **unterstreichen** (**unterstrich, unterstrichen**)   *to emphasize, underline*
18. **ergänzen**   *to add to, supplement*

---

1. The possessive pronoun **sein** *(its)* refers in this case to **der Europarat**.

2. Note that **werden** is the future auxiliary of three passive infinitives: **aufgenommen werden**, **ergänzt werden**, and **bereichert werden**.

FRAUEN WERDEN VERZWEIFELT GESUCHT[3]

S eit dem Fall der Mauer haben mehr als 1,5 Millionen
Menschen die neuen Bundesländer verlassen. Vor allem gut
ausgebildete junge Frauen gehen in den Westen. Forscher am
Berlin-Institut für Bevölkerung und Entwicklung warnen vor einem
„europaweit einzigartigen Frauenmangel".   5

In einigen Regionen gibt es einen Männerüberschuss von bis
zu 25 Prozent. Es wurde festgestellt: Gut ausgebildete, schon
berufstätige Frauen zwischen 18 bis 29 Jahren verlassen ihre
ostdeutsche Heimat, aber viele junge Männer bleiben mit schlechter
Ausbildung und ohne Beruf zurück. Außerdem fehlen in den neuen   10
Bundesländern wegen der Abwanderung der Frauen schon jetzt
etwa 100 000 Kinder.

Als Ursache sehen die Forscher die eklatanten Bildungsunterschiede
zwischen den Jungen und Mädchen im Osten an. Fast 60 Prozent
aller Schüler (oder besser gesagt Schülerinnen) mit Gymnasienabschluss   15
sind junge Frauen. In den vergangenen Jahren schafften deutlich
weniger Jungen als Mädchen auch nur den Hauptschulabschluss.

„Zusammen mit einer hohen Arbeitslosigkeit und den
schlechteren Chancen auf einen Ausbildungsplatz führt dieses
Bildungsgefälle dazu, dass viele junge Frauen ihr Glück in   20
Westdeutschland versuchen", sagte der Leiter der Studie. „Die
Frauen suchen sich einen Partner mit ähnlichem Bildungsniveau—
und finden diesen nicht in Ostdeutschland."

Title **verzweifelt** desperate(ly)
2 **verlassen (verließ, verlassen;
verlässt)** to leave, abandon
vor allem above all
5 **einzigartig** unique
Mangel (*m.*) lack, scarcity
6 **Überschuss** (*m.*), ¨e excess
7 **von bis zu** of up to
10 **außerdem** in addition

13 **als Ursache** as the cause
eklatant striking, ~~brilliant~~
Unterschied (*m.*), -e difference,
dissimilarity
16 **deutlich** marked(ly)
19 **Ausbildung** (*f.*) training,
education
20 **Gefälle** (*n.*), – decline

---

3. Based on „Frauen verzweifelt gesucht", *sueddeutsche.de*, May 30, 2007.
© sueddeutsche.de GmbH / Süddeutsche Zeitung GmbH.

KAPITEL 15

15.1 Reflexive Pronouns

A reflexive pronoun object refers back to the subject of the verb and thus *reflects* the subject. Both the subject and the pronoun refer to the same person, thing, or idea. In English the reflexive pronoun is expressed by attaching *-self* to a singular object pronoun or *-selves* to a plural one. Reflexive pronouns function as either direct or indirect objects.

A. As a direct object (reflexive pronouns in accusative case)

ich sehe mich   *I see myself*
du siehst dich   *you see yourself*
wir sehen uns   *we see ourselves*
ihr seht euch   *you see yourselves*

B. As an indirect object (reflexive pronouns in dative case)

Ich kaufe mir einen Wagen.
   I am buying myself a car.
Du kaufst dir einen Wagen.
   You're buying yourself a car.
Wir kaufen uns einen Wagen.
   We're buying ourselves a car.
Kauft ihr euch einen Wagen?
   Are you buying yourselves a car?

C. *Sich:* third-person (accusative and dative cases)

In the third-person singular and plural, the reflexive pronoun is **sich**, meaning *himself, herself, itself, themselves, yourself,* or *yourselves* depending on the subject. **Sich** is used as both the direct and the indirect object.

er sieht sich   *he sees himself*
sie sieht sich   *she sees herself*
sie sehen sich   *they see themselves*
Sie sehen sich   *you see yourself* or: *you see yourselves*

Sie hat sich einen Fernseher gekauft.
   She bought herself a television.

Sie haben sich ein Geschenk gekauft.
They bought themselves a gift.
Was haben Sie sich gekauft?
What did you buy yourself/yourselves?

When a plural or compound subject occurs reflexively, the best translation may be *each other* or *one another*.

Mein Bruder und ich verstehen uns gut.
My brother and I understand each other well.
Mein Bruder und seine Frau lieben sich.
My brother and his wife love each other.
Wir gaben uns die Hand, und sie umarmten sich.
We shook hands with each other, and they hugged each other.

15.2 Reflexive Verbs

Many German verbs become reflexive by adding reflexive pronouns. Note the variation in meaning when this happens.

Der Soldat verletzte den Zivilisten.
The soldier injured the civilian.
Der Soldat verletzte sich.
The soldier injured himself. (The soldier got hurt.)

Ich wasche das Auto.
I'm washing the car.
Ich wasche mich.
I'm washing myself.
Ich wasche mir das Gesicht und dann wasche ich mir die Haare.
I'm washing my face, and then I'm going to wash my hair.

Note that in situations involving personal items such as body parts or clothing, English uses a possessive adjective where the German generally uses a reflexive construction to indicate that the involved action is being done to oneself: **Sie zieht sich den Mantel an**. *(She's putting her coat on.)*

Numerous verbs in German must have reflexive pronouns to complete their meaning. The English equivalents of the German reflexives generally do not have reflexive pronouns.

sich befinden   *to be located; to be feeling*
sich empfehlen   *to say good-bye; to commend oneself*

sich setzen   *to take one's seat*
sich wenden   *to turn around*

It is quite common in German for an inanimate noun to be the subject of a reflexive verb. Attempts to translate these combinations literally into English are awkward at best. Instead, use some form of passive construction. Consider the following examples.

Das Problem löst sich ohne viel Anstrengung.
The problem is being solved without much effort.
Die Industrie der Stadt beschränkt sich auf Schiffbau.
The city's industry is restricted to shipbuilding.
Diese Theorie entwickelte sich über viele Jahre.
This theory was developed over a number of years.

Some German reflexive verbs have idiomatic meanings and the reflexive pronoun is not necessarily translated into English. Dictionaries indicate transitive *(tr. V.)* and reflexive forms *(refl. V.)* as follows.

erinnern   *(tr. V.) to remind;* **erinnern**   *(refl. V.) to remember*
versprechen   *(tr. V.) to promise;* **versprechen**   *(refl. V.) to mispronounce*
vor/stellen   *(tr. V.) to present;* **vor/stellen**   *(akk. refl. V.) to introduce oneself; (dat. refl. V.) to imagine*

You must be careful to differentiate.

ich erinnere ihn   *I remind him*   er erinnert mich   *he reminds me*
ich erinnere mich   *I remember*   er erinnert sich   *he remembers*
ich stelle mich vor   *I introduce myself*
ich stelle mir etwas vor   *I imagine something*

15.3 Position of the Reflexive Pronoun in Main Clauses

In main clauses, the reflexive pronoun usually immediately follows the finite verb.

Der Herzog sah sich nicht als einen normalen Menschen, sondern als einen Übermenschen. **(sich sehen)**
The duke saw himself not as a normal human being but rather as a superhuman.
Den Schmuck zog sich die Herzogin nicht an. **(sich anziehen)**
The duchess did not put on the jewelry.

Dieses Buch befasst sich mit der Kolonialpolitik Englands. (**sich befassen**)
This book deals with the colonial policy of England.
Wir befassen uns mit einem schwierigen Problem. (**sich befassen**)
We are dealing with a difficult problem.

In compound tenses, the reflexive pronoun follows the auxiliary while the main verb stands at the end of the clause.

Unter solchen Bedingungen hat sich der Widerstand langsam aber sicher gebildet. (**sich bilden**)
Under such circumstances, the resistance came about slowly but surely.
Die westlichen Staaten der Vereinigten Staaten haben sich in den letzten Jahrzehnten äußerst schnell entwickelt. (**sich entwickeln**)
The western states of the United States have developed very rapidly in the past decades.

This word order also holds true for questions, unless the subject is a pronoun.

Hat sich die Frau verletzt? *Did the woman injure herself?*
Hat sie sich verletzt? *Did she injure herself? (Did she get hurt?)*
Wie befinden Sie sich heute? *How are you feeling today?*

15.4 Suffixes *-bar* and *-lich*

A. Suffix *-bar*

Many verbs can be the basis for compounds formed with the suffix **-bar**. This common German suffix corresponds to English *-able, -ible,* or *-ful*.

trennen *to separate* **trennbar** *separable*
Die zwei Argumente sind einfach nicht **trennbar**.

essen *to eat* **essbar** *edible*
Nach dem Atomkraftunfall in Tschernobyl wurde das Gemüse im ganzen Land **unessbar**.

danken *to thank* **dankbar** *thankful*
Für seine schnelle Reaktion sind wir dem Rettungsteam sehr **dankbar**.

B. Suffix -*lich*

German speakers add the suffix **-lich** to verbs, nouns, and adjectives. The corresponding English suffixes are usually -*able* after verbs and -*ly* after nouns and adjectives.

fragen	*to question*	**fraglich**	*questionable*
ganz	*whole, entire*	**gänzlich**	*wholly, entirely*
Monat	*month*	**monatlich**	*monthly*

Note that the suffix **-lich** may cause an umlaut to occur on the stem vowel of the original word: **ganz, gänzlich; Jahr, jährlich.**

Grundwortschatz

Abschnitt (*m.*), **-e**	*section, paragraph*	**Fortschritt** (*m.*), **-e**	*progress*
sich ändern	*to change*	**Gesicht** (*n.*), **-er**	*face*
sich an/siedeln	*to settle*	**leider**	*unfortunately*
außerordentlich	*extraordinary*	**Nachteil** (*m.*), **-e**	*disadvantage*
sich befassen mit	*to deal with, to concern oneself with*	**sich nieder/lassen (ließ ... nieder, niedergelassen; lässt ... nieder)**	*to settle down, establish oneself*
sich befinden (befand, befunden)	*to be located; to be, feel; to find oneself*		
		plötzlich	*suddenly*
sich beschränken auf	*to limit oneself to, be limited to*	**schrecklich**	*frightful, terrible, dreadful, awful, horrible, hideous*
bezeichnen	*to designate, denote, call*	**Titel** (*m.*), **–**	*title*
		verletzen	*to injure*
Bürger (*m.*), **–;** **Bürgerin,** (*f.*), **-nen**	*citizen*	**sich verletzen**	*to get hurt, injure oneself*
		sich vermehren	*to multiply*
Bürger (*pl.*)	*middle class, citizens*	**versprechen (versprach, versprochen; verspricht)**	*to promise*
dunkel	*dark*		
Durchschnitt (*m.*), **-e**	*average, cross section*	**wachsen (wuchs, ist gewachsen; wächst)**	*to grow*
eingehend	*thoroughly, in detail*		
sich entwickeln	*to develop, evolve*	**(sich) waschen (wusch, gewaschen; wäscht)**	*to wash*
erinnern an	*to remind about/of*		
sich erinnern (an)	*to remember*		
sich finden	*to find oneself, turn out to be*		

Übungssätze

1. Die ersten Universitäten entwickelten sich im 12. Jahrhundert in Italien (Bologna, Salerno, Padua), dann entstanden die Universitäten in Paris, Cambridge und Oxford.

2. In Berlin befinden sich heute zwei weltbekannte Hochschulen: die Humboldt-Universität und die Freie Universität.

3. In diesem Abschnitt des Buches werden wir uns mit den religiösen Bewegungen befassen.

4. Knapp 57 Millionen Menschen bekennen sich in Deutschland zu einer christlichen Konfession.

5. Unter den Widerstandskämpfern im Dritten Reich befanden sich nicht nur Geistliche aus den verschiedenen Konfessionen, sondern auch Bürger, Soldaten, Studenten und Politiker vor allem der linken Bewegungen.

6. Der politische Widerstand gegen Hitler änderte sich mit der Zeit; schon Mitte der 30er Jahre nahm er unter den normalen Bürgern zu.

7. In Kafkas Novelle „Die Verwandlung" lesen wir etwas Fantastisches: der Erzähler findet sich in ein riesiges Ungeziefer verwandelt.

8. Die Familie des Helden kümmert sich sehr um die Reaktionen der Nachbarn. Der Held und sein Vater verstehen sich überhaupt nicht.

9. Unter solchen Bedingungen vermehren sich die Probleme außerordentlich schnell.

10. Selbst der meistversprechende technische Fortschritt bringt Nachteile und Probleme mit sich.

11. Ich habe mir gestern ein vielversprechendes Buch gekauft. Es verspricht Beiträge von mehreren Experten auf dem Gebiet Völkerwanderung und -Stämme.

1. **entstehen (entstand, ist entstanden)** *to come into being, emerge*
4. **knapp** *just barely*
   sich bekennen (bekannte, bekannt) *to profess*
   Konfession (*f.*), **-en** *denomination, religion*
5. **unter** *among*
   Widerstand (*m.*), **-̈e** *resistance*
   Geistliche (*pl.*) *clergy*
   linke *left-wing*

7. **riesig** *gigantic*
   Ungeziefer (*n.*), **–** *vermin, pestiferous insect*
   verwandelt *transformed, metamorphosed*
8. **sich kümmern um** *to mind, worry about*
   Nachbar (*m., n-noun*), **-n** *neighbor*
   überhaupt *generally, really, at all*
9. **Bedingung** (*f.*), **-en** *condition*
10. **mit sich bringen (brachte, gebracht)** *to entail*

12. Die Literaturauswahl in diesem Buch konzentriert sich leider, dem amerikanischen Brauch gemäß, auf Werke in englischer Sprache.

13. Während der Völkerwanderung haben sich die Bajuwaren im heutigen Bayern niedergelassen.

14. Unter den ursprünglichen Völkern im äquatorialen Afrika haben sich Zwergvölker entwickelt; sie wachsen im Durchschnitt nicht über 150 cm groß.

15. Das kleine Kind zeigte seiner Mutter seine frisch gewaschenen Hände: „Ich wusch mir selber die Hände", sagte er stolz. Die ziemlich strenge Mutter antwortete: „Warum hast du dir nicht auch das Gesicht gewaschen"

16. Nun erinnere ich mich an den Titel des Buches. Es heißt: „Der Soldatenhandel deutscher Fürsten nach Amerika".

17. Die Soldaten aus Hessen befanden sich in einer außerordentlich schwierigen Situation. Der Herzog interessierte sich nur für Geld. Er wusch seine Hände in Unschuld.

12. **Literaturauswahl** (*f.*) *choice of references, bibliography*
    sich konzentrieren auf *to concentrate on*
13. **Bajuwaren** (*pl.*) *Bavarians*
    Bayern *Bavaria*
14. **Zwergvölker** (*pl.*) *pygmies*
    groß *tall*
15. **stolz** *proudly*
    ziemlich *seemingly*
16. **Soldatenhandel** (*m.*) *soldier trade*
    Fürst (*m., n-noun*), **-en** *ruler, prince*
17. **sich interessieren für** *to be interested in*
    Unschuld (*f.*) *innocence*

 Leitfragen zum Lesetext auf **academic.cengage.com/german/korb**

DIE HESSEN IM AMERIKANISCHEN FREIHEITSKRIEG

In amerikanischen Geschichtsbüchern sind die hessischen Soldaten schon immer als „Söldner" bezeichnet worden. Diese Bezeichnung ist ungenau. Durch sie wird die lang gehegte Voreingenommenheit gegen diese Soldaten verewigt.

5   Im engeren Sinne des Wortes verkauft ein Söldner seine eigenen Dienste und eventuell sein Leben. Dies war jedoch bei den hessischen Soldaten nicht der Fall. Sie sind der Tyrannei und Geldsucht ihrer

Title **Hesse** (*m., n-noun*), **-n** Hessian
2 **Söldner** (*m.*), **–** *mercenary*
3 **ungenau** *inaccurate*
  hegen *to cultivate*
4 **Voreingenommenheit** (*f.*) *prejudice*
  verewigen *to perpetuate*
6 **Dienst** (*m.*), **-e** *service*
7 **Geldsucht** (*f.*) *avarice*

Fürsten zum Opfer gefallen. Ganze Regimente deutscher Soldaten sind von ihren Landesvätern an höchstbietende fremde Länder, besonders England, verkauft worden. Dieser Abschnitt deutscher Geschichte ist von Friedrich Kapp in seinem Buch „Der Soldaten- handel deutscher Fürsten nach Amerika: ein Beitrag zur Kulturge- schichte des achtzehnten Jahrhunderts" (Berlin, 1874) eingehend beschrieben worden.

Im Juli 1776 kamen 7000 deutsche Soldaten aus Hessen und verschiedenen anderen Fürstentümern unter dem Befehl des General- leutnants von Heister in Staten Island an. Sie wurden dem Kommando des Generals Howe unterstellt. In den nächsten Jahren stieg die Zahl bis auf fast 30 000. Von diesen kehrten jedoch nur ungefähr 17 000 wieder in ihre Heimat zurück. Tausende sind auf dem Schlachtfeld gefallen und andere haben sich in Amerika angesiedelt. Von den Deserteuren und Kriegsgefangenen haben sich viele in Pennsylvania und Virginia niedergelassen und sind mit der Zeit amerikanische Bürger geworden.

8 **Opfer** *(n.),* **–** *victim, sacrifice*
   zum Opfer fallen (fiel, ist gefallen; fällt) *to fall victim to*
9 **Landesvater** *(m.),* ∸ *"father of the country,"* ruler
   höchstbietend *highest bidding*
16 **Befehl** *(m),* **-e** *command*
17 **Generalleutnant von Heister**
   Lieutenant General von Heister
18 **unterstellen** *to place under*
19 **bis auf** *to, up to*
21 **auf dem Schlachtfeld fallen (fiel, ist gefallen; fällt)** *to die on the battlefield*
22 **Kriegsgefangene** *(f. or m.),* **-n** *prisoner of war*

WIEDERHOLUNG 3

PARACELSUS *final* : *omit p. 156*

Theophrastus Bombastus von Hohenheim (1493–1541), genannt Paracelsus und in der Schweiz geboren, ist eine der
interessantesten Persönlichkeiten der Frührenaissance. Er
wird als Gelehrter, Arzt, Forscher, Schriftsteller und Bahnbrecher in
5   verschiedenen Wissenschaften angesehen. Er verachtete Bücherwissen
und sah in der Erforschung der Natur die dringlichste Aufgabe der
Wissenschaftler. Für Paracelsus war der Mensch der Mittelpunkt der
Welt, ein Spiegel des Makrokosmos. Einsicht in den Makrokosmos,
die große Welt, bedeutete für ihn daher auch Einsicht in den Mikro-
10   kosmos, den Menschen.

Paracelsus wird als einer der Begründer der modernen Chemie
angesehen. Als Arzt bereitete er die meisten seiner Arzneien im
eigenen Labor zu. In seiner alchimistischen Küche fand er neue
Heilmittel, besonders metallische und mineralische. Diese waren bis
15   dahin als giftig angesehen worden. Paracelsus empfahl z.B. Salz mit
starkem Jodgehalt als Heilmittel gegen Kropf. Mit der Einführung
chemischer Arzneimittel wurde er der Vater der modernen Chemothe-
rapie.

Als Arzt machte sich Paracelsus auch in der Chirurgie einen
20   Namen. Damals wurden Operationen nicht von akademisch gebildeten Ärzten ausgeführt, sondern von Badern. Paracelsus hingegen
wirkte nicht nur als beratender Arzt, sondern auch als Chirurg. Er

---

4 **Bahnbrecher** (*m.*), – *pioneer*
5 **verachten** *to despise*
   Bücherwissen (*n.*) *book learning*
6 **Erforschung** (*f.*), **-en** *investigation, study*
   dringlich *pressing, urgent*
8 **Einsicht** (*f.*), **-en** *knowledge, insight*
12 **zu/bereiten** *to prepare, mix*
13 **alchimistische Küche** (*f.*), **-n** *alchemist's laboratory*

14 **Heilmittel** (*n.*), – *medicine*
20 **gebildet** *trained, educated*
21 **Bader** (*m.*), – *barber* (obsolete usage)
   hingegen *on the other hand*
22 **wirken** *to act, work*
   beraten (beriet, beraten; berät) *to advise*

führte Operationen selbst aus. Damit verhalf er der Chirurgie zu
einem gewissen Ansehen. Als Chirurg kamen ihm seine außerordent-
lichen Kenntnisse in der Anatomie sehr zugute, denn die Bader und
auch die meisten Ärzte verstanden wenig von der Anatomie. Dieses
Studium war damals noch weithin verpönt.

Auch in der Psychologie und in der Psychiatrie hat Paracelsus
grundlegende Arbeit geleistet. Er hat auch schon psychologische
Heilmittel befürwortet. Als erster machte er einen Unterschied
zwischen Teufelsbesessenheit und Irrsinn. Dies hat wahrscheinlich
manchem Irrsinnigen das Leben gerettet, denn im Mittelalter wurden
viele „Teufelsbesessene" hingerichtet.

Mit seiner Schrift „Von der Bergsucht" legte Paracelsus den
Grundstein für die moderne Lehre von Gewerbekrankheiten und
Gewerbehygiene. Er studierte die eigenartigen Krankheiten der
Bergbauarbeiter und suchte auch entsprechende Heilmittel dagegen.
Durch seine vielen Versuche mit Quecksilber ist Paracelsus selbst an
einer gewerbsmäßigen Vergiftung gestorben. Er liegt in der kleinen St.
Sebastians-Kirche in der Stadt Salzburg begraben.

23 **damit** *with that*
   verhelfen (verhalf, verholfen;
   verhilft) *to help, aid*
24 **gewiss** *certain*
   Ansehen (*n.*) *prestige, respect*
25 **zugute kommen (kam, ist**
   gekommen) *to be helpful*
27 **weithin** *to a large extent*
   verpönt *taboo, despised*
29 **leisten** *to perform*
30 **befürworten** *to propose*
   als erster machte er ... *he was the*
   first one to make . . .
   Unterschied (*m.*), **-e** *difference,*
   distinction
31 **Teufelsbesessenheit** (*f.*) *being*
   possessed by the devil
   Irrsinn (*m.*) *insanity*

33 **hin/richten** *to execute*
34 **Bergsucht** (*f.*) *black lung disease*
35 **den Grundstein legen** *to lay the*
   foundation
   Gewerbekrankheit (*f.*), **-en**
   occupational disease
36 **eigenartig** *peculiar, characteristic*
37 **Bergbauarbeiter** (*m.*), **–** *miner*
   entsprechend *corresponding*
   dagegen *for them* (only in this
   context)
38 **Quecksilber** (*n.*) *quicksilver,*
   mercury
39 **gewerbsmäßig** *occupational*
   Vergiftung (*f.*), **-en** *poisoning*

Das obeliskförmige Grabmal trägt in der obersten Schriftenplatte die Inschrift: „Des Philippus Theophrastus Paracelsus, der durch die Alchimie einen so großen Ruhm in der Welt erworben hat, Bildnis und Gebeine. Bis sie wieder mit ihrer Haut umgeben sein werden." Unter
45 einem kreisrunden Reliefbildnis steht noch die Verkündigung: „Hier liegt begraben Philippus Theophrastus, der berühmte Doktor der Medizin, welcher auch die schrecklichsten Wunden, Lepra, Podagra und Wassersucht und andere unheilbar scheinende Krankheiten durch seine wunderbare Kunst heilte. Und es brachte ihm auch Ehre ein,
50 dass er sein Hab und Gut unter die Armen verteilen ließ. Im Jahre 1541, am 24. September, vertauschte er das Leben mit dem Tode."
  In mancher Beziehung war Paracelsus noch ein mittelalterlicher Mensch. Aber in seinen wissenschaftlichen und sozialen Anschauungen wird er vielfach als eine der hervorragendsten Gestalten der
55 Frührenaissance angesehen.

41 **obeliskförmig** *in the form of an obelisk*
    Grabmal *(n.),* **¨er** *tombstone*
    tragen (trug, getragen; trägt) *to bear*
    oberst- *uppermost*
    Schriftenplatte *(f.),* **-n** *inscribed slab*
43 **Ruhm** *(m.) fame, honor, glory*
    erwerben (erwarb, erworben; erwirbt) *to attain*
    Bildnis *(n.),* **-se** *likeness*
44 **Gebeine** *(pl.) skeleton, bones*
    Haut *(f.),* **¨e** *skin, hide*
    umgeben *to surround, be together*
45 **kreisrund** *circular*
    Verkündigung *(f.),* **-en** *announcement*
47 **Wunde** *(f.),* **-n** *wound*
    Lepra *(f.) leprosy*
    Podagra *(n.) podagra, gout*

48 **Wassersucht** *(f.) dropsy*
    scheinen (schien, geschienen) *to appear*
49 **Ehre ein/bringen (brachte ... ein, eingebracht)** *to win honors and fame*
50 **dass** *that*
    Hab und Gut *worldly possessions*
    unter *among*
    verteilen lassen (ließ, gelassen; lässt) *to divide up*
51 **vertauschen** *to exchange*
52 **Beziehung** *(f.),* **-en** *respect, relationship*
53 **Anschauung** *(f.),* **-en** *view, idea*
54 **vielfach** *widely, frequently*
    hervorragend *outstanding*

KAPITEL 16

16.1 Modal Auxiliaries Express Modalities

Modal auxiliary verbs in German function similarly to English verb forms like *can, must, may, should,* and *would.* Modal auxiliaries do not describe the actual performance of an action. Instead, modals express modalities or attitudes about the activity in the sentence: **dürfen** expresses permission, **können** expresses ability, **mögen** expresses desire, **müssen** expresses necessity, **sollen** expresses obligation, and **wollen** indicates volition.

German modal auxiliaries, unlike English modals, have a complete conjugational system similar to other weak verbs. Note the variety of possible meanings in English for the infinitive of the German modal auxiliaries.

Infinitive	Past	Past participle	Present	
dürfen	durfte	gedurft	darf	*to be allowed/ permitted to, may*
können	konnte	gekonnt	kann	*to be able to, can*
mögen	mochte	gemocht	mag	*to like (to)*
müssen	musste	gemusst	muss	*to have to, must*
sollen	sollte	gesollt	soll	*to be supposed to, should, ought*
wollen	wollte	gewollt	will	*to want to, intend*

Möchten, the present subjunctive form of **mögen**, is a high-frequency verb form expressing intention. It means *would like to.*

16.2 Conjugation of the Modals

A. Present tense

The modals have irregular forms for **ich, du, er/sie/es.**

	dürfen	können	mögen *subjunctive*
ich	darf	kann	mag/möchte
du	darfst	kannst	magst/möchtest
er/sie/es	darf	kann	mag/möchte
wir	dürfen	können	mögen/möchten
ihr	dürft	könnt	mögt/möchtet
sie/Sie	dürfen	können	mögen/möchten

	müssen	sollen	wollen
ich	muss	soll	will
du	musst	sollst	willst
er/sie/es	muss	soll	will
wir	müssen	sollen	wollen
ihr	müsst	sollt	wollt
sie/Sie	müssen	sollen	wollen

–Darf ich hier sitzen? –Natürlich dürfen Sie das.
> *"May I (am I permitted to) sit here?"*
> *"Yes, of course you may/are permitted."*

Er kann das nicht verstehen. Seine Eltern können es auch nicht verstehen.
> *He cannot understand that. His parents can't understand it either.*

Ich mag nicht arbeiten, aber wer mag denn arbeiten?
> *I don't like to work, but then who likes to work?*

–Was möchten Sie heute machen? –Ich möchte im Bett liegen und mein Buch lesen.
> *"What would you like to do today?"*
> *"I'd like to lie in bed and read my book."*

Ich muss mit Ihnen sprechen. Was müssen wir tun?
> *I have to speak with you. What must we do?*

Die heutige Vorlesung soll um 10 Uhr beginnen. Wir sollen nicht spät sein.
> *Today's lecture is supposed to begin at 10 o'clock. We ought not to be late.*

Sie will arbeiten, aber ich will nicht. Was wollen Sie tun?
> *She wants to work, but I don't want to. What do you want to do?*

Note that the first- and third-person forms of **wollen**, **ich will/sie will**, mean *I want to* and *she wants to*. These forms are misleadingly similar in their appearance to English *will*.

Remember: **ich werde** = *I will*; **ich will** = *I want to*.

B. Past tense

In the simple past, modals are conjugated like weak verbs. There are no umlauts on modals in the past tense.

ich durfte   *I was allowed to/permitted to*
du konntest   *you were able to, could*
~~er mochte~~   *he wanted (to)*
wir mussten   *we had to*
ihr solltet   *you were supposed to, should have*
sie wollten   *they wanted to*

[handwritten note: no umlaut — don't confuse! with möchte]

16.3 Modals and the Dependent Infinitive

Modals generally occur in combination with an infinitive. Whereas in English, the modal and the infinitive are generally located together, in German the modal stands in second position and the infinitive stands in final position. As with the auxiliary verbs (**haben**, **sein**, **werden**), you must go to the end of the clause to complete the verb.

A. Modals with present infinitive

An einem klaren Abend kann man viele Sterne sehen.
On a clear evening one can see many stars.
Ich will draußen unter freiem Himmel schlafen und die Sterne sehen.
I want to sleep outside under the open sky and see the stars.
Der Philosoph musste sich immer fragen: Was kann ein Mensch wissen? Was soll ein Mensch in dieser Situation tun? Was darf er hoffen?
The philosopher always had to ask himself: What can a human being know? What should a person do in this situation? What is he allowed to hope for?

B. Modals with past infinitive

Er kann diese Tatsachen nicht gewusst haben. Er muss seinen Freund gefragt haben.
He cannot have known these facts. He must have asked his friend.
Diese Geschichte muss wahr gewesen sein.
This story must have been true.

[handwritten note: past infinitive: to have asked, etc. past participle + haben/sein]

C. Modals with passive infinitive

Die Beobachtungen der Archäologin mussten bestätigt werden.
The observations of the archaeologist had to be confirmed.
Die Beobachtungen ihres Vorgängers müssen bestätigt worden sein.
The observations of her predecessor must have been confirmed.
Die neuen Beobachtungen werden bestätigt werden müssen.
The new observations will have to be confirmed.

D. Modals in the future tense

Modalities are frequently expressed in the future tense with **werden** as the helping verb and a double infinitive in the final position of the clause.

Unsere Freunde werden uns bei der Arbeit helfen können.
Our friends will be able to help us with our work.
Er wird bald nach Hause gehen müssen.
He will have to go home soon.

E. Modals with implied infinitive

Modal verbs are also used without a dependent infinitive. In such sentences, you will often find **das** as the direct object, with the verb **tun** implied.

Das sollst du nicht. (= Das sollst du nicht tun.)
You should not do that.
Das habe ich nicht gewollt. (= Ich habe das nicht tun wollen.)
I didn't want (to do) that.

Other sources of information that help imply an omitted infinitive are adverbs and prepositional phrases, such as those that indicate motion or direction.

Ich muss in die Vorlesung. (= Ich muss in die Vorlesung gehen.)
I have to go to the lecture.
Wann willst du wieder nach Deutschland? (= Wann willst du wieder nach Deutschland fahren?)
When do you want to go to Germany again?

Note that **mögen** + object without infinitive means *to like*; **möchten** + object without infinitive means *would like*.

Ich mag deinen neuen Freund.
I like your new friend.
Ich möchte eine Tasse Tee.
I would like a cup of tea.

16.4 Fractions

In German fractions, the numerator is expressed by a cardinal number while the denominator is expressed by a cardinal number + the suffix **-tel** (from 4 through 19) or **-stel** (20 and above). The only denominators that do not follow this pattern are **halb-** *(half)* and **Drittel** *(third)*.

ein halb-	*one half*	drei Viertel	*three fourths*
ein Drittel	*one third*	sieben Achtel	*seven eighths*
zwei Drittel	*two thirds*	ein Zwanzigstel	*one twentieth*
ein Viertel	*one fourth*	ein Hundertstel	*one hundredth*

Decimals in German are indicated by means of a decimal comma instead of a decimal point.

drei Komma drei Prozent aller Schulanfänger ...
three point three percent of all first-graders . . .
Ein halbes Pfund Tomaten kostet € 1,50.
A half pound of tomatoes costs € 1.50.

Grundwortschatz

Alter *(n.)*	age	**ganz**	whole, quite
Aufklärung *(f.)*	enlightenment	**helfen (half,**	to help
Ausnahme *(f.)*, **-n**	exception	**geholfen; hilft)**	
Ausschnitt *(m.)*, **-e**	excerpt	**heutig**	today's, current
Begriff *(m.)*, **-e**	concept	**nie**	never
berechnen	to calculate	**schließlich**	finally
damalig	then,	**Schwierigkeit** *(f.)*, **-en**	difficulty
	of that time	**Stern** *(m.)*, **-e**	star
darum	therefore,	**teilen**	to divide
	for all that	**Teilung** *(f.)*, **-en**	division
durch/führen	to carry out,	**teilweise**	partially
	execute	**tun (tat, getan)**	to do
Entfernung *(f.)*, **-en**	distance	**Verfahren** *(n.)*, **–**	process
Erkenntnis *(f.)*, **-se**	knowledge,	**Vernunft** *(f.)*	reason
	perception	**Vorlesung** *(f.)*, **-en**	lecture
fest/stellen	to determine	**weder ... noch**	neither . . . nor
Freiheit *(f.)*, **-en**	freedom		

Übungssätze

1. Viele Leute mögen moderne Musik und Kunst nicht. Mein Freund mag sie auch nicht, aber ich mag beide sehr.
2. Ich will Ihnen keine Schwierigkeiten bereiten.
3. Rauchen ist ungesund. Das darfst du und sollst du auch nicht tun.
4. Nach dem Versailler Vertrag (1919) musste Deutschland alle deutschen Kolonien abtreten. Das damalige Deutschland war nur ein Achtel so groß wie seine Kolonien.
5. Ohne Wasser werden die Pflanzen im Garten nicht gedeihen können, und schließlich werden sie sterben.
6. Sie müssen darum regelmäßig bewässert werden. Es gibt keine Ausnahme.
7. Vierundzwanzig kann durch acht geteilt werden. Das Resultat dieser Teilung ist drei.
8. Die heutige Vorlesung über Kants „Kritik der reinen Vernunft" sollte um halb zehn (9.30 Uhr) anfangen, aber der Professor wurde krank und konnte nicht vorlesen.
9. Die Produktionskosten müssen bis auf einen Drittel reduziert werden. Diese Reduzierung darf aber nicht auf Kosten der Qualität durchgeführt werden.
10. Weder das eine noch das andere hilft uns in dieser Situation. Darum müssen wir weiter suchen.
11. Ein Elektromagnet kann durch Einschalten oder Ausschalten des Stromes beliebig magnetisch und wieder unmagnetisch gemacht werden.
12. Mit diesem Verfahren wird man viele Fundstellen von vorgeschichtlichen Menschen datieren können. So können die Beobachtungen der Archäologen viel genauer bestätigt werden.

2. **bereiten**   *to cause*
4. **Vertrag** *(m.)*, **⁻e**   *treaty*
   ab/treten (trat ... ab, abgetreten;
   tritt ... ab)   *to surrender, cede*
5. **gedeihen (gedieh, ist gediehen)**
   to thrive
6. **regelmäßig**   *regular, regularly*
   bewässern   *to water (a plant)*

9. **auf Kosten**   *at the expense*
11. **ein/schalten**   *to switch on*
    aus/schalten   *to switch off*
    beliebig   *as desired, arbitrarily*
12. **Fundstelle** *(f.)*, **-n**   *archeological site, dig*
    vorgeschichtlich   *prehistoric*

13. Das Alter der Erde werden wir wahrscheinlich nie ganz genau feststellen können.

14. Mit diesen Instrumenten konnte die Entfernung der Sterne berechnet werden.

15. Die Erinnerung kann in der Hypnose ganz oder teilweise erhalten, sie kann vollständig erloschen, aber auch außerordentlich gesteigert werden.[1]

16. Weder Kant noch seine Kollegen an der Universität in Königsberg können sich eine solche Reaktion auf diese Frage vorgestellt haben.

17. Das „Ding an sich" ist unsichtbar, die Welt kann aber durch den Filter des Verstandes wahrgenommen werden.

15. **Erinnerung** (*f.*), **-en** *memory*
erhalten (erhielt, erhalten; erhält) *to retain, obtain*
vollständig *completely*
erlöschen (erlosch, ist erloschen; erlischt) *to wipe out, extinguish*
16. **Kollege** (*m., n-noun*), **-n** *colleague*
sich vor/stellen *to imagine*

17. **Ding an sich** (*n.*), **Dinge an sich** (*pl.*) *thing in itself, i.e., independent of human perception*
unsichtbar *invisible, imperceptible*
wahr/nehmen (nahm ... wahr, wahrgenommen; nimmt ... wahr) *to perceive*

 Leitfragen zum Lesetext auf **academic.cengage.com/german/korb**

„WAS IST AUFKLÄRUNG?"

Immanuel Kant (1724–1804), einer der größten Philosophen Deutschlands, ist ein Kind der Aufklärung und zugleich ihr Überwinder. Er lebte sein ganzes Leben in Königsberg, wo er auch an der Universität Professor für Philosophie war. Kant bemühte sich um die Fragen: Was kann ich wissen? Was soll ich tun? Was darf ich hoffen? Die erste dieser Fragen war ihm aber am wichtigsten. In drei Kritiken stellte er ein System der Logik, Ethik und Ästhetik auf. In der „Kritik der reinen Vernunft" (1781) untersuchte er die Grenzen der menschlichen Erkenntnis. Kants „Kritik" nach kann die Welt nur

5

2 **zugleich** *simultaneously*
3 **Überwinder** (*m.*), **–** *conqueror*

5 **sich bemühen um** *to concern oneself with*
7 **auf/stellen** *to formulate, advance*

---

1. Series of three passive infinitives all built on one single auxiliary **werden** in final position.

10 durch den Filter des Verstandes gesehen und nur mit solchen Begriffen wie „Zeit", „Raum", „Identität", „Kausalität" usw. beschrieben werden. Wir können nicht wissen, wie die „Dinge an sich" wirklich sind.

15 Mit einer anderen Frage wollte Kant eins der wichtigsten Themen seiner Zeit ansprechen. Die folgende Passage ist ein bekannter Ausschnitt aus seinem Text, „Was ist Aufklärung?".[2]

„Zu dieser Aufklärung aber wird nichts erfordert als Freiheit; und zwar die unschädlichste unter allem, was nur Freiheit heißen mag, nämlich die: von seiner Vernunft in allen Stücken öffentlichen Ge-
20 brauch zu machen. Nun höre ich aber von allen Seiten rufen: räsoniert nicht! Der Offizier sagt: räsoniert nicht, sondern exerziert! Der Finanzrat: räsoniert nicht, sondern bezahlt! Der Geistliche: räsoniert nicht, sondern glaubt! (Nur ein einziger Herr in der Welt sagt: räsoniert, so viel ihr wollt, und worüber ihr wollt; aber gehorcht!) Hier ist
25 überall Einschränkung der Freiheit. Welche Einschränkung aber ist der Aufklärung hinderlich, welche nicht, sondern ihr wohl gar beförderlich? – Ich antworte: Der öffentliche Gebrauch seiner Vernunft muss jederzeit frei sein, und der allein kann Aufklärung unter Menschen zustande bringen; der Privatgebrauch derselben aber darf
30 öfters sehr enge eingeschränkt sein, ohne doch darum den Fortschritt der Aufklärung sonderlich zu hindern ...

Wenn denn nun gefragt wird: leben wir jetzt in einem aufgeklärten Zeitalter? so ist die Antwort: Nein, aber wohl in einem Zeitalter der Aufklärung ..."

15	**an/sprechen (sprach ... an, angesprochen; spricht ... an)** *to address*	24	**gehorchen** *to obey*
17	**erfordern** *to require, call for, need*	25	**Einschränkung** *(f.),* **-en** *limitation*
18	**was nur ... heißen mag** *whatever one wants to call . . .*	26	**hinderlich** *hindering, obstructive*
19	**nämlich** *namely, that is*	27	**beförderlich** *favorable, conducive*
20	**Gebrauch** *(m.)* *use*	28	**jederzeit** *at all times*
	räsonieren *to reason, be rational*		**der allein** *that alone, only that (one)*
21	**exerzieren** *to drill*	29	**zustande bringen (brachte, gebracht)** *to bring about*
22	**Finanzrat** *(m.),* **⸚e** *finance minister*		**derselben** *of the same*
	geistlich *spiritual*	30	**öfters** *often*
23	**Herr** *(m.),* **-en** *lord; here:* *Friedrich II*		**ein/schränken** *to limit*
		31	**sonderlich** *particularly*
		32	**wenn** *whenever, if*

---

2. Immanuel Kant, "Was ist Aufklärung?", first published in *Berlinische Monatsschrift,* Dezember 1784. *Kants Werke,* Ed. E. Cassirer, Berlin, 1912, Volume IV

KAPITEL 17

17.1 Perfect Tenses of Modals

Modal verbs have two forms of the past participle.

A. Regular form

A regular form is used when a dependent infinitive, usually **tun**, is not expressed but understood.

Er hat es gedurft.   *He was allowed to do it.*
Er hat es gekonnt.   *He was able to do it.*
Er hat es gemusst.   *He had to do it.*
Er hat es gesollt.   *He was supposed to do it.*
Er hat es gewollt.   *He wanted to do it.*
Er hat es gemocht.   *He liked it.*

Any one of these statements might occur, e.g., in response to the question: **Warum hat er das getan?** *(Why did he do that?)*

B. Double infinitive

Identical with the infinitive, the second form is used when a dependent infinitive is expressed. This construction is commonly called a *double infinitive.*

Wir haben eine andere Methode benutzen müssen.
  We had to use a different method.
Kolumbus hatte seine Theorie nicht beweisen können.
  Columbus had not been able to prove his theory.
Die siebenjährige Pilotin hat das Flugzeug fliegen dürfen.
  The seven-year-old pilot was allowed to fly the airplane.
Ich habe diesen Flug niemals vergessen können.
  I have never been able to forget that flight.

Note that a *double infinitive* made up of the modal and the dependent infinitive also occurs in the future tense. Pay close attention: the finite verb in the perfect tense is **haben** and in the future tense the finite verb is **werden**.

Ich habe eine andere Methode benutzen müssen. *(present perfect)*
  I had to use a different method.
Ich werde eine andere Methode benutzen müssen. *(future)*
  I will have to use a different method.

All modals in the perfect tense occur with the helping verb **haben**. When you come upon a form of **haben**, check the end of the clause and pick up the double infinitive or regular form of the past participle (if there is one) in order to translate the entire verb unit. When you encounter such a double infinitive (following **haben**) at the end of a clause, remember that the infinitive of the modal actually represents a past participle.

17.2 Double Infinitive with Other Verbs

Hören *(to hear)*, **sehen** *(to see)*, and **lassen** *(to let)* also form perfect tenses with a double infinitive.

> Habt ihr das Flugzeug kommen hören?
> *Did you hear the plane coming?*
> Wir haben das Flugzeug abstürzen sehen.
> *We saw the airplane crashing.*
> Sie haben den Verletzten auf der Straße liegen lassen.
> *They left the injured man lying in the street.*

Note that the future tense of these verbs plus a dependent infinitive also results in a double infinitive standing at the end of a clause. Be careful to differentiate.

> Wir haben den Zug kommen hören. *(present perfect)*
> *We heard the train coming. vs.*
> Wir werden den Zug kommen hören. *(future)*
> *We will hear the train coming.*

17.3 Objective vs. Subjective Meanings of Modal Auxiliaries

Unlike other verbs, modal verbs express a mode or an attitude and may be used *objectively* to show the attitude of the subject toward the situation or *subjectively* to indicate the attitude of the person speaking with regard to the content of the statement.

1. Objective statement

   When used objectively, the modal indicates the attitude of the subject toward the situation.

   > Der Schüler kann gut Deutsch sprechen.
   > [This is a fact of the pupil's ability.]

Die Schülerin muss eine Prüfung schreiben.
[This is a fact of necessity.]
Die Lehrerin will die Hausaufgaben nicht lesen.
[This is a fact of the teacher's (lack of) desire.]

2. Subjective statement

When used subjectively, the modal indicates the attitude or opinion of the speaker regarding the statement.

Die Reise soll schön sein.
[You don't know for sure until you've taken the trip.]
Der Archäologe will einen neuen Dinosaurier entdeckt haben.
[The archaeologist's claim provides no immediate proof about the new dinosaur.]
Er muss seine Gründe haben.
[Surely he must have reasons.]

A. *Dürfen*

1. Objectively, **dürfen** expresses permission in the positive and prohibition in the negative.[1]

Man darf in der Raucherabteilung rauchen.
Smoking is permitted in the smoking section.
Du darfst nicht rauchen.
You must not smoke.
Man darf diese Tatsache nicht außer Acht lassen.
We must not disregard this fact.

2. Subjectively, **dürfen** may be used negatively to express disbelief or improbability.

Das darf nicht wahr sein.
That can't be true.

B. *Können*

1. Objectively, **können** may express an ability, a possibility, or permission.

Als Kind habe ich das Klavier sehr gut spielen können.
As a child, I was able to play the piano very well.

---

1. Note that **nicht dürfen** translates into English as *must not,* as well as *not allowed.*

Mit dem Zug kann man schnell reisen, aber mit einem Flugzeug kann man noch schneller reisen.
It's possible to travel fast by train, but with an airplane one can travel even faster.
Kann ich schwimmen gehen?
Can I go swimming?

2. Subjectively, **können** indicates a fairly certain assumption:

Morgen kann es regnen.
(I sense) It's likely to rain tomorrow.
Er kann gut gespielt haben.
(I haven't seen him, but I assume) He was a good player.

C. *Mögen*

1. Objectively, **mögen** indicates a liking for something or desire for an activity.

Die Schüler mögen ihren Lehrer.
The pupils like their teacher.
Das Kind mag die Hausaufgaben nicht machen.
The child doesn't like to do the homework.

2. Subjectively, **mögen** indicates a possibility, an estimate, or a question of uncertainty.

Das mag stimmen.
That may be true.
Der Flug mag drei bis vier Stunden dauern.
The flight could last three to four hours.
Wo mag mein Freund jetzt sein?
Where (on earth) is my friend now?

D. *Müssen*

1. Objectively, **müssen** indicates compulsion, obligation, or an absolute necessity.[2]

Im Alter von sechs Jahren müssen alle Kinder zur Schule gehen.
At the age of six, all children must go to school.
Ich habe meinen Vater im Krankenhaus besuchen müssen.
I had to visit my father in the hospital.

---

2. Note that **nicht müssen** means *not to have to.*

Man muss Geld haben.
You have to have money.

2. Subjectively, **müssen** indicates a form of conviction based on evidence or other grounds.

Mein Freund hat einen neuen Mercedes gekauft. Er muss sehr viel Geld haben.
My friend has bought a new Mercedes. He must have a lot of money.

E. *Sollen*

1. Objectively, **sollen** indicates an order, a moral duty, or a commandment.

Der Angeklagte soll seinen Namen laut und klar angeben.
The accused should state his name loudly and clearly.
Älteren Leuten gegenüber soll man immer höflich sein.
You should always be polite to your elders.
„Du sollst nicht stehlen!"
"Thou shalt not steal."

2. Subjectively, **sollen** means *to be supposed to* or *to be said to.*

Diese Aufgabe soll sehr schwer sein.
This lesson is said to be very difficult.
Der Saurier soll ein Schrecken gewesen sein.
The dinosaur was supposedly a terror.

F. *Wollen*

1. Objectively, **wollen** expresses a wish or an intention.

Wir haben die neue Erfindung sehen wollen.
We wanted to see the new invention.
Wir wollten eben anfangen.
We were just about to begin.

2. Subjectively, **wollen** means to claim to.

Die Russen wollen diese Erfindung gemacht haben.
The Russians claim to have made this invention.

allgemein	general	**Hausaufgabe** (f.), **-n**	homework,
im Allgemeinen	in general		assignment
Aufsatz (m.), **⁻e**	essay,	**herrschen**	to rule, govern,
	composition		prevail
Ausland (n.)	foreign country,	**Name** (m., n-noun), **-n**	name
	abroad	**niemals**	never
bedeutend	significant,	**riesig**	gigantic
	considerable,	**schätzen**	to estimate; to
	meaningful		value
bislang	so far, as yet	**Schüler** (m.), **-;**	pupil, student
dauern	to last	**Schülerin** (f.), **-nen**	
eben	just now, now	**Stellung** (f.), **-en**	position
empfehlen (empfahl,	to recommend	**unzählig**	countless
empfohlen;		**vergessen (vergaß,**	to forget
empfiehlt)		**vergessen; vergisst)**	
erwarten	to expect	**Verhältnis** (n.), **-se**	relation,
fliegen (flog, ist	to fly		situation
geflogen)		**zuerst**	first, first of all
Flug (m.), **⁻e**	flight	**Zug** (m.), **⁻e**	train
(sich) fürchten vor	to be afraid of	**Zustand** (m.), **⁻e**	condition
Grund (m.), **⁻e**	ground, reason		
aus diesem Grunde	for this reason		

 Lösungen zu Ubungssätzen auf **academic.cengage.com/german/korb**

1. Die Astrologie will aus dem Lauf und der Stellung der Sterne die Zukunft der Menschen deuten.

2. Als Hausaufgabe haben die Schüler einen langen Aufsatz schreiben müssen. Das Thema hat sich jeder Schüler selbst wählen dürfen.

3. Der amerikanische Student konnte sich in Deutschland verständigen: Er konnte fließend Deutsch.

4. Viele Forscher haben bei diesen Versuchen ihr Leben riskiert; wir dürfen das nicht vergessen.

5. Das Dritte Gebot lautet: „Du sollst den Namen des Herrn, deines Gottes, nicht missbrauchen." Aber im Namen Gottes wurden

1. **Lauf** (m.), **⁻e** *course, path*
   deuten *to interpret, construe*
2. **wählen** *to select, choose*
3. **(sich) verständigen** *to make oneself understood; to communicate*

fließend *fluent*
5. **Gebot** (n.), **-e** *commandment*
   lauten *to say, read*
   missbrauchen *to misuse, speak in vain*

unzählige Menschen getötet, und in seinem Namen wurden und werden noch heute Kriege geführt.

6. Man darf die Lösung dieser Frage nicht in der nahen Zukunft erwarten. Ich schätze, es wird eine lange Zeit dauern.

7. Da sprach der Herr zu Kain: „Wo ist dein Bruder Abel?" Er sprach: „Ich weiß es nicht; soll ich meines Bruders Hüter sein?"

8. Wir haben unzählige Aufsätze von diesem Autor lesen müssen, aber bislang habe ich die Gründe seiner Argumente niemals verstehen können.

9. Dieses Buch über den Namen der Stadt Berlin wurde mir empfohlen; es soll sehr anregend sein.

10. In den späteren Jahren seines Lebens wurde der Künstler immer kränker. Aus diesem Grunde hat er die Arbeit einstellen müssen.

11. In einem Interview sagte er: „Ich habe eben mit der Arbeit anfangen wollen."

12. Interessante Verhältnisse herrschen in der Natur. Elefanten sollen sich zum Beispiel vor Mäusen fürchten.

13. Andere Zustände herrschen im Ausland als hier bei uns, und das darf man nicht vergessen.

14. Im Allgemeinen sollen die Arbeitsverhältnisse hier bei uns bedeutend besser sein.

15. Wegen der Dunkelheit haben wir langsamer fahren müssen. Ich schätze, die Reise hat gut zwei Stunden länger gedauert.

16. Der Autofahrer hat den Zug nicht kommen sehen.

17. Nach dem zweiten Unfall hat er nicht mehr fahren wollen.

18. Im 1. Buch Moses heißt es: „Im Schweiße deines Angesichts sollst du dein Brot essen." Das heißt: Der Mensch muss sich seinen Lebensunterhalt durch harte Arbeit verdienen.

19. Jetzt, nach vielen Jahren, will der Politiker ein Frontkämpfer gewesen sein. Er hat jedoch während des Krieges niemals eine Kugel pfeifen hören.

20. Man darf eine Lösung des Welternährungsproblems durch eine Züchtung neuer Pflanzensorten allein nicht erwarten.

7. **Hüter** (*m.*), – *keeper, protector*
10. **ein/stellen** *to stop*
12. **Maus** (*f.*), ̈e *mouse*
13. **bei uns** *at home, in our country*
15. **Dunkelheit** (*f.*) *darkness*
17. **Unfall** (*m.*), ̈e *accident*
18. **Schweiß** (*m.*) *sweat*
    Angesicht (*n.*), **-e** *face, brow*
    Lebensunterhalt (*m.*) *livelihood*
    verdienen *to earn*
19. **Frontkämpfer** (*m.*), – *combat soldier*
    jedoch *however*
    Kugel (*f.*), **-n** *bullet*
    pfeifen (**pfiff, gepfiffen**) *to whistle*
20. **Züchtung** (*f.*), **-en** *cultivation, breeding*
    Sorte (*f.*), **-n** *variety, kind*

GRÖßTER RAUBSAURIER IN PATAGONIEN ENTDECKT[3]

Amerikanische und argentinische Wissenschaftler entdeckten im Rahmen der Ausgrabungen für das „Dinosaur Project 2000" die fossilen Überreste des wahrscheinlich größten fleischfressenden Sauriers, der je gelebt hat. Mehrere Urzeitriesen wurden in Patagonien entdeckt. Bislang glaubten die Forscher, es handelte sich um Einzelgänger, jedoch die neuen Funde weisen auf ein Gruppenleben hin. „Man glaubte immer, sie waren alleine – jetzt wissen wir, sie lebten in Rudeln", sagt der Mitentdecker Philip Currie.

(...)

Die neu entdeckten Raubsaurier lebten vor rund 100 Millionen Jahren, waren schwerer als der T-Rex und hatten auch kürzere Beine. Sie haben eine optische Ähnlichkeit zum Tyrannosaurus. Besonders kennzeichnend sind ihre langen schmalen Schädel mit rasiermesserscharfen Zähnen und Krallen. Currie glaubt, die Urzeitjäger dürfen ihre Beute mit chirurgischer Präzision zerlegt haben. Der T-Rex soll eine Nussknacker-Strategie gebraucht haben – er zerdrückte das lebende Opfer einfach in seinem gigantischen Maul.

„Ich glaube, er muss widerlich ausgesehen haben", so Currie's Kommentar. Der furchterregende Fleischfresser darf etwa 14 m

Title	**Saurier** *(m.), – saurian, dinosaur*	15	**rasiermesserscharf** *razor-sharp*
	Patagonien *(South American region) Patagonia*	16	**Urzeitjäger** *(m.), – prehistoric hunter*
2	**im Rahmen** *in the framework*		**Beute** *(f.) prey*
3	**Überreste** *(pl.), remains*		**chirurgisch** *surgical*
4	**fleischfressend** *carnivorous*		**zerlegen** *to dissect*
	der je gelebt hat *that ever lived*	17	**Nussknacker** *(m.), – nutcracker*
	Urzeitriese *(m.),* **-n** *prehistoric giant*	18	**zerdrücken** *to crush*
6	**hin/weisen auf** *to point to; indicate*	19	**Maul** *(n.) mouth, muzzle*
8	**Rudel** *(m.), – herd, pack*	20	**widerlich** *revolting, repulsive*
14	**schmal** *narrow*	21	**furchterregend** *frightening, horrific*
	Schädel *(m.), – skull*		

---

3. Artikel gekürzt und adaptiert nach Klaus Hofbauer © ExpeditionZone 1999–2007.

lang gewesen sein. Das macht ihn noch größer als das bisher größte
Raubtier, der Gigantosaurus, um knapp 1,5 m. Der T-Rex war mit
rund 12 m noch etwas kleiner. Die Forscher nehmen an, dieses Tier
mag ein Verwandter des Gigantosaurus gewesen sein. 25

Für die Paläontologen ist jedoch nicht die Größe des Tieres so
bedeutend, sondern die Tatsache, dass sie gleich mehrere Indi-
viduen fanden. Das Team hat seiner neuen Spezies einen süd-
amerikanischen Namen gegeben: „Mapusaurus roseae". Der Name
„Mapusaurus" kommt von dem Wort „Erde" in der Sprache der 30
Mapuche, des Indiovolks Westpatagoniens. „Roseae" kommt von
der rötlichen Färbung des Sandsteins, wo die Versteinerungen gefunden wurden.

23 **um knapp** *by about*

KAPITEL 18

18.1 Coordinating Conjunctions

Coordinating conjunctions connect, compare, contrast and/or establish relations between pairs or series of individual words, phrases, or clauses. Once you have learned their meanings, coordinating conjunctions present no special problem for translation.

aber	*but, however*	jedoch	*however*
allein	*but, only*	oder	*or*
denn	*since, because, for*	sondern	*but (rather)*
entweder ... oder		und	*and*
either . . . or		weder ... noch	*neither . . . nor*

Complete statements connected by coordinating conjunctions demonstrate independent word order with no change resulting from the occurrence of a coordinating conjunction:

x V1 s do io S Adverbs IO DO V2 , conjunction x V1 s do io S Adverbs IO DO V2. For example:

> Die Fahrt nach Griechenland war schön, **und** die Ausgrabung soll nächste Woche in Athen anfangen.
> *The trip to Greece was lovely, and the excavation is supposed to begin in Athens next week.*
>
> **Entweder** die Firma sagt den Arbeitern höhere Löhne zu, **oder** die Arbeiter werden ab übermorgen streiken.
> *Either the company promises the workers higher wages, or the workers will strike beginning the day after tomorrow.*

The conjunction **sondern** follows a negative and is followed by an alternative item or statement. **Sondern** is best translated as *but, rather* or *on the contrary.*

> Das Gemälde ist nicht von Monet, sondern von Manet.
> *The painting is not by Monet but rather by Manet.*
>
> Unser Haus ist kein Museum, sondern es ist ein Institut für bildende Kunst.
> *Our establishment is not a museum; on the contrary, it is an institute of fine arts.*

18.2 Subordinating Conjunctions

Subordinating conjunctions establish connections between independent clauses and clauses dependent upon them to complete the idea in the dependent clause. The following subordinate conjunctions introduce dependent clauses:

als	*when*	nachdem	*after*
als ob	*as if*	ob	*whether*
bevor	*before*	obgleich, obwohl	*although*
bis	*until*	seit, seitdem	*since*
da	*since, because*	sobald	*as soon as*
damit	*so that*	solange	*as long as*
dass	*that*	sooft	*as often as*
ehe	*before*	während	*while*
falls	*if; in case*	weil	*because* (not: *while*)
indem	*by (+ verb + -ing)*	wenn	*if; when*
je nachdem	*according to, depending on*	wenn (immer)	*when(ever)*
		wie	*how*

The finite verb in a dependent clause introduced by a subordinating conjunction no longer stands in second position, but rather stands at the very end of the dependent clause:

x V1 s do io S Adverbs IO DO V2 , conjunction x s do io S Adverbs IO DO V2 **V1**. For example:

> Es ist gewiss, dass er heute Abend mit uns kommen **wird**.
> *It is certain that he will come with us this evening.*
> Es ist gewiss, dass er zu diesem Thema kein Wort gesagt **hat**.
> *It is certain that he said not one word on this topic.*
> Ich weiß nicht, ob das richtig oder falsch **ist**.
> *I don't know whether that is true or false.*
> Ich weiß nicht, wie dieses Theaterstück aufgeführt **wird**.
> *I don't know how this theater play is produced.*
> Ich weiß nicht, wie dieses Theaterstück in diesem Theater aufgeführt werden **soll**.
> *I don't know how this theater play is supposed to be produced in this theater.*

Translating tip:

When a subordinating conjunction introduces a clause, look for the finite verb at the end of the clause. If the finite verb is an auxiliary (**sein**,

haben, **werden**, or a modal), the participle or infinitive will stand immediately before the auxiliary. To translate the dependent clause, begin with the subordinating conjunction followed by the subject, then all parts of the verb (located at the end of the clause), then the complements of the dependent verb, generally in reverse order. The main clause is translated likewise, beginning with the subject followed by the verb and its complements.

Dependent clauses are always set off by commas.

Dependent clauses often precede the main clause. In such cases, the dependent clause is set off by a comma followed immediately by the main verb, standing in the second position of the sentence as a whole:

Conjunction x s do io S Adverbs IO DO V2 **V1** , **V1** s do io S Adverbs IO DO V2. For example:

> Als Mozart noch ein kleines Kind gewesen **ist**, **spielte** er schon Konzerte am Hof.
> *When Mozart was still a small child, he was already playing concerts at court.*
> Weil sein Vater viel Geld verdienen **wollte**, **musste** der Junge viele Konzerte spielen.
> *Because his father wanted to earn a lot of money, the youth had to play many concerts.*
> Wenn sie auf Reisen **waren**, **blieb** seine Mutter meist zu Hause.
> *When they were on trips, his mother usually stayed at home.*

Should a double infinitive (**Kapitel 17**) occur in a dependent clause, the double infinitive holds its final position in the clause, preceded immediately by the finite auxiliary verb.

> Ich weiß nicht, ob er mit uns **hat** kommen können.
> *I don't know whether he was able to come with us.*
> Ich weiß nicht, ob er diese Arbeit heute für uns **wird** tun können.
> *I don't know whether he will be able to do this work for us today.*

18.3 Learn to Differentiate

Several subordinating conjunctions are identical in appearance to other parts of speech. Word order and punctuation are important aids to help you differentiate.

A. *Während:* subordinating conjunction vs. genitive preposition

[handwritten: while]

[handwritten: during]

Während can be a subordinating conjunction, meaning *while,* or a genitive preposition, meaning *during.* **Während**, **da**, and **damit** can always be recognized as subordinating conjunctions by the position of the finite verb. If the finite verb is the last element of the clause, these words are subordinating conjunctions.

> Während Hans auf der Universität war, musste Fritz arbeiten.
> *While Hans was attending university, Fritz had to work.*
> Während dieser Zeit war ich in München.
> *During this time I was in Munich.*

B. *Da:* subordinating conjunction vs. adverb

[handwritten: since]

[handwritten: there, then]

Da, as a subordinating conjunction, means *since, because;* as an adverb it means *there, then.* In example 2, *then* is superfluous in the English translation.

> Da ich nicht wusste, wo ich war, bat ich um Auskunft.
> *Since I didn't know where I was, I asked for help.*
> Sobald ich Auskunft bekam, da wusste ich wieder, wo ich war.
> *As soon as I got help, [then] I knew again where I was.*
> Da stand direkt vor mir mein Hotel.
> *There, right in front of me stood my hotel.*

C. *Damit:* subordinating conjunction vs. preposition

[handwritten: so that]

[handwritten: with that (da-compound)]

Damit can be a subordinating conjunction, meaning *so that, in order that,* or a preposition, meaning *therewith, with it, with that.*

> Wir haben die neuen Werkzeuge gekauft, damit wir besser
> arbeiten können.
> *We bought the new tools so that we can work better.*
> Hier sind die neuen Werkzeuge. Damit können wir besser arbeiten.
> *Here are the new tools. With them we can work better.*

D. *Indem* vs. *in dem*

Indem is a subordinating conjunction. **In dem**, on the other hand, is just **in** + pronoun or article, meaning *in which, in that.*

> Der Schauspieler wurde bekannt, indem er die Hauptrolle in
> Herzogs neuem Film spielte.
> *The actor became famous by playing the title role in Herzog's
> new movie.*

Das Buch, in dem seine Theorie erklärt wird, heißt *Das politische Theater.*
The book in which his theory is explained is called The Political Theater.
In dem Buch steht auch viel zum Thema Politik.
In that book there is also a lot on the topic of politics.

Indem (one word) means *while, in that, because of the fact that,* or often *by* plus the *-ing* form of the verb, e.g., *by playing.* **Indem** can be recognized by the final position of the finite verb.

18.4 *Wenn auch, auch wenn (even if, even though, even when)*

Diese Zimmer sind immer kalt, auch wenn sie geheizt sind.
These rooms are always cold, even when they are heated.
Wenn das Zimmer auch geheizt war, so war es doch kalt.
Even though the room was heated, it still was cold.

Note that **auch** may precede or follow **wenn** and may be separated from it within the same clause without changing the meaning of this expression.

18.5 "False Friends"

German and English are related languages and have many cognates and related words. At the same time it is important to be aware of words that are identical or similar in appearance or sound but that have completely different meanings. Mark these words in your dictionary and make a point of differentiating.

Listed on pages 178–179 are common "false friends." An extensive annotated German-English glossary of common false cognates and misleading expressions can be found on the World Wide Web at: http://german.about.com/library/blfalsef.htm

"False Friends"

aktuell	relevant, up-to-date	**her**	here, this way
also	thus, so	**Kapitel** (n.)	chapter
arm	poor	**Kind** (n.)	child
Art (f.)	species, type, class	**Kinder** (pl.)	children
bald	soon	**konsequent**	consistent
Band (m.)	volume	**Konzepte** (pl.)	notes
Band (n.)	tie, bond	**Last** (f.)	burden, load
bei	at, while, during, with	**man**	one, someone
bekommen	to receive	**Mittel** (n.)	means
bilden	to form, shape, educate	**Not** (f.)	need, necessity
Bildung (f.)	education	**pathetisch**	lofty, solemn, expressive
blank	shining, bright	**Pest** (f.)	plague
brav	well-behaved, good	**plump**	clumsy, awkward
breit	broad, wide	**Rat** (m.)	advice
Brief (m.)	letter	**ringen**	to struggle for
Chef (m.)	boss, chief	**Roman** (m.)	novel
damit	with that, with them; thereupon	**rot**	red
		See (m.)	lake
denn	because, for	**See** (f.)	sea, ocean
eventuell	possible	**sensibel**	sensitive
Fall (m.)	case, instance, matter, affair	**sensitiv**	hypersensitive
		stehen	to stand, be written down
fast	almost, nearly		
fehlen	to lack, be missing	**tot**	dead
Gift (n.)	poison	**weil**	because, since
groß	tall, high; large, great, immense	**wer**	who
		wo	where
hell	clear, bright	**will**	want

Grundwortschatz

Ähnlichkeit (f.), **-en**	similarity	**gründen**	to found
Ausdruck (m.), **⁼e**	expression	**jedoch**	however
aus/führen	to carry out, execute, perform	**leicht**	light, easy
		manchmal	sometimes
Ausgrabung (f.), **-en**	excavation	**mit/teilen**	to tell, communicate
benutzen	to use		
bitten (bat, gebeten)	to ask, request	**nachdem**	after
um Rat bitten	to ask for advice	**nach/weisen (wies ... nach, nachgewiesen)**	to prove, show
Ding (n.), **-e**	thing	**verbessern**	to improve
einmal	once	**vorläufig**	for the time being, temporarily
(sich) entscheiden (entschied, entschieden)	to decide		
erfahren (erfuhr, erfahren; erfährt)	to learn, find out	**Wetter** (n.)	weather
		Zuschauer (m.), **–; Zuschauerin** (f.), **-nen**	viewer, audience member
Erfahrung (f.), **-en**	experience		
erzeugen	to produce	**zustande kommen (kam ... zustande, ist zustande gekommen)**	to come about, be produced
Fahrt (f.), **-en**	trip		
Feld (n.), **-er**	field		
Gewicht (n.), **-e**	weight		

Übungssätze

1. Da der deutsche Kaiser Karl V. (1510–1556) auch König von Spanien war und als solcher Kolonien in der Neuen Welt besaß, ging in seinem Reich die Sonne nicht unter.

2. Während seines Lebens hat sich der Kaiser entscheiden müssen, wie er sein Reich unter seine drei Söhne teilen sollte.

3. Auch wenn sie unterschiedliche politische und rechtliche Standpunkte vertraten, haben sich die zwei Seiten entschieden, dass eine Zusammenarbeit möglich sein sollte.

4. Beide Seiten stellten fest, dass eine Einigung über Arbeitsbedingungen nicht zustande kommen konnte, wenn die Fragen über die Versicherung nicht zuerst geklärt wurden.

5. Die Überquerung des Atlantischen Ozeans von Cristoph Kolumbus im Jahr 1492 führte zur Neuentdeckung Amerikas für die Europäer. Kolumbus selbst hat nie erfahren, dass er nicht den Wasserweg nach Indien, sondern einen neuen Kontinent entdeckt hatte.

6. Wenn eine Biene ein Feld mit vielen Blüten entdeckt hat, teilt sie dies den anderen Bienen in ihrem Stock mit, indem sie einen eigenartigen Tanz ausführt.

7. Da sich die Berliner Humboldt-Universität im sogenannten Ostsektor der Stadt befand, wurde 1948 die Freie Universität Berlin gegründet. Die neue Universität bekam ihren Namen, weil sie im „freien" Teil der Stadt war.

8. Als im Jahre 1876 Schliemann mit den Ausgrabungen vom „goldreichen Mykenä" anfing, hatte er schon unzählige Goldschmiedekunstwerke im „homerischen Troja" entdeckt und ausgegraben.

1. **unter/gehen (ging ... unter, ist untergegangen)** *to set, sink*
3. **unterschiedlich** *different*
   vertreten (vertrat, vertreten; vertritt) *to advocate, defend*
4. **Versicherung** (*f.*), **-en** *insurance*
   klären *to clarify*
5. **Überquerung** (*f.*), **-en** *crossing*
6. **Biene** (*f.*), **-n** *bee*

6. **Blüte** (*f.*), **-n** *blossom*
   Stock (*m.*), **⁻e** *hive*
   Tanz (*m.*), **⁻e** *dance*
8. **Schliemann** (*Heinrich Schliemann [1822–1890], archaeologist*)
   Mykenä *Mycenae (ancient Greek city)*
   Goldschmied (*m.*), **-e** *goldsmith*
   Troja *Troy*

9. Das Innere des großen Königspalasts von Troja hat, wenn der Archäologe es auch nicht gleich erkannte bzw. glauben wollte, viel Ähnlichkeit mit den Palästen von Mykenä oder Tiryns.

10. Je nachdem, ob eine dramatische Handlung in den Zuschauern Identifikation oder Entfremdung erzeugt, teilt der Autor die Dramen des frühen zwanzigsten Jahrhunderts in klassische und epische Formen ein.

11. Da die Anhänger der Aufklärung im 18. Jahrhundert die Vernunft zum Maßstab aller Dinge erheben wollten, kamen viele Fragen zum Offenbarungsglauben zustande.

12. Wenn die Musik auch etwas sentimental war, war sie doch schön.

13. Louis Pasteur wies durch seine Versuche nach, dass die Gärung durch die Lebenstätigkeit kleiner Pilze und Bakterien zustande kommt, und zeigte, wie man sie verhindern kann.

14. Indem Berlin wieder die Bundeshauptstadt geworden ist und fast die ganze Regierung nach Berlin verlegt worden ist, wurde Bonn zu einem wichtigen, wenn auch nicht mehr so großen Verwaltungs- und Forschungszentrum.

15. Als der Kaiser um Rat bat, schlug ihm der Graf vor, dass er seine Luftschiffe gegen die englische Flotte schicken sollte.

9. **Palast** *(m.),* **̈e** *palace*
   bzw. (= beziehungsweise) *either/or; respectively*
   Tiryns *Tiryns (ancient Greek city)*
10. **Handlung** *(f.),* **-en** *action, plot*
    Entfremdung *(f.)* *alienation*
11. **Anhänger** *(m.),* **–** *adherent, follower*
    Maßstab *(m.),* **̈e** *criterion, measure*
    erheben (erhob, erhoben) *to raise, elevate*

11. **Offenbarungsglaube** *(m., n-noun)* *belief in revelation*
13. **Gärung** *(f.)* *fermentation*
    Lebenstätigkeit *(f.),* **-en** *activity*
    Pilz *(m.),* **-e** *fungus, mushroom*
14. **verlegen** *(f.)* *to transfer, shift*
    Verwaltung *administration*
15. **Luftschiff** *(n.),* **-e** *airship, Zeppelin*
    Flotte *(f.),* **-n** *fleet*

 Leitfragen zum Lesetext auf **academic.cengage.com/german/korb**

DER ZEPPELIN IM ERSTEN WELTKRIEG

Unter der Leitung von Graf Zeppelin startete schon 1900 der erste Zeppelin, der „LZ1". In den folgenden Jahren wurden die Luftschiffe immer größer und schneller.

Nachdem der Erste Weltkrieg ausgebrochen war, wurden
Zeppeline von der Marine und dem Heer übernommen. Sie wurden
zuerst für Aufklärungsflüge über der Nordsee gegen die englische
Flotte und später zum Bombenabwurf über England eingesetzt. Als
die Zeppeline über England und London ihre ersten Luftangriffe
machten, erregten sie großen Schrecken, denn es gab keine erfolgreiche Abwehr gegen sie, wenn sie in einer Höhe von 4000 m flogen.
Weder die englischen Jagdflugzeuge noch die Artilleriegranaten
konnten so eine Höhe erreichen. Jedoch in verhältnismäßig kurzer
Zeit verbesserten die Engländer ihre Flugabwehr, indem sie ihre
Jagdflugzeuge und die Flak (Flugzeugabwehrkanone) verbesserten.
Nun konnten sie die Zeppeline mit Phosphormunition angreifen. Da
die Zeppeline mit brennbarem Wasserstoff gefüllt waren, genügte
manchmal nur ein Treffer, um das Luftschiff in einen riesigen Feuer-
ball zu verwandeln. Die angreifenden Luftschiffe erlitten nun schwere
Verluste, und für die Mannschaft wurde ein Flug gegen England ein
„Himmelfahrtskommando".

Obwohl die Zeppeline kaum taktischen Wert hatten, hatten sie
doch in den ersten Kriegsjahren einen gewissen psychologischen und
strategischen Wert. Je tiefer sie ins englische Hinterland eindrangen,
desto mehr Streitkräfte und Artillerie mussten zur Abwehr in England
bleiben und konnten daher nicht in den Entscheidungsschlachten in
Frankreich eingesetzt werden.

4 **aus/brechen (brach ... aus, ist ausgebrochen; bricht ... aus)** *to start, break out*
5 **übernehmen (übernahm, übernommen; übernimmt)** *to take over*
6 **Aufklärungsflüge** *(pl.) reconnaissance flights*
7 **Bombenabwurf** *(m.),* ̈-e *bombing* **ein/setzen** *to engage, use*
9 **erregen** *to arouse, cause*
10 **Abwehr** *(f.) defense*
12 **erreichen** *to attain, reach*
13 **Flugabwehr** *(f.) air defense*

15 **an/greifen (griff ... an, angegriffen)** *to attack*
16 **genügen** *to suffice*
18 **um ... zu verwandeln** *to transform* **erleiden (erlitt, erlitten)** *to suffer*
20 **Himmelfahrtskommando** *(n.),* **-s** *suicide mission*
23 **ein/dringen (drang ... ein, ist eingedrungen)** *to penetrate*
24 **Streitkräfte** *(pl.) armed forces*
25 **Entscheidungsschlacht** *(f.),* **-en** *decisive battle*

19.1 Relative Pronouns

A relative pronoun introduces an attributive clause, that is, a clause that refers back to and modifies a noun or a pronoun. Consider the following examples.

> The artist *who* painted this work has lived in Rome since 1957.
> He is the artist *whom* we discuss in this chapter.

In the first example, the relative pronoun is *who* and the attributive clause, *who painted this work,* modifies the noun *artist.* In the second example, *whom* introduces the clause *whom we discuss in this chapter,* which refers to *artist.* This noun is called the antecedent of the relative pronoun.

In German, the relative pronoun always agrees in number and gender with its antecedent. Note that in English, the function of the relative pronoun in its clause is indicated by its declensional form: *who* is the subject; *whom* is the direct object.

The relative pronouns in German are based on the definite article system; as relative pronouns the **der**-words are declined as follows.[1]

	Masculine	Feminine	Neuter	Plural
Nominative:	der *who, which, that*	die	das	die
Accusative:	den *whom, which, that*	die	das	die
Dative:	dem *(to/for) whom, which, that*	der	dem	denen
Genitive:	dessen *whose, of whom, of which*	deren	dessen	deren

different!

---

1. Forms of **welch-** are also used as relative pronouns.

	Masculine	Feminine	Neuter	Plural	
Nominative:	welcher	welche	welches	welche	*who, which*
Accusative:	welchen	welche	welches	welche	*whom, which*
Dative:	welchem	welcher	welchem	welchen	*(to/for) whom, which*
Genitive:	(no genitive forms)				

19.2 Recognizing Relative Clauses

Der Künstler, **der** dieses Werk malte, lebt seit 1957 in Rom.
The artist who painted this work has lived in Rome since 1957.

Die Ausstellung bietet einen Blick in die Werke eines Künstlers,
der Amerikaner ist, **der** aber seit 1957 in Rom lebt.
*The exhibit offers a look into the works of an artist who is an
American, but who has been living in Rome since 1957.*

Hier können Sie Werke sehen, **welche** vorher nie ausgestellt
worden sind.
Here you can see works that have never been exhibited before.

Dieses Gemälde wird allgemein als das beste Werk angesehen,
das der Künstler produzierte.
*This painting is generally recognized as the best work that the
artist produced.*

Es ist ein Bild, in **dem** der Künstler noch einmal Graffiti darstellt.
It is a picture in which the artist once again represents graffiti.

All German relative clauses are set off from the main clause by commas. *The finite verb stands last in a relative clause.*[2]

Diese Geschichten, **die von den meisten Kindern gelesen
werden**, sind sehr bekannt.
*These stories, which are read by most children, are very well-
known.*

Der Wolf, **der ein paar Minuten früher angekommen war**, lag im
Bett der Großmutter.
*The wolf, who had arrived a couple minutes earlier, was lying in
the grandmother's bed.*

Das Haus, **in dem die Großmutter wohnte**, war in einem Wald.
The house in which the grandmother lived was in a forest.

Und wo war der Korb, **den sie ihrer Großmutter hatte geben
wollen**?
*And where was the basket that she had wanted to give to her
grandmother?*

When a form of **der**, **die**, **das**, or **welch-** (or a preposition plus one of
these forms) directly follows a comma, check the end of the clause. If

---

2. Except in the double infinitive construction, discussed in **Kapitel 18**, e.g., **Und wo war
der Korb, den sie ihrer Großmutter hatte geben wollen?**

the finite verb, or a double infinitive, is the last element, you are dealing with a relative clause.

Translating tips:

First, translate the pronoun after having determined the noun to which the pronoun refers and the pronoun's function in the relative clause. If the relative pronoun is the subject of its clause, the pronoun will be the first word in the translation, followed by the verb and its objects and adverbs generally in reverse order. If the relative pronoun isn't the subject, it should still be the first word translated, followed by the clause's subject (usually located right after the non-subject relative pronoun), then the verb and its complements. At times, it is best to translate a relative clause as a separate sentence so as to avoid awkward formulations.

19.3 *Welch-* as Relative Pronoun, Indefinite Pronoun, and Interrogative Pronoun

As a relative pronoun, **welch-** means *who, which,* or *that.* As an indefinite pronoun, **welch-** means *some* or *any.* As an interrogative pronoun **welch-** means *which?* or *which one?*

> Das ist die Situation, welche wir vermeiden wollten.
> *That's the situation which we wanted to avoid.*
> Hast du Geld? Ja, ich habe noch welches.
> *Do you have money? Yes, I still have some.*
> Welcher Wagen wird von welchem Fahrer gefahren?
> *Which vehicle is being driven by which driver?*

19.4 Case of Relative Pronoun Indicates Function

The case of the pronoun depends on its function in the relative clause.

A. Relative pronoun in the nominative = subject

The verb in the clause must agree in number, meaning that the relative pronoun can provide valuable information regarding the antecedent.

> Der Schriftsteller, **der** das Buch schrieb, heißt Günther Grass.
> *The author **who** wrote the book is Günther Grass.* (m. sing.)
> Die Schriftstellerin, **die** das Buch schrieb, heißt Christa Wolf.
> *The author **who** wrote the book is Christa Wolf.* (f. sing.)
> Das Buch, **das** auf dem Tisch liegt, heißt *Kassandra.*
> *The book **that** is lying on the table is called* Cassandra. (n. sing.)

Die Schriftsteller, **die** die Bücher schrieben, heißen Grass und Wolf.

*The authors **who** wrote the books are Grass and Wolf.* (pl.; verb ends in **-en**)

B. Relative pronoun in the accusative = direct object (or object of accusative preposition)

Der Schriftsteller, **den** die Kritiker loben, heißt Günther Grass.

. . . ***whom*** *the critics are praising . . .* (m. sing.)

Die Schriftstellerin, **die** die Kritiker loben, heißt Christa Wolf.

. . . ***whom*** *the critics are praising . . .* (f. sing.)

Das Buch, **das** die Kritiker besprechen, heißt „Kassandra".

. . . ***which*** *the critics are discussing . . .* (n. sing.)

Die Schriftsteller, über **die** die Kritiker diskutieren, heißen Grass und Wolf.

. . . ***whom*** *the critics are discussing . . .* (pl.; object of preposition)

C. Relative pronoun in the dative = indirect object (or object of dative preposition or verb)

Der Schriftsteller, **dem** sie den Preis geben, heißt Günther Grass.

. . . ***to whom*** *they are giving the prize . . .* (m. sing.)

Die Schriftstellerin, **der** sie den Preis geben, heißt Christa Wolf.

. . . ***to whom*** *they are giving the prize . . .* (f. sing.)

Das Buch, mit **dem** ich arbeite, heißt „Kassandra".

. . . ***with which*** *I am working . . .* (n. sing.; object of dative preposition)

Die Schriftsteller, **denen** sie die Preise geben, heißen Grass und Wolf.

. . . ***to whom*** *they are giving the prizes . . .* (dative pl.)

D. Relative pronoun in the genitive = possessive + noun

Der Schriftsteller, **dessen** Buch wir alle lesen wollen, heißt Günther Grass.

. . . ***whose*** *book we all want to read . . .* (m. sing.)

Die Schriftstellerin, **deren** Buch wir alle lesen wollen, heißt Christa Wolf.

. . . ***whose*** *book we all want to read . . .* (f. sing.)

Das Buch, **dessen** Titel „Kassandra" ist, liegt auf dem Tisch.
   ... *whose* title is ... (n. sing.)
Die Schriftsteller, über **deren** Bücher wir alle diskutieren, heißen
  Grass und Wolf.
   ... *whose* books we are all discussing ... (pl.; object of
  preposition)

19.5 *Was* as a Relative Pronoun

A. Generalized antecedents

Was is used as a relative pronoun after neuter entities, such as **alles**,
vieles, **nichts**, **etwas**, **das**.

Alles, was ich weiß, ...
   Everything that I know ...
Etwas, was die Kritiker nicht mögen, ...
   Something that the critics don't like ...
Es gibt nichts mehr, was man wissen muss.
   There is nothing else that a person needs to know.

B. Neuter superlative antecedents

Was is used after a neuter superlative.

Das Interessanteste, was ich gehört habe, war ...
   The most interesting thing (that) I heard was ...
Das Allerschlimmste, was passieren kann, ist ...
   The very worst (thing) that can happen is ...

C. Non-specified antecedents

Was is used as a relative pronoun when there is no specific antecedent.

Er erzählte uns, was schon jeder wusste.
   He told us what everyone already knew.
Der Wolf wusste, was er wollte.
   The wolf knew what he wanted.

D. Whole statements as antecedents

Was is used as a relative pronoun referring to an entire preceding statement and then usually means *a fact that* or *something that*.

Er hat diesen Staatsstreich allein durchgeführt, was man kaum glauben konnte.

He carried out this coup d'état all by himself, something that one could hardly believe.

Die Wahlergebnisse wurden nicht bestritten, was ich einfach nicht verstehen kann.

The election results weren't contested, a fact that I simply cannot understand.

Grundwortschatz

Abenteuer (n.), -	adventure	**gehören zu**	to belong to
alles	everything	**(gehörte, gehört)**	
Anblick (m.)	sight	**Gemälde** (n.), **-n**	painting
beschreiben	to describe	**Gerechtigkeit** (f.)	justice
(beschrieb,		**Häuptling** (m.), **-e**	chief, chieftain
beschrieben)		**Held** (m., n-noun), **-en**	hero
Ei (n.), **-er**	egg	**hören (hörte, gehört)**	to hear
Einleitung (f.), **-en**	introduction, prelude	**(Kraft)Fahrzeug** (n.), **-e**	(motor) vehicle
Eltern (pl.)	parents	**legen**	to lay, place
entsprechen	to correspond to	**nichts**	nothing
(entsprach,		**prägen**	to shape, form, coin
entsprochen;			
entspricht)		**Raum** (m.), ⸚e	room, space
etwas	something	**vieles**	much
erkennen (erkannte,	to recognize	**Übersetzung** (f.), **-en**	translation
erkannt)		**Wagen** (m.), -	wagon, vehicle, car
im Ganzen	on the whole		
gegenseitig	each other, one another	**Weise** (f.), **-n**	way, manner
		auf diese Weise	in this way

 Lösungen zu Übungssätzen auf **academic.cengage.com/german/korb**

Übungssätze

1. Das Beste, was ein Mensch besitzen kann, ist Gesundheit.
2. Das Wort Automobil bedeutet „Fahrzeug, welches sich *von selbst* bewegt", im Gegensatz zu „Wagen", der von einem Pferd gezogen wird.

2. **im Gegensatz zu** *in contrast to*

3. Von den 4,3 Millionen Kraftfahrzeugen, die im Jahr in Deutschland hergestellt werden, gehen rund 55 Prozent in den Export.
4. Zu diesem Experiment wurden Tiere verwendet, deren Eltern gegen diese Krankheit immun waren. Auf diese Weise konnte man feststellen, welche von den jungen Tieren anfällig waren.
5. Die Vögel bauen Nester, in die sie ihre Eier legen.
6. Das Straußenei, dessen Inhalt etwa 24 Hühnereiern entspricht, soll sehr schmackhaft sein.
7. An der Grenze zu Frankreich liegt das politisch sehr interessante Saarland, dessen Hauptstadt Saarbrücken heißt.
8. Saarbrücken hat mehrere Hochschulen, die auch von vielen Studenten aus dem benachbarten Frankreich besucht werden.
9. Die hellen Räume, in denen man die Gemälde aus dieser Periode besichtigen kann, wurden von Mies van der Rohe entworfen.
10. Das Gemälde, in dem sich der Künstler zum ersten Mal mit diesem Thema beschäftigte, wird auf S. 58 des Katalogs beschrieben.
11. Die „Neue Zeitschrift für Musik", deren Gründer Robert Schumann war, erschien zum ersten Mal 1834.
12. Clara Schumann war eine gefeierte Musikerin, die den Wandel des Virtuosentums im 19. Jahrhundert entscheidend prägte.
13. Der Monotheismus ist ein Glaube, nach welchem nur ein Gott verehrt wird. Beispiele sind das Judentum, das Christentum, der Islam.
14. Die Hindus glauben, dass der Mensch, der in einer niederen Kaste geboren wird, auf diese Weise für die Sünden eines früheren Lebens büßen muss.
15. Alles, was aus der Erde kommt, muss wieder zu Erde werden.

3. **her/stellen** *to produce*
4. **fest/stellen** *to determine*
   anfällig *susceptible*
5. **Vogel** (*m.*), ¨ *bird*
6. **Straußenei** (*n.*), **-er** *ostrich egg*
   Huhn (*n.*), ¨**er** *chicken*
   schmackhaft *tasty*
7. **Saarland** (*n.*) *federal state in southwest Germany*
8. **benachbart** *neighboring, adjacent*
9. **Ludwig Mies van der Rohe (1886–1969)** (*German-American architect*)
9. **entwerfen (entwarf, entworfen; entwirft)** *to design*
12. **feiern** *to celebrate*
   Wandel (*m.*) *change, transformation*
   Virtuosentum (*n.*) *virtuosity*
   entscheidend *decisive*
13. **verehren** *to worship*
14. **Kaste** (*f.*), **-n** *caste*
   Sünde (*f.*), **-n** *sin*
   büßen *to atone*

16. Es gibt kaum ein anderes Datum als den 9. November, das mit so vielen Umwälzungen und wichtigen Ereignissen in der neueren deutschen Geschichte verbunden ist. In dieser Beziehung muss man die Jahre 1919, 1923, 1938 und 1989 erwähnen.

17. Karl Mays Abenteuer- und Reiseromane, die in der ganzen Welt von Millionen gelesen wurden, gehören zu der Kategorie „Trivialliteratur".

18. Es gibt kaum ein deutsches Kind, welches noch nie von Mays Cowboyhelden „Old Shatterhand" oder dem Indianerhäuptling „Winnetou" gehört hat.

16. **Umwälzung** (*f.*), **-en**   *revolution, upheaval*
Ereignis (*n.*), **-se**   *event*

16. **verbunden sein**   *to be coupled with*
17. **Trivialliteratur** (*f.*)   *pulp fiction*

 Leitfragen zum Lesetext auf **academic.cengage.com/german/korb**

KARL MAYS AMERIKABILD UND -REISE

Karl May, der 1842 in großer Armut in Ernstthal geboren wurde und 1912 in seiner „Villa Shatterhand" in Radebeul starb, gehört seit Generationen weltweit zu den beliebtesten und meistgelesenen deutschen Schriftstellern. Die deutschsprachige

5   Gesamtauflage seiner Abenteuer- und Reiseerzählungen, die im wilden Westen Nordamerikas und im Orient des 19. Jahrhunderts spielen, überschreitet 80 Millionen. Übersetzungen liegen in 30 Sprachen vor.

Durch die Augen von seinem Indianerhäuptling Winnetou und
10   dem Cowboyhelden Old Shatterhand lernten Millionen von Deutschen einen wilden Westen kennen, in dem das Gute immer gewinnt und das Böse immer verliert. Old Shatterhand und Winnetou sind engste Freunde, die sich gegenseitig respektieren und

1   **Ernstthal**   (*eastern German town of*) *Ernstthal*
2   **Radebeul**   (*eastern German town of*) *Radebeul (near Dresden)*
3   **beliebt**   *popular*
4   **meistgelesen**   *most frequently read*
5   **Gesamtauflage** (*f.*)   *total circulation, total number of books in print*

7   **überschreiten (überschritt, überschritten)**   *to exceed*
8   **vor/liegen (lag ... vor, vorgelegen)**   *to be available*
13   **eng**   *close*
    gegenseitig   *each other, one another*

lieben. Der Autor, der sich mit Old Shatterhand identifizierte, malte eine Welt, in der der weiße Held seinem roten Bruder immer beisteht und ihm in jeder Situation helfen will.

In diesem Sinne beschreibt sich Old Shatterhand zum Beispiel in *Old Surehand I:* „Vor allen Dingen bin ich Mensch, und wenn ein andrer Mensch sich in Not befindet und ich ihm helfen kann, so frage ich nicht, ob seine Haut eine grüne oder eine blaue Farbe hat." (*Old Surehand I*, Freiburg, 1894, S. 242)

Nicht alles, was der fantasievolle Schriftsteller in seinen unzähligen Werken beschrieb, entsprach der wahren Geschichte des „wilden Westens" ganz. Die amerikanische Indianerwelt, über die Karl May wohl sehr viel gelesen hatte, war letztendlich eine Gegend, die der Autor selber mit eigenen Augen nie sah. Die einzige Reise, die Karl May in die USA machte, führte ihn im Herbst 1908 hauptsächlich nach New York und Boston. Der wildeste und westlichste Punkt seines Amerikabesuchs stellten die Niagarafälle dar. Auf dem Indianerreservat, den er damals besuchte, konnte der Mann, der Old Shatterhand sein wollte, keinen Winnetou finden.

16 **bei/stehen (stand ... bei, beigestanden)** *to aid, support*
17 **in diesem Sinne** *in this spirit*
19 **sich in Not befinden (befand, befunden)** *to be in danger*

25 **letztendlich** *in the final analysis*
28 **führen nach** *to lead to, to take to*
hauptsächlich *mainly, primarily*

KAPITEL 20

20.1 Demonstrative Pronouns

A. Replacing personal pronouns

Der, **die**, **das**, and **die**, used as demonstrative pronouns, assume the meaning of the pronouns they have replaced and mean *he, she, it, that, this, they, that one, those ones,* etc. Forms of **der**, **die**, **das**, and **die** are the most frequently occurring demonstrative pronouns and are declined like relative pronouns (**Kapitel 19**).

> –Kennen Sie den Filmemacher Volker Schlöndorff? –Nein, **den** kenne ich nicht.
> *"Do you know the filmmaker Volker Schlöndorff?"*
> *"No, I don't know him."* or: *"No, I'm not familiar with that one."*
> –Er hat den Film „Homo Faber" gedreht. –Ach, wirklich? **Den** kenne ich schon, **der** ist wirklich gut.
> *"He made the movie* Homo Faber.*"*
> *"Oh, really? I know that one; it's really good."*

The genitive forms **dessen** and **deren** are used primarily as demonstrative adjectives, meaning that they occur in combination with a noun; they indicate possession and refer back to the last-mentioned noun.

> Mein Bruder besucht seinen Freund und **dessen** Familie.
> *My brother is visiting his friend and his (friend's) family.*
> Die Beschreibung der Maschine und **deren** Gebrauch finden Sie auf der ersten Seite des Buchs.
> *You will find the description of the machine and its (i.e., the machine's) use on the first page of the book.*

As demonstrative pronouns, forms of **der**, **die**, **das**, and **die** are used for emphasis, and—in spoken utterances—they generally receive a strong stress. Unlike the relative pronouns, demonstratives have no effect on word order.

B. Antecedents of relative pronouns

Demonstrative forms of **der**, **die**, **das**, and **die** are often used as antecedents of relative pronouns.

Die Polizei kennt **den**, der das Auto gestohlen hat.
The police know the one who stole the car.
Das ist nicht **der**, den wir suchen.
That is not the one we are looking for.
Das sind die Ansichten **derer**, die gegen uns sind.
These are the views of those who are against us.
[As an antecedent, **derer** is used instead of **deren**.]

C. Preceding genitives in a series

Forms of **der**, **die**, **das**, **die** may stand directly before a genitive article.

Die Gesetze Deutschlands und **die** der Vereinigten Staaten sind
verschieden.
The laws of Germany and those of the United States are different.
Der Name des neuen Buches und **der** des alten sind sich sehr
ähnlich.
The name of the new book and that of the old one are very similar.

20.2 Other Demonstratives

A. *Das (this, that, or those)*

Das may be used as a demonstrative pronoun with either a singular
or plural verb to indicate *this, that,* or *those* when no specific noun antecedent exists.

Das ist die wichtige Information.
That is the important information.
Das sind die Bände mit den schönsten Bildern.
Those are the volumes with the most beautiful pictures.

It is possible for an entire clause to be referred to by the demonstrative
pronoun **das**.

Die Architekten entwarfen eine Vielfalt von Plänen. **Das** hat uns
sehr beeindruckt.
The architects designed a variety of plans. That impressed us a lot.

B. *Dies-* and *jen-* (this and *that*)

Dieser and **jener** are also used frequently as demonstrative pronouns,
in which case they are declined with the same endings as the **der**-words.

If the antecedent of **dieser** is unspecified or an entire clause, the shortened neuter form, **dies**, often occurs.

> **Dies** ist mein Vater.
> *This is my father.*
> Von den zwei Artikeln ist **dieser** der interessantere.
> *Of the two articles, this one is the more interesting.*

Dies- and **jen-** often occur as demonstrative adjectives together with a noun that is being pointed out for emphasis.

> **Dieser Mann** ist mein Vater. *This man is my father.*
> **Dieses Buch** finde ich am interessantesten. Es war viel besser als **jenes**.
> *I find this book the most interesting. It was much better than that one.*

Dieser and **jener** can also mean *the latter* and *the former* (see also **Kapitel 5**). In this literary usage, **dies-** refers to the person or object that is closer at hand, **jen-** to the one that is farther away.

> Beide Dirigenten haben die Philharmonie geleitet; **jener** am Anfang des Jahrhunderts, **dieser** am Ende des Jahrhunderts.
> *Both directors led the philharmonic orchestra: the former at the beginning of the century, the latter at the end of the century.*

C. Derjenige, diejenige, dasjenige; diejenigen (the one, he, she, it, those, etc.)

> **Diejenigen**, die noch nicht untersucht worden sind, müssen zurückbleiben.
> *Those who have not yet been examined must remain behind.*
> Die Polizei sucht **denjenigen**, der das Geld gestohlen hat.
> *The police are looking for the one who stole the money.*
> Das Belohnungsgeld wird **demjenigen** ausgezahlt werden, der den Missetäter anzeigt.
> *The reward money will be paid to the one who identifies the culprit.*

Note that this demonstrative pronoun is usually followed by a relative clause.

Since the first part of the demonstrative pronoun is declined like a definite article and the second part takes adjective endings, you can easily differentiate singular and plural by remembering that **die** + **-en** is the plural form.

D. *Derselbe, dieselbe, dasselbe; dieselben*
   (the same one, the same thing, he, she, it, etc.)

This group of demonstratives functions in a fashion similar to forms of **derjenige**.

> Der neu entdeckte Dinosaurier hat **dieselben** Eigenschaften wie der Tyrannosaurus rex.
> *The newly discovered dinosaur has the same characteristics as the Tyrannosaurus rex.*
> **Dasselbe** wurde bei der letzten Entdeckung beobachtet.
> *The same thing was observed in the case of the last discovery.*
> Auch unsere deutschen Mitarbeiter benutzen diese Methode, seit sie **dieselbe** kennen.
> *Our German co-workers have also been using this method since they became acquainted with it.*

20.3 Suffixes *-los*, *-fach*, and *-mal*

A. *-los (less, without)*

arbeitslos	*unemployed*	furchtlos	*fearless*
atemlos	*breathless*	geldlos	*without money*
bewegungslos	*motionless*	machtlos	*powerless*
brotlos	*breadless*	obdachlos	*homeless*
erfolglos	*unsuccessful*	sprachlos	*speechless*
farblos	*colorless*	zahllos	*countless*

B. *-fach (-fold, times)*

dreifach	*three times*	vielfach	*many times, manifold*
mehrfach	*several times*	zehnfach	*ten times*

Note, however:

einfach   *simple*

C. *-mal (time, times)*

damals	*at that time*	oftmals	*frequently*
einmal	*once*	viermal	*four times*
jedes Mal	*every time*	zigmal	*over and over,*
keinmal	*never*		*a thousand times*
manchmal	*sometimes*		

[handwritten: English equivalent: the umpteenth time]

Ausgabe (f.), **-n**	expenditure; edition	**vergleichen** **(verglich, verglichen)**	to compare
Band (m.), **ⁱ-e**	volume		
Darstellung (f.), **-en**	representation	**Verlag** (m.), **-e**	publishing house, publishers
ein/führen (in)	introduce (to)		
Einteilung (f.), **-en**	division, arrangement	**verständlich**	intelligible
		v.H. (vom Hundert)	percent
-fach	times, -fold	**vorhanden sein**	to be present
falsch	false, wrong	**vorher/gehen**	to precede
führen (zu)	to lead (to)	**(ging ... vorher, ist**	
gar	even, very, quite	**vorhergegangen)**	
Handlung (f.), **-en**	act, action	**vor/schlagen**	to suggest, propose
Inhalt (m.), **-e**	content, contents	**(schlug ... vor,**	
Menge (f.), **-n**	amount	**vorgeschlagen;**	
neulich	recently	**schlägt ... vor)**	
Rate (f.), **-n**	rate	**wirken**	to work, be engaged, to have an effect
sammeln	to collect		
Schaden (m.), **ⁱ-**	damage		
Sinn (m.), **-e**	meaning, sense		
Tod (m.)	death	**Wirtschaft** (f.), **-en**	industry, economy

 Lösungen zu Übungssätzen auf **academic.cengage.com/german/korb**

Übungssätze

1. In dieser Untersuchung wurden die Schulzeugnisse von über 1000 Kindern gesammelt und mit denen ihrer Eltern und Großeltern verglichen.
2. Die allgemeine Methode war dieselbe wie in den vorhergehenden Studien.
3. Andere Methoden sind vorgeschlagen worden, z.B. die, die der nächste Abschnitt des Buches behandelt.
4. „Wenn zwei das Gleiche tun, so ist es noch lange nicht dasselbe." Das heißt: Nicht nur die Handlung ist wichtig, sondern auch wer sie aus welchem Motiv ausführt.
5. Die Beobachtungen von Nelson, wie diejenigen der anderen Autoren, konnten von uns bestätigt werden.
6. Die neuen Wirtschaftstheorien sind nur dem verständlich, der die höhere Mathematik beherrscht.

1. **Schulzeugnis** (n.), **-se** *report card*   6. **beherrschen** *to master*
   Großeltern (pl.) *grandparents*

7. Mit der Komposition seiner großen C-Dur Sinfonie hat Franz Schubert wahrscheinlich 1825 begonnen. Das Charakteristische an dieser Sinfonie ist deren Beginn.

8. Schuberts große C-Dur Sinfonie, deren langsame Einleitung Schumann begeisterte und später so beeinflusste, entdeckte dieser um 1840 in Wien.

9. Die durchschnittliche Zuwachsrate der Ausgaben des Staates für die deutsche Forschung und Entwicklung betrug in den Jahren zwischen 1980 und 1990 12,7 v.H., die der Wirtschaft 13,1 v.H.

10. Verglichen mit den Zahlen der Arbeitslosen in den alten Bundesländern waren die in den neuen Ländern zwei- bis dreimal so hoch.

11. „Was du nicht willst, das man dir tu', / Das füg' auch keinem andern zu." Dies bezeichnet man als die „Goldene Regel".

12. Manchmal wollen kinderlose Ehepaare auch ein etwas älteres Kind adoptieren.

13. Ein Adoptivkind erhält den Familiennamen dessen, der es adoptiert hat.

14. Der Kranke blieb manchmal nächtelang schlaflos. Dies machte sein Leiden nur noch unerträglicher und führte am Ende zu seinem Tod.

15. Arzneimittel, die in zu großer Menge oder in falscher Weise dem Kranken zugeführt wurden, wirkten als Gifte.

16. Im engeren Sinne bezeichnet man diejenigen Stoffe als Gifte, die zu Gesundheitsschäden bei Menschen und Tieren führen.

17. Die historischen Vorurteile gegenüber „den" Deutschen sind noch vielfach in der Bevölkerung ihrer Nachbarländer vorhanden. Dies zeigte neulich eine Rundfrage in einem niederländischen Wochenmagazin.

18. Der vorliegende Band führt den Leser furchtlos in die Kontroversen der neuesten deutschen Geschichte ein.

8. **langsam** *slow*
   begeistern *to fill with enthusiasm*
9. **Zuwachs** *(m.)* *growth, increase*
10. **Bundesland** *(n.),* **⁻er** *federal state*
    die neuen (Bundes)Länder *the new federal states (formerly East German states)*
11. **zu/fügen** *to do unto, inflict upon*
    bezeichnen *to call, describe*
12. **Ehepaar** *(n.),* **-e** *married couple*
14. **nächtelang** *for whole nights, for nights at a time*

14. **Leiden** *(n.),* **–** *suffering*
    unerträglich *unbearable*
15. **Arzneimittel** *(n.),* **–** *medicine*
    zu/führen *to administer*
    Gift *(n.),* **-e** *poison*
17. **Vorurteil** *(n.),* **-e** *prejudice, bias*
    Rundfrage *(f.),* **-n** *questionnaire, inquiry*
18. **vor/liegen (lag ... vor, vorgelegen)** *to be under discussion or consideration*

19. Der Autor hat sein Buch in zwei Teile gegliedert, von denen der erste die Geschichte chronologisch darstellt und der zweite strukturelle Zusammenhänge erhellen soll. Jenen fand ich wegen der chronologischen Darstellung sehr verständlich, bei diesem bin ich aber in den Unmengen von Details hilflos stecken geblieben.

19. **gliedern** *to arrange, organize*
Zusammenhang (*m.*), ⸚e *connection, relationship*
erhellen *to clear up, illuminate*

19. **stecken bleiben (blieb ... stecken, ist stecken geblieben)** *to come to a standstill, get lost*

 Leitfragen zum Lesetext auf **academic.cengage.com/german/korb**

BUCHBESPRECHUNG

JÜRGEN MIROW: *GESCHICHTE DES DEUTSCHEN VOLKES: VON DEN ANFÄNGEN BIS ZUR GEGENWART*, GERNSBACH, CASIMIR KATZ VERLAG, NEUAUFLAGE 1996. NEU BEARBEITETE UND AKTUALISIERTE TASCHENBUCHAUSGABE, 2004. VIER BÄNDE, ZUSAMMEN 1510 S. MIT ZAHLR. ABB., KARTEN U. GRAFIKEN.

Der Autor dieses Bandes stellt vor allem die Geschichte des einfachen Volkes dar – das wird hier in seiner Gesamtheit wie in der Mannigfaltigkeit seiner Lebensäußerungen in ein neues Licht gestellt. Das, was diesen Autor am meisten interessiert, ist

10 nicht nur die Frage nach den Lebensumständen, nach Arbeit, Ernährung und Wohnen, sondern auch die nach Glauben und Mentalität, nach den Denkgewohnheiten der Menschen. Diese Darstellung erreicht durchgängig ein hohes Maß an Anschaulichkeit und Lesbarkeit.

15 Derjenige, der an zwischeneuropäischen Beziehungen interessiert ist, wird sich mehrfach darüber freuen, wie immer wieder bei den

3 **Neuauflage** (*f.*) **-n** *new edition, reprint*
S. (Seite) *page*
5 **zahlr. (zahlreich)** *numerous*
Abb. (Abbildung) *illustration*

7 **Gesamtheit** (*f.*) *entirety*
8 **Äußerung** (*f.*), **-en** *expression*
10 **Umstand** (*m.*), ⸚e *circumstance*
12 **Gewohnheit** (*f.*), **-en** *habit*
13 **durchgängig** *throughout*

verschiedenen Epochen vergleichend auf Entwicklungen im benachbarten Europa Bezug genommen wird. Dasselbe findet man bei der Behandlung von Sachfragen. Die Einteilung in neun Epochen bezieht die vorgeschichtlichen Zeiten ein und reicht bis kurz vor die Wende.

Aus dem Inhalt: 1. Vorspiel zur deutschen Geschichte. 2. Die Deutschen im hohen Mittelalter: 960–1250. 3. Die Deutschen im späten Mittelalter: 1250–1470. 4. Von der bürgerlichen Frühblüte zum Vernichtungskrieg: 1470–1648. 5. Zeitalter der Fürstenhöfe: 1648–1780. 6. Aufsteigendes Bürgertum und beharrende Fürstenmacht: 1780–1850. 7. Industrialisierung und kleindeutscher Obrigkeitsstaat: 1850–1918. 8. Umstrittener Pluralismus und Nationalsozialismus: 1918–1945. 9. Fortgeschrittener Industrialismus und gegensätzliche Ordnungssysteme und deren Nachwirkungen: seit 1945.

Das Wesentliche an der Neuauflage des Titels „Geschichte des deutschen Volkes" ist seine Ergänzung durch ein entscheidendes Kapitel, „Die Deutschen in der Gegenwart seit 1989", das die deutsche Geschichte seit der Wiedervereinigung von DDR und BRD am 3. Oktober 1990 beleuchtet. In dieser Ergänzung wird das Thema der Einwanderungsbewegung aus Osteuropa behandelt und über die Frage nach dem Weg zur multikulturellen Gesellschaft sowie die Probleme der Wirtschaft von Deutschland diskutiert. Kritiker finden Mirows Opus „hervorragend geplant", „souverän gegliedert" und vor allem „frei von Polemik und Schönfärberei".

18 **Bezug nehmen (nahm, genommen; nimmt)** *to make reference*
19 **Sachfrage** *(f.), -n factual inquiry*
20 **ein/beziehen (bezog ... ein, einbezogen)** *to include*
   Wende *(f.) the period surrounding the fall of the Berlin Wall*
23 **Frühblüte** *(f.) early prosperity*
24 **Fürstenhof** *(m.), ⁻e principality*
25 **auf/steigen (stieg ... auf, ist aufgestiegen)** *to ascend*
   beharren *to persevere, persist*

26 **kleindeutsch** *united Germany excluding Austria*
   Obrigkeitsstaat *(m.) authoritarian state*
28 **fort/schreiten (schritt ... fort, ist fortgeschritten)** *to progress*
29 **gegensätzlich** *opposing, contradictory*
32 **entscheidend** *decisive*
35 **beleuchten** *to illuminate*
40 **Schönfärberei** *(f.) glossing things over*

IM WILDEN, WILDEN WESTEN BLÜHTE DIE FANTASIE[1]

Nicht die Dichterfürsten Goethe, Schiller und Lessing sind die auflagenstärksten deutschen Autoren, es ist der verkrachte sächsische Volksschullehrer Karl May (1842–1912). In mehr als 200 Millionen verkaufter Bücher in über 40 Sprachen hat
5 der Sohn einer armen Weberfamilie seine Leser mit den fantastischen Erzählungen von Winnetou, Old Shatterhand und Kara Ben Nemsi in die Sehnsuchtsräume der wilhelminischen Zeit – Amerika, Orient und Afrika – entführt, ohne selbst dort gewesen zu sein. Jedenfalls nicht, während er seine zahlreichen Bücher schrieb.
10 Sein Wissen recherchierte er in Büchern, Zeitschriften und Zeitungen.

   Der Mahagoni-Schreibtisch aus dem späten Biedermeier um 1850, an dem Deutschlands erfolgreichster Jugendschriftsteller seine Geschichten erfand und der ihn sein Leben lang begleitete,
15 steht sonst im Karl-May-Museum in Radebeul. Jetzt bildet er als Leihgabe zusammen mit dem verstellbaren Stuhl den Mittelpunkt in der vom September bis Januar andauernden Ausstellung „Karl May – Imaginäre Reisen" im Deutschen Historischen Museum (DHM) in Berlin.
20   Sie ist eine liebevoll, aber keineswegs unkritisch arrangierte Hommage an einen Mann, dessen Helden in einer damals noch weitgehend

---

2 **auflagenstärkst-** *most widely published*
3 **verkracht** *failed, disreputed*
7 **Sehnsuchtsräume** *(pl.) dream worlds*
10 **recherchieren** *to research*
12 **Biedermeier** *style circa 1815–1845*

15 **sonst** *otherwise*
   Radebeul *German town of Radebeul*
16 **Leihgabe** *(f.)*, **-n** *loan*
   verstellbar *adjustable*
21 **weitgehend** *largely*

---

1. Slightly adapted from the original by Dieter W. Rockenmeier http://www.nz-online.de/artikel.asp?art=691601&kat=49&man=4, © *Nürnberger Zeitung* (31.08.2007)

unbekannten, exotischen Welt den alten Kampf zwischen
Tugenden und Lastern ausfochten, so dass er die moralischen
Leitbilder ganzer Generationen beeinflusst hat. „Damit hat Karl
May zur Ideenbildung in Deutschland beigetragen", sagte der
Generaldirektor des Museums. Es ist das Wechselspiel von Fiktion
und Wirklichkeit, das die Ausstellungskuratoren auch ohne rundes
Jubiläum an Karl May fasziniert. Laut dem Kuratoren, sei die
Ausstellung „dem Zeitgeist geschuldet und zunehmend objektiviert".

Mays Versuch, mit den Schilderungen atemberaubender
Abenteuer den Weg vom Kolportageschreiber zum Volksschriftsteller
und damit zum Literaten zu gehen, imponiert noch heute.
Seine Chance war die Einbettung in das deutsche Kaiserreich mit
dessen gehobenem Interesse am Lesen. Dies führte damals hinzu,
dass der einstige kleine Betrüger, der acht Jahre im Gefängnis
gesessen und sich aus seiner Zelle in die weite Welt geträumt hatte,
in ständigen Wildwest- oder Orient-Verkleidungen jahrzehntelang
steif und fest behaupten konnte, alle Abenteuer selbst erlebt zu
haben.

Die gut gegliederte Präsentation mit 500 Exponaten auf zwei
Etagen der DHM-Ausstellungshalle von I. M. Pei umfasst große
Teile seines Nachlasses, das zum ersten Mal ausgestellt wird. Als
großzügiger Leihgeber fungiert der Bamberger Karl-May-Verlag.
Nicht nur zahlreiche Gemälde, Zeichnungen und Fotografien
sondern auch Zeugnisse indianischer und afrikanischer Kultur
erschließen den kulturgeschichtlichen Zusammenhang der
Erzählungen des Schriftstellers. Tropenhelm und Reiseapotheke,

23 **aus/fechten (focht...aus,**
   ausgefochten; ficht...aus) *fight out*
24 **Leitbild** *(n.),* **-er** *role model*
25 **Ideenbildung** *(f.)* *fashioning of
   ideas*
26 **Wechselspiel** *(n.),* **-e** *interplay*
29 **geschuldet (+ Dativ)** *owing/
   indebted to*
30 **atemberaubend** *breathtaking*
31 **Kolportageschreiber** *(m.),* **–** *hack
   writer*
32 **imponieren** *to impress*
33 **Einbettung** *(f.)* *integration*
34 **gehoben** *elevated, lofty*
35 **einstig** *erstwhile*

37 **Verkleidung** *(f.),* **-en** *costume*
   jahrzehntelang *for decades*
38 **steif und fest** *obstinately*
39 **erlebt zu haben** *to have
   experienced*
40 **Exponaten** *(pl.)* *exhibition pieces*
42 **Nachlass** *(m.)* *legacy, literary
   remains*
43 **Leihgeber** *(m.),* **-** *lender*
   fungieren *to function*
45 **Zeugnisse** *(pl.)* *testimonials,
   evidence*
46 **erschließen (erschloss,
   erschlossen)** *open up, unlock*

persönliche Dokumente aber auch die legendären Gewehre namens
Silberbüchse, Bärentöter und Henrystutzen, die Karl May als
50 angeblich authentische Waffen mit anderen Souvenirs in seiner
Radebeuler „Villa Shatterhand" zeigte, stellen die Exotik dar, die
May erlebt haben will.

 Die Ausstellung möchte eine Phase deutscher Kulturgeschichte
kritisch beleuchten und sie dennoch mit Sympathie verstehen,
55 und dies ist der Ausstellung wunderbar gelungen. In der Nazi-
Zeit instrumentalisiert und in den Anfangsjahren der DDR sogar
verboten, reiten Karl Mays edle Helden einer christlichen Moral
heute über Filmleinwand, Fernsehschirm und Freilichtbühne.
Doch auch seine Bücher finden immer wieder Interessenten.
60 Dafür spricht am Ende der Ausstellung jener völlig zerlesene Band
Winnetou III, der 1904 erschien.

48	**Gewehr** *(n.)*, **-e**	*rifle, firearm*	54 **dennoch**	*nonetheless*
49	**Silberbüchse**	*"Silver-Flint"*	60 **zerlesen**	*well-thumbed*
	Bärentöter	*"Bear-Killer"*		
	Henrystutzen	*"Henry's Carbine"*		

KAPITEL 21

21.1 *Wer* and *Was* Used as Interrogative and Relative Pronouns

A. As interrogative pronouns

The interrogatives **wer** *(who)* and **was** *(what)* generally occur with singular verbs. **Wer** is used to inquire about persons and has declensional forms closely related to **der**. **Was** inquires about things, concepts, or actions.

Nominative:	wer	*who*	was	*what*
Accusative:	wen	*whom*	was	*what*
Dative:	wem	*(to) whom*		
Genitive:	wessen	*whose*		

Wer ist dieser Mann?　*Who is this man?*
Was ist sein Beruf?　*What is his occupation?*
Wen besuchen Sie in Europa?　*Whom are you visiting in Europe?*
Was machen Sie dort?　*What are you doing there?*
Was wollen Sie kaufen?　*What do you want to buy?*
Mit wem haben Sie gesprochen?　*With whom did you speak?*
Wem gehört dieses Buch?　*To whom does this book belong?*
Wessen Wörterbuch ist das?　*Whose dictionary is that?*

In the event that these interrogatives act as a predicate complement with the verb **sein**, keep in mind that the verb agrees in number not with the singular interrogative but (as always) with the subject that follows the verb in these questions.

Wer sind diese Leute?　*Who are these people?*
Was sind ihre Namen?　*What are their names?*

B. As relative pronouns

When no clear antecedent exists, the relative pronouns **wer**, **wen**, **wem**, and **wessen** are used to indicate the person in question, and **was** is used to refer to things, concepts, or actions. In this case, **wer** means *he who, whoever,* or *anyone who.* **Was** means *what, whatever, that which,* or *that* (see also **Kapitel 19**).

Wer nicht für uns ist, ist gegen uns.
　Whoever is not for us is against us.

Wer zuletzt lacht, lacht am besten.
He who laughs last, laughs best.
Wir wissen nicht, was wir machen wollen.
We don't know what we want to do.
Ich weiß nicht, mit wem ich sprechen soll.
I do not know with whom I'm supposed to speak.
Wessen Wagen das ist, möchte die Polizei erfahren.
The police would like to find out whose car that is.

Maxims or warnings are often expressed with a relative clause introduced by **wer**, **wen**, **wem**, or **wessen** preceding the main clause, which
then begins with a demonstrative pronoun **der**, **den**, **dem**, or **dessen**.

Wer sich der Einsamkeit ergibt, ach, der ist bald allein.
Anyone who is devoted to loneliness will soon be all alone.
Wen Gott vernichten will, den schlägt er mit Blindheit.
Whomever God wishes to destroy, he strikes with blindness.

21.2 Verb-First Constructions

A. Questions

Questions not introduced by interrogatives begin with the finite verb. The
presence of the question mark makes identification simple. Always be sure
to check the end of the sentence for dependent verbs or prefixes.

Kann die Wirtschaft im Osten von Frauen gerettet werden?
Can the economy in the east be saved by women?
Haben sie die Ursache des Problems entdecken können?
Were they able to discover the cause of the problem?

B. Omission of *wenn* in conditional clauses

In conditional clauses, **wenn** is often omitted in favor of a verb-first
construction. Conditional verb-first constructions are followed by result clauses, usually introduced by **dann** or **so**.

Wenn man Erfolg haben will, (dann) muss man arbeiten.
Will man Erfolg haben, (dann) muss man arbeiten.
If we want to be successful, (then) we must work.
Wenn eine musikalische Komposition verloren geht, verliert die
ganze Welt einen Schatz.

Geht eine musikalische Komposition verloren, (so) verliert die
ganze Welt einen Schatz.
If a musical composition is lost, the whole world loses a treasure.

C. Imperatives

Verb-first constructions also introduce imperatives that express com-
mands or requests. There are three different imperative forms corresponding to the three German words for **you**: **du**, **ihr**, **Sie**. Most short
imperatives are punctuated with an exclamation point (!). Here are the
du-forms and **ihr**-forms for some common verbs.

Infinitive	du-form[1]	ihr-form[2]
gehen	Geh(e)!	Geh(e)t!
nehmen	Nimm!	Nehm(e)t!
schreiben	Schreib(e)!	Schreib(e)t
sein	Sei ... !	Seid ... !

The **du**-imperative of most verbs consists of the indicative **du**-form minus the **-st** ending and the subject. The **ihr**-imperative is identical with
the indicative **ihr**-form minus the subject. These two forms are seldom
used in scholarly writing.

The **Sie**-form is the most frequent imperative in scholarly writing. It is
formed by inverting the word order of the formal **Sie**-construction. The
only irregular form is **seien Sie**.

Gehen Sie sofort nach Hause!   *Go home immediately!*
Nehmen Sie bitte Platz!   *Please take a seat!*
Schreiben Sie Ihren Namen!   *Write your name!*
Seien Sie ehrlich mit mir!   *Be honest with me!*
Vergleichen Sie die zwei Beispiele.   *Compare the two examples.*

Note that the subject **Sie** is not translated into English.

D. Verb first followed by *wir (let's . . . !)*

Wir following the verb in this verb-first construction is equivalent
to English *let us*. An exclamation point may or may not follow this

---

1. The final **-e** is often dropped.

2. In elevated speech, for example, in literary works, an **-e-** may be added before the final **-t**.

construction. It can be differentiated from a question by the absence of a question mark and from a conditional clause by the absence of the following **so** or **dann** clause.

> Fangen wir an!   *Let's begin.*
> Nehmen wir an, dass ...   *Let us assume that . . .*
> Versuchen wir diese Methode!   *Let us try this method.*

But:

> Fangen wir heute an?   *Do we begin today?*
> Nehmen wir das an, dann ...   *If we assume that, then . . .*
> Versuchen wir diese Methode, so ...
>   *If we try this method, then . . .*

21.3 Feminine Noun Suffixes

A. Suffix *-ung*

Added to verb stems, this suffix forms feminine nouns that often correspond to English nouns ending in *-ing*, *-tion*, or *-ment*. Here is a list of some of these words with which you have become familiar and which you should have no difficulty translating.

beobachten	*to observe*	Beobachtung
bestimmen	*to determine*	Bestimmung
bewegen	*to move*	Bewegung
bezahlen	*to pay*	Bezahlung
einführen	*to introduce*	Einführung
entwickeln	*to develop*	Entwicklung
erfahren	*to experience*	Erfahrung
identifizieren	*to identify*	Identifizierung
lösen	*to solve*	Lösung
trennen	*to separate*	Trennung

This close verb–noun relationship should assist you in expanding your active reading vocabulary. In addition, since *all* words that end in the suffix **-ung** are feminine singular, and the plural form of these words is *always* **-ungen**, you should begin to depend on such words as reliable sources to help you decode sentences in which they occur.

Note the difference between the feminine verb forms ending in **-ung** (*-tion*, *-ment*) and the neuter noun forms identical to the infinitive ending in **-en** (*-ing*) in the examples on the next page.

die Beobachtung	das Beobachten
the observation	*the observing*
die Bewegung	das Bewegen
the movement	*the moving*

B. Suffixes *-heit, -keit, -igkeit*

Added to adjectives, these suffixes form feminine abstract nouns corresponding to English nouns ending in *-ity* or *-ness*. Keep this relationship in mind to assist you in defining the multitude of feminine nouns like the following.

ähnlich	*similar*	Ähnlichkeit
blind	*blind*	Blindheit
empfindlich	*sensitive*	Empfindlichkeit
ewig	*eternal*	Ewigkeit
fähig	*capable*	Fähigkeit
genau	*exact*	Genauigkeit
hilflos	*helpless*	Hilflosigkeit
krank	*sick*	Krankheit
möglich	*possible*	Möglichkeit
verantwortlich	*responsible*	Verantwortlichkeit

All words ending in the suffixes **-heit**, **-keit**, **-igkeit**, and their plurals, which always end in **-en**, represent another set of reliable aids in the decoding process.

Grundwortschatz

beispielsweise	*for example*	**Ursache** (f.), **-n**	*cause*
bisher	*until now, up to now*	**verlieren (verlor,**	*to lose*
erweisen (erwies,	*to show, prove*	**verloren)**	
erwiesen)		**Verstand** (m.)	*mind, reason*
farbig	*colored*	**vor allem**	*above all*
Gesellschaft (f.),	*society, company*	**vor/stellen**	*to present*
-en		**sich vor/stellen**	*to introduce*
gewiss	*certain*	(acc.)	*oneself*
hingegen	*on the other hand*	**sich vor/stellen**	*to imagine*
innerhalb	*within, inside of*	(dat.)	
Leiden (n.), –	*suffering*	**Wahrheit** (f.), **-en**	*truth*
leiten	*to conduct, lead*	**weit**	*wide, far, extensive*
lieben	*to love*	**Wörterbuch**	*dictionary*
mehrere	*several, some, a few*	(n.), **⁝er**	
rationell	*efficient, economical*	**Zitat** (n.), **-e**	*quote*
sogenannt	*so-called*	**Zusammenhang**	*connection,*
Strahl (m.), **-en**	*ray, beam*	(m.), **⁝e**	*relationship*

Übungssätze

1. Wer die Reifeprüfung, das Abitur, der deutschen höheren Schulen bestanden hat, darf an Universitäten und Hochschulen studieren.
2. Wem Gott will rechte Gunst erweisen, / Den schickt er in die weite Welt, / Dem will er seine Wunder weisen / In Berg und Wald und Strom und Feld. (Eichendorff)
3. Wird ein Lichtstrahl durch ein Prisma geleitet, dann entsteht ein farbiges Band, das man das Spektrum nennt.
4. Wer Theologie studiert, der will lernen, was bisher in der Kirche über Gott gelehrt worden ist, vor allem, was die Heilige Schrift von Gott zu erkennen gibt.
5. Wen die Götter lieben, der stirbt jung. (Plutarch)
6. Der Staat ist im letzten Jahrhundert so mächtig geworden, dass der Mensch sich heute fragen muss: „Was ist und wo ist noch Freiheit?"
7. Wer über gewisse Dinge (Atombombe, Rüstungswettlauf usw.) den Verstand nicht verliert, der hat keinen zu verlieren.
8. Jeder schwimmende Körper verdrängt so viel Wasser, wie er wiegt. Verdrängt er weniger Wasser, als sein Gewicht beträgt, so sinkt er.
9. Wissen Sie, wie der Intelligenzquotient (IQ) berechnet wird? IQ = Intelligenzalter / Lebensalter × 100. Ist z.B. ein Kind 10 Jahre alt und hat ein Intelligenzalter von 12 Jahren, so ist sein IQ 120.
10. Sind Sie der Meinung, dass die demokratische Gesellschaft eine Nivellierung der Kultur mit sich bringt und damit zur Massenkultur führt? Ich kann mir so eine Entwicklung gut vorstellen.
11. Ist Ihnen dieser Ausdruck nicht bekannt, schlagen Sie ihn im Wörterbuch nach.

1. **Reifeprüfung** (*f.*), **-en = Abitur** (*n.*) *final comprehensive examination*
   höhere Schule (*f.*), **-n** *secondary school*
   bestehen (bestand, bestanden) *to pass*
2. **recht** *real, true*
   Gunst (*f.*) *favor*
   weisen (wies, gewiesen) *to show*
4. **Heilige Schrift** (*f.*) *Holy Scriptures*
   zu erkennen geben (gab, gegeben; gibt) *to reveal*
6. **mächtig** *powerful*
7. **Rüstungswettlauf** (*m.*) *arms race*

8. **schwimmen (schwamm, ist geschwommen)** *to swim, float*
   verdrängen *to displace*
   soviel ... wie *as much . . . as*
9. **Intelligenzalter** (*n.*) *mental age*
   Lebensalter (*n.*) *chronological age*
10. **Nivellierung** (*f.*), **-en** *leveling*
    mit sich bringen (brachte, gebracht) *to bring about, entail*
11. **nach/schlagen (schlug ... nach, nachgeschlagen; schlägt nach)** *to look up*

12. Wer einmal lügt, dem glaubt man nicht, selbst dann, wenn er die Wahrheit spricht.
13. Es bleibt ungewiss, was die Ursachen von Schumanns Krankheit waren.
14. Was diese Krankheit verursacht, wer sie bekommt, wer nicht, das sind komplexe Fragen, mit denen sich Generationen von Wissenschaftlern beschäftigt haben.
15. Wer nicht sehen will, der ist am blindesten.
16. Jetzt beschäftigen wir uns etwas näher mit einem berühmten Zitat des sogenannten „Frauendichters des 18. Jahrhunderts", Friedrich Schiller:

    „Ehret die Frauen! Sie flechten und weben / Himmlische Rosen ins irdische Leben."

12. **lügen**   *to tell a lie, lie*
14. **verursachen**   *to cause*
16. **flechten (flocht, geflochten; flicht)**   *to braid*

16. **weben**   *to weave*
    himmlisch   *heavenly*
    irdisch   *earthly, human*

  Leitfragen zum Lesetext auf **academic.cengage.com/german/korb**

Robert Schumanns Partitur Wiedergefunden[1]

W er sich für die Musik Robert Schumanns interessiert, erlebte eine Überraschung bei Sotheby's in München, als das Autograph seiner zweiten Sinfonie in C-Dur op. 61 vorgestellt wurde. Das Manuskript war seit mehreren Jahrzehnten verloren. Man glaubte, es wurde im Zweiten Weltkrieg bei der Bombardierung von Leipzig vernichtet. Die Wiederauffindung der kompletten Sinfonie eines der wichtigsten Komponisten der Romantik gilt deshalb bei Musikwissenschaftlern als Sensation.

5

Title **Partitur** *(f.),* **-en**   *full score*
3 **Autograph** *(n.),* **-e**   *handwritten original*
  Dur *(n.)*   *major (music)*
6 **vernichten**   *to destroy*
  Wiederauffindung *(f.),* **-en**   *rediscovery*

7 **gelten (galt, gegolten; gilt)**   *to mean, be considered (as)*
8 **deshalb**   *therefore, for that reason*

---

1. Based on Renate Schostack's "Robert Schumann: Original-Partitur wiedergefunden," *Frankfurter Allgemeine Zeitung,* Oct. 27, 1994.

Das Konvolut umfasst 236 numerierte Seiten. Goldenfarbige
Schnörkel verzieren den originalen Einband von 1846, auf dessen
Lederrücken steht: „Symphonie Nr. 2"; der Name des Autors fehlt.
Clara Schumann schenkte das Manuskript dem Dirigenten Julius Rietz
bei einer Aufführung der Sinfonie im Spätjahr 1855. Ihr Mann befand
sich zu dieser Zeit in der Heilanstalt von Endenich bei Bonn. Wer die
Geschichte seines Leidens und tragischen Endes kennt, weiß, dass der
Komponist bald danach im Sommer 1856 starb.

Die Partitur, mit schwarzer Tinte geschrieben, erweist mit ihren
unzähligen Korrekturen die Schaffensweise des Komponisten. Jeder
Satz ist am Ende von seiner Hand datiert. So liest man zum Beispiel
unter dem ersten Satz: „Dresden am 8. Mai 1846 im Garten." Die
Sinfonie, für ihren wunderbaren langsamen Satz in C-Moll berühmt,
wurde 1846 uraufgeführt. Mendelssohn leitete das Leipziger Gewand-
haus Orchester. *for the very first time | or something that is very very very old*

9 **Konvolut** (n.), -e *bundle/sheaf of papers*
   um/fassen *to comprise, contain*
10 **Schnörkel** (m.), – *flourish (writing)*
   verzieren *to adorn, ornament*
11 **Lederrücken** (m.), – *leather spine (of book)*
14 **Heilanstalt** (f.), -en *sanatorium*

16 **danach** *thereafter*
18 **Schaffensweise** (f.), -n *creative process*
19 **Satz** (m.), ⁻e *movement* (music)
22 **uraufgeführt** *premiered; performed for the first time*
23 **Leipziger Gewandhaus** (*concert hall in Leipzig*)

KAPITEL 22

22.1 Infinitives with *zu*

Infinitives dependent on verbs other than the modals and **hören, sehen, lassen,** and **werden** are prepositional infinitives preceded by **zu**. This common combination occurs with active infinitives, e.g., **zu lesen, zu fahren;** past infinitives, such as **gelesen zu haben, gefahren zu sein;** passive infinitives, e.g., **gelesen zu werden, gefahren zu werden;** and past passive infinitives, such as **gelesen worden zu sein, gefahren worden zu sein.**

A. Verb complements

Infinitives with **zu** complete a number of German verbs, a few of which are **an/fangen** and **beginnen** (both meaning *to begin*), **auf/hören** (*to cease*), **brauchen** (*to need*), **scheinen** (*to appear*), **versprechen** (*to promise*), **verstehen** (*to understand how*), and **versuchen** (*to try*).

> Es hat angefangen zu regnen. Jetzt beginnt es zu schneien.
> *It started to rain. Now it's beginning to snow.*
> Es hat aufgehört zu regnen.   *It stopped raining.*
> Für diesen Kurs brauchst du das Buch nicht gelesen zu haben.
> *For this course you don't need to have read that book.*
> Der Professor scheint diese Woche nicht in seinem Büro zu sein.
> Er scheint schon nach Deutschland gefahren zu sein.
> *The professor does not appear to be in his office this week. He seems to have gone to Germany already.*
> Er hat versprochen, hier zu sein.   *He promised to be here.*
> Sie versteht es, schnell gute Bücher zu schreiben.
> *She understands how to write good books rapidly.*

These prepositional infinitives stand at the end of the clause, but in English they must be translated immediately after the verb upon which they depend.

B. Infinitive phrases

A prepositional infinitive that is modified and extended by objects, adverbs, or prepositional phrases functions much like a dependent clause, except that it never has a subject. Note that most infinitive phrases are set off by commas and that the infinitive must be translated first followed by its object and modifiers.

Kolumbus versuchte, einen neuen Weg nach Indien zu finden.
Columbus tried to find a new route to India.
Als er in der neuen Welt ankam, glaubte er, Indien entdeckt zu haben.
When he arrived in the new world, he believed he had discovered India.
Das vorliegende Buch ist ein Versuch, die Entwicklung der Außenpolitik der Vereinigten Staaten darzustellen.
The book under consideration is an attempt to show the development of the foreign policy of the United States.

When used with the infinitive stem of a separable verb, e.g., **dar/stellen** *(to show)*, **zu** stands between the prefix and the simple verb. If you need to look up the verb in the dictionary, leave out **zu**.

Infinitive phrases may contain modifying clauses or phrases, set off by commas that separate the infinitive from the rest of the clause. Remember that the infinitive must be nonetheless translated immediately after the main verb.

Das vorliegende Buch ist ein Versuch, die Entwicklung der Außenpolitik der Vereinigten Staaten, wie sie von heutigen Geschichtsforschern verstanden wird, darzustellen.
The book under consideration is an attempt to show the development of the foreign policy of the United States, as it is understood by present historians.

C. Prepositional infinitives with *um, ohne, (an)statt*

1. **um ... zu** *(in order to)*

   Infinitive phrases introduced by **um** indicate the purpose, consequence, or effect of the action in the main clause. Translate this combination *in order to* + infinitive.

   Der Herzog schickte Soldaten nach Amerika, um seine Schatzkammer mit Geld zu füllen.
   The duke sent soldiers to America in order to fill his coffers with money.
   Lady Milford hat das Geschenk zurückgegeben, um dem Herzog zu zeigen, dass sie seine Handlung ablehnte.
   Lady Milford returned the present in order to show the duke that she rejected his action.

Die Studenten haben Schillers Drama gelesen, um neue Ein-
sichten in die Geschichte dieser Zeit zu gewinnen.
*The students read Schiller's drama in order to gain new insights
into the history of this period.*

2. **ohne ... zu** (*without . . . -ing*) and **(an)statt ... zu** (*instead of . . . -ing*)

Infinitive phrases introduced by **ohne** indicate that the situation in
the main clause can exist regardless of the situation in the infinitive
phrase. **Ohne ... zu** + infinitive translates *without . . . -ing*.

Die Wissenschaftler suchten das Gen, das blind macht, ohne
genau zu wissen, was sie suchten.
*The scientists sought the gene that causes blindness without
knowing exactly what they were seeking.*
Der Arzt verließ das Krankenhaus, ohne den Patienten besucht
zu haben.
The doctor left the hospital without having visited the patient.

Infinitive phrases introduced with **anstatt** or **statt** explain a situation
that might be expected, instead of the one that actually occurs in the
main clause. **(An)statt ... zu** translates *instead of . . . -ing*.

Die Artillerie musste in England bleiben, anstatt in Frankreich
eingesetzt zu werden.
*The artillery had to remain in England instead of being de-
ployed in France.*
Statt ins Kino zu gehen, bin ich zu Hause geblieben.
Instead of going to the movie theater, I stayed at home.

22.2 Idiomatic Prepositional Phrases

Many verbs occur with prepositions in idiomatic combinations. A few
have parallel structures in English, for example **vergleichen mit** and *to
compare with*; **arbeiten an** and *to work on*. For the many combinations
that do not parallel the English, one must rely on a good dictionary
and note the idiomatic meanings. Consider the following entry from
Langenscheidt's New College German Dictionary for **halten**, which basically means in English *to hold, to stop*:

~ *für acc.* consider *s.o.* (to be), think *s.o.* is, (mis)take *s.o.* for; *er
hält ihn für den Besitzer usu.* he thinks he's the owner; *ich halte
es für richtig, dass er absagt* I think he's right to refuse, I think it's
right that he should refuse; *ich hielte es für gut, wenn wir gingen*

I think we should go, I think it would be a good idea if we went;
fur wie alt hältst du ihn? how old do you think he is?; *wofür ~
Sie mich (eigentlich)?* who do you think I am?

Here is a list of some of the most common idiomatic verb-preposition
combinations and their meanings.

denken an	Er denkt an uns.
to think about	*He's thinking about us.*
erinnern an	Er erinnert mich an meinen Bruder.
to remind of; remind about	*He reminds me of my brother.*
sich erinnern an	Er erinnert sich gut an uns.
to remember	*He remembers us well.*
sich gewöhnen an	Wir gewöhnen uns an das Wetter hier.
to get used to, become accustomed to	*We're getting used to the weather here.*
glauben an	Er glaubt an Gott.
to believe in	*He believes in God.*
leiden an	Sie leidet an Rückenschmerzen.
to suffer from	*She suffers from backache.*
teil/nehmen an	Nehmen Sie an einem Filmkurs teil?
to take part in	*Do you take part in a film course?*
zweifeln an	Wir zweifeln an den Resultaten.
to doubt	*We doubt the results.*
achten auf	Ich muss auf meine Linie achten.
to pay attention to	*I have to pay attention to my waistline.*
antworten auf	Antworten Sie auf die Frage!
to answer	*Answer the question!*
sich freuen auf	Ich freue mich auf das Wochenende.
to look forward to	*I'm looking forward to the weekend.*
hoffen auf	Wir hoffen auf gutes *Wetter.*
to hope for	*We are hoping for good weather.*
warten auf	Auf wen warten Sie?
to wait on / for	*For whom are you waiting?*
bestehen aus	Das Buch besteht aus 30 Kapiteln.
to consist of	*The book consists of 30 chapters.*
sich beschäftigen mit	Er beschäftigt sich mit Film.
to deal with, be busy with	*He deals with film.*
fragen nach	Hat sie nach uns gefragt?
to ask about	*Did she ask about us?*

sich sehnen nach	Sie sehnt sich nach Deutschland.
to long for, to miss	*She longs for Germany.*
schmecken nach	Das Essen schmeckt nach Knoblauch.
to taste of	*The meal tastes of garlic.*
sich freuen über	Er freut sich über deinen Besuch.
to be pleased about	*He's pleased about your visit.*
klagen über	Klage nicht über deine Freunde!
to complain about	*Don't complain about your friends.*
lachen über	Alle lachen über mich.
to laugh about	*Everyone is laughing about me.*
nach/denken über	Er denkt über seine Ziele nach.
to reflect upon	*He's thinking hard about his goals.*
sprechen (reden) über	Sprechen wir über deutsches Kino!
to talk about	*Let's talk about German cinema!*
streiten über	Wir streiten immer über Geld.
to fight about	*We always fight about money.*
bitten um	Ich bitte um Erlaubnis.
to request	*I'm requesting permission.*
sich kümmern um	Er kümmert sich um seine alte Mutter.
to worry about, take care of	*He takes care of his elderly mother.*
halten von	Was halten Sie von mir?
to consider, think of	*What do you think of me?*
sich fürchten vor / Angst haben vor	Er fürchtet sich vor dem Hund. Er hat Angst vor dem Hund.
to fear, be afraid of	*He's afraid of the dog.*
schützen vor	Die Mauer schützt sie vor den Feinden.
to protect from	*The wall protects them from the enemies.*
warnen vor	Warnen Sie ihn vor der Gefahr!
to warn about	*Warn him about the danger!*

Third-person pronouns representing an inanimate object or a concept do not usually occur as objects of prepositions, but are replaced by **da(r)** + preposition. **Warnen Sie ihn vor der Gefahr!** becomes **Warnen Sie ihn davor!** See **Kapitel 26** for details.

Grundwortschatz

an/deuten	to indicate, mention briefly	**glauben (an)**	to believe (in)
anstatt, statt	instead (of)	**halten (hielt, gehalten; hält)**	to hold, stop
bemerken	to notice	**halten für**	to consider
beweisen (bewies, bewiesen)	to prove	**hoffen (auf)**	to hope (for)
		imstande sein	to be able
bitte	please	**jederzeit**	any time, at all times, always
ehren	to honor	**Kino** (n.), **-s**	cinema, movie theater
ein/gehen (ging ... ein, ist eingegangen)	to go into, enter	**Menschheit** (f.)	mankind, humanity
Einzelheit (f.), **-en**	detail	**näher**	more closely, in greater detail
Filmemacher (m.), **–; Filmemacherin**, (f.), **-nen**	filmmaker, film director	**Satz** (m.), **¨e**	sentence, theorem, movement (music)
fort/fahren (fuhr ... fort, ist fortgefahren; fährt ... fort)	to continue	**Sicherheit** (f.)	security, safety
		sichern	to protect
gefallen (gefiel, gefallen)	to please, be pleasing	**Sohn** (m.), **¨e**	son
		unter	under, among
es gefällt mir	I like it, it is pleasing to me	**versuchen**	to try
		warten (auf)	to wait (for)
		Wille (m., n-noun)	will
gelingen (gelang, ist gelungen)	to succeed	**Ziel** (n.), **-e**	goal, aim
		zugleich	also, at the same time
es gelingt ihm	he is successful		

 Lösungen zu Übungssätzen auf **academic.cengage.com/german/korb**

Übungssätze

1. Ein Land kann es sich nicht erlauben, materiell reich und geistig arm zu sein. (John F. Kennedy)
2. Willst du immer weiter schweifen? / Sieh! das Gute liegt so nah. / Lerne nur das Glück ergreifen, / Denn das Glück ist immer da. (Goethe)
3. Da Kolumbus daran glaubte, Indien gefunden zu haben, erhielten die Ureinwohner des Landes den Namen „Indianer".

1. **sich erlauben** *to afford, permit oneself*
2. **schweifen** *to roam*
   Glück (*n.*) *good fortune, happiness*
2. **ergreifen (ergriff, ergriffen)** *to take hold of, seize*
3. **Ureinwohner** (*m.*), *– original inhabitant, native*

4. In diesem Buch haben wir versucht, die dringenden Probleme anzudeuten.
5. Das deutsche Kinopublikum der sechziger Jahre wartete und hoffte sehr auf anständige deutsche Filme.
6. Fast alle Charaktere in Fassbinders Filmen leiden an einem kaputten Leben und sehnen sich nach einem neuen Anfang.
7. Um den Kritikern besser zu gefallen, braucht der arme junge Musiker nichts anderes zu tun, als seine eigenen Kompositionen etwas häufiger zu spielen.
8. Viele Menschen arbeiten, um zu essen, einige dagegen essen, um arbeiten zu können.
9. Wir werden im Folgenden nur physikalische Prinzipien betrachten, ohne auf technische Einzelheiten näher einzugehen.
10. Röntgenstrahlen sind imstande, undurchsichtige Körper zu durchdringen.
11. Das Ziel der Vereinten Nationen ist, den Frieden und die Sicherheit unter den Nationen zu sichern.
12. Um nach dem Einbruch der Hunnen die Grenzen seines Weltreiches besser verteidigen zu können, teilte Theodosius 395 das Römische Reich unter seinen Söhnen auf. Den östlichen Teil mit der Hauptstadt Konstantinopel nennt man in der Geschichte das Oströmische Reich, den westlichen Teil mit der Hauptstadt Rom das Weströmische Reich.
13. In Deutschland bedeutet Lehrfreiheit, dass kein Lehrer gezwungen werden darf, etwas zu lehren, was er für falsch hält. Er darf aber die Lehrfreiheit nicht dazu gebrauchen, die Verfassung anzugreifen.

4. **dringend** *urgent, pressing*
5. **anständige** *decent*
6. **fast** *nearly*
8. **dagegen** *on the other hand*
9. **im Folgenden** *in the following (text)*
10. **undurchsichtig** *opaque*
    durchdringen (durchdrang, durchdrungen) *to penetrate*
12. **Einbruch** *(m.),* ¨e *invasion*
    verteidigen *to defend*
    auf/teilen *to divide*

13. **Lehrfreiheit** *(f.)* *freedom of instruction*
    zwingen (zwang, gezwungen) *to force, coerce*
    dazu *for (the purpose of)*
    Verfassung *(f.),* **-en** *constitution*
    an/greifen (griff ... an, angegriffen) *to attack*

14. Immanuel Kant (1724–1804) formulierte seinen Kategorischen Imperativ wie folgt: „Handle so, dass die Maxime deines Willens jederzeit zugleich als Prinzip einer allgemeinen Gesetzgebung gelten könnte."

15. Anstatt sich zu beherrschen und Selbstüberwindung zu zeigen, haben die Hörer während der Vorlesung über den Professor gelacht. Das hat ihm extrem missfallen.

14. **Maxime** (f.), **-n** *maxim, principle*
Gesetzgebung (f.), **-en** *legislation (law)*
gelten (galt, gegolten; gilt) *to be considered, be valid*
könnte (subjunctive of **können**) *could*

15. **sich beherrschen** *to control oneself, restrain oneself*
Selbstüberwindung (f.) *self-control*
Hörer (m.), **–** *listener; student attending a lecture*

 Leitfragen zum Lesetext auf **academic.cengage.com/german/korb**

DER NEUE DEUTSCHE FILM

In den sechziger und siebziger Jahren erlebte der deutsche Film im Westen Deutschlands eine neue Blüte. Unter dem Motto „Papas Kino ist tot" gelang es einer Gruppe von jungen Filmemachern, Mitte der sechziger die veralteten Lustspiele der fünfziger
5 Jahre mit dem „Neuen Deutschen Film" zu ersetzen. Wollen wir versuchen, dieses Phänomen zu erklären, so müssen wir das System der öffentlichen Spielfilm-Förderung als erstes erwähnen. Finanzielle Unterstützung vom Bundesminister des Innern und vom Kuratorium Junger Deutscher Film hat den jungen Filmemachern geholfen, eine
10 Reihe von bemerkenswerten Filmen zu drehen und dabei eine erstaun-

1 **erleben** *to experience*
2 **Blüte** (f.), **-n** *flowering, blossoming*
3 **es gelang einer Gruppe** *a group succeeded*
4 **veraltet** *outdated*
Lustspiel (n.), **-e** *comedy*
7 **Förderung** (f.), **-en** *sponsorship, grant*

8 **Unterstützung** (f.), **-en** *support*
Bundesminister des Innern *Federal Secretary of the Interior*
Kuratorium (n.), **Kuratorien** *board of trustees*
10 **bemerkenswert** *noteworthy*
drehen *to make, shoot (a film)*
dabei *in the process*

liche Vielfalt an Genres und Themen zu behandeln. Zugleich schien es auch eine Periode zu sein, in der sich ein erstaunliches Talent auf der deutschen Filmszene zusammenfand. Beginnen wir mit Alexander Kluge.

Alexander Kluge verstand es, in „Abschied von gestern" (1966) gekonnt fiktive und dokumentarische Elemente zu vermischen. Für diese bahnbrechende Arbeit, deren Titel auch eindeutig einen neuen Beginn andeutet, bekam Kluge den Sonderpreis auf den Filmfestspielen von Venedig. Jahr für Jahr sammelte er weitere Filmpreise dazu. Plötzlich kam eine Industrie, die seit dem Zweiten Weltkrieg viel Mühe hatte, Anschluss an das internationale Niveau zu finden, wieder in vollen Schwung. Anstatt nur noch Hollywood Spielfilme sehen zu wollen, fingen die Deutschen nun an, Filme in der eigenen Sprache wieder als Weltklassefilme anzusehen. 1977/78 wurden fast 60 deutsche Kinofilme produziert, von denen gut die Hälfte zum Neuen Deutschen Film gehörte. Neben Kluge gab es Filmemacher wie Werner Herzog, Margarethe von Trotta und Rainer Werner Fassbinder.

Fassbinder, das sogenannte „Enfant terrible des Neuen Deutschen Filmes", versuchte in Filmen wie „Katzelmacher" (1968), „Die Ehe der Maria Braun" (1978) und „Berlin Alexanderplatz" (1980) einerseits die Situation der Außenseiter in der deutschen Gesellschaft darzustellen, und auf der anderen Seite die deutsche Geschichte dieses Jahrhunderts zu dokumentieren. In nur 13 Jahren produzierte Fassbinder über 40 Filme und Fernsehserien. 1970, 1971, 1972, 1978, 1979 und 1982 bekam der kontroverse Filmemacher Bundesfilmpreise, und kurz vor seinem Tod 1982 wurde er für „Veronika Voss" mit dem Goldenen Bären der Berliner Filmfestspiele geehrt.

---

11 **Vielfalt an** *variety of*
13 **sich zusammen/finden (fand ... zusammen, zusammengefunden)** *to come together*
16 **gekonnt** *skillfully*
   vermischen *to mix, combine*
17 **bahnbrechend** *pioneering, epoch-making, trend-setting*
   eindeutig *clearly*
19 **Venedig** *Venice*
   dazu *in addition, additionally*

20 **plötzlich** *suddenly*
21 **Mühe** *(f.)* *trouble, effort*
   Anschluss finden (fand, gefunden) *to catch up*
22 **in Schwung kommen (kam, ist gekommen)** *to get going*
   Spielfilm *(m.),* **-e** *feature film*
25 **gut** *easily*
30 **„Katzelmacher"** *"tom cat"* (pejorative slang term)

23.1 Extended-Adjective Constructions

Adjectives and participles may also be modified by attributes of their own. The resulting extended-adjective constructions—often prepositional phrases—precede the noun that they modify and may be one of several adjectives in a series. As a result of extended-adjective constructions the limiting words (**der**-words and **ein**-words) appear to the untrained eye to have become disconnected from the noun that they introduce. Consider the following examples in which the extended-adjective constructions are highlighted.

> Die **in New York wohnenden** Menschen ...
> *The people living in New York ...*
> Die **seit Jahren in New York wohnenden** Menschen ...
> *The people who have been living in New York for years ...*
> Dieses **in Deutschland gebaute** Flugzeug ...
> *This airplane, which was built in Germany ...*
> Eine **für diesen Baustil charakteristische** Eigenschaft ...
> *A feature that is characteristic for this building style ...*

The article and its noun are separated by an extended-adjective construction. The adjectives or participles immediately preceding the nouns are modified themselves by prepositional phrases (**in New York**; **seit Jahren in New York**; **in Deutschland**; **für diesen Baustil**). After translating the article or **der**-word, you cannot proceed with the prepositional phrase but must first translate the noun modified by that article or **der**-word. The adjective or participle is translated next (often as a relative clause), followed by the preceding modifiers grouped in meaningful units. As a general rule, translate the modifier units from right to left, beginning from the participle and working back to the first modifier after the article.

23.2 Recognizing Extended-Adjective Constructions

Extended-adjective constructions are particularly common in journalistic and expository writing. Direct translations into English and sometimes even immediate comprehension are almost impossible in all but the shortest extended-adjective constructions. Keep your eyes open: Anytime a limiting word is followed by a preposition or another limiting word instead of the noun that it introduces, you are dealing with an extended-adjective construction.

The most common signals for these constructions are as follows.

1. Limiting adjective (article, **ein**-word, **der**-word, **alle**, **viele**, numbers, and others) followed by a preposition instead of a noun (as in all of the examples above).

> alle noch zu Hause bei den Eltern lebenden Studenten ...
> *all students who are still living at home with their parents ...*
> zwei mit Hilfe eines Pfadfinders die Straße überquerende alte Damen ...
> *two old ladies crossing the street with the help of a boy scout ...*

2. Limiting adjective followed by another limiting adjective or a pronoun.

> die unser Leben beherrschenden Kräfte
> *the forces controlling our lives*[1]
> das die Natur liebende Kind
> *the child that loves nature; the nature-loving child*
> ein alle Freuden des Lebens genießender Mann
> *a man who enjoys all the pleasures of life; a man enjoying all the pleasures of life*
> ein sich täglich erweiterndes Gebiet
> *a field which is being extended daily*

23.3 Translating Extended-Adjective Constructions

As soon as you recognize an extended-adjective construction, place an opening parenthesis after the limiting adjective. Then find the noun modified by the limiting adjective. This noun is preceded directly by an adjective or most often a participle. Place the closing parenthesis after this adjective or participle.

> Die (im Jahre 1386 gegründete) Universität Heidelberg ...

The words within the parentheses constitute an extended adjective and modify **Universität Heidelberg**. In translating the extended adjective, begin with the last word (the adjective or participle) within the

---

1. Though the German expression **unser Leben** is singular, the equivalent in English, *our lives*, is plural. Remember that in translating such culturally specific items, the appropriate equivalent is often similar yet different.

parentheses and work backward toward the limiting adjective. Translate words that obviously belong together as a unit (**im Jahre 1386**).

> *The University of Heidelberg, which was founded in the year 1386, . . .*

If you translate by using a relative clause, put the clause into the present or past tense, depending on the context of the whole sentence. Usually present participles will call for a present tense and past participles for a past tense. With adjectives, only the context is a reliable guide. Observe the sequence of the translation in this sentence.

```
 1  2       3      4       7              6      5
```
Das U-Boot versenkte den (mit Waffen und Treibstoff beladenen) Dampfer.
> *The submarine sank the steamer, which was loaded with arms and fuel.*

Here are further examples.

> Das auf diesem Wege entdeckte Land ...
>> *The country that was discovered in this way . . .*
>
> Unser ausländischer Freund kennt die in diesem Lande herrschenden Zustände.
>> *Our foreign friend knows the conditions that exist in this country.*
>
> Mein Mitarbeiter vollendete die im letzten Jahr von mir begonnene Arbeit.
>> *My co-worker completed the work that I started last year.* or:
>> *My co-worker completed the work that was begun by me in the past year.*
>
> Die uns von der Natur gegebenen Triebe ...
>> *The instincts that nature gave us . . .* or:
>> *The instincts given to us by nature . . .*
>
> Diese von den alten Griechen geschaffenen Grundgedanken der heutigen Atomphysik ...
>> *These basic ideas of modern atomic physics, which were developed by the ancient Greeks . . .*
>
> Außerordentlich groß ist die in den letzten Jahren auf den Markt gekommene Zahl von Videos.
>> *The number of videos placed on the market in the last few years is exceedingly large.*

Translations of past participles in extended-adjective constructions may be rendered using either an active or a passive verb construction (see the third and fourth examples above). If the passive construction in

English is awkward, you may turn it into an active one without changing the meaning.

Note that the entire noun unit (**diese Grundgedanken der heutigen Atomphysik**; **die Zahl von Videos**) should be translated before translating the extended adjective. Breaking up units that belong together and translating them as separate words often leads to confusion. When the connections in a sentence continue to seem unclear, look again at how you group units of words.

Grundwortschatz

Anzahl (f.)	number	**Maßnahme** (f.), **-n**	measure, precaution
Aufbau (m.)	construction		
Ausstellung (f.), **-en**	exhibition, exhibit	**Rad** (n.), **¨er**	wheel
		stehen (stand, gestanden)	to stand
Bezeichnung (f.), **-en**	term, designation	**Verbindung** (f.), **-en**	connection
Fahrrad (n.), **¨er**	bicycle	**Vergleich** (m.), **-e**	comparison
Franzose (m., n-noun), **-n; Französin** (f.), **-nen**	Frenchman/-woman	**zum Vergleich**	as a comparison
		verhältnismäßig	relative, comparative
Gebäude (n.), **–**	building		
Gelegenheit (f.), **-en**	opportunity	**vermeiden (vermied, vermieden)**	to avoid
gering	small, slight		
häufig	frequent		
insgesamt	all together, all in all	**vor** (+ amount of time)	(amount of time) ago
Kopf (m.), **¨e**	head	**zerstören**	to destroy
laufen (lief, ist gelaufen; läuft)	to run	**Zerstörung** (f.), **-en**	destruction
		Zusammenarbeit (f.)	cooperation

 Lösungen zu Übungssätzen auf **academic.cengage.com/german/korb**

past participle

Übungssätze

1. Nehmen wir zum Vergleich das (vor zehn Jahren ausgeführte) Experiment.
2. Der mit zwanzig neugeborenen Säuglingen vorgenommene Versuch führte wieder zum gleichen Ergebnis wie der erste Versuch.

2. **neugeboren** *newborn*
   Säugling (m.), **-e** *infant*

2. **vor/nehmen (nahm ... vor, vorgenommen; nimmt ... vor)**
   to undertake

3. Dieses noch am Anfang seiner technischen Entwicklung stehende Gebiet verlangt ein umfangreiches wissenschaftliches Studium.
4. Die (vor zwei Jahren in der niederländischen Stadt Utrecht ausgerichtete) Ausstellung über Banken in der Schweiz versuchte, die korrupte Verbindung zwischen Kunst und der Bankenwelt aufzuzeigen.
5. Der am 13. August 1961 begonnene Mauerbau bedeutete eine neue Phase im Leben der Ostberliner. Die durch den Mauerbau geschockte Welt musste fast 30 Jahre warten, bevor die Mauer abgerissen werden sollte.
6. In dem für heute Abend zu lesenden Text wird der im Jahre 1889 geborene und 1938 gestorbene Nobelpreisträger Carl von Ossietzky diskutiert.
7. Gemeinsam mit Kurt Tucholsky leitete Carl von Ossietzky eine für Menschenrechte und gegen Nationalsozialismus kämpfende Zeitschrift. Ab 1926 wurde Ossietzky der allein stehende Herausgeber von „Die Weltbühne".
8. Der Kopf des alten Franzosen war unvergesslich: Sein stoppeliges Gesicht, die lange Nase und der tief in die Stirn gezogene Filzhut machten ihn zu einer unverwechselbaren Figur.
9. Bei einem Rundgang durch das festlich für Weihnachten geschmückte Weiße Haus sprach die Frau des US-Präsidenten über die in das Kriegsgebiet abkommandierten Truppen.
10. Die in der Einleitung ihres neuen Buches besprochene Zusammenarbeit mit Experten auf dem Gebiet der Kindererziehung hat die Frau des Präsidenten auch bei dieser Gelegenheit ziemlich häufig erwähnt.
11. Am 6. August 1945, morgens um Viertel nach acht, wurde die von 400 000 Menschen bewohnte Stadt Hiroschima zu neunzig Prozent durch die erste Atombombe zerstört.

3. **verlangen** *to require, demand*
   umfangreich *extensive*
4. **aus/richten** *to organize, install*
   auf/zeigen *to show, indicate*
5. **Mauerbau** *(m.)* *construction of the Berlin Wall*
   ab/reißen (riss ... ab, abgerissen) *to tear down*
7. **gemeinsam** *jointly, together*
   Herausgeber *(m.), –* *editor*
8. **unvergesslich** *unforgettable*
   stoppelig *stubbly, bristly*
   Nase *(f.), -n* *nose*

8. **Stirn** *(f.), -en* *forehead, brow*
   Filzhut *(m.), ⸚e* *felt hat*
   unverwechselbar *unmistakable*
9. **Rundgang** *(m.), ⸚e* *tour*
   festlich *festive*
   Weihnachten *(n.)* *Christmas*
   schmücken *to decorate, trim*
   ab/kommandieren *to order off, detail, detach (military)*
10. **Erziehung** *(f.)* *education, training*
    erwähnen *to mention*
11. **bewohnt** *inhabited*

12. Auf einem wenige Tage später im Herzen der zerstörten Stadt aufgenommenen Foto ist das Ausmaß der Zerstörung zu sehen.
13. Die Anzahl der am Aufbau des neuen Stadtzentrums beteiligten Baufirmen war verhältnismäßig gering. Zwei oder drei Firmen haben drei Viertel der Aufträge bekommen.
14. Um an Gebäuden einen Brand zu vermeiden, bringt man an den Gebäuden, nach einem schon[2] 1753 von B. Franklin gemachten Vorschlag, Blitzableiter an.
15. „Draisine" war die Bezeichnung für die im Jahre 1817 vom Förstermeister Karl von Drais erfundene Laufmaschine, die ein Vorgänger des heutigen Fahrrads war.

12. **Herz** (*n.*), **-en** *heart*
    auf/nehmen (nahm ... auf, aufgenommen; nimmt ... auf) *to take (a photograph)*
    Ausmaß (*n.*) *extent*
13. **beteiligt** *involved, participating*
    Auftrag (*m.*), **⁻e** *contract*
    bekommen (bekam, bekommen) *to receive* (not: *become*)

14. **Brand** (*m.*), **⁻e** *fire*
    an/bringen (brachte ... an, angebracht) *to install, attach*
    Vorschlag (*m.*), **⁻e** *suggestion*
    Blitzableiter (*m.*), **–** *lightning rod*
15. **Förstermeister** (*m.*), **–** *forester*
    Vorgänger (*m.*), **–** *predecessor*

 Leitfragen zum Lesetext auf **academic.cengage.com/german/korb**

AM ANFANG WAR DIE DRAISINE

Wenn wir heute unser Fahrrad besteigen, kommt es uns wohl kaum in den Sinn, dass auch dieses Fahrzeug eine verhältnismäßig lange Entwicklung hatte. Das erste, unseren modernen Rädern vorangehende Fahrzeug war eine aus Holz gebaute Laufmaschine. Sie wurde von einem in Mannheim lebenden Förstermeister, Karl von Drais, 1817 erfunden und später nach ihm die Draisine benannt.

5

1 **besteigen (bestieg, bestiegen)** *to get on*
2 **in den Sinn kommen (kam, ist gekommen)** *to occur (to)*

4 **voran/gehen (ging ... voran, ist vorangegangen)** *to precede*
7 **benennen (benannte, benannt)** *to name, call*

---

2. In this instance, the adverb **schon** occurs between the limiting word and the preposition. In such a case, proceed as usual, placing the opening parenthesis after the limiting word: **einem (schon ... gemachten)**.

Diese Laufmaschine ähnelte dem modernen Fahrrad nur insofern, als sie zwei hintereinander angebrachte Räder und einen Sattel
10 hatte und mit den Händen gesteuert werden konnte. Jedoch musste
sich der im Sattel Sitzende mit den Füßen abwechselnd durch Absto-
ßen auf der Erde fortbewegen, fast wie beim Laufen. Natürlich erregte
dieser Anblick viel Gelächter unter den Zuschauenden, besonders,
wenn das noch nicht mit einer Bremse ausgestattete Fahrzeug zu
15 schnell über eine mit Kopfsteinpflaster belegte Straße bergab sauste.
    Etwa vierzig Jahre später kam die erste wichtige Verbesserung.
Ein Instrumentenmacher namens Fischer führte das mit einer
Tretkurbel am Vorderrad versehene Fahrrad ein. Erst 1885 wurde das
mit einer Kette am Hinterrad getriebene Fahrrad in England erfun-
20 den. Nach vielen anderen Verbesserungen erreichte das Fahrzeug
seine heute bevorzugte Form, die meistens eine Handbremse und bei
einem Rennrad bis zu zwanzig Gänge, und im Falle des heute von
vielen jungen Leuten sehr beliebten Mountainbikes sogar Federung
aufweist.

8	**ähneln** *to resemble*		15	**belegen** *to cover*
9	**insofern, als** *in so far as, in that*			**bergab** *downhill*
	hintereinander *one behind the other*		18	**Tretkurbel** *(f.),* **-n** *pedal crank*
	an/bringen (brachte ... an, angebracht) *to arrange, mount*			**versehen (versah, versehen; versieht)** *to equip*
11	**abwechselnd** *alternating(ly)*		19	**treiben (trieb, ist getrieben)** *to drive*
12	**ab/stoßen (stieß ... ab, abgestoßen)** *to push off*		21	**bevorzugt** *preferred*
	sich fort/bewegen *to propel oneself*		22	**bis zu** *up to*
	erregen *to cause*			**Gang** *(m.),* **⁼e** *gear (speed)*
14	**aus/statten** *to equip*		23	**Federung** *(f.)* *suspension, spring system*
15	**Kopfsteinpflaster** *(n.)* *cobblestone pavement*		24	**auf/weisen (wies ... auf, aufgewiesen)** *to exhibit, have*

KAPITEL 24

24.1 Other Types of Extended-Adjective Constructions

A. Extended-adjective constructions without limiting adjective

> (Sich bei den Olympischen Spielen in Peking treffende)[1] Sportler
> repräsentieren (Frieden liebende) Menschen aus aller Welt.
> *Athletes meeting at the Olympic games in Beijing represent*
> *peace-loving people from all over the world.*
> (Aus den alten Mythen herstammende) Träume von Ruhm und
> Ehre mischen sich mit ganz pragmatischen (auf wertvolle
> Werbeverträge ausgerichtete) Hoffnungen.
> *Dreams of fame and glory stemming from the ancient myths mix*
> *with completely pragmatic hopes aimed at valuable advertising*
> *contracts.*

The majority of constructions without limiting adjectives involve plural
nouns and are introduced by a preposition.

B. Extended-adjective constructions introduced by a preposition followed by another preposition

> Der Inhalt des letzten Kapitels handelt von (aus der Tiefe des
> Planeten hervorquellenden) Rauchwolken.
> *The contents of the last chapter deal with smoke clouds belching*
> *forth from the depths of the planet.*
> Der Heilpraktiker arbeitet ausschließlich mit (von der Natur
> gegebenen) Heilmitteln.
> *The homeopathic doctor works exclusively with homeopathic*
> *remedies that occur naturally.*

C. Participles used as nouns

> das (in der Schule vor vielen Jahren) Gelernte
> *what was learned in school many years ago*
> das (auf Seite 26) Gesagte
> *what was said on page 26*

---

1. Parentheses in the example sentences provide an aid for reading or translating. They are
normally not part of the sentence.

24.2 Extended Adjectives plus Unextended Adjectives

In a construction with both extended and unextended adjectives or participles *(all having the same adjective ending)* before the noun, unextended adjectives and participles are translated before the noun. The extended construction usually ends after the first adjective or participle.

> diese (für den Präsidenten schwierige) militärische Aufgabe
> *this military mission, which is (was) difficult for the president*
> die (im Lande herrschenden) politischen und sozialen Zustände
> *the political and social conditions prevailing in the country*
> die (zum ersten Mal in diesem Buch erzählten) lustigen
> Geschichten
> *the funny stories told in this book for the first time*

Even if the unextended modifier precedes the extended modifier and the two modifiers are separated by a comma, translate as above.

> die lustigen, (zum ersten Mal in diesem Buch erzählten)
> Geschichten
> *the funny stories told in this book for the first time*

24.3 Multiple Extended Adjectives

When a noun is modified by several extended adjectives, awkward translation may be avoided without altering meaning by dividing the long German sentence into shorter English sentences.

> Dieser (mit vielen Ehren in Deutschland ausgezeichnete,) (von
> seiner Heimat geflüchtete,) (jetzt in den Vereinigten Staaten
> lebende) große Filmregisseur war einer der Gründer der
> heutigen Filmindustrie.
> *This great film director, who had received many honors in Germany, was one of the founders of the contemporary film industry. He fled from his native country and is now living in the United States.*
> Der Film bietet ein (ausgezeichnetes, auf der Wahrheit basiertes)
> Bild der (von bestem Idealismus getragenen) Leidenschaft des
> ehemaligen Nobelpreisträgers.
> *The movie offers an excellent picture of the former Nobel Prize recipient's suffering born of the best idealism. This picture is based on truth.*

Lösungen zu Übungssätzen auf **academic.cengage.com/german/korb**

Übungssätze

1. Dieses 1816 zuerst erschienene, später laufend ergänzte, 1838 ins Deutsche übersetzte Buch hatte einen großen Einfluss auf die Psychiatrie ausgeübt.
2. Paracelsus veröffentlichte seine für die damalige Zeit bahnbrechenden neuen Erkenntnisse in verschiedenen Schriften.
3. Von uns gewonnene Versuchsergebnisse erscheinen in den nächsten Mitteilungen der „Zeitschrift für medizinische Beiträge".
4. Für jeden am Erziehungswesen Interessierten ist ein grundlegendes Verständnis der Technik und der Grundsätze des „Programmierten Unterrichts" heute unerlässlich.

1. **laufend** *continuously*
2. **bahnbrechend** *pioneering, revolutionary*
3. **Versuchsergebnisse** *(pl.)* *experimental findings*

3. **Mitteilung** *(f.),* **-en** *issue, report*
4. **Erziehungswesen** *(n.)* *educational system*
   unerlässlich *indispensable*

5. Dieses umfangreiche, hervorragend mit 366 vorzüglichen Farbbildern ausgestattete Werk wird mit einer vom Autor selbst aus dem Englischen übersetzten Abhandlung über die Welt der Mythen eingeleitet.

6. Das auf Seite 72 über Shakespeares „Hamlet" Gesagte gilt auch zum Teil für Tom Stoppards 1966 uraufgeführte Komödie „Rosenkranz und Güldenstern sind tot".

7. Das 1939 von Goodwin und Stone entworfene, heute noch als Museum benutzte Gebäude stellt eines der ersten Beispiele des Internationalen Stils in den Vereinigten Staaten dar.

8. Die Künstler des Expressionismus legten keinen Wert auf die Wirklichkeit und brachten statt dessen das im Inneren, im Geiste Geschaute zum Ausdruck.

9. Körperliche Bewegung auszudrücken gehörte zu den Grundsätzen der sich dem naturalistischen Darstellungs-Denken entfremdeten, gleichzeitig den „modernen" Denk- und Erlebnisformen verpflichteten Kunst des Expressionismus.

10. Schauen wir zum Beispiel die von E. L. Kirchner im Jahre 1911 in Berlin großformatig gemalten Straßenszenen an, so gewinnen wir ein neues Verständnis des Begriffes „körperliche Bewegung".

11. Macchiavellis Name und die von ihm geprägte, oft umstrittene Staatsform sind bis zur Gegenwart ein Begriff und werden es wohl in der Zukunft bleiben.

12. Durch Anwendung des heute im Unterricht über die Währungsunion Gelernten soll jeder aufmerksame Student nun den Wert der deutschen Mark und des „Euro" unterscheiden können.

13. Das neue Selbstbewusstsein der Ostdeutschen ist im allgemeinen für in den alten Bundesländern lebende Westdeutsche schwer zu verstehen.

---

5. **umfangreich** *extensive, voluminous*
   vorzüglich *excellent*
   ausgestattet mit *replete with, furnished with*
   Abhandlung (f.), **-en** *treatment*
6. **uraufgeführt** *premiered*
8. **zum Ausdruck bringen (brachte, gebracht)** *to express (to bring to expression)*
9. **körperlich** *physical*

9. **aus/drücken** *to express*
   sich entfremden *to alienate (oneself), become alienated*
   sich verpflichten *to commit or pledge (oneself), be dedicated to*
10. **malen** *to paint*
11. **prägen** *to coin, form, determine the shape of*
    umstritten *controversial*
12. **Währungsunion** (f.) *currency union*
    aufmerksam *attentive*

14. Dresden galt schon immer als eine Stätte der Kunst und Kultur. Heute bietet sie viele historische Sehenswürdigkeiten und gilt auch als ein Zentrum von Wissenschaft, Technik und moderner Industrie.

15. Die Dresdner Semperoper, die schon zweimal zerstört und wiedererrichtet wurde, gilt als ein hervorragendes Beispiel der bis in die Gegenwart hinein fortsetzenden Dauerhaftigkeit der Stadt an der Elbe.

16. Das originelle im Jahre 1838 vom Baumeister Gottfried Semper entworfene Opernhaus wurde 1869 vom Feuer zerstört. Der zweite, im Jahre 1871 wieder von Semper entworfene Bau fiel in der Schrecknacht des 13. Februar 1945 dem Luftangriff auf Dresden zum Opfer. 1977 bis 1985 wurde die nochmals wiedererrichtet.

14. **Stätte** *(f.),* **-n** *historic site*
Sehenswürdigkeiten
(pl.) *attractions*
15. **Oper** *(f.),* **–** *opera house*
wieder/errichten *to reconstruct*
Dauerhaftigkeit *(f.)* *durability*
Elbe *(f.)* *the Elbe river*

16. **Schrecknacht** *(f.)* *night of terror*
[nearly all of Dresden was destroyed by fire bombs]
Luftangriff *(m.),* **-e** *air attack*

 Leitfragen zum Lesetext auf **academic.cengage.com/german/korb**

CARL OSSIETZKY: VOM IDEALISMUS GETRAGENE LEIDENSCHAFT[1]

Der am 3.10.1889 in Hamburg geborene Carl von Ossietzky, eines der streitbarsten und mutigsten Publizisten der Weimarer Republik, infizierte sich 1938 im KZ Papenburg-Esterwegen und starb bald darauf an Tuberkulose in Berlin. Zwei

2 **streitbar** *pugnacious, disputatious*
mutig *brave*
3 **KZ = Konzentrationslager** *(m.),* **–** *concentration camp*

4 **bald darauf** *soon thereafter*

1. Shortened and adapted from Stephan Reihnardt's "Carl von Ossietzky: Vom Idealismus getragene Leidenschaft," *Rowohlt Revue,* Frühjahr 1995, S. 7.

Jahre zuvor wurde Ossietzky Friedensnobelpreisträger. Diese
Preisverleihung repräsentierte eine schallende Ohrfeige für die
Machthaber des Dritten Reiches und eine Bestätigung für die aus
Deutschland vertriebenen politischen Flüchtlinge.

Ossietzky begann seine Karriere als Hilfsschreiber beim Ham-
burger Amtsgericht. In der „Demokratischen Vereinigung" fand
der junge—im Geist Kants, der Aufklärung und der 1848er erzo-
gene—Verfechter der Menschenrechte eine Organisation, die
seinen intellektuellen und politischen Absichten sehr nah stand. Sie
wollte in Deutschland eine Demokratie durchsetzen und sich für
den Abbau sozialer Spannungen und für weltweite Abrüstung
einsetzen.

1920 wurde Ossietzky Redakteur der „Berliner Volkszeitung".
Gemeinsam mit Kurt Tucholsky arbeitete er bei der „Weltbühne",
zunächst als Mitarbeiter und dann als Leitartikler, ab 1926 auch als
Herausgeber. Ein freier, undogmatischer, von nichts und niemandem
korrumpierbarer Geist, stritt Ossietzky als parteipolitisch unab-
hängiger Radikaldemokrat für die erste deutsche Republik. Er fand
Freunde aber auch viele Feinde inmitten einer sich mehr und mehr
dem Wahn des Nationalsozialismus hingebenden Gesellschaft.

---

5 **zuvor** *earlier*
6 **Preisverleihung** *(f.)* *award*
  schallen *to resound*
  Ohrfeige *(f.),* **-n** *slap in the face*
7 **Machthaber** *(pl.)* *dictatorial powers*
8 **vertreiben (vertrieb, vertrieben)** *to exile, banish*
9 **Hilfsschreiber** *(m.),* – *assistant recorder*
10 **Amtsgericht** *(n.)* *district court*
11 **1848er** *(pl.)* *revolutionaries of 1848*
12 **erziehen (erzog, erzogen)** *to train, educate*
  Verfechter *(m.),* – *defender*
13 **Absicht** *(f.),* **-en** *aim, intention*
14 **durch/setzen** *to push through, bring about*

15 **Abbau** *(m.)* *breaking down*
16 **sich ein/setzen für** *to support, champion*
18 **Weltbühne** *(f.),* **-n** *world stage*
19 **Leitartikler** *(m.),* – *lead-story writer*
21 **korrumpierbar (von)** *corruptible (by)*
  streiten (stritt, gestritten) *to fight/stuggle/argue*
22 **unabhängig** *independent*
23 **inmitten** *in the middle of, in the midst of*
24 **Wahn** *(m.)* *insanity*
  sich hingeben (gab ... hin, hingegeben; gibt ... hin) *to resign oneself to, submit, yield*

Ossietzkys vom Idealismus getragene Leidenschaft galt nicht nur der Vitalisierung der Weimarer Republik, sondern auch der Stärkung des republikanischen Geistes und des Selbstbewusstseins mündiger Bürger. Ossietzkys Leben und sein publizistisches Werk sind ein Dokument des aufrechten Ganges.

25 **galt (gelten)** *was dedicated to*
28 **mündiger Bürger** *of responsible citizens*

29 **des aufrechten Ganges** *of mankind (of* homo erectus)

KAPITEL 25

25.1 Additional Extended-Adjective Constructions

A. Extended-adjective constructions within extended-adjective constructions

When you come to the signal for a second extended-adjective construction, usually a preposition after a limiting adjective, set it off with brackets. Translate the second construction after the first one.

> Kürzlich fragte mich einer der (an das [schon seit Jahren baufällige] Balkongeländer gelehnten) Mieter, wann das Haus renoviert werden soll.
> *Recently one of the tenants leaning on the balcony railing, which has been dilapidated now for years, asked me when the building is to be renovated.*
> Die (während der Nacht mit dem [aus Frankreich kommenden] Zug eingetroffenen) Touristen fanden keine Unterkunft.
> *The tourists who arrived during the night on the train coming from France did not find any lodging.*

These constructions are relatively rare. Practice in recognizing signals, such as a preposition followed by an article followed by another preposition, should alert you that these units always must be isolated and translated only after identifying the sentence element that they are modifying.

B. Extended-adjective constructions with *zu* + present participle

This construction is quite common in extended-adjective constructions. **Zu** plus a present participle is best translated with *to be, can be, may be, must be* + past participle.

> die (zu schreibende) Aufgabe
> *the assignment to be written* (or: *the assignment that must be written*)
> die (für morgen vorzubereitende) Aufgabe
> *the assignment to be prepared for tomorrow*
> die (in unserem Museum zu sehenden) Kunstwerke
> *the works of art that can be seen in our museum* (or: *to be seen . . .*)

Note that in the case of present participles of verbs with separable prefixes, e.g., **vor/bereiten** *(to prepare),* **zu** becomes part of the participial adjective: **vorzubereitend**.

25.2 Participial Phrases

Similar to participles in extended-adjective constructions, participial phrases are constructions in which a present or past participle occurs with modifiers to indicate time, manner, or cause. The participial phrase always refers to the subject of the sentence in which it is found. Since they function similarly to dependent clauses, participial phrases are set off by commas.

Note when translating that the present or past participle is the last element of the German construction, but it is translated first in English.

A. Participial phrases indicating time

> Von seinem historischen Treffen mit dem deutschen Kanzler zurückkehrend, rief der Premierminister seine Berater zusammen.
> *Returning from his historic meeting with the German chancellor, the prime minister called his advisors together.*
> In „der neuen Welt" angekommen, versuchten die Vertriebenen ein neues Leben zu beginnen.[1]
> *Having arrived in "the new world," the exiles tried to begin a new life.*

B. Participial phrases indicating manner

> Eine Politik der Verbundenheit mit West Berlin fördernd, entschied sich Präsident Truman im Mai 1948 für die „Berliner Luftbrücke".
> *Promoting a policy of solidarity with West Berlin, President Truman decided in May 1948 for the "Berlin airlift."*
> Die Warnungen der Sowjets ignorierend, versorgten die Amerikaner Berlin durch die Luftbrücke mit Lebensmitteln.
> *Ignoring the warnings of the Soviets, the Americans provided Berlin with food via the airlift.*

---

1. Such statements in English must be conveyed using *having* + past participle to indicate that the descriptive action took place in the past: **in New York angekommen** = *having arrived in New York.*

C. Participial phrases indicating cause

> Von allen Frieden liebenden Nationen abgeschnitten, fand der Kriegsführer keine neuen Alliierten.
> *Cut off from all peace-loving nations, the warlord found no new allies.*
> Endlich unterschrieben, konnte der Vertrag für gültig gehalten werden.
> *Having finally been signed, the contract could be considered valid.*

25.3 *Ist (war)* + *zu* + Infinitive

This construction translates most often to the English, *can be / could be* + past participle. For example:

> Die Geschichte der Familie Mendelssohn **ist** von ihren Briefen und Tagebüchern sehr gut **zu verstehen**.
> *The history of the Mendelssohn family **can be understood** very well from their letters and journals.*
> Der Nachweis für diese Theorie **ist** in der Einleitung seines neuen Buches **zu finden**.
> *The evidence of this theory **can be found** in the preface of his new book.*
> Der Erfolg der jüngeren Generation **war** nicht mehr **aufzuhalten**.
> *The success of the younger generation **could** no longer **be checked**.*

Note that in verbs with separable prefixes, **zu** stands between the prefix and the verb, as in **auf*zu*halten**. Other possible translations are *is to be / was to be* + past participle or *must be / had to be* + past participle.

Keep in mind that the future tense of **sein** + **wohl** expresses probability in the present.

> Diese Art von Nachweisen **wird wohl** in verwandten Werken **zu finden sein**.
> *This type of proof **can probably be found** in related works.*
> Der Unfall bei dem Atomkraftwerk **wird wohl** auf menschliche Fehler **zurückzuführen sein**.
> *The accident at the atomic power plant **can probably be traced back** to human error.*

Context will help you determine whether the **sein** + **zu** + infinitive should be translated *can be* or *must/should be*. Situations in which a time limit is set generally translate *must/should be*.

> Dieses Buch ist bis Montag zu lesen.
> *This book must/should be read by Monday.*
> Der Bericht ist genau zu überprüfen, bevor er dem Ausschuss vorzulegen ist.
> *The report should/must be checked thoroughly before it can be presented to the committee.*

Grundwortschatz

ab/schneiden (schnitt ... ab, abgeschnitten)	to cut off	**im Wesentlichen**	essentially
		Kraftwerk *(n.)*, **-e**	power plant
		Kreis *(m.)*, **-e**	circle
auf/halten (hielt ... auf, aufgehalten; hält ... auf)	to stop, check, delay	**Lebensmittel** *(pl.)*	food, victuals
		Nachweis *(m.)*, **-e**	proof, detection, determination
brennen (brannte, gebrannt)	to burn	**Rohstoff** *(m.)*, **-e**	raw material
		sicher	certain, sure, safe
Droge *(f.)*, **-n**	drug	**Truppe** *(f.)*, **-n**	troop
ein/schließen (schloss ... ein, eingeschlossen)	to include	**umfangreich**	extensive
		versehen (versah, versehen; versieht)	to equip, provide
entfernen	to remove		
ernten	to harvest	**versorgen**	to provide, supply
fördern	to support, foster, promote	**vollenden**	to complete, end, finish
Gebrauchsgut *(n.)*, **⁼er**	consumer item	**vollständig**	complete, entire
Gehalt *(m)*, **-e**	content, amount	**Zweck** *(m.)*, **-e**	purpose
Himmelskörper *(m.)*, **–**	celestial body	**zwingen (zwang, gezwungen)**	to force, coerce

 Lösungen zu Übungssätzen auf **academic.cengage.com/german/korb**

Übungssätze

1. Es ist zu erwähnen, dass das Neue nicht immer das Beste ist.
2. Bereits 1507 im Wesentlichen vollendet, wurde Kopernikus' Studie „Über die Kreisbewegungen der Himmelskörper" erst 1543 veröffentlicht.

3. Von der Kirche gezwungen, musste Galileo Galilei im 17. Jahrhundert seine revolutionären Ideen widerrufen.
4. Der Fortschritt war, wie auf anderen Gebieten, auch hier nicht aufzuhalten.
5. Die bei dieser Methode zu beachtenden Vorsichtsmaßregeln sind unbedingt einzuhalten.
6. Das deutsche Luftschiff „Hindenburg", mit brennbarem Wasserstoff gefüllt, ist 1937 in Lakehurst in Flammen aufgegangen.
7. Auf Basis solcher unvollständigen Nachweise war eine erfolgreiche Untersuchung des damaligen Chefs des Staatssicherheitsdienstes nicht durchzuführen.
8. Ursprünglich nur für Versuchszwecke Anwendung findend, ist diese Droge heute in vielen Gebieten der Pharmazie vorzufinden.
9. Das Ernten dieser Drogen ist in derjenigen Vegetationsperiode vorzunehmen, in welcher die Pflanzen bzw. die zu erntenden Pflanzenteile den größten Gehalt an wirksamen Bestandteilen enthalten.
10. Von diesen neuen Methoden sind keine Wunder zu erwarten.
11. Die aus der gefährdeten Stadt entfernten Kunstschätze sind jetzt im neuen Museum ausgestellt.
12. In chronologischer Reihenfolge angelegt und zwar mit den Post-Impressionisten des späten 19. Jahrhunderts beginnend, befinden sich die Gemälde und Skulpturen im hinteren Gebäude des Museums.
13. Der noch zu diskutierende Beitrag von Professor Müller handelt über altägyptische Mythen.

3. **widerrufen (widerrief, widerrufen)** *to deny, recant*
5. **beachten** *to observe*
   Vorsichtsmaßregel (*f.*), **-n** *precautionary measure*
   unbedingt *absolute, absolutely*
   ein/halten (hielt ... ein, eingehalten; hält ... ein) *to observe, adhere to*
6. **brennbar** *combustible*
   Wasserstoff (*m.*) *hydrogen*
   auf/gehen (ging ... auf, ist aufgegangen) *to go up*
7. **Staatssicherheitsdienst** (*m.*) (*former GDR*) *secret police force*
8. **vor/finden (fand ... vor, vorgefunden)** *to find*
9. **vor/nehmen (nahm ... vor, vorgenommen; nimmt ... vor)** *to undertake, do*
   Bestandteil (*m.*), **-e** *component, constituent, ingredient*
11. **gefährden** *to endanger*
   Schatz (*m.*), **⁻e** *treasure*
   aus/stellen *to exhibit*
12. **Reihenfolge** (*f.*), **-n** *order, sequence*
   an/legen *to arrange, set up*
13. **ägyptisch** *Egyptian*

14. Eine umfangreiche Einleitung in Art, Wesen und Verständnis altägyptischer Mythen führt den Leser in die Vorstellungswelt der pharaonischen Ägypter ein und macht ihn mit den bedeutendsten Mythen dieser Zeit bekannt.

15. Jahrzehntelang durch die Mauer vom Westen abgeschnitten, war Berlin im Wesentlichen als Symbol der deutschen Teilung und Zentrum des „Kalten Krieges" anzusehen.

14. **Vorstellung** (f.), **-en** *imagination, idea*   14. **bekannt/machen** *to introduce*

Leitfragen zum Lesetext auf **academic.cengage.com/german/korb**

DIE „ROSINENBOMBER"

Die während des Zweiten Weltkrieges über Berlin fliegenden alliierten Bomber brachten der Stadt Tod und Verheerung. Nur drei Jahre später wieder nach Berlin fliegend, wurden amerikanische und britische Flugzeuge von der Bevölkerung West-Berlins mit Jubel begrüßt. Von Juni 1948 bis Mai 1949 brachten sie den West-Berlinern alles, was diese zum Lebensunterhalt brauchten. Durch die von den sowjetischen Truppen durchgeführte Blockade isoliert, mussten die 2,5 Millionen Einwohner vollständig durch die „Luftbrücke" versorgt werden. Dies schloss nicht nur Lebensmittel und Medikamente, sondern auch Kohle, Rohstoffe, Maschinenteile und Gebrauchsgüter aller Art mit ein. Da Berlin auch von der Stromversorgung abgeschnitten war, wurde sogar ein ganzes Kraftwerk eingeflogen, um die Stadt mit elektrischem Strom zu versorgen. Bei schlechtem Wetter landete alle zwei bis drei Minuten ein Flugzeug, bei gutem sogar öfter. Etwa 500 Großflugzeuge flogen über 200 000 Einsätze und beförderten eine Fracht von fast 1 500 000 Tonnen.

Die für ihren Humor und ihre Schlagfertigkeit bekannten Berliner, und besonders die Kinder, zu denen die Piloten kleine aus Betttüchern selbstgemachte Fallschirme mit daran hängenden

Title **Rosine** (f.), **-n** raisin
6 **Lebensunterhalt** (m.), **-e** subsistence
9 **Luftbrücke** (f.) air lift ("air bridge")
12 **Stromversorgung** (f.) electrical current supply

16 **Einsatz** (m.), **-̈e** mission
befördern to haul, transport
17 **Schlagfertigkeit** (f.) quick wit
19 **Betttuch** (n.), **-̈er** bed sheet
Fallschirm (m.), **-e** parachute

20 Süßigkeiten abwarfen, gaben den Flugzeugen den Spitznamen „Rosinenbomber." Dank der Luftbrücke überstanden die West-Berliner die elfmonatige Blockade. Diese sichtbare Verbundenheit mit Berlin als Vorposten westlicher Politik und Lebenskultur förderte eine während der fünfziger Jahre in ganz Westdeutschland immer

25 stärker werdende Bereitschaft zur Zusammenarbeit mit dem Westen.

20 **Spitzname** *(m., n-noun)*, **-n** *nickname*

23 **Vorposten** *(m.)*, – *outpost*

25 **Bereitschaft** *(f.)* *readiness, preparedness*

WIEDERHOLUNG 5

Buchbesprechung: *Die Familie Mendelssohn 1729 bis 1847. Nach Briefen und Tagebüchern.* Herausgegeben von Sebastian Hensel. Mit zeitgenössischen Abbildungen und einem Nachwort von Konrad Feilchenfeldt. Insel-Verlag, Frankurt, 1995 (Taschenbuch 2002). 935 S.

ÜBER DIE FAMILIE MENDELSSOHN[1]

A braham Mendelssohn, ein erfolgreicher Bankier, der sich nach seinem Schwager Mendelssohn Bartholdy nannte, soll einmal geseufzt haben: „Früher war ich der Sohn meines Vaters, jetzt bin ich der Vater meines Sohnes". Der Vater, das war der Philosoph Moses Mendelssohn, der Freund Lessings; der Sohn war der Komponist Felix Mendelssohn Bartholdy. Eine bemerkenswerte Familie, die Mendelssohns, die im geistigen und künstlerischen Leben zwischen Aufklärung und Romantik (und darüber hinaus) eine wichtige Rolle gespielt haben. Moses' Tochter Dorothea heiratete in zweiter Ehe Friedrich Schlegel; Felix' Schwester Fanny war ebenfalls Komponistin, ihr Werk wird erst in der Gegenwart angemessen gewürdigt.

Sebastian, Fannys einziger Sohn aus der Ehe mit dem Maler Wilhelm Hensel, fasste, ursprünglich nur für seine Kinder, Briefe und Aufzeichnungen der früheren Generationen in einer „Familien Biographie" zusammen, die bis zum Todesjahr Fannys und Felix' (beide starben im Abstand von einigen Monaten 1847) reicht; 1879 erschien sein Werk im Druck. Es war damals auch eine politische Stellungnahme: Hensel betont, schon Moses Mendelssohn

3 **zeitgenössisch** *contemporary*
6 **sich nennen nach (nannte, genannt)** *to be called by the name of*
12 **darüber hinaus** *beyond that*
15 **ebenfalls** *likewise*
   angemessen *appropriate, adequate*
16 **würdigen** *to appreciate, value*
19 **Aufzeichnungen** *(pl.)* *documents, papers*

20 **zusammen/fassen** (here:) *to collect, put together*
21 **Abstand** *(m.),* ⁻e *interval*
22 **im Druck erscheinen (erschien, ist erschienen)** *to appear in print*
23 **Stellungnahme** *(f.),* **-n** *opinion, point of view*

---

1. Slightly adapted from the original by Albert Gier, *Neue Zürcher Zeitung*.

habe die Klippe des „schalsten Kosmopolitismus" vermieden und den deutschen Standpunkt eingenommen; die Geschichte der folgenden Generationen ist die Geschichte einer geglückten Assimilation, die die Konversion zum protestantischen (Felix und Fanny) oder zum katholischen Christentum (Dorothea Schlegel und ihre Schwester Henriette, die als Erzieherin in Paris lebte) einschloss.

In diesem Buch ist sehr Unterschiedliches zu finden: Details aus dem alltäglichen Leben der Zeit, nicht nur in den zahlreichen Reisebriefen, sondern auch von Anekdoten über die Großen, etwa über Goethe, der den elfjährigen Felix Mendelssohn 1821 für zwei Wochen zu sich einlud; vor allem aber erfährt man den Reiz einer sehr kultivierten Gesellschaft, die in künstlerischer Aktivität und in der Diskussion über ästhetische Gegenstände ganz selbstverständlich zum Bewusstsein ihrer selbst gelangte.

Die festen Grundlagen bilden dabei bürgerliche Weltvorstellungen, die natürlich Patina angesetzt haben. So mahnt Abraham Mendelssohn Bartholdy seine Tochter Fanny, sich „ernster und emsiger zum einzigen Beruf eines Mädchens, zur Hausfrau, zu bilden", und ihr Sohn vermerkt dies mit offensichtlicher Zustimmung. Es mag uns empören, wie hier eine große musikalische Begabung an ihrer Entfaltung gehindert wurde; freilich zeigen diese Aufzeichnungen vor allem, dass die Lebensverhältnisse komplexer waren, als es der Hochmut der Nachgeborenen wahrhaben will.

24 **habe die Klippe ... vermieden ... und eingenommen** *managed to avoid the precipice (. . .) and adopted (. . .)*
„schalter Kosmopolitismus" *"hackneyed cosmopolitanism"*
26 **glücken** *to succeed*
29 **Erzieherin** *(f.),* **-nen** *governess*
32 **die Großen** *the great (names)*
etwa *take for example*
34 **Reiz** *(m.) charm, allurement, fascination*
37 **zum Bewusstsein ihrer selbst gelangen** *to arrive at an awareness of itself*
38 **bilden** *to establish, shape*
38 **dabei** *at the same time, in the process*
39 **Patina an/setzen** *to build up patina, wear thin*
40 **emsig** *diligently*
42 **vermerken** *to note*
44 **an ihrer Entfaltung** *in her development*
45 **Lebensverhältnisse** *(pl.) circumstances surrounding one's life*
46 **Hochmut** *(m.) pride, arrogance, haughtiness*
Nachgeborene *(pl.,* adj. as noun*) later generations*
wahrhaben wollen *to want to admit/accept/acknowledge*

Eine Neuausgabe dieses sympathischen Buchs war überfällig: Die letzte vollständige Ausgabe (aus der auch die Schwarzweiß-illustrationen übernommen worden sind) datiert von 1924. Die zwei Bände sind jetzt in einem starken Taschenbuch komprimiert; neben dem Nachwort und seiner Stammtafel wurden nützliche Register (Personen, musikalische und literarische Werke) hinzugefügt.

50

47	**sympathisch** *engaging*		52	**Register** *(n.), –* *index*
50	**komprimieren** *to compress*			**hinzu/fügen** *to add, supplement*
51	**Stammtafel** *(f.),* **-n** *family tree*			

KAPITEL 26

26.1 *Da(r)-* compounds

A. *Da(r)-* compounds used to replace a pronoun

Da(r)- compounds consist of **da(r)** plus one of the following prepositions: **an, auf, aus, bei, durch, für, gegen, hinter, in, mit, nach, neben, über, um, unter, von, vor, zu, zwischen**. The **-r-** is inserted when the preposition begins with a vowel.

Da(r)- generally replaces a personal or demonstrative pronoun which refers to a singular or plural inanimate object or an idea. Translate the preposition first, then **da(r)-** as *it, them, that, this, those, these.*

> In der Mitte des Zimmers steht ein Tisch, und **darauf** finden Sie die gesuchten Papiere.
> *In the middle of the room is a table, and on it you will find the papers you were looking for.*
> Hier sind die Bücher. **Darin** können Sie die Informationen finden, die Sie gesucht haben.
> *Here are the books. In them you can find the information you were looking for.*
> In der Ausstellung sind die Pinsel des Künstlers zu sehen. **Damit** hat er seine letzten Werke gemalt.
> *In the exhibit you can see the artist's brushes. He painted his last works with them.*

B. *Da(r)-* compounds anticipating clauses

Da(r)- compounds may also anticipate clauses (usually **dass**-clauses) or infinitive phrases that complete idiomatic combinations of verbs or nouns and prepositions. In some instances this type of **da(r)**-compound is best translated with a preposition + *the fact that* or a preposition + gerund (verb ending in *-ing*); at other times the **da(r)**-compound has a strictly functional purpose requiring no translation:

> Viele Leute glaubten nicht **daran**, dass die Erde rund ist.
> *Many people did not believe (in the fact) that the earth is round.*

Die Mannschaft des Schiffes klagte **darüber**, dass die Reise zu
lange dauerte.
*The ship's crew complained (about the fact) that the trip lasted
too long.*
In diesem Artikel ist der Autor **damit** beschäftigt, die Basilika in
Assisi zu beschreiben.
*In this article the author is busy describing the basilica in
Assisi.*
Der große Beitrag dieses Malers bestand **darin**, die perspektivi-
sche Malerei zu fördern.
*This painter's great contribution consisted in promoting perspec-
tive painting.*

Idiomatic prepositional phrases are discussed in **Kapitel 22**. A list of
common combinations is located on pages 214–215.

C. Idiomatic uses of *da(r)-* compounds

Note that the following **da(r)-** compounds have idiomatic meanings.

1. **dabei** *on the verge of; in the process* [just about]

   Er war gerade dabei, eine neue Entdeckung zu machen.
   He was just on the verge of making a new discovery.
   Seine festen Grundlagen bilden dabei bürgerliche
   Weltvorstellungen.
   *In the process, his firm fundamentals shape middle-class ideas of
   the world.*

2. **dagegen** *on the other hand, however*

   Im Süden sind die meisten Kirchen katholisch, im Norden
   dagegen protestantisch.
   *Most of the churches in the south are Catholic; in the north,
   however, they are Protestant.*

3. **daher** *therefore, for that reason*

   [handwritten: idiomatic word; not really a da-compound]

   Das Projekt kostet zu viel Geld, und daher wird es nicht
   ausgeführt.
   *The project costs too much money, and for that reason it won't
   be carried out.*

4. **damit**   *so that, in order that*

Die Musiker sollen etwas leiser spielen, damit die Solistin gehört werden kann.
The musicians should play somewhat more softly, so that the soloist can be heard.

5. **darauf**   *thereupon, after that*

Die zwei Diplomaten gaben sich die Hand, und gleich darauf unterschrieben sie den Vertrag.
The two diplomats shook hands and immediately after that signed the treaty.

6. **dazu**   *in addition*

Jeder hat dazu eine kurze Rede gehalten.
In addition, each of them gave a short speech.

26.2 *Wo(r)-* compounds

Wo(r)- compounds, consisting of **wo(r)** + preposition, are used as interrogatives.

Womit fangen wir an?
What do we begin with? (or: *With what ... ?*)
Wozu gebrauchen Sie dieses Instrument?
What do you use this instrument for? (or: *For what [purpose] ... ?*)
Worauf muss er warten?
What does he have to wait for? (or: *For what ... ?*)

Wo(r)- compounds may introduce relative clauses, in which case they replace a relative pronoun object of a preposition, e.g., **das Haus, *in dem ...* = das Haus, *worin ...*** . They mean *which* or *what*.

Das Haus, **worin** er lange gewohnt hatte, wurde zerstört.
The house in which he had lived a long time was destroyed.
Das Thema, **womit** wir uns heute beschäftigen, heißt ...
The topic with which we are dealing today is ...
Ich weiß nicht, **woran** er gedacht hat.
I don't know what he was thinking about.
Ich weiß auch nicht, **wovon** er gesprochen hat.
I also don't know what he talked about.

Only references to inanimate objects and ideas occur in **wo(r)-** compounds.

26.3 *Hier-* compounds

Hier- is combined similarly, but less often, with prepositions to form the following compounds: **hierauf, hieraus, hierbei, hierdurch, hierfür, hiergegen, hierin, hiermit, hiernach, hierüber, hierunter, hierzu.**

Translate the preposition first, then **hier** as *this*.

> **Hierauf** werden wir später zurückkommen.
> *We will come back to this later.*
> **Hierin** muss ich Ihnen recht geben.
> *I have to admit you are right in this (matter).*
> **Hiermit** beschließen wir unsere Unterhaltung.
> *With this we conclude our conversation.*
> **Hierzu** braucht man viel Zeit und Geld.
> *A lot of time and money are needed for this.*

26.4 Adverbs of Direction in Prepositional Phrases

The most frequent adverbs of direction that combine with prepositions are **hin** and **her**. **Hin** indicates direction away from the speaker and toward another point; **her** indicates direction toward the speaker. When the directional adverb comes at the end of the prepositional phrase, it emphasizes where the situation or action is headed to or coming from. In either case, **hin** and **her** are not translated into English.

> Die Feinde sind nach allen Richtungen hin geflohen.
> *The enemies fled in all directions.*
> Die Vögel sind vom Süden her gekommen.
> *The birds came from the south.*

Do not be distracted by **hin** or **her** or other "extra" adverbs of direction that do not translate. Some that occur fairly commonly are:

von ... aus *from*	Von diesem Standpunkt aus gesehen ... *Seen from this perspective ...*
um ... herum *around*	Sie sitzen um den Tisch herum. *They sit around the table.*
über ... hinaus *beyond*	Darüber hinaus möchte ich sagen ... *Furthermore, I'd like to say ...*
von ... her *from*	Sie kommt vom Flughafen her. *She's coming from the airport.*
zu ... her *to, toward*	Komm zu mir her! *Come to me!*

zu ... hin *to, toward*   Geh zu ihr hin! *Go to her!*
nach ... hin *to, toward*   Nach Bonn fahren wir nicht mehr hin.
  We're not going to Bonn anymore.

26.5 Introductory *es* Not the Real Subject

German speakers often use the word **es** as a placeholder to give a sentence the form of a normal statement. In these situations, **es** is a filler with no grammatical function, so the finite verb does not agree with it but with the true subject of the sentence. **Es** may be eliminated entirely or translated as *there*.

Es bestehen zwei Möglichkeiten.
  There are two possibilities. (or: *Two possibilities exist.*)
Es sind mehrere Möglichkeiten zu erwähnen.
  Several possibilities should be mentioned.
Es bildet sich eine Gruppe von Menschen auf der Straße.
  A group of people forms in the street.

Note that the expression **es gibt** *(there is, there are)* functions quite differently. Here, **es** is the true subject, so **gibt** is always singular. You must ascertain whether the object of the expression is singular or plural before translating.

Es gibt 25 Studenten in diesem Zimmer. Gestern gab es 50.
  There are 25 students in this room. Yesterday there were 50.
Es gibt nur eine Möglichkeit.
  There is only one possibility.

See **Kapitel 30** for further discussion the expression of **es gibt**.

26.6 Clauses without a Subject—*es* Implied

When an impersonal statement anticipates a **dass**- clause, the impersonal pronoun **es** is sometimes omitted. The translation nonetheless includes the impersonal *it*.

Bekannt ist, dass ...
  It is known that ...
In vielen Fällen kann gesagt werden, dass ...
  In many cases it can be said that ...
Dabei konnte festgestellt werden, dass ...
  In the process it could be determined that ...

Grundwortschatz

Abhandlung *(f.)*, **-en**	*treatise, discussion*	**derart**	*in such a way, to such an extent*
achten auf	*to pay attention to*		
allerdings	*certainly, to be sure, of course*	**Gefahr** *(f.)*, **-en**	*danger*
		gestalten	*to fashion, form*
Basilika *(f.)*, **Basiliken**	*basilica*	**hinauf**	*up, upward*
		hin/weisen auf (wies ... hin, hingewiesen)	*to refer to, point to*
beschäftigen	*to employ, occupy*		
beschäftigt sein mit	*to be busy with*	**malen**	*to paint*
sich beschäftigen mit	*to deal with, engage in*	**Malerei** *(f.)*	*painting*
		Regen *(m.)*	*rain*
beschließen (beschloss, beschlossen)	*to decide*	**Standpunkt** *(m.)*, **-e**	*position, standpoint, perspective*
betrachten	*to look at, to observe*	**Übung** *(f.)*, **-en**	*exercise, practice*
		Wahl *(f.)*, **-en**	*choice, vote*
Decke *(f.)*, **-n**	*ceiling*	**wählen**	*to choose, to vote*
		Wand *(f.)*, **ẏe**	*wall*

 Lösungen zu Übungssätzen auf **academic.cengage.com/german/korb**

Übungssätze

1. Bei Regenwetter kommt der Regenwurm aus dem Boden heraus, daher sein Name. Es gibt viele davon im Regenwald.
2. Betrachten wir das erste Beispiel. Daraus können wir klar ersehen, was das Problem ist.
3. Das Blut besteht aus dem Blutplasma und den darin verteilten Blutkörperchen.
4. Darüber hinaus sind noch einige andere Eigenschaften dieser Körperchen zu erwähnen.
5. Worauf basiert das deutsche Wahlsystem?–Jeder Deutsche, der das 18. Lebensjahr vollendet hat, ist wahlberechtigt.
6. Die große Gefahr in diesem Wahlkampf besteht darin, dass viele der Wahlberechtigten nicht zum Wählen hingehen, und dass die Radikalen dadurch gewählt werden.

1. **Regenwurm** *(m.)*, **ẏer** *earthworm* **heraus/kommen (kam ... heraus, ist herausgekommen)** *to come out*
2. **ersehen aus (ersah, ersehen; ersieht)** *to see from, to understand from*
3. **verteilen** *to distribute* **Blutkörperchen** *(n.)*, **–** *blood corpuscle*
5. **basieren auf** *to be based upon* **wahlberechtigt** *entitled to vote*

7. Von einem politischen Standpunkt aus kann so eine Handlung nicht gerechtfertigt werden.
8. 448 v. Chr. kam der Perserkrieg zu einem Ende. Gleich darauf beschäftigte sich Perikles mit dem Wiederaufbau der Akropolis.
9. Die Ruinen der Akropolis geben ein Bild davon, wie hoch entwickelt die Baukunst der Griechen vor 2500 Jahren war.
10. Die Erde wandert in einem Jahr ein Mal um die Sonne. Dadurch entstehen die vier Jahreszeiten.
11. Sonnenwärme kann zum Betrieb von Heizungsanlagen verwendet werden. Hiermit beschäftigen sich viele Forscher.
12. Naheliegend scheint, die Sonnenwärme auszunutzen, auch um Kälte zu erzeugen, z.B. zur Klimatisierung. In dem vorliegenden Beitrag werden hierzu geeignete Vorschläge gemacht.
13. In diesem Bericht wird mit Fakten, nicht mit Vorurteilen operiert.
14. Luftbilder werden von einem Satelliten aus gemacht. Dadurch sollen wir mehr über die uns noch nicht so gut bekannten Himmelskörper erfahren.
15. Es werden hier verschiedene Experimente zum ersten Mal beschrieben, womit allerdings nur ein Anfang gemacht wird.
16. Hierzu verwendet man den auf Seite 15 beschriebenen Apparat.
17. Eine Basilika ist ein länglicher, frühchristlicher Bau, dessen doppelte Säulengänge und Apsen (oder Altarnischen) dazu benutzt wurden, Gottesdienste aber auch Gerichtsverhandlungen abzuhalten.
18. Eine Suggestivfrage ist z.B. die folgende: „Ist nicht die Winkelsumme im Dreieck 180 Grad?" – Worauf der Schüler nur ja oder nein antworten kann, und wobei ihm nahegelegt wird, ja zu sagen.
19. Eine solche Frage weist darauf hin, dass der Lehrer nur feststellen möchte, ob der Schüler seine Aufgaben getan hat oder nicht.
20. Hiermit beschließen wir die heutigen Übungen.

7. **rechtfertigen** *to justify*
8. **v. Chr. = vor Christus** B.C.
   Perserkrieg (*m.*) *Persian war*
   Perikles *Pericles (495–429 B.C.)*
9. **Baukunst** (*f.*) *architecture*
11. **Heizungsanlage** (*f.*), **-n** *heating plant*
12. **naheliegend** *obvious, reasonable*
   aus/nutzen *to utilize*
   vorliegend *under consideration*
13. **Vorurteil** (*n.*), **-e** *prejudice*
14. **Luftbild** (*n.*), **-er** *aerial photo*
17. **länglich** *long*

17. **Säulengang** (*m.*), **⁻e** *colonnade*
   Apsis (*f.*), **Apsen** *apse*
   Altarnische (*f.*), **-n** *altar niche, altar recess*
   Gottesdienst (*m.*), **-e** *religious service*
   Gerichtsverhandlung (*f.*), **-en** *court procedure, trial*
   ab/halten (hielt ... ab, abgehalten; hält ... ab) *to hold, celebrate*
18. **Winkel** (*m.*), **–** *angle*
   nahe/legen *to suggest*

DIE KUNST UND DIE KIRCHE[1]

Die Künstler des frühen Mittelalters malten flächig und konzentrierten sich darauf, metaphysische Beziehungen darzustellen: Christus wurde größer gemalt als die Engel und diese wiederum größer als die Menschen. Gott, so glaubte dagegen der Franziskanermönch Roger Bacon, hatte die Welt so geschaffen, wie es die Lehrsätze der euklidischen Geometrie vorschrieben. Deshalb sollten sich die Künstler bei der Abbildung danach richten. Als einer der ersten förderte der Franziskaner die „perspektivische Malerei", wie sie später genannt wurde.

Für die Europäer begründete der neue Stil eine fundamental veränderte Weltsicht. Zunehmend verlagerte sich ihr Interesse von den metaphysischen auf die physischen Beziehungen. Christus und der Mensch wurden – in einem dreidimensionalen euklidischen Raum – alle im selben Maßstab dargestellt.

Die Basilika San Francesco in Assisi, mit deren Bau nicht lange nach Bacons Abhandlung begonnen wurde, war mit perspektivisch-illusionistischen Bildern ausgestattet. An den Wänden und Decken fanden sich Szenen aus dem Leben des heiligen Franziskus, wobei auf eine möglichst naturgetreue Dreidimensionalität geachtet wurde. Damit war die Basilika eine der ersten Kathedralen, die dazu bestimmt war, den Betrachter aus seiner eigenen Welt in die des heiligen Franziskus zu versetzen. Die Wirkung war derart eindrucksvoll, dass die Basilika, noch bevor sie ganz fertiggestellt war, zum meistbesuchten Gotteshaus der westlichen Christenheit wurde.

1 **flächig** *flat, two-dimensional*
2 **sich konzentrieren auf** *to concentrate on*
4 **wiederum** *in (his/her) turn, in return*
6 **Lehrsatz** *(m.),* ⁻e *theorem, doctrine*
 vor/schreiben (schrieb ... vor, vorgeschrieben) *to dictate, prescribe*
 deshalb *for that reason*

7 **sich richten nach** *to conform to*
11 **zu/nehmen (nahm ... zu, zugenommen; nimmt ... zu)** *to increase*
 sich verlagern von ... auf *to shift from to*
14 **Maßstab** *(m.)* *scale*
19 **naturgetreu** *true to nature*
20 **bestimmt sein zu** *to be destined to*
22 **versetzen** *to transplant*

1. *THE SCIENCES*, Nov./Dec. 1995.

27.1 Subjunctive

The verb tenses you learned about in earlier chapters were in the indicative mood, expressing facts and real conditions. In order to imply doubt or express wishes, improbability, and statements contrary to fact, German, like English, uses the subjunctive mood.

English has few commonly used subjunctive forms. Some of them are *if he knew, if he were, so be it, long live the king.* German, however, has a full conjugational system for the various tenses of the subjunctive mood.

German has two types of subjunctive. In this chapter you will learn about subjunctive II or the *general subjunctive,* whose forms are based on the past stem. Subjunctive I, also known as the *special subjunctive,* based on the infinitive stem of the verb, is discussed in detail in **Kapitel 28**.[1]

27.2 Subjunctive II

Subjunctive II is primarily used to express uncertainty, doubt, and hypothetical situations. It indicates imaginary situations and conjectures—situations that have not (yet) taken place or that might be or have been possible.

A. Present subjunctive II

The present subjunctive expresses conjectures in present as well as in future time.

> Wäre ich reich, so **hätte** ich viel Geld und **könnte** alles kaufen, was ich **wollte**.
> *If I were rich, then I would have a lot of money and could buy everything that I wanted.*

The forms are derived from the stem of the past indicative plus subjunctive endings. If an English subjunctive equivalent does not exist, translate with the simple past or *would* + infinitive.

---

1. We begin our discussion of the subjunctive with subjunctive II because in many instances you will need to recognize its forms when learning the uses of subjunctive I.

1. Weak verbs

   sagen *to say*

   ich sagte *(if) I said; I would say*
   er/sie/es sagte *(if) he/she/it said; he/she/it would say*
   wir sagten *(if) we said; we would say*
   sie/Sie sagten *(if) they/you said; they/you would say*

2. Strong verbs

   kommen *to come*

   ich käme *(if) I came; I would come*
   er/sie/es käme *(if) he/she/it came; he/she/it would come*
   wir kämen *(if) we came; we would come*
   sie/Sie kämen *(if) they/you came; they/you would come*

   laufen *to run*

   ich liefe *(if) I ran; I would run*
   er/sie/es liefe *(if) he/she/it ran; he/she/it would run*
   wir liefen *(if) we ran; we would run*
   sie/Sie liefen *(if) they/you ran; they/you would run*

   fahren *to drive*

   ich führe *(if) I drove; I would drive*
   er/sie/es führe *(if) he/she/it drove; he/she/it would drive*
   wir führen *(if) we drove; we would drive*
   sie/Sie führen *(if) they/you drove; they/you would drive*

   haben *to have*

   ich hätte *(if) I had; I would have*
   er/sie/es hätte *(if) he/she/it had; he/she/it would have*
   wir hätten *(if) we had; we would have*
   sie/Sie hätten *(if) they/you had; they/you would have*

   sein *to be*

   ich wäre *(if) I were; I would be*
   er/sie/es wäre *(if) he/she/it were; he/she/it would be*
   wir wären *(if) we were; we would be*
   sie/Sie wären *(if) they/you were; they/you would be*

Umlauts added to the stem vowel (**a, o, u**) of strong verbs are a key clue that you are dealing with the hypothetical subjunctive mood.

Forms of present subjunctive weak verbs, e.g., **sagte**, and plural strong verbs without an umlaut, e.g., **liefen**, are identical to past indicative forms. Pay close attention to context and recognizable subjunctive verbs occurring in the sentence; if one verb in a conditional sentence is in the subjunctive, the other verbs also must be in the subjunctive.

> Er spielte mehr Musik, wenn er mehr Zeit hätte.
> *He would play more music, if he had more time.*

Note this frequently used idiomatic form:

> es gäbe   *(if) there were; there would be*

B. Past subjunctive II

The past of subjunctive II consists of **hätte** or **wäre** + past participle and means *would have* + past participle.

> er hätte gesagt   *(if) he had said; he would have said*
> er wäre gekommen   *(if) he had come; he would have come*
> er hätte gehabt   *(if) he had had; he would have had*
> er wäre gewesen   *(if) he had been; he would have been*
> es hätte gegeben   *(if) there had been; there would have been*

Modal verbs and their dependent infinitives occur as double infinitives with **hätten** in the past subjunctive.

> ich hätte gehen sollen   *I should have gone*
> sie hätte schreiben können   *she could have written*

C. Future subjunctive II

The future subjunctive consists of the subjunctive of **werden** + infinitive. **Würde** in this construction, which occurs frequently with weak verbs, is equivalent to English *would.*

> ich würde sagen   *I would say; (if) I were to say*
> du würdest arbeiten   *you would work; (if) you were to work*
> er würde suchen   *he would seek; (if) he were to seek*
> wir würden lernen   *we would learn; (if) we were to learn*
> ihr würdet fragen   *you would ask; (if) you were to ask*
> sie/Sie würden antworten   *they/you would answer; (if) they/you*
>   *were to answer*

27.3 Suppositions of Conditions Contrary to Fact

Observe the similarity between the German and English constructions in expressing unreal conditions in **wenn**-clauses.

> Wenn ich das wüsste, ...
> > *If I knew that . . .*
> Wenn ich das gewusst hätte, ...
> > *If I had known that . . .*
> Wäre er gekommen, so ...
> > *If he had come, (then) . . . or Had he come, (then) . . .*
> Hätte er das gewusst, so ...
> > *If he had known that, (then) . . . or Had he known that,*
> > *(then) . . .*
> Käme er, so ...
> > *If he were coming, (then) . . . or If he came, (then) . . .*

Note that the subjunctives without auxiliaries express present conditions (the first and last examples), while past participles with the subjunctive of **haben** or **sein** express past conditions (the second, third, and fourth examples). In conditional clauses, **wenn** may be omitted in favor of a verb-first construction, followed by a result clause usually introduced by **dann** or **so** (the third, fourth, and fifth examples).

Study the following result clauses for the preceding examples.

> Wenn ich das wüsste, **würde ich es Ihnen sagen.**
> > *If I knew that, I would tell (it to) you.*
> Wenn ich das gewusst hätte, **dann wäre ich gekommen.**
> > *If I had known that, (then) I would have come.*
> Wäre er gekommen, **so hätten wir unseren Freund besucht.**
> > *If he had come, (then) we would have visited our friend.*
> Hätte er das gewusst, **so wäre er gekommen.**
> > *Had he known that, (then) he would have come.*
> Käme er, **so gingen wir ins Kino.**
> > *If he were coming, we would be going to the movies.*
> Gäbe es mehr Zeit, **so spielte er das Lied noch einmal.**
> > *If there were more time, he would play the song again.*

In translating a result clause with or without **würde**, use *would* with the present or past infinitive.

Hätte ich mehr Geld, so führe ich nach Deutschland.
*If I had more money, I **would** go to Germany.*
Wenn es regnete, würden wir zu Hause spielen.
*If it were to rain, we **would** play at home.*
Wenn ich nicht gekommen wäre, wäre mein Vater beleidigt
gewesen.
*If I hadn't come, my father **would** have been offended.*
Wenn Kolumbus Amerika nicht entdeckt hätte, so hätte es
jemand anders getan.
*If Columbus had not discovered America, someone else **would**
have done it.*

27.4 *Wenn-* Clauses or Result Clauses Standing Alone

Contrary-to-fact wishes may be expressed using subjunctive II in a
wenn-clause (with or without **wenn**). Such expressions often include
nur *(if only . . .)* or **doch** *(really)* to make the wish more emphatic.

Wenn ich das nur wüsste! (Wüsste ich das nur!)
If only I knew that!
Wenn nur ein Arzt hier wäre!
If only a doctor were here!
Hätte ich nur Zeit gehabt! (Wenn ich nur Zeit gehabt hätte!)
If only I had had time!
Das hätte ich doch nicht geglaubt.
I really would not have believed that.

27.5 *Als ob, als wenn (as if, as though)*

Als ob and **als wenn** are always followed by the subjunctive.

Er tat, als ob (wenn) er nichts gehört hätte.
He acted as though he had heard nothing.
Sie benahm sich, als ob sie seine Mutter wäre.
She acted as if she were his mother.
Die Bewohner bleiben auf der Insel, als ob kein Sturm käme.
*The inhabitants remain on the island, as if there weren't a storm
coming.*

Note the position of the finite verb when **wenn** or **ob** is omitted. It does
not stand at the end of the clause but directly follows **als**.

Die Bewohner bleiben auf der Insel, als käme kein Sturm.

The inhabitants remain on the island, as if there weren't a storm coming.

Es schien, als bewegte sich der Sturm in eine neue Richtung.

It seemed as though the storm were moving in a new direction.

Grundwortschatz

anders	*different, otherwise*	**richtig**	*right, correct*
Bewohner *(m.)*, **–;**	*inhabitant*	**Sieger** *(m.)*, **–;**	*victor*
Bewohnerin *(f.)*, **-nen**		**Siegerin** *(f.)*, **-nen**	
		Spielzeug *(n.)*, **-e**	*toy*
erreichen	*to reach, attain*	**Teilnahme** *(f.)*	*participation*
folgendermaßen	*as follows*	**(sich) überlegen**	*to think (about), ponder*
Größe *(f.)*, **-n**	*size, magnitude*	**voraus/sagen**	*to predict*
Insel *(f.)*, **-n**	*island*	**wahr**	*true*
Jahrestag *(m.)*, **-e**	*anniversary*	**Werkzeug** *(n.)*, **-e**	*tool*
Kenntnis *(f.)*, **-se**	*knowledge*	**Wirkung** *(f.)*, **-en**	*effect, consequence*
Mund *(m.)*, **⁻er**	*mouth*		
noch einmal	*once more, again*	**wohl**	*probably, likely*
noch immer	*still*		

 Lösungen zu Übungssätzen auf **academic.cengage.com/german/korb**

Übungssätze

1. Der Naturforscher Weisman fragte sich, was wohl aus Mozart geworden wäre, wenn er auf den Samoainseln geboren wäre.

2. Wäre ich eine Frau, so würde ich rebellieren gegen jeden Anspruch des Mannes, aus der Frau sein Spielzeug zu machen. (Mahatma Gandhi)

3. Sie: „Wenn Sie mein Mann wären, würde ich Ihnen Gift geben." Er: „Wenn Sie meine Frau wären, würde ich es nehmen."

4. Hätten wir gewusst, wie groß die Gefahr war, so wären wir vorsichtiger gewesen.

5. Das Resultat eines Kernwaffenkrieges wäre wohl ein Krieg ohne Sieger. Es gäbe nur Verlierer.

1. **Naturforscher** *(m.)*, **–** *scientist*
   was wohl *just what*
   Samoainseln *Samoa Islands*
2. **Anspruch** *(m.)*, **⁻e** *claim, demand*
3. **Gift** *(n.)*, **-e** *poison*
4. **vorsichtig** *cautious, careful*
5. **Kernwaffenkrieg** *(m.)*, **-e** *nuclear war*

6. Die verhältnismäßig schnelle Erschließung des Westens der USA wäre ohne die Einwanderer aus allen Ländern Europas nicht möglich gewesen.
7. Wäre uns dieses Verfahren bekannt gewesen, so hätten wir woh eine ganz andere Versuchsmethode angewandt.
8. Wenn Sie die nötigen mathematischen Kenntnisse gehabt hätten, hätten Sie diese Aufgabe ausführen können.
9. Die Bevölkerungszahlen der Insel sind viel schneller gestiegen, als man vor zehn Jahren hätte voraussagen können.
10. Viele Inselbewohner hätten einen höheren Lebensstandard erreicht, wenn es auf der Insel eine bessere Infrastruktur gegeben hätte.
11. Gewisse Menschen hätten Tugend, wenn sie Geld hätten. (Jean Paul)
12. Nehmen wir an, in einer Stadt von der Größe Chicagos würde ein neues Wohlfahrtssystem eingeführt werden. Was wären wohl die unmittelbaren Wirkungen?
13. Hätten die Menschen mehr Arbeit, dann würde der Lebensstandard bestimmt steigen.
14. Die Bewohner in dieser Gegend von Südamerika arbeiten noch immer mit ihren alten Werkzeugen, als hätten sie niemals von modernen Arbeitsmethoden gehört.
15. Was ist ein Name? Was uns Rose heißt,
    Wie es auch hieße, würde lieblich duften. (Shakespeare)
16. Wie oft hört man heute aus dem Munde eines älteren Studenten den Satz: „Wenn ich noch einmal anzufangen hätte, würde ich es anders machen."
17. Existierte die amerikanische Blockade gegen Kuba nicht, so würde sich die wirtschaftliche Lage der Insel schnell erholen.
18. Es wäre für die Kubaner wohl eine positive Entwicklung, wenn es bald zu dieser Situation eine Lösung gäbe.
19. Wenn es nur wahr wäre!

6. **verhältnismäßig** *relatively*
   Erschließung (*f.*), **-en** *opening, development*
   Einwanderer (*m.*), **–** *immigrant*
9. **Bevölkerungszahl** (*pl.*), **-en** *total population (statistics)*
12. **an/nehmen (nahm ... an, angenommen; nimmt ... an)** *to assume, accept*

12. **unmittelbar** *immediate, direct*
15. **wie es auch** *no matter how (what) it*
    lieblich *lovely, sweet*
    duften *to smell (sweet)*
17. **sich erholen** *to recover*
18. **bald** *soon*

DAS ATTENTAT ZU SARAJEWO

Am 28. Juni 1914 fielen zwei Schüsse in Sarajewo, die eine Weltkatastrophe auslösten. Der österreichische Thronfolger, Erzherzog Franz Ferdinand, und seine Gemahlin wurden von einem jungen serbischen Studenten durch zwei Schüsse getötet. Einer der Verschwörer, Vaso Cubrilovic, der an dem Attentat teilnahm, war später Geschichtsprofessor an der Belgrader Universität. Der 1914 erst siebzehnjährige, politisch engagierte Student wurde wegen Teilnahme an der Verschwörung zu sechzehn Jahren schweren Kerkers verurteilt. Wäre er damals älter gewesen, so wäre er gehängt worden.

In einem Interview für United Press am 40. Jahrestag des Attentates äußerte er sich folgendermaßen: „Wenn ich gewusst hätte, welche tragische Entwicklung die Weltgeschichte durch diesen Mord nehmen würde, hätte ich es mir bestimmt anders überlegt. Ich will nicht sagen, dass ich heute für Österreich eintreten würde, aber heute weiß ich, dass Meuchelmord nicht der richtige Weg ist, um politische Ziele, auch wenn sie richtig sind, zu erreichen."

Ohne den Mord von Franz Ferdinand wäre es wohl nicht zu der Julikrise von 1914 gekommen, Österreich-Ungarn hätte Serbien das große Ultimatum nicht gestellt. Und doch meinen die meisten Historiker, dass der Krieg zwischen den Großmächten wahrscheinlich so oder so ausgebrochen wäre. Auch wenn der Mord des Erzherzogs unterblieben wäre, hätte es höchstwahrscheinlich keine friedliche Lösung zu den Spannungen zwischen ihnen gegeben.

5

10

15

20

---

1 **Schuss** (*m.*), ⸚e   *shot*
  Schüsse fielen   *shots were fired*
3 **Erzherzog** (*m.*), -e   *archduke*
5 **Verschwörer** (*m.*), -n   *conspirator*
8 **Kerker** (*m.*), –   *prison*
  schwerer Kerker   *hard labor*
9 **verurteilen**   *to condemn*

14 **ein/treten für (trat ... ein, ist eingetreten; tritt ... ein)**   *to side with*
15 **Meuchelmord** (*m.*), -e   *assassination*
22 **unterbleiben (unterblieb, ist unterblieben)**   *not to take place*

28.1 Subjunctive I

In **Kapitel 27** you learned how subjunctive II expresses uncertainty, doubt, and hypothetical situations. These uses of the subjunctive, although they are much more structured in German, are not totally unlike the English conditional *would* and subjunctive. In **Kapitel 28**, you will learn the forms and uses of subjunctive I, which has no direct equivalent in English. Subjunctive I is used primarily to express indirect discourse, to report things that are *supposedly* true, or to report speech for which the writer does not take responsibility.

> Im Bericht steht, die Tagung sei wichtig, man habe sehr viel zu tun.
> *The report says the meeting is (supposed to be) important; (supposedly) they have a lot to do.*

Indirect discourse forms are used quite frequently in German to convey that the reporter does not take responsibility for what is being said. Doubt may or may not be involved. In English this is made clear by using words and expressions like *allegedly, according to . . . , apparently,* etc. In German these expressions are less necessary as a result of the subjunctive forms used for this purpose.

The forms of subjunctive I derive from the stem of the infinitive plus subjunctive endings. The most common forms found in formal writing are third-person singular forms, e.g., **man habe** or **die Tagung sei**. The **ich**-forms and plural **wir-** and **sie**-forms are generally identical to their indicative counterparts. As a result, they have limited use and are often replaced by subjunctive II. Note that the forms of **sein** are distinctive throughout.

A. Present tense subjunctive I

1. Weak and strong verbs

	sagen	**geben**	**kommen**	**fahren**	**werden**
ich	sage	gebe	komme	fahre	werde
du	sagest	gebest	kommest	fahrest	werdest
er/sie/es	sage	gebe	komme	fahre	werde
wir	sagen	geben	kommen	fahren	werden
ihr	saget	gebet	kommet	fahret	werdet
sie/Sie	sagen	geben	kommen	fahren	werden

2. **Haben** and **sein**

	haben	**sein**
ich	habe	sei
du	habest	sei(e)st
er/sie/es	habe	sei
wir	haben	seien
ihr	habet	seiet
sie/Sie	haben	seien

Your key to identifying the most frequently found forms is a *third-person singular* subject together with a verb ending in **-e**. (Otherwise you will see this verb ending only with **ich**.) The single exception to this rule is **sei**.

B. Past tense subjunctive I

Subjunctive I past tense consists of the subjunctive of **haben** (generally only with third-person singular forms) or **sein** (in singular and plural) plus the past participle.

er/sie/es habe gesagt
er/sie/es habe gegeben
er/sie/es habe gehabt
er/sie/es sei gekommen   sie seien gekommen
er/sie/es sei geworden   sie seien geworden
er/sie/es sei gewesen   sie seien gewesen

Note that **hätte** or **wäre** + past participle is used with conjugational forms where subjunctive I and indicative are identical. The context will alert you to the use of subjunctive II forms in indirect discourse.

> Im Bericht steht weiter, dass drei Repräsentanten die letzte Tagung verpasst hätten. Nur einer von ihnen habe eine legitime Ausrede. Die anderen seien einfach zu Hause geblieben.
> *The report said further that three of the representatives had missed the last meeting. Only one of them is said to have a legitimate excuse. (According to the report) the others simply stayed at home.*

C. Future subjunctive I

Subjunctive I future consists of the subjunctive of **werden** + infinitive, which translates as *would* + infinitive.

Er sagte, er werde kommen.   *He said he would come.*
Sie sagten, sie würden kommen.   *They said they would come.*
Wir sagten, wir würden kommen.   *We said we would come.*

28.2 Subjunctive I in Indirect Discourse

Indirect discourse is usually introduced by verbs of thinking, believing, or saying. A direct quotation is: **Er sagte: „Ein Sturm kommt."** *(He said, "A storm is brewing.")* In indirect discourse, a statement is reported: **Er sagte, dass ein Sturm komme.** *(He said that a storm was brewing.)*

By using the subjunctive, a German writer stresses his/her role in reporting information given by a third party. By using the subjunctive, the writer need not constantly remind the reader (by periodically saying: *"and the author further states"*) that the statements continue to be reported.

In indirect discourse, German usually uses subjunctive I when the forms are clearly different from their indicative counterparts. Otherwise, e.g., with plural subjects, subjunctive II may be used. There is *no time difference* between the two forms, and to a certain extent they are used interchangeably.

The relationship between the tense of the verb in the introductory statement and the tense of the reported speech plays a decisive role in translating the subjunctive form. In German, the tense of the original statement is reflected in the reported speech. In the English translation, however, the tense of the reported speech depends on the tense used in the introductory statement. Examine the translations of the following subjunctives.

Er sagt, dass er es wisse. Er sagt, dass sie es wüssten.
  He says that he knows it. He says that they know it.
Er sagte, dass er es wisse. Er sagte, dass sie es wüssten.
  He said that he knew it. He said that they knew it.
Er sagt, dass er es gewusst habe. Er sagt, dass sie es gewusst hätten.
  He says that he knew it. He says that they knew it.
Er sagte, dass er es gewusst habe. Er sagte, dass sie es gewusst hätten.
  He said that he had known it. He said that they had known it.

In general, when dealing with indirect discourse, translate the present subjunctive in the *same* tense used in the introductory verb (*says* and *said* in the first and second examples). Translate a past subjunctive in a tense *before* that of the introductory verb (as in the third and fourth examples).

Note in the following example that when **dass** is omitted, normal word order is used in the indirect statement. The finite verb is in the second position.

> Er sagte, er habe es gewusst.   *He said that he had known it.*

28.3 Indirect Questions

The subjunctive is used regularly in indirect questions, introduced by **ob** *(whether)* or by interrogatives such as **wer**, **wann**, **wo**, **womit**. Subjunctives in indirect questions are translated like those in indirect discourse.

> Sie fragte mich, ob die Preise gestiegen seien und was ich gekauft hätte.
> *She asked me whether the prices had risen and what I had bought.*
> Der Verkäufer fragte uns, wo unser Geld sei.
> *The salesman asked us where our money was.*
> Ich habe ihn gefragt, warum er das wissen wolle.
> *I asked him why he wanted to know that.*
> Er wollte wissen, womit wir bezahlen würden.
> *He wanted to know how we intended to pay.*

28.4 Other Uses of Subjunctive I

A. Indicating a wish or a command

Subjunctive I can be used in a main clause to express a wish that can be fulfilled or to express a request or command.

> Es möge wahr sein.   *May it be true!*
> Gott segne die Königin!   *God save the queen.*
> So sei es!   *So be it.*

See **Kapitel 29** for further examples of this construction.

B. Expressing information questionable to the writer

The subjunctive I can be used to indicate disbelief regarding information about a third party and unsatisfactory explanations. One possible translation in these situations is *supposedly* + verb.

Die Brücke ist nicht rechtzeitig vollendet worden, weil das Geld
dafür **gefehlt habe**.

*The bridge wasn't completed on time because the money for fin-
ishing it was (supposedly) lacking.*

Es habe zu viele Bauprojekte auf einmal **gegeben**.

*(Supposedly) There were too many building projects all at the
same time.*

Grundwortschatz

Anhänger *(m.)*, **–;**	*adherent, believer*	**Forderung** *(f.)*, **-en**	*demand, request*
Anhängerin		**sich fühlen**	*to feel*
(f.), **-nen**		**Furcht** *(f.)*	*fear*
an/nehmen	*to assume, accept*	**Geburt** *(f.)*, **-en**	*birth*
(nahm ... an,		**gehen (ging,**	*to go, walk*
angenommen;		**ist gegangen)**	
nimmt ... an)		**Wie geht es**	*How are you?*
aus/sprechen	*to voice, express,*	**Ihnen?**	
(sprach ... aus,	*pronounce*	**Es geht mir gut.**	*I am well (fine).*
ausgesprochen;		**inzwischen**	*meanwhile, in the*
spricht ... aus)			*meantime*
behaupten	*to maintain,*	**Lebewesen** *(n.)*, **–**	*living being,*
	assert, claim		*creature*
bereits	*already,*	**stammen**	*to come from,*
	as early as		*stem from*
berufstätig	*employed,*	**Tagung** *(f.)*, **-en**	*convention,*
	working		*meeting*
	in a job	**teil/nehmen**	*to take part,*
ehemalig	*former*	**(nahm ... teil,**	*participate*
Einheit *(f.)*	*unity, unit*	**teilgenommen;**	
erweitern	*to expand,*	**nimmt ... teil)**	
	broaden	**Tugend** *(f.)*, **-en**	*virtue*
Fähigkeit *(f.)*, **-en**	*talent, capacity,*	**üben**	*to practice*
	ability	**um ... willen**	*for the sake of . . .*
fordern	*to ask, demand,*	**zusammen/fassen**	*to summarize*
	claim		

Übungssätze

1. Bereits 1750 sprach B. Franklin die Vermutung aus, dass der Blitz elektrischer Natur sei.[1]
2. Von vielen Leuten wird angenommen, dass sich der Lebensstandard immer weiter verbessern werde.
3. Man möge es glauben oder nicht.
4. Eine junge Frau fragte eine Verkäuferin, was für ein Buch für ihren zehnjährigen Sohn am geeignetsten sei. Die Verkäuferin wollte wiederum wissen, wofür sich der Junge interessiere.
5. Viele Amerikaner glaubten lange Zeit, dass der Kauf Alaskas für 7,2 Million Dollar eine Dummheit gewesen sei.
6. Wer hätte gewusst, dass diese „tiefgefrorene Eiskiste", wie man Alaska damals nannte, eines Tages zu einem der beliebtesten Touristenziele des Landes werden sollte?
7. Mein Freund fragte mich, wie es mir gehe. Ich antwortete: „Danke, es geht mir gut", obwohl es nicht wahr war.
8. Von Sokrates stammt die Meinung, Tugend sei lehrbar; wenn jemand das sittlich Gute wirklich erkannt habe, so werde er es auch üben. Von dieser Meinung, die immer eine Lieblingsmeinung der Rationalisten gewesen ist, sind wir weit abgekommen.
9. Der Polizist fragte den Studenten, wo er am Sonntag gewesen sei und was er den ganzen Tag gemacht habe.
10. Vor hundert Jahren ließ die erste deutsche Ärztin durch ein Schild verkünden, dass es in Berlin von nun an eine Ärztin mit eigener Heilpraxis gebe.

1. **Vermutung** (*f.*), **-en** *idea, conjecture*
4. **wiederum** *in return, in (his/her) turn*
5. **Kauf** (*m.*), **⸚e** *purchase*
   Dummheit (*f.*), **-en** *folly*
6. **Eiskiste** (*f.*), **-n** *icebox*
8. **lehrbar** *teachable*
   sittlich *moral(ly)*
   Lieblingsmeinung (*f.*), **-en** *favorite idea*

8. **ab/kommen von (kam ... ab, ist abgekommen)** *to get away (from)*
9. **Polizist** (*m.*, *n-noun*), **-en** *policeman*
10. **Schild** (*n.*), **-er** *sign*
    verkünden *to announce*
    Heilpraxis, (*f.*), **Heilpraxen** *medical practice*

---

1. Note that, if the statement is still true or believed today, it normally is expressed in the present tense in English, even though the introductory verb is in the past tense.

11. Laut einem Fernsehbericht gebe es inzwischen rund 260 000 berufstätige Ärzte und Ärztinnen im Lande. Damit zähle die Bundesrepublik zu den medizinisch bestversorgten Ländern der Welt.

12. Der Direktor wollte wissen, wie viele Personen an der Tagung teilnehmen würden. Er hat wohl nicht damit gerechnet, dass so viele daran interessiert waren.

13. Anhänger des Glaubens an die Seelenwanderung meinen, dass der Mensch vor seiner Geburt in anderen Lebewesen (auch in Pflanzen und Tieren) verkörpert war und dass er auch nach dem Tode wieder in andere Körper, höhere oder niedere, eingehen müsse, je nachdem wie er als Mensch gelebt hat.

14. Immanuel Kant forderte, etwas Gutes solle man nicht um eines Lohnes willen oder aus Furcht vor Strafe tun, sondern allein darum, weil es gut ist.

15. Die Stadtplaner behaupten, es sei heute in Berlin einfach unmöglich ein Haus zu bauen, das die gleichen Qualitäten wie ein Altbau hat. Zur gleichen Zeit mache die übertriebene Forderung nach Licht, Luft und Sonne einen kompakten Städtebau unmöglich.

16. Um ihre Fähigkeiten in der deutschen Sprache so schnell wie möglich zu erweitern, nahm die junge Ausländerin im Wintersemester an noch einem Sprachkurs teil.

17. Die Sprachlehrerin behauptete, Deutsch sei leicht auszusprechen und je mehr man übe, desto leichter werde es, alles korrekt auszusprechen.

---

11. **laut** (+ *dative object*) *according to*
    Fernsehbericht (*m.*), **-e** *television report*
    zählen zu *to belong to, be classed with, be among*
    versorgen *to provide, take care of*
12. **rechnen mit** *to count on*
13. **Seelenwanderung** (*f.*), **-en** *transmigration of souls*
13. **verkörpert** *embodied*
    je nachdem *depending on*
14. **Lohn** (*m.*), **⸚e** *reward, pay*
    Strafe (*f.*), **-n** *punishment*
15. **Stadtplaner** (*m.*), **–** *city planner*
    Altbau (*m.*), **-ten** *old building, prewar building*
    übertreiben (**übertrieb, übertrieben**) *to exaggerate*

In Gesamt-Westdeutschland sind die Ostdeutschen Einwanderer

In seinem im Jahre 2003 geschriebenen Aufsatz „Ossis sind Türken"[1] betrachtet der Autor Toralf Staud ehemalige Ostdeutsche als Immigranten im Westdeutschland. Ihm nach seien Irritationen zwischen Ost- und Westdeutschen oft Konflikte zwischen Erwartungen einer Mehrheitsgesellschaft, dass man sich anpasse, und Forderungen der Zuwanderer, etwas von seiner Identität behalten zu dürfen. Mit der folgenden Szenebeschreibung aus Wolfgang Beckers 2003 Spielfilm *Good bye, Lenin!* behauptet Staud, dass ein „Ostler" aus einem völlig anderen Land stamme:

„ ... der Filmheld Alex [besucht] kurz vor den Wiedervereinigungsfeiern seinen in den Westen geflohenen Vater. Unerkannt betritt er die schmucke Villa in Wannsee, setzt sich zu seinen Halbgeschwistern vor den Fernseher und schaut das *Sandmännchen.* Die beiden Kinder fragen, wie er heiße, woher er komme. Alex antwortet: ‚Ich komme aus einem anderen Land.' Er sagt nicht, er sei aus der DDR. Er sagt nicht, er komme aus ‚der Zone'. Alex sagt auch nicht: ‚Ich bin einer eurer armen Brüder und Schwestern.' (Obwohl das in dieser Konstellation nicht einmal gelogen gewesen wäre und einen hübschen Szenenwitz abgegeben hätte.) Schon gar nicht sagt er, er sei Ostdeutscher. Alex sagt: Er komme aus einem

5	**Mehrheitsgesellschaft** *(f.)* *majority (of society)*	13	**das Sandmännchen** *sandman (cartoon figure)*
9	**Ostler** *(m.),* – *East German (slang)*	18	**lügen (log, gelogen)** *to lie, to fib*
11	**fliehen (floh, ist geflohen)** *to flee* **unerkannt** *unrecognized*	19	**einen hübschen Szenenwitz abgegeben hätte** *would have been a cute joke*
12	**schmuck** *pretty* **Wannsee** *southwestern Berlin suburb*	20	**schon gar nicht** *certainly not*

5

10

15

20

---

1. Excerpt from Toralf Staud's „Ossis sind Türken. 13 Jahre Einheit: In Gesamt-Westdeutschland sind die Ostdeutschen Einwanderer." © DIE ZEIT 02.10.2003 Nr.41. The entire text can be read at: http://www.zeit.de/2003/41/Einwanderer?page=all

völlig anderen Land als die beiden West-Berliner Kinder. Das ist die schlichte Wahrheit. Wäre sie in den vergangenen 13 Jahren beachtet worden, wäre der Prozess der Deutschen Einheit anders – und wahrscheinlich erfolgreicher – verlaufen."

25 „Seit dem Mauerfall und der Wiedervereinigung beherrschen Missverständnisse und wohlmeinende Lebenslügen über ‚die Ostdeutschen' Politik und Öffentlichkeit. ‚Der Westen' redete sich und den Ostlern ein, eigentlich sei man sich gar nicht so fremd. Nun wachse zusammen, was zusammengehöre. Alles werde gut.
30 Ganz schnell. Tatsächlich aber sind die Ostdeutschen – genau wie Alex sagt – aus einem völlig anderen Land gekommen."

22	**beachten** *to heed, pay attention to*	26	**Lebenslüge** *(f.)*, **-n** *self-delusion, grand delusion*
24	**verlaufen (verlief, ist verlaufen; verläuft)** *to take its course, turn out*	28	**ein/reden** *to persuade, convince*
26	**wohlmeinend** *well-meant*	30	**tatsächlich** *in fact, in reality*

KAPITEL 29

29.1 Special Uses of Subjunctive I

The uses of subjunctive I illustrated in **A** and **C** below occur mainly in relatively short independent clauses. The verb endings are **-e** for singular and **-en** for plural subjects, with the exception of **sei**. *May, let,* or *should* used with the verb will usually convey the meaning of these constructions.

A. Wishes and exhortations (see also *Kapitel 28*)

> Gott sei gelobt!
> *(Let/May) God be praised!*
> Er ruhe in Frieden!
> *May he rest in peace.*

B. Assumptions in scientific writing

> A sei ein Punkt auf der Linie X Y.
> *Let A be a point on the line X Y.*
> Die Linien A B und C D seien den Linien E F und G H parallel.
> *Let the lines A B and C D be parallel to lines E F and G H.*

C. Common phrases

> Es sei erwähnt, dass ...
> *Let it be mentioned that . . .* or: *It should be mentioned that . . .*
> Es sei darauf hingewiesen, dass ...
> *It should be pointed out that . . .*
> Es seien nur einige Beispiele erwähnt.
> *Let us (me) mention just a few examples.*
> Es sei denn, ...
> *Unless . . .*

D. Formulas and directions

Man at the beginning of a sentence and followed by a subjunctive I ending in **-e** is best translated into English with an imperative.

> Man nehme ein Pfund Butter, zwölf Eier, ...
> *Take a pound of butter, twelve eggs, . . .*
> Man denke an die Schwierigkeiten ...
> *Think of the difficulties . . .*

29.2 *Lassen*

The principal parts of **lassen** are infinitive: **lassen**; past: **ließ**; perfect: **gelassen**; present: **lässt**. This verb has a variety of uses, mostly in connection with other verbs.

A. *Lassen*

Lassen can be translated as *to let, allow, leave; to cause or arrange for something.*

> Man lässt die Suppe eine Stunde kochen.
>> *You let the soup cook for an hour.*
> Lassen Sie den Koch hinein!
>> *Let the cook enter (go in)!*
> Ich habe meinen Schlüssel im Auto stecken lassen.
>> *I left my key in the car.*
> Wir ließen den Wagen vor dem Haus stehen.
>> *We left the car standing in front of the house.*
> Ich muss das Auto reparieren lassen.
>> *I have to have the car repaired.* or: *I must get the car repaired.*

B. *Sich lassen* (without object)

This active construction, with an inanimate object or idea as a subject, acts as a substitute for the passive voice with **können** and means *can, could,* or *is able to.*

> Das lässt sich machen. (= Das kann gemacht werden.)
>> *That can be done.*
> Das ließ sich machen. (= Das konnte gemacht werden.)
>> *That could be done.*
> Das neue Computerprogramm lässt sich leicht lernen.
>> *The new computer program can be learned easily/is easy to learn.*
> Die ganze Arbeit ließ sich nicht an einem Nachmittag erledigen.
>> *The entire job could not be finished in one afternoon.*
> Das Verfahren hat sich wiederholen lassen.
>> *The process could be repeated. (We were able to repeat the process.)*

Note that a double infinitive is used with the perfect tenses of **lassen** (last example above).

C. *Sich lassen* (with object)

Used with an object, **sich lassen** means *to cause, have (something) done (by someone for oneself)*.

> Er lässt sich die Aufgabe erklären.
> *He is getting the assignment explained. (He is having the assignment explained.)*
> Unsere Lehrerin ließ uns die Hausaufgaben noch einmal machen.
> *Our teacher made us do the homework again.*
> Die Gemeinde hat sich eine neue Kirche bauen lassen.
> *The congregation had a new church built.*
> Der Pfarrer lässt sich auch ein Haus bauen.
> *The pastor is having a house built, as well.*

Grundwortschatz

auf/fallen	*to attract*	**klar**	*clear*
(fiel ... auf, ist	*attention,*	**loben**	*to praise*
aufgefallen;	*be noticeable,*	**malen**	*to paint*
fällt ... auf)	*be striking*	**Maler** *(m.)*, **-;**	*painter*
auf/richten	*to set up, erect*	**Malerin** *(f.)*,	
beachten	*pay attention to*	**-nen**	
Beziehung *(f.)*, **-en**	*relation,*	**nämlich**	*namely, that is*
	connection	**Schau** *(f.)*, **-en**	*show, exhibition*
einzelne	*individual,*	**Spur** *(f.)*, **-en**	*track, trace,*
	isolated		*footstep*
ergänzen	*to complete*	**ständig**	*constant*
etwa	*approximately*	**Thema** *(n.)*,	*topic, theme*
Fachmann *(m.)*,	*expert, specialist*	**Themen** *(pl.)*	
Fachfrau *(f.)*,		**Verfügung** *(f.)*, **-en**	*disposal, order*
Fachleute *(pl.)*		**zur Verfügung**	*to be available*
Flut *(f.)*, **-en**	*flood*	**stehen (stand,**	
gegenüber	*as compared to*	**gestanden)**	
Gruppe *(f.)*, **-n**	*group*	**veröffentlichen**	*to publish, release*
Haupt *(n.)*, **¨-er**	*head, chief*	**Zeichen** *(n.)*, **–**	*sign, symbol*
hell	*bright*	**Zeitalter** *(n.)*, **–**	*age, era*

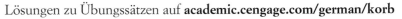

Übungssätze

1. Als Erstes sei auf die Schwierigkeiten dieser Arbeit hingewiesen.
2. Die Fläche des Materials sei der XZ-Ebene parallel und der positiven Y-Achse zugekehrt.
3. Lass uns sagen, das Problem sei damit gelöst.
4. Die zum ersten Mal im Jahre 1905 von Albert Einstein veröffentlichte Relativitätstheorie lässt sich folgendermaßen formulieren: $E = mc^2$.
5. Diese Theorie hat sich experimentell beweisen lassen.
6. Nur einzelne dieser Versuche seien hier genannt.
7. Seit etwa Mitte des zwanzigsten Jahrhunderts lebt der Mensch in einer Welt, die voller technischer Entwicklungen ist. Man denke nur an die Raketen im Weltraum, die moderne Medizin, die Automation in der Industrie usw.
8. Der Leser mache sich Folgendes klar: Wozu wir im Westen viele Jahrhunderte Zeit hatten, nämlich zur Entwicklung von Frühzeit- zum Atomzeitaltermenschen, mussten und müssen andere Länder in einem Menschenleben durchmachen.
9. Es sei noch erwähnt, dass ein Krieg zwischen den Großmächten fast nicht zu vermeiden war.
10. In den fünfzehn Jahren relativen Friedens nach den Perserkriegen hat Perikles die Akropolis bauen lassen.
11. In nur fünfzehn Jahren (447 bis 432 vor Christus) ließ sich der berühmte Parthenon, der Tempel der jungfräulichen Stadtgöttin Athene bauen.
12. Man vergleiche hierzu Abb. 221 bis 225 und beachte dabei besonders die Details.
13. Der Legende nach ließ Dionysios von Syrakus während der Mahlzeiten ein Schwert über dem Haupt des Damokles an einem Pferdehaar aufhängen. Wenn sich heute jemand in ständiger Gefahr befindet, so sagt man, dass über ihm das Damoklesschwert hänge.

2. **Fläche** (*f.*), **-n** *surface*
   Ebene (*f.*), **-n** *plane*
   zu/kehren *to turn to*
8. **durch/machen** *to experience, undergo*
10. **Perserkriege** (*pl.*) *Persian Wars (fought 490–448 B.C.)*

11. **jungfräulich** *virginal*
13. **Mahlzeit** (*f.*), **-en** *meal, repast*
    Schwert (*n.*), **-er** *sword*
    Pferdehaar (*n.*), **-e** *horsehair*
    auf/hängen *to suspend*

14. Sprichwörter lassen sich oft schwer in eine andere Sprache übersetzen. Man denke an ein Beispiel wie: „der langen Rede kurzer Sinn". Das bedeutet: „um es kurz zu machen".

15. Die wachsende Bedeutung des Nahen Osten als Wirtschaftspartner lässt das Interesse an dieser Region, ihrer Kultur und ihren Problemen schneller wachsen, als man es vor einigen Jahren hätte voraussagen können.

16. Die Verlage haben sich schnell auf diese Situation eingestellt, die Flut der Bücher zum Thema Naher Osten ist kaum noch zu überblicken.

17. Es sei schließlich darauf hingewiesen, dass dieses vor kurzem veröffentlichte Buch für Fachleute geschrieben ist.

18. Der Herr hat's gegeben, der Herr hat's genommen, der Name des Herrn sei gelobt. (Hiob 1, 21)

19. Die Künstler des „Neuen Realismus", dessen Bezeichnung aus dem 1961er Manifest des Kunstkritikers Pierre Restény stammte, verwendeten Stereotypen, die von den Massenmedien geprägt wurden.

20. Zusammen mit Jean Dubuffet gehört Cy Twombly einer Gruppe Malern an, in deren Werk der Einfluss von Graffiti sehr auffällt. Besonders in Twomblys Malerei gibt es auch klare Spuren vom Neuen Realismus.

14. **Sprichwort** (*n.*), **-̈er** *saying, proverb, maxim*
Sinn (*m.*) *meaning, sense*
„der langen Rede kurzer Sinn" *"to make a long story short"*
16. **sich ein/stellen auf** *to adjust to, adapt oneself to*

16. **überblicken** *to survey, view, look over*
17. **hin/weisen (wies ... hin, hingewiesen)** *to indicate, point out*
vor kurzem *a short time ago, quite recently*
19. **verwenden** *to utilize, use*

EIN MALER, DER SPUREN MALT: CY-TWOMBLY-RETROSPEKTIVE IN BERLIN[1]

Die Tournee, die das New Yorker Museum of Modern Art für Cy Twombly ausgerichtet hat, findet ihren Abschluss in Berlin. Die Gesellschaft der Freunde der Nationalgalerie ermöglichte die einzige Station der Retrospektive in Europa. Einige

5 wenige Bilder konnten nicht die Reise nach Berlin antreten, dafür kamen andere hinzu.

Die Berliner Nationalgalerie, die Mies van der Rohe entworfen hat, besitzt gegenüber dem New Yorker Museum ein Plus: austarierte, helle Räume, in die das Tageslicht immer wieder einbricht, so dass

10 Twomblys Faszination mit Weiß noch stärker auffällt. Dies ist nicht unwichtig für den amerikanischen Maler, der sich auf seiner Suche nach einem historischen und sentimentalen Arkadien an das Mittelmeer und an Italien gebunden hat.

Die Beziehungen Twomblys zu den fünfziger oder sechziger

15 Jahren fallen in der umfangreichen Schau auf. Das Überhandnehmen von Graffiti in den Bildern, das an die Aktivität der Affichisten im Umkreis des Nouveau Réalisme und an die Kompositionen des

2 **Abschluss** (*m.*), ⸚e *conclusion*
5 **einige wenige** *only a few*
  an/treten (trat ... an, angetreten; tritt ... an) *to set out on*
  dafür *for them, in place of them*
6 **hinzu/kommen (kam ... hinzu, ist hinzugekommen)** *to be added*
8 **aus/tarieren** *to balance out*
9 **ein/brechen (brach ... ein, ist eingebrochen; bricht ... ein)** *to enter, break into*

11 **Suche** (*f.*), **-n** *search*
12 **Arkadien** (*n.*) *Arcadia*
13 **Mittelmeer** (*n.*) *Mediterranean Sea*
  sich binden an (band, gebunden) *to feel compelled by*
15 **Überhandnehmen** (*n.*) *prevalence, spread*
  Affichist (*m., n-noun*), **-en** *poster artist*
17 **Nouveau Réalisme** *"new realism"*

---

1. Shortened from the original by Werner Spies, *Frankfurter Allgemeine Zeitung,* 1/96, pp. 12–13.

Italieners Rotella[2] denken lässt, fällt auf. Dieser Phase gehen Arbeiten voran, in denen sich ein autistischer Mitteilungsdrang ausdrückt. Die Überproduktion von Zeichen ohne Botschaft gehört ebenso zu dieser Übergangszeit wie die endlosen Kurven und Zirkelschläge, die die großen graugrundierten Bildformate füllen.

18 **an ... denken lässt** *makes one think of . . .*
19 **voran/gehen** (+ *dative*) (**ging ... voran, ist vorangegangen**) *to precede*
   Mitteilungsdrang (*m.*) *urge to communicate*
   sich ausdrücken *to be expressed*

20 **ebenso** *likewise, in the same way*
21 **Zirkelschlag** (*m.*), **⸚e** *circular stroke*
22 **graugrundiert** *having a gray background*
   Bildformat (*n.*), **-e** *picture format*

2. Mimmo Rotella, Italian painter who worked in the mid-1960s with compositions made from fragments of old posters and billboards.

KAPITEL 30

30.1 Idiomatic Meanings of Subjunctive Modals

For a review of modal verbs and the differences between objective and subjective meanings of modals, refer to **Kapitel 17**. Modals may be used in the general subjunctive to express imagined and hypothetical possibilities, uncertain or less-than-certain assumptions, astonishment, wishes, and politeness. Keeping in mind the following basic meanings will help you translate subjunctive modals frequently used in situations like those in the examples.

dürfte   *might (be), probably (is, was)*
könnte   *could, would (might) be able to*
möchte   *would like to*
möchte gern   *would like to*
müsste   *would have to, would be necessary*
sollte   *should*
wollte   *wish(ed)*

Here are some example sentences.

Das dürfte möglich sein.   *That might be possible.*
Das dürfte die Antwort gewesen sein.
   That might have been the answer. or: *That probably was the answer.*
Es könnte vorkommen, dass ...   *It could happen that . . .*
Wir möchten feststellen, ob ...   *We would like to determine if . . .*
Wir möchten gern mehr darüber hören.
   We would like to hear more about that.
Ich sollte heute Abend arbeiten, anstatt ins Theater zu gehen.
   I should be working this evening instead of going to the theater.
Ich wollte, diese Aufgabe wäre leichter.
   I wish this lesson were easier.

30.2 *Es* in Idiomatic Expressions

Es occurs quite regularly in idiomatic expressions. Examples of some of the most common expressions are given in the following pages, but there are many other idioms of this type. Whenever one of the common meanings of a verb does not make sense in your translation, check the idiomatic uses of the verb in your dictionary.

A. *Es gibt   (there is, there are)*

You know already from **Kapitel 4** and **Kapitel 26** that **es gibt** translates in the singular or plural depending on its object.

> Es gibt nur einen guten Grund dafür.
> *There is only one good reason for that.*
> Es gibt keine guten Gründe, so was zu sagen.
> *There aren't any good reasons to say such a thing.*

Note these other idiomatic usages:

> Was gibt's?   *What's the matter?*
> Was gibt's Neues?   *What's new?*
> Es gibt nichts.   *There's nothing at all.*
> Es gibt gar nichts Derartiges.   *There is nothing like that.*
> Es wird sich schon geben.   *It will occur in due course.*
> Es gibt viel zu tun.   *There's a lot to do / to be done.*

B. Weather Expressions

Es plus a verb denoting a weather condition, e.g., **es regnet**, is translated *it's raining*.

> –Regnet es oder schneit es? –Im Moment hagelt es.
> — *Is it raining or snowing?* — *Right now it's hailing.*
> Es stürmte richtig: es donnerte und blitzte.
> *It was really storming: it was thundering and lightning.*

C. *Gelingen (gelang, gelungen)   (to succeed, to be successful)*

Some verbs form idioms with **es** as an impersonal subject and a dative object. In English, however, the equivalent construction has a personal subject that derives from the dative object in the German expression.

> **es** gelingt **mir**   *I succeed, I am successful*
> **es** gelingt **ihm**   *he succeeds, he is successful*
> **es** gelang **uns**   *we succeeded, we were successful*
> **es** ist **ihnen** gelungen   *they succeeded, they were successful*

> Es gelang dem Forscher, eine gute Lösung zu finden.
> *The researcher succeeded in finding a good solution.*
> Ob es der Stadt gelingen wird, dieses Unternehmen bis nächstes
> Jahr zu vollenden, ist unsicher.
> *It is uncertain whether the city will succeed in completing this
> undertaking by next year.*

Do not confuse this verb with the weak verb **gelangen** (*to arrive, reach*).

> Der Brief ist an die falsche Adresse gelangt.
> *The letter arrived at the wrong address.*

D. *Es kommt auf ... an* (*it depends on, it's a question of*)

An/kommen means *to arrive*. Note the meaning of the idiomatic expression **es kommt auf** + object **an**.

> Es kommt auf die Umstände an.
> *It depends on the circumstances.*
> Es kommt nicht nur auf uns an.
> *It doesn't depend solely on us.*
> Es kommt darauf an, wie groß die Gefahr ist.
> *It is a question of how great the danger is.*
> Worauf kommt es denn an? Es kommt darauf an, ob ...
> *What does it depend on? It depends on whether . . .*

E. *Es handelt sich um* (*we are dealing with, it's a question of*)

To recognize this common use of the verb **handeln** (which has multiple meanings), look for **es**, **sich**, and **um** in the same clause.

> Es handelt sich noch einmal um ein geheimnisvolles Phänomen.
> *Once again it's a question of a mysterious phenomenon.*
> In dem früheren Buch handelte es sich um quantitative Ergebnisse.
> *In the earlier book we were dealing with quantitative results.* or:
> *The earlier book dealt with quantitative results.*
> In diesem Fall handelt es sich ganz klar darum, die verschiedenen Gesichtspunkte zu erkennen.
> *In this case it is clearly a question of recognizing the different points of view.*
> Wir wussten, dass es sich damals um mehrere unterschiedliche Meinungen gehandelt hatte.
> *We knew that we had been dealing with several distinct opinions at that time.*

Lösungen zu Übungssätzen auf **academic.cengage.com/german/korb**

Übungssätze

1. Als Alexander der Große auf einem seiner Eroberungszüge Diogenes sah, der trotz des Krieges seinen philosophischen Betrachtungen nachging, soll er gesagt haben: „Wenn ich nicht Alexander wäre, möchte ich wohl Diogenes sein."

2. Der erste Aufstieg mit einem Ballon gelang den Brüdern Montgolfier in Frankreich im Juni 1783.

3. Kurz danach gab es auch einen Flug mit einem neuartigen Wasserstoffballon, der aber landen musste, weil es so stark regnete.

1. **Eroberungszug** (*m.*), **⁻e** *war of conquest*
   trotz *in spite of*
   nach/gehen (ging ... nach, ist nachgegangen) *to pursue*

2. **Aufstieg** (*m.*), **-e** *ascent*
3. **Wasserstoffballon** (*m.*), **-s** *hydrogen balloon*

4. Ob der Versuch unternommen werden wird, hängt davon ab, wie viel Geld zur Verfügung stehen wird.
5. Dieses Experiment zu finanzieren, dürfte dem Staat zu kostspielig sein. Es kommt immer auf das Geld an.
6. Wir wissen, dass es sich hier um Fragen handelt, die dem Laien nicht absolut klar und verständlich sind.
7. Die in diesem Buch angewandte Terminologie dürfte nur einem exklusiven Kreis von Fachleuten verständlich sein.
8. Hier handelt es sich um eine der Fragen, auf die es weder deduktiv noch empirisch eine absolut sichere Antwort gibt.
9. Frau Prof. Dr. Warnke gelangte zu ihrer Lösung mit Hilfe der in Band I auf S. 327 angeführten Informationen.
10. Möchten Sie sich mit der Philosophie des 19. Jahrhunderts beschäftigen, so sollten Sie Arthur Schopenhauer nicht übersehen.
11. Wenn ein Gott diese Welt gemacht hat, so möchte ich nicht dieser Gott sein; ihr Jammer würde mir das Herz zerreißen. (Schopenhauer)
12. Impfungen gegen ansteckende Viruskrankheiten gibt es erst seit 1796, als es dem Forscher Edward Jenner gelang, eine Impfung gegen Pocken zu entdecken.
13. Würde es sich hier um eine Mischinfektion handeln, so müsste eine andere Methode angewandt werden.
14. Ich möchte kurz darauf hinweisen, dass es noch eine andere Möglichkeit gibt.
15. Dem Verfasser gelang es, einen guten Überblick über den gegenwärtigen Stand der Kafkaforschung zu vermitteln, und darüber hinaus Kafkas Briefe in ein ganz neues Licht zu stellen.
16. Damit dürfte er ein wichtiger Name in der vergleichenden Literaturwissenschaft werden.
17. Mir ist es leider nicht gelungen, meine Kenntnisse auf diesem Gebiet zu erweitern. Es hat zu viele neuartige Phänomene gegeben.

---

5. **kostspielig** *expensive*
6. **Laie** (*m., n-noun*), **-n** *layman; novice*
8. **sicher** *reliable, sure*
10. **übersehen** (**übersah, übersehen; übersieht**) *to overlook*
11. **Jammer** (*m.*) *misery*

11. **zerreißen** (**zerriss, zerrissen**) *to break, tear up*
12. **Impfung** (*f.*), **-en** *vaccination*
    an/stecken *to infect*
    Pocken (*pl.*) *smallpox*
13. **Mischinfektion** (*f.*), **-en** *mixed (compound) infection*

18. Man vermutet, dass die geheimnisvolle Unternehmung des Staats-sekretärs auch unmittelbar mit dem Friedensvertrag zusammen-hängt.
19. Es sollte möglich sein, das Angenehme mit dem Nützlichen zu verbinden.
20. Zwar weiß ich viel, doch möcht' ich alles wissen. (Goethes „Faust")

19. **angenehm** *pleasant*
    nützlich *practical, useful*

 Leitfragen zum Lesetext auf **academic.cengage.com/german/korb**

DER NAME BERLIN[1]

Im Jahre 1237 wurde Berlin das erste Mal in einer Urkunde erwähnt, und von daher errechnen wir das Alter der Stadt. Was der Name „Berlin" bedeutet, ist nicht bekannt. Lange Zeit glaubte man, es handle sich um eine slawische Siedlung und versuchte, das Wort „Berlin" aus slawischen Wörtern herzuleiten. Heute scheint sicher zu sein, dass Berlin eine germanische Siedlung war – die später mit slawischen „wasserwendischen" Siedlungen wie Köpenick zusam-menwuchs.

Viele Leute glauben, der Name dürfte mit dem Wappentier Berlins, dem Bären, zusammenhängen und könnte vielleicht ein kleines „Bärlein" bezeichnen, wie es eine Sage um den Markgrafen Albrecht glauben machen möchte: dieser habe auf der Bärenjagd

5

10

2	**errechnen** *to calculate*	11	**um** *surrounding*
4	**slawisch** *Slavic*		**Markgraf** (*m., n-noun*), **-en** *margrave (Prussian royalty)*
5	**her/leiten** *to derive*		**Markgraf Albrecht** (*1100–1170*)
7	**wasserwendisch** *waterfront*	12	**glauben machen** *to make one believe*
	Köpenick (*Berlin city district*)		
9	**Wappentier** (*n.*), **-e** *heraldic animal*		

---

1. Excerpted and modified from *Städteporträt: Berlin,* Ingeborg Braa/Sigrid Kumm, Inter Nationes, 1992.

eine Höhle mit einem jungen Bären gefunden und an dieser Stelle die Stadt gegründet. Aber wenn „Bär" eine Sachbezeichnung ist,

15 von der der Name abgeleitet wurde, dann bezeichnet dieses Wort nicht das Tier, sondern nach einem alten Wörterbuch „einen starken, aus Steinen gemauerten Querdamm".

Werfen wir einen kurzen Blick auf das Wappen der Stadt, worauf man heute noch beides findet: Bär und Mauer.

20 Das von 1338 bis 1448 gebräuchliche Siegel zeigt das Wappentier Berlins, den Bären, in lockerer Verbindung mit dem Adler Brandenburgs oder Cöllns. Das erstmals 1460 nachgewiesene, bis 1700 benutzte Siegel zeigt den landesherrlichen Adler, der mit seinen Krallen auf dem Berliner Bären reitet. Ob diese Darstellung die Unterwerfung

25 Berlins unter die kurfürstliche Gewalt symbolisieren sollte, ist umstritten, scheint aber möglich.

Nach der Revolution von 1918 wurde aus der Monarchie eine Republik, und die Stadt Berlin erhielt ein neues Wappen: Der Bär steht jetzt aufrecht und trägt eine rote Mauer-Krone. Westberlin

30 erhielt 1954 ein etwas verändertes Wappen: Darauf ist der Bär der gleiche geblieben, doch seine Krone ist golden und zeigt Stadtmauern und Blätter.

Neuere Untersuchungen legen den Schluss nahe, dass „Berlin" wohl eher von einem Personennamen gebildet wurde, vielleicht von

35 „Berlichingen" oder verkürzt „Berlingen". Jedenfalls soll der Name der Stadt schwäbischen Ursprungs sein, wie anlässlich der 750-Jahrfeier eine Abhandlung von Hans Scholz im Berliner „Tagesspiegel" ausführlich begründete.

14	**Sachbezeichnung** (*f.*) *technical term*	24	**Unterwerfung** (*f.*), **-en** *submission*
15	**ab/leiten** *to derive*	25	**kurfürstlich** *electoral*
17	**aus Steinen gemauert** *built of stone*		**Gewalt** (*f.*) *power, dominion, might*
	Querdamm (*m.*) *lateral embankment*	29	**aufrecht/stehen (stand ... aufrecht; aufrechtgestanden)** *to stand erect*
20	**gebräuchlich** *common, customary*	32	**Blatt** (*n.*), **¨-er** *leaf*
21	**locker** *loose*	33	**nahe/legen** *to suggest*
22	**Brandenburg** (*German state*)	36	**schwäbisch** *Swabian*
	Cölln (*Berlin city district*)		**anlässlich** *on the occasion of*
23	**landesherrlich** *sovereign*	37	**„Tagesspiegel"** (*a daily newspaper in Berlin*)

ENTGRENZUNG: GEDANKEN ZU EINER TRANSNATIONALEN LITERATUR[1]

VOM NATIONALEN ...

In diesem Lesebuch wird alles andere als das Einheimische besungen, hier kommt das Andere zum Zug, das Fremde, das Nichtdazugehörige. Bestimmendes Auswahlkriterium war sozusagen die Negation des Schweizerischen. Eingang in diese Anthologie fand nur, wer nicht zur hiesigen Mehrheitskultur gehört, wer nicht aus Westeuropa oder den USA kommt. Kurz: Die Andern – ein Kameruner, eine Kolumbianerin, ein Chilene, ein Türke, ein Libyer, eine Albanierin. Es war die Herkunft, die über die Aufnahme in dieses Buch entschied. Einzige Bedingung war, dass die Autorinnen und Autoren in der Schweiz wohnen, dass sie sich innerhalb der festen Grenzen aufhalten, die das helvetische Territorium ausmachen, dass sie eine Aufenthaltsbewilligung haben für dieses Fleckchen Erde, das die nationale Identität festlegt.

Ein Taha Khalil, eine Radka Donnell oder ein Daniel Perez stehen für die andere Schweizer Literatur. Die exotische. Die fremdsprachige. Die fremdartige. Mit „Eine andere Sehnsucht", „am Walensee" oder „Don Juans Abgang" schreiben sie das Kontrastprogramm zur nationalen Literatur. Ob es eine einheimische Litera-

Title **Entgrenzung** (*f.*) *"redefining a boundary"*	12 **Aufenthaltsbewilligung** (*f.*), **-en** *residency permit*
2 **zum Zug kommen** *to get a chance*	13 **Fleckchen** (*n.*) *speck*
3 **nichtdazugehörig** *not belonging (to)*	14 **Taha Khalil, Radka Donnell, Daniel Perez** (*authors in the anthology*)
bestimmend *decisive*	
4 **Eingang** (*m.*), **⸚e** *entry, acceptance*	17 **Walensee** (*lake in northeastern Switzerland*)
9 **Aufnahme** (*f.*) *inclusion*	**Abgang** (*m.*), **⸚e** *departure*
11 **sich auf/halten** *to spend time*	
helvetisch *Swiss*	

---

1. Shortened from original by Ina Boesch, in *Küsse und eilige Rosen: Die fremdsprachige Schweizer Literatur: Ein Lesebuch,* herausgegeben von Chudi Bürgi, Anita Müller und Christine Tresch, mit Fotos von Dominique Meienberg, 1998.

turspezies überhaupt gibt, müsste eine Loetschersche Kommission
20 eruieren; ob sie jedoch fündig würde oder nicht, spielt eigentlich
keine Rolle, denn unbestritten wurde bei der Auswahl zu diesem
Reader an eine nationale Literatur gedacht. Sozusagen als Vexierbild,
in dem das Andere plötzlich aufscheint. Und dieses Andere, das
heisst diese anderen Literaturen gehören nur zusammen, weil sie
25 nicht dazugehören. Denn was verbindet die ausgewählten Autorinnen und Autoren ausser der Tatsache, dass sie als fremd wahrgenommen werden und sich, mag sein, auch fremd fühlen?

Dennoch gilt: „Sozial zu existieren heisst immer auch wahrgenommen zu werden, und zwar als distinkt wahrgenommen zu
30 werden."[2] Also ist eine solche Selektion mittels Unterscheidung gar
nicht so abartig – sie verschafft Aufmerksamkeit. Und sie folgt einer
langen Tradition von Lesebüchern, die auf Unterscheidungsmerk-
malen basieren, der Unterscheidung zwischen den Geschlechtern,
zwischen Religionen, Kulturen und Sprachen. Welches jeweils zum
35 Zug kommt, hat unter anderem auch mit dem Zeitgeist zu tun.
Denken wir an Bücher aus den siebziger Jahren, an Reader wie
„Afrikanische Frauen" oder „Asiatische Frauen", als die Kategorie
Frau als das Andere entdeckt und definiert wurde. Erinnern wir uns
an Bücher mit Texten von AutorInnen aus Afrika, Asien und
40 Lateinamerika, als die Kategorie Dritte Welt als das Andere gefunden und benannt wurde. Vergessen wir nicht die Literatur von
Minderheiten oder von Gastarbeitern, sie machten in den sechziger
Jahren das Andere aus. Heute, im Zeitalter der Globalisierung,
besinnt man sich, so paradox das tönt, eher wieder auf das Eigene,

19 **überhaupt** *altogether, anyway*
Loetschersche Kommission *a literature prize commission (after the Swiss author Hugo Loetscher)*
20 **eruieren** *to determine*
jedoch *however, still though*
fündig werden *to get lucky, hit paydirt*
22 **Vexierbild** *(n.)* *picture puzzle*
23 **auf/scheinen** *to appear, become evident*
29 **wahr/nehmen (nahm ... wahr, wahrgenommen; nimmt ... wahr)** *to perceive*

30 **mittels** *by means of*
31 **abartig** *abnormal*
Aufmerksamkeit verschaffen *to draw attention*
33 **Merkmal** *(n.)*, **–** *characteristic*
39 **AutorInnen** *(pl.)* *male* and *female authors*
42 **Gastarbeiter** *(m.)*, **–** *immigrant workers* (literally: *"guest workers"*)
44 **sich besinnen auf** *to think about*
das Eigene *that which is proper to the self*
eher wieder *once again likely*

2. Singer, Mona. "Fremd-Wahrnehmung, Unterscheidungsweisen und Definitionsmacht"
In: *Die Philosophin,* Frühling 1997.

also steht das Nationale beziehungsweise die Unterscheidung in SchweizerInnen und AusländerInnen im Vordergrund.

… ZUM TRANSNATIONALEN

Ich gestehe, ich wünschte mir heute, am Ende dieses Jahrtausends und hundertfünfzig Jahre nach der Gründung des schweizerischen Bundesstaats, etwas anderes. Nämlich ein Buch mit einer Auswahl von AutorInnen unabhängig des Kriteriums Herkunft, ein Lesebuch mit Texten von SchriftstellerInnen, die wie in der Philosophie der Aufklärung in erster Linie Mitglieder der Menschheit und damit WeltbürgerInnen sind und nicht Mitglieder einer Nation. Nur: Bis es zu diesem Paradigmenwechsel und zu einem Weltstaat kommt, in dem eine universale Freizügigkeit herrscht,[3] ist diese Auswahl legitim und aus der Perspektive des Zentrums auch ganz eigennützig, denn „unter Grenzen leiden zwar am meisten diejenigen, die ausgegrenzt werden, aber die grössten Verluste erleiden letztlich wohl jene, die sich abgrenzen, sich nicht öffnen für das, was von aussen kommt".[4] Also möchte ich zu meinem Egoismus stehen und drei Wünsche formulieren: Für die Schweiz erwarte ich von den ausgegrenzten Literaturschaffenden, die innerhalb der Schweizer Grenzen leben und arbeiten, einen fremden Blick auf unser Land, Erkenntnisse, die uns im harmlosesten Fall bereichern und im besten Fall aufrütteln. Spiegelung und Widerspruch. Für

45 **also** *thus*	56 **Freizügigkeit** *(f.) freedom of*
beziehungsweise *alternatively*	*movement*
46 **im Vordergrund stehen** *to be of*	58 **eigennützig** *selfish*
immediate importance, be in the	59 **aus/grenzen** *to exclude, ignore*
foreground	60 **sich ab/grenzen von** *to distance*
50 **nämlich** *namely, that is (to say)*	*(separate) oneself from*
55 **Wechsel** *(m.), – change, shift*	66 **auf/rütteln** *to shake up, wake up*

3. Fisch, Hansjörg. „Der letzte Hort der Diskriminierung." In: NZZ vom 13./14. Dezember 1997.
4. Ackermann, Irmgard. Vorwort zu *Über Grenzen. Berichte, Erzählungen, Gedichte von Ausländern*. München, 1987.

die nationale Literatur, sofern es sie denn gibt, erhoffe ich von den Rändern her neue Impulse, Texte, die den Slogan „The empire writes back" zu einem Markenzeichen von Erneuerung und Dynamik machen. Für die Sprache schliesslich wünsche ich mir Offenheit und Lebendigkeit.

An der Peripherie wird also geortet, was dereinst eine transnationale Literatur sein könnte, eine Literatur, die universelle menschliche Erfahrungen vermittelt, Grenzübergänge zwischen den Kulturen und den Geschlechtern schafft und die Begrenzungen der Sprache auslotet. Eine entgrenzte Literatur.

67 **erhoffen** *to hope for, expect*
68 **von den Rändern her** *(coming) from the extremities*
69 **Markenzeichen** (*n.*) *trademark*
72 **geortet werden** *to be located*
   dereinst *some day, one day*

74 **vermitteln** *to mediate, bring about*
75 **Begrenzung** (*f.*), **-en** *boundary, limitation*
76 **aus/loten** *to explore in detail*

APPENDICES, VOCABULARY, INDEX

APPENDIX A

The German Case System

German uses a signal called *case* to identify the function of nouns and pronouns within a sentence. The ending of the pronoun and the definite or indefinite article indicate case. Note that the boldfaced endings for each gender follow a pattern: As long as they are put in their proper

Gender	Pronoun/Article	Nominative
		Subject/Predicate
Masculine	pronoun definite article indefinite article negation/possessive relative pronoun	**er** **der** Mann ein Mann kein Mann/ mein Mann **, der ...**
Feminine	pronoun definite article indefinite article negation/possessive relative pronoun	**sie** **die** Frau ein**e** Frau kein**e** Frau/ mein**e** Frau **, die ...**
Neuter	pronoun definite article indefinite article negation/possessive relative pronoun	**es** **das** Kind ein Kind kein Kind/ mein Kind **, das ...**
Plural	pronoun definite article negation/possessive relative pronoun	**sie** **die** Männer/ Frauen/Kinder kein**e**/mein**e** **, die ...**
Interrogative		**Wer?**

cases, the nouns and pronouns in the sentence can be moved around in a variety of ways that effect emphasis and style without changing the essential meaning of the sentence. The word order system is outlined in the Sentence Formula following the case system table.

Accusative	Dative	Genitive
Direct Object/ Object of Accusative Preposition	Indirect Object/ Object of Dative Preposition or Verb	Possession/ Object of Genitive Preposition
ihn **den** Mann einen Mann keinen Mann/ meinen Mann , **den** ...	**ihm** **dem** Mann einem Mann keinem Mann/ meinem Mann , **dem** ...	**(seinet-)** **des** Mann(e)s eines Mannes keines Mannes/ meines Mannes , **dessen** ...
sie **die** Frau eine Frau keine Frau/ meine Frau , **die** ...	**ihr** **der** Frau einer Frau keiner Frau/ meiner Frau , **der** ...	**(ihret-)** **der** Frau einer Frau keiner Frau/ meiner Frau , **deren** ...
es **das** Kind ein Kind kein Kind/mein Kind , **das** ...	**ihm** **dem** Kind einem Kind keinem Kind/ meinem Kind , **dem** ...	**(seinet-)** **des** Kind(e)s eines Kindes keines Kindes/ meines Kindes , **dessen** ...
sie **die** Männer/ Frauen/Kinder keine/meine , **die** ...	**ihnen** **den** Männern/ Frauen/Kindern keinen + **n**/ meinen + **n** , **denen** ...	**der** Männer/ Frauen/Kinder keiner/meiner , **deren** ...
Wen?	**Wem?**	**Wessen?**

Note that the conjugated verb (V1) is always in the second position in a German statement. The first position does not necessarily have to be and often is not the subject, but rather new, important information that is answering a specific question. The other primary syntactical elements making up a German statement follow this formulaic pattern:

Sentence Formula: X V1 n a d N Adverbs D A V2
time/manner/place
(wann/wie/wo)

any item in the formula can be **X** in first position

V1 = the conjugated main verb
n = nominative pronoun (subject)
a = accusative pronoun (direct object)
d = dative pronoun (indirect object)
N = Nominative Noun (Subject)
Adverbs of time/manner/place
D = Dative Noun (Indirect Object)
A = Accusative Noun (Direct Object)
V2 = final component of compound verb (prefixes, participles, infinitive)

German case and word order allow at least two variations whereas the English is basically limited to expressing actions in syntax from left to right:

German	English translation
Der Mann küsst die Frau. Er küsst sie.	*The man kisses the woman. He kisses her.*
Die Frau küsst der Mann. Sie küsst er.	*The man kisses the woman. He kisses her.*
Die Frau küsst den Mann. Sie küsst ihn.	*The woman kisses the man. She kisses him.*
Den Mann küsst die Frau. Ihn küsst sie.	*The woman kisses the man. She kisses him.*
Der Mann bringt der Frau das Kind. Er bringt es ihr.	*The man brings the child to the woman. He brings it to her.*
Der Frau bringt der Mann das Kind. Ihr bringt er es.	*The man brings the child to the woman. He brings it to her.*
Das Kind bringt der Mann der Frau. Es bringt er ihr.	*The man brings the child to the woman. He brings it to her.*

Note in the following examples a) that V1 is the conjugated verb agreeing in number with the subject whereas V2 (always in final position of the clause) completes a compound verb, and b) that the order of the adverbs and objects as well the order of the objects themselves depends on whether the objects are nouns or pronouns.

WANN			WIE	WO
Im Jahr 1717	streitet	Bach	mit dem Herzog	in Dresden.
X = time	V1	N	Adverb of manner	Adverb of place

In the year 1717, Bach argues in Dresden with the duke.

Wo	hat	er	für 100 Dukaten	seiner neuen Frau	den Ring	gekauft?
X = place	V1	n	Adverb of manner	D	A	V2

In Arnstadt	hat	er	ihn	ihr	für 100 Dukaten	gekauft.
X = place	V1	n	a	d	Adverb of manner	V2

Where did he buy his new wife the ring for 110 ducats? In Arnstadt, he bought it for her for 100 ducats.

APPENDIX B

Strong and Irregular Verbs

This list includes common German verbs that change vowels when conjugated. Verbs with identical stems plus a prefix are not listed, as they take the same changes. Thus, you find **fangen** *to catch* (**fing**, **gefangen**; **fängt**), but not **an/fangen** *to begin* or **empfangen** *to receive*.

To use this list, remove the prefix from the verb form that appears in the reading text (e.g., [**an**]**fangen** or [**emp**]**fangen**, and then find the conjugated stem-form (**fing**, **gefangen**; **fängt**) in the list. Reattach the prefix to the infinitive of the strong/irregular verb and look up the meaning of the complete verb in your dictionary. See **Kapitel 8** for more information on verbs with prefixes.

Infinitive		Past	Past Participle	Present
backen	*bake*	buk, backte	gebacken	bäckt
befehlen	*command*	befahl	befohlen	befiehlt
beginnen	*begin*	begann	begonnen	beginnt
beißen	*bite*	biss	gebissen	beißt
bergen	*hide*	barg	geborgen	birgt
bersten	*burst*	barst	geborsten	birst
bewegen	*induce*	bewog	bewogen	bewegt
biegen	*bend*	bog	gebogen	biegt
bieten	*offer*	bot	geboten	bietet
binden	*bind*	band	gebunden	bindet
bitten	*beg, ask*	bat	gebeten	bittet
blasen	*blow*	blies	geblasen	bläst
bleiben	*remain*	blieb	geblieben	bleibt
brechen	*break*	brach	gebrochen	bricht
brennen	*burn*	brannte	gebrannt	brennt
bringen	*bring*	brachte	gebracht	bringt
denken	*think*	dachte	gedacht	denkt
dringen	*press*	drang	gedrungen	dringt
dünken	*seem*	dünkte, deuchte	gedünkt, gedeucht	dünkt, deucht
dürfen	*be allowed*	durfte	gedurft	darf
empfehlen	*recommend*	empfahl	empfohlen	empfiehlt
essen	*eat*	aß	gegessen	isst
fahren	*drive*	fuhr	gefahren	fährt
fallen	*fall*	fiel	gefallen	fällt
fangen	*catch*	fing	gefangen	fängt
fechten	*fight*	focht	gefochten	ficht
finden	*find*	fand	gefunden	findet
flechten	*braid*	flocht	geflochten	flicht

Infinitive		Past	Past Participle	Present
fliegen	*fly*	flog	geflogen	fliegt
fliehen	*flee*	floh	geflohen	flieht
fließen	*flow*	floss	geflossen	fließt
fressen	*devour*	fraß	gefressen	frisst
frieren	*freeze*	fror	gefroren	friert
gären	*ferment*	gor, gärte	gegoren, gegärt	gärt
gebären	*bear*	gebar	geboren	gebiert
geben	*give*	gab	gegeben	gibt
gedeihen	*thrive*	gedieh	gediehen	gedeiht
gehen	*go*	ging	gegangen	geht
gelingen	*succeed*	gelang	gelungen	gelingt
gelten	*be valid*	galt	gegolten	gilt
genesen	*recover*	genas	genesen	genest
genießen	*enjoy*	genoss	genossen	genießt
geschehen	*happen*	geschah	geschehen	geschieht
gewinnen	*gain*	gewann	gewonnen	gewinnt
gießen	*pour*	goss	gegossen	gießt
gleichen	*resemble*	glich	geglichen	gleicht
gleiten	*glide*	glitt	geglitten	gleitet
graben	*dig*	grub	gegraben	gräbt
greifen	*seize*	griff	gegriffen	greift
haben	*have*	hatte	gehabt	hat
halten	*hold*	hielt	gehalten	hält
hängen	*hang*	hing	gehangen	hängt
heben	*lift*	hob	gehoben	hebt
heißen	*be called*	hieß	geheißen	heißt
helfen	*help*	half	geholfen	hilft
kennen	*know*	kannte	gekannt	kennt
klingen	*sound*	klang	geklungen	klingt
kommen	*come*	kam	gekommen	kommt
können	*can*	konnte	gekonnt	kann
kriechen	*creep*	kroch	gekrochen	kriecht
laden	*load*	lud	geladen	lädt (ladet)
lassen	*let*	ließ	gelassen	lässt
laufen	*run*	lief	gelaufen	läuft
leiden	*suffer*	litt	gelitten	leidet
leihen	*lend*	lieh	geliehen	leiht
lesen	*read*	las	gelesen	liest
liegen	*lie*	lag	gelegen	liegt
lügen	*tell a lie*	log	gelogen	lügt
meiden	*shun*	mied	gemieden	meidet
messen	*measure*	maß	gemessen	misst
mögen	*like, may*	mochte	gemocht	mag
müssen	*must*	musste	gemusst	muss
nehmen	*take*	nahm	genommen	nimmt
nennen	*name*	nannte	genannt	nennt
pfeifen	*whistle*	pfiff	gepfiffen	pfeift

Infinitive		Past	Past Participle	Present
preisen	*praise*	pries	gepriesen	preist
quellen	*gush*	quoll	gequollen	quillt
raten	*advise*	riet	geraten	rät
reiben	*rub*	rieb	gerieben	reibt
reißen	*tear*	riss	gerissen	reißt
reiten	*ride*	ritt	geritten	reitet
rennen	*run*	rannte	gerannt	rennt
riechen	*smell*	roch	gerochen	riecht
ringen	*wring; wrestle*	rang	gerungen	ringt
rinnen	*flow, run*	rann	geronnen	rinnt
rufen	*call*	rief	gerufen	ruft
saufen	*drink, guzzle*	soff	gesoffen	säuft
schaffen	*create*	schuf	geschaffen	schafft
scheiden	*part*	schied	geschieden	scheidet
scheinen	*appear*	schien	geschienen	scheint
schelten	*scold*	schalt	gescholten	schilt
schieben	*shove*	schob	geschoben	schiebt
schießen	*shoot*	schoss	geschossen	schießt
schlafen	*sleep*	schlief	geschlafen	schläft
schlagen	*strike*	schlug	geschlagen	schlägt
schleichen	*sneak*	schlich	geschlichen	schleicht
schließen	*shut*	schloss	geschlossen	schließt
schmeißen	*throw*	schmiss	geschmissen	schmeißt
schmelzen	*melt*	schmolz	geschmolzen	schmilzt
schneiden	*cut*	schnitt	geschnitten	schneidet
schreiben	*write*	schrieb	geschrieben	schreibt
schreien	*cry*	schrie	geschrie(e)n	schreit
schreiten	*stride*	schritt	geschritten	schreitet
schweigen	*be silent*	schwieg	geschwiegen	schweigt
schwimmen	*swim*	schwamm	geschwommen	schwimmt
schwinden	*vanish*	schwand	geschwunden	schwindet
schwingen	*swing*	schwang	geschwungen	schwingt
schwören	*swear*	schwur, schwor	geschworen	schwört
sehen	*see*	sah	gesehen	sieht
sein	*be*	war	gewesen	ist
senden	*send*	sandte, sendete	gesandt, gesendet	sendet
sieden	*boil*	sott, siedete	gesotten, gesiedet	siedet
singen	*sing*	sang	gesungen	singt
sinken	*sink*	sank	gesunken	sinkt
sinnen	*think*	sann	gesonnen	sinnt
sitzen	*sit*	saß	gesessen	sitzt
sollen	*should*	sollte	gesollt	soll
spinnen	*spin*	spann	gesponnen	spinnt
sprechen	*speak*	sprach	gesprochen	spricht
sprießen	*sprout*	spross	gesprossen	sprießt
springen	*spring*	sprang	gesprungen	springt
stechen	*sting, pierce*	stach	gestochen	sticht

Infinitive		Past	Past Participle	Present
stecken	*stick, put*	stak, steckte	gesteckt	steckt
stehen	*stand*	stand	gestanden	steht
stehlen	*steal*	stahl	gestohlen	stiehlt
steigen	*climb*	stieg	gestiegen	steigt
sterben	*die*	starb	gestorben	stirbt
stinken	*stink*	stank	gestunken	stinkt
stoßen	*push*	stieß	gestoßen	stößt
streichen	*delete*	strich	gestrichen	streicht
streiten	*quarrel*	stritt	gestritten	streitet
tragen	*carry, wear*	trug	getragen	trägt
treffen	*hit*	traf	getroffen	trifft
treiben	*drive*	trieb	getrieben	treibt
treten	*step*	trat	getreten	tritt
trinken	*drink*	trank	getrunken	trinkt
trügen	*deceive*	trog	getrogen	trügt
tun	*do*	tat	getan	tut
verderben	*spoil*	verdarb	verdorben	verdirbt
verdrießen	*vex*	verdross	verdrossen	verdrießt
vergessen	*forget*	vergaß	vergessen	vergisst
verlieren	*lose*	verlor	verloren	verliert
wachsen	*grow*	wuchs	gewachsen	wächst
waschen	*wash*	wusch	gewaschen	wäscht
weben	*weave*	wob, webte	gewoben, gewebt	webt
weichen	*yield*	wich	gewichen	weicht
weisen	*show*	wies	gewiesen	weist
wenden	*turn*	wandte, wendete	gewandt, gewendet	wendet
werben	*woo, solicit*	warb	geworben	wirbt
werden	*become*	wurde, ward	geworden	wird
werfen	*throw*	warf	geworfen	wirft
wiegen	*weigh*	wog	gewogen	wiegt
winden	*wind*	wand	gewunden	windet
wissen	*know*	wusste	gewusst	weiß
wollen	*want (to)*	wollte	gewollt	will
zeihen	*accuse*	zieh	geziehen	zeiht
ziehen	*pull* move	zog	gezogen	zieht
zwingen	*force*	zwang	gezwungen	zwingt

APPENDIX C

Choosing and Using a Dictionary

Finding the right dictionary for your purposes and learning to use it effectively are key to accurate translating, reading, and researching in German. You should consider a number of dictionaries before settling on the best one for your purposes.

Pocket dictionaries with 50,000 to 70,000 entries are handy for carrying around and looking up common items, but are stopgaps with drawbacks: lack of clarity (caused by small print and other space-saving approaches) and a lack of completeness. Online dictionaries also offer convenience, but are lacking in completeness and detail.

Serious students and researchers should consider a standard, hardcover dictionary containing 150,000 to 300,000 entries which clearly outlines its system of entries and the information that it contains. Read through the introductory outline of the dictionaries you are considering. In each check some key words, including (1) examples of contemporary jargon in your field to see if the dictionary is up to date; (2) several noun entries to see how gender and plural forms are presented; (3) compound nouns to check the extent to which the dictionary lists compounds; (4) irregular verbs, paying particular attention to whether principal parts are listed as separate cross-referenced entries, whether **haben/sein**-auxiliary verbs are given, and how various types of verbs (transitive, intransitive, reflexive) are denoted; (5) common abbreviations and those related to your field; and (6) proper nouns and names. **The ease with which you are able to find and understand these entries should be the deciding factor in your selection.**

To test whether a standard dictionary makes it easy for you to find and understand its entries, pay attention to the following aspects:

1. **Clarity of physical presentation:** Can you read the print? Are several print types employed to clarify different meanings of the same word? Does the dictionary use boldface, italics, and a numbering system?
2. **Clarity of definitions:** Does the dictionary supply authentic examples of modern usage in context? How are idioms listed? Are the translations themselves idiomatic?

3. **Focus:** Has the foreign reader been taken into consideration? Are the predicates and principal parts of irregular/strong verbs listed as main entries? Does the dictionary provide a sufficient number of compound nouns?
4. **Special lists of entries:** Do the lists assist you? Does the extra listing make it easier for you to find the specialized information in the dictionary?

Here, for example, are features highlighted by Collins Publishers in describing their 2006 edition of *Collins German Unabridged Dictionary:*

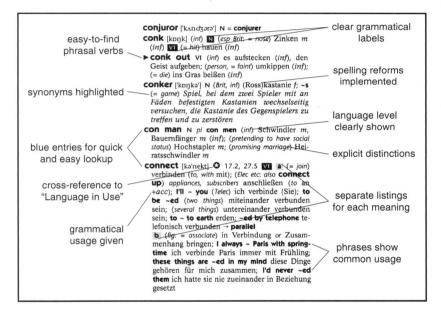

Using Your Dictionary

Before looking up a word, ascertain its function in the original text. A good dictionary makes clear to you whether a word is used as an adjective, adverb, conjunction, preposition, etc. Keep in mind that many German words can function in more than one way and have more than one meaning.

It is not always necessary to understand every word exactly to understand a text. Trust your intuition, your understanding of the general context, and your reading of a word's function. Sometimes all you need to recognize is that a verb alerts you to movement or that an adjective describes something. Keep reading and use the text and context to decide if that verb conveys a rapid or a slow mode of moving, whether that adjective is a positive or a negative one.

When a precise definition becomes necessary, keep the following in mind:

1. The meaning listed first is NOT necessarily the meaning you want. Reconsider the context and other definitions offered in the dictionary entry. Cross-check meaning: once you've got what you think is the correct English translation, look up that word in the English part of the dictionary and see how the German definition matches the word in the original.
2. With so many German compounds, it's unlikely to find a separate entry for each word. Learn to look up words under the basic stems. Pay attention to boldface entries and use the context to help you interpret the German meaning.
3. Reread your dictionary's introduction: "How To Use This Dictionary" and review how it uses abbreviations and other symbols.
4. If your English translation doesn't make any sense, reread the text, concentrate on what you do understand, reconsider the possibilities of what you don't quite understand and, if necessary, expand the dictionary search.
5. Make notes in your dictionary! If you have marked a word numerous times, add it to your personal active vocabulary list.

APPENDIX D

German Script

The German Alphabet

GERMAN FORM		GERMAN NAME	ROMAN FORM	
a	𝔄	ah	a	A
b	𝔅	bay (bé)	b	B
c	ℭ	tsay (tsé)	c	C
d	𝔇	day (dé)	d	D
e	𝔈	ay (é)	e	E
f	𝔉	eff	f	F
g	𝔊	gay	g	G
h	𝔥	hah	h	H
i	𝔍	ee	i	I
j	𝔍	yott	j	J
k	𝔎	kah	k	K
l	𝔏	ell	l	L
m	𝔐	emm	m	M
n	𝔑	enn	n	N
o	𝔒	oh	o	O
p	𝔓	pay (pé)	p	P
q	𝔔	koo	q	Q
r	𝔑	err (trilled or uvular *r*)	r	R
ſ, s	𝔖	ess	s	S
t	𝔗	tay (té)	t	T
u	𝔘	oo	u	U
v	𝔙	fow (*as in* fowl)	v	V
w	𝔚	vay (vé)	w	W
x	𝔛	icks	x	X
y	𝔜	üpsilon	y	Y
z	𝔷	tset	z	Z
ä	𝔄̈	ah Umlaut	ä	Ä
ö	𝔒̈	oh Umlaut	ö	Ö
ü	𝔘̈	uh Umlaut	ü	Ü
ch		tsay-hah	ch	
ck		tsay-kay	ck	
ß		ess-tset	ß	
tz		tay-tset	tz	

In **Kapitel 18** you encountered the following reading in Roman script. Comparing the two forms will assist you in learning to recognize German script, used widely in older academic German texts.

Der Zeppelin im Ersten Weltkrieg

Unter der Leitung von Graf Zeppelin startete schon 1900 der erste Zeppelin, das „LZ 1". In den folgenden Jahren wurden die Luftschiffe immer größer und schneller.

Nachdem der 1. Weltkrieg ausgebrochen war, wurden Zeppeline von der Marine und dem Heer übernommen. Sie wurden zuerst für Aufklärungsflüge in der Nordsee gegen die englische Flotte und später zum Bombenabwurf über England eingesetzt. Als die Zeppeline über England und London ihre ersten Luftangriffe machten, erregten sie einen großen Schrecken, denn es gab keine erfolgreiche Abwehr gegen sie, wenn sie in einer Höhe von 4000 m flogen. Weder die englischen Jagdflugzeuge noch die Artilleriegranaten konnten so eine Höhe erreichen. Jedoch in einer verhältnismäßig kurzen Zeit verbesserten die Engländer ihre Flugabwehr, indem sie ihre Jagdflugzeuge und die Flak (Flugzeugabwehrkanone) verbesserten. Nun konnten sie die Zeppeline mit Phosphormunition angreifen. Da die Zeppeline mit brennbarem Wasserstoff gefüllt waren, genügte manchmal nur ein Treffer, um das Luftschiff in einen riesigen Feuerball zu verwandeln. Die angreifenden Luftschiffe erlitten nun schwere Verluste, und für die Mannschaft wurde ein Fahrt gegen England ein „Himmelfahrtskommando".

Obwohl die Zeppeline wenig taktischen Wert hatten, hatten sie jedoch in den ersten Kriegsjahren einen gewissen psychologischen und strategischen Wert. Je tiefer sie ins englische Hinterland eindrangen, desto mehr Streitkräfte und Artillerie mußten zur Abwehr in England bleiben und konnten daher nicht in den Entscheidungsschlachten in Frankreich eingesetzt werden.

VOCABULARY

This vocabulary list consists of basic vocabulary and words used frequently in *German for Reading Knowledge*. Basic definitions given here do not attempt to compete with a good dictionary. Meanings are specific to uses in this textbook and are not necessarily correct for uses in other contexts. Check your dictionary for further information.

abartig abnormal
Abb. = Abbildung *(f.)*, **-en** illustration
Abbau *(m.)* mining; dismantling
Abenteuer *(n.)*, **–** adventure
aber but, however
Abfall *(m.)*, **ːe** garbage; **Abfall** *(m.)* **von** revolt against
ab/fassen to write, compose
Abgang *(m.)*, **ːe** departure
ab/halten (hielt ... ab, abgehalten, hält ... ab) to hold, celebrate
Abhandlung *(f.)*, **-en** treatise, discussion
ab/hängen von (hing ... ab, abgehangen) to be dependent upon
abhängig dependent
ab/kommen (kam ... ab, ist abgekommen) to come away, deviate
ab/lehnen to reject
ab/leiten to derive
ab/nehmen (nahm ... ab, abgenommen; nimmt ... ab) to decrease, take off
ab/reißen (riss ... ab, abgerissen) to tear down
Abschied *(m.)*, **-e** departure, farewell
Abschluss *(m.)*, **ːe** conclusion
ab/schneiden (schnitt ... ab, abgeschnitten) to cut off
Abschnitt *(m.)*, **-e** section, paragraph
Absicht *(f.)*, **-en** intention, design
Abstand *(m.)*, **ːe** interval, distance
ab/stoßen (stieß ... ab, abgestoßen; stößt ... ab) to push off, repel
Abteilung *(f.)*, **-en** department, section
ab/treten (trat ... ab, abgetreten; tritt ... ab) to surrender, cede
abwechselnd alternating(ly)
Abwehr *(f.)* protection (against)
abwehrend in defense
achten auf to pay attention to
Advokat *(m., n-noun)*, **-en** lawyer
ähneln to resemble
ahnen to suspect
ähnlich similar

Ähnlichkeit *(f.)*, **-en** similarity
aktuell relevant, up-to-date
all- all, every
alle all
allein alone, only, but
alleinstehend single, living on one's own
allerdings certainly, to be sure, of course
alles everything
allgemein general; **im Allgemeinen** in general
allmählich gradual, by degrees
als as; when; than
also thus, therefore
alt old
Alter *(n.)* age
Altertum *(n.)* antiquity
an/bieten (bot ... an, angeboten) to offer for sale
Anblick *(m.)* sight
an/bringen (brachte ... an, angebracht) to install, arrange, mount
an/dauern to last, continue
ander- other, different
ändern (sich) to change
anders different, otherwise
Änderung *(f.)*, **-en** change, alteration
an/deuten to point out
anfällig susceptible
Anfang *(m.)*, **ːe** beginning, origin, start
an/fangen (fing ... an, angefangen; fängt ... an) to begin
anfangs in the beginning
an/führen to cite, state
Angabe *(f.)*, **-n** statement, estimate, information
an/geben (gab ... an, angegeben; gibt ... an) to state, quote, indicate; to boast
angeblich alleged
angemessen appropriate, adequate
angenehm pleasant
Angesicht *(n.)*, **-e** face, brow
angesichts in view of, in face of
Anhang *(m.)*, **ːe** appendix
Anhänger *(m.)*, **–**; **Anhängerin** *(f.)*, **-nen** believer, fan
an/kommen (kam ... an, ist angekommen) to arrive; **an/kommen auf** to be dependent upon; **es kommt darauf an** it depends
an/langen an to arrive at
Anlass *(m.)*, **ːe** cause, occasion
anlässlich on the occasion of

an/legen to arrange, set up

an/nehmen (nahm ... an, angenommen; nimmt ... an) to assume, accept

an/passen (sich) to adapt to

Anpassung (*f.*) adjustment, adaptation

Anrede (*f.*), **-n** greeting, form of address

an/regen to stimulate

Anregung (*f.*), **-en** stimulation, suggestion

Ansager (*m.*), **–; Ansagerin** (*f.*), **-nen** announcer

an/schauen to look at, view

Anschauung (*f.*), **-en** idea, view

an/schließen (schloss ... an, angeschlossen) to attach; **sich an/schließen** to follow

Anschluss (*m.*) annexation

Ansehen (*n.*) prestige, respect

an/sehen (sah ... an, angesehen; sieht ... an) to regard, look at

Ansicht (*f.*), **-en** view, opinion

an/siedeln (sich) to settle

an/sprechen (sprach ... an, angesprochen; spricht ... an) to address

Anspruch (*m.*), **⁓e** claim, demand

anständig decent

anstatt instead (of)

Anstieg (*m.*), **-e** rise

anstelle instead, in place of

an/stellen to employ

anstrengend strenuous

atemlos breathless

Antike (*f.*) antiquity

Antwort (*f.*), **-en** answer

antworten to answer

an/wachsen (wuchs ... an, ist angewachsen; wächst ... an) to grow, expand

an/wenden (wandte ... an, angewandt) to use, employ

Anwendung (*f.*), **-en** use, application

Anzahl (*f.*) number

an/zeigen to indicate, show

an/ziehen (zog ... an, angezogen) to attract

Arbeit (*f.*), **-en** work

arbeiten to work

arbeitslos unemployed

arm poor

Armut (*f.*) poverty

Art (*f.*), **-en** kind, type, species

-artig resembling, like

Arznei (*f.*), **-en** medicine

Arzt (*m.*), **⁓e; Ärztin** (*f.*), **-nen** physician

auch also, too

auf on, upon

Aufbau (*m.*) construction

auf/bauen to build up, synthesize

auf einmal suddenly

auf/fallen (fiel ... auf, ist aufgefallen; fällt ... auf) to attract attention, be noticeable, strike

auf/fordern to call upon, command, invite

Aufführung (*f.*), **-en** performance

Aufgabe (*f.*), **-n** task

auf/halten (hielt ... auf, aufgehalten; hält ... auf) to stop

auf/heben (hob ... auf, aufgehoben) to suspend, repeal

Auflage (*f.*), **-n** edition

auf/listen to list

aufmerksam attentive

Aufmerksamkeit (*f.*), **-en** attention

Aufnahme (*f.*), **-n** photograph; reception; uptake

auf/nehmen (nahm ... auf, aufgenommen; nimmt ... auf) to take in, admit; to absorb; to record

aufrecht upright

aufrecht/erhalten (erhielt ... aufrecht, aufrechterhalten; erhält ... aufrecht) to maintain

auf/richten to set up, erect

Aufsatz (*m.*), **⁓e** essay, composition

Aufschwung (*m.*) prosperity, stimulus

Aufstand (*m.*) revolt

auf/steigen (stieg ... auf, ist aufgestiegen) to rise

auf/stellen to set up, prepare, advance, formulate

Aufstieg (*m.*), **-e** ascent

Auftrag (*m.*), **⁓e** order, commission

auf/treten (trat ... auf, ist aufgetreten; tritt ... auf) to appear, occur

auf/wachsen (wuchs ... auf, ist aufgewachsen) to grow up

auf/weisen (wies ... auf, aufgewiesen) to show, have

aufwendig expensive

Aufzeichnungen (*pl.*) documents, papers

auf/zeigen to show, indicate

Auge (*n.*), **-n** eye; **vor Auge führen** to present, imagine

aus out of, from

aus/beuten to exploit

aus/bilden to train

aus/brechen (brach ... aus, ist ausgebrochen; bricht ... aus) to break out

Ausbruch (*m.*), **⁓e** outbreak

Ausdauer (*f.*) perseverance

aus/dehnen to expand, enlarge

Ausdruck (*m.*), **⁓e** expression, term

Auseinandersetzung (*f.*), **-en** exchange, altercation

Ausfuhr (*f.*) export

aus/führen to carry out, perform, execute

ausführlich   detailed

Ausgabe *(f.)*, **-n**   expenditure; edition

aus/geben (gab ... aus, ausgegeben; gibt ... aus)   to spend

Ausgrabung *(f.)*, **-en**   excavation

aus/grenzen   to exclude, ignore

aus/kommen (kam ... aus; ist ausgekommen)   to get along with

Ausland *(n.)*   foreign country, abroad

Ausländer *(m.)*, **–; Ausländerin** *(f.)*, **-nen**   foreigner

ausländisch   foreign

aus/leihen   to lend

aus/lösen   to precipitate

Ausmaß *(n.)*, **-e**   extent, impact

Ausnahme *(f.)*, **-n**   exception

aus/nutzen   to utilize

aus/richten   to direct; to organize, install

aus/schalten   to switch off

Ausschau *(m.)*   watch out

ausschließlich   exclusive

Ausschnitt *(m.)*, **-e**   excerpt

aus/schütten   to pour out, empty out

außer   besides, except for

außerhalb   outside of

äußern   to express, say

außerordentlich   extraordinary

Außenseiter *(m.)*, **–**   outsider

äußerst   very, extremely

Äußerung *(f.)*, **-en**   expression

aus/sprechen (sprach ... aus, ausgesprochen; spricht ... aus)   to voice, express, pronounce

aus/sterben (starb ... aus, ist ... ausgestorben; stirbt ... aus)   to die out, become extinct

aus/statten   to equip, endow

Ausstattung *(f.)*, **-en**   equipment, endowment

aus/stellen   to exhibit

Ausstellung *(f.)*, **-en**   exhibition, exhibit

aus/üben   to exert

Auswahl *(f.)*   selection

aus/wählen   to choose, select

aus/wandern   to emigrate

aus/zahlen   to pay out, make payment

Auszug *(m.)*, **⸚e**   excerpt

Autor *(m.)*, **-en; Autorin** *(f.)*, **-nen**   author

Bahnbrecher *(m.)*, **–**   pioneer

bald   soon

Band *(m.)*, **⸚e**   volume

Bär *(m., n-noun)*, **-en; Bärin** *(f.)*, **-nen**   bear

basieren auf   to be based upon

Basilika *(f.)*, **Basiliken**   basilica

Bau *(m.)*, **-e, -ten**   construction, building

bauen   to build

Bauer *(m., n-noun)*, **-n; Bäuerin** *(f.)*, **-nen**   farmer, peasant

Baukunst *(f.)*   architecture

beachten   to pay attention to

Beachtung *(f.)*   attention, notice

beantworten   to answer, reply to

bedecken   to cover

bedeuten   to mean, signify

bedeutend   significant, considerable, meaningful

Bedeutung *(f.)*, **-en**   meaning, significance

bedienen (sich)   to make use of

Bedingung *(f.)*, **-en**   condition

Bedrohung *(f.)*, **-en**   threat

bedürfen (bedurfte, bedurft; bedarf)   to require

beeinflussen   to influence, manipulate

beenden   to finish, complete

befassen (sich) mit   to deal with, to concern oneself with

Befehl *(m.)*, **-e**   command

befehlen (befiel, befohlen; befiehlt)   to order

befinden (sich) (befand, befunden)   to be located; to be; to feel

beförderlich   favorable, conducive

befördern   to transport

befürworten   to advocate

begeistern   to fill with enthusiasm

beginnen (begann, begonnen)   to begin

begraben   buried

begreifen (begriff, begriffen)   to understand, conceive

Begrenzung *(f.)*, **-en**   boundary, limitation

Begriff *(m.)*, **-e**   concept; word

begründen   to found, prove, substantiate

Begründer *(m.)*, **–; Begründerin** *(f.)*, **-nen**   founder

begrüßen   to greet

behandeln   to handle, treat, deal with

Behandlung *(f.)*, **-en**   treatment

beharren   to persevere, persist

behaupten   to maintain, assert, claim

beherrschen   to master, rule; **sich beherrschen**   to control oneself

bei   at; while, during; with; **bei uns**   in our country/family, here

beide   both

Beispiel *(n.)*, **-e**   example; **zum Beispiel (z.B.)** for example (e.g.)

beispielsweise   for example

bei/stehen (stand ... bei, beigestanden)   to aid, support

Beitrag *(m.)*, **⸚e**   contribution

bei/tragen (trug ... bei, beigetragen; trägt ... bei)   to contribute

bekämpfen   to combat

Bekämpfung (*f.*), **-en**   combat, fight
bekannt   (well) known
bekannt machen   to introduce
Bekannte (*f. or m.*), **-n**   acquaintance
bekommen (**bekam, bekommen**)   to get, receive
Belastung (*f.*), **-en**   burden, stress
belegen   to cover
beleuchten   to light
beliebt   popular
beliefern   to deliver
bemerken   to notice
bemerkenswert   noteworthy
benachbart   neighboring, adjacent
Benehmen (*n.*)   behavior
benennen (**benannte, benannt**)   to name, call
benutzen   to use
Benzin (*n.*)   gasoline
beobachten   to observe
Beobachtung (*f.*), **-en**   observation
beordern   to order, command
beraten (**beriet, beraten; berät**)   to advise
berechnen   to calculate
Bereich (*m.*), **-e**   realm, sphere
bereichern   to enrich, enhance
bereiten   to cause, prepare
bereits   already, as early as
Bereitschaft (*f.*)   readiness, preparedness
Berg (*m.*), **-e**   mountain
bergen (**barg, geborgen; birgt**)   to conceal
Bericht (*m.*), **-e**   report
berichten   to report
berücksichtigen   to consider, take into consideration
Beruf (*m.*), **-e**   occupation, profession
berufstätig   employed, working in a job
beruhen auf   to be based on, rest on, depend on
beruhigen   to quiet, pacify, mitigate
berühmt   famous
berühren   to touch
Besatzung (*f.*), **-en**   occupation
beschäftigen   to employ, occupy; **sich beschäftigen mit**   to deal with, engage in
bescheiden   modest, moderate
beschleunigen   to accelerate
beschließen (**beschloss, beschlossen**)   to decide
beschränken (**sich**) **auf**   to limit oneself to, be limited to
beschreiben (**beschrieb, beschrieben**)   to describe
beschützen   to protect
beseitigen   to eliminate, do away with
besetzen   to occupy
Besiedlung (*f.*), **-en**   settlement

besinnen (**sich**)   to call to mind
Besitz (*m.*), **-e**   possession
besitzen (**besaß, besessen**)   to possess, have
besonders   especially
besprechen (**besprach, besprochen; bespricht**)   to discuss
besser   better
Bestandteil (*m.*), **-e**   component, ingredient
bestätigen   to confirm
Bestätigung (*f.*), **-en**   confirmation
bestehen auf (**bestand, bestanden**)   to insist on, persist in, hold out for
bestehen aus (**bestand, bestanden**)   to consist of
besteigen (**bestieg, bestiegen**)   to climb; to ascend
bestimmen   to ascertain, define
bestimmt   certain, definite; **bestimmt sein**   to be destined
Bestimmung (*f.*), **-en**   determination, definition
Besuch (*m.*), **-e**   visit
besuchen   to visit, attend
beteiligt   involved
Beteiligung (*f.*), **-en**   participation
betonen   to emphasize, stress
betrachten   to observe
Betrachter (*m.*), **–**; **Betrachterin** (*f.*), **-nen**   viewer
Betrachtung (*f.*), **-en**   reflection, observation
betragen (**betrug, betragen; beträgt**)   to amount to
Betragen (*n.*)   behavior
betreffen (**betraf, betroffen; betrifft**)   to affect, touch
betreiben (**betrieb, betrieben**)   to carry out
Betrieb (*m.*), **-e**   operation, plant
Bett (*n.*), **-e**   bed
Bevölkerung (*f.*), **-en**   population
bevorzugt   preferred
bewässern   to water (a plant)
bewegen   to move
Bewegung (*f.*), **-en**   movement
beweisen (**bewies, bewiesen**)   to prove
bewirken   to effect, cause, bring about
Bewohner (*m.*), **–**; **Bewohnerin** (*f.*), **-nen**   inhabitant
Bewusstsein (*n.*)   consciousness
bezahlen   to pay
bezeichnen   to designate, denote, call, characterize
Bezeichnung (*f.*), **-en**   term, designation
bezeugen   to declare, testify to
Beziehung (*f.*), **-en**   relation, connection
Bibliothek (*f.*), **-en**   library
bieten (**bot, geboten**)   to offer

Bild *(n.)*, **-er** picture, photograph
bilden to form; to educate; to be
Bildung *(f.)* education, training
billig cheap
Bindung *(f.)*, **-en** bond, tie
bis until
bis auf to, up to
bisher hitherto, until now
bislang so far, as yet
bis zu up to
bitte please
bitten (bat, gebeten) to ask, request
Blatt *(n.)*, **̈-er** sheet of paper; leaf;
    Blumenblatt petal
blau blue
bleiben (blieb, ist geblieben) to stay,
    remain
Blick *(m.)*, **-e** look, view
bloß mere
blühen to bloom, blossom
Blut *(n.)* blood
Blüte *(f.)*, **-n** blossom
Blütezeit *(f.)*, **-en** golden age
Boden *(m.)* ground, territory
Boot *(n.)*, **-e** boat
böse evil, angry
Botschaft *(f.)*, **-en** message
Brand *(m.)*, **̈-e** fire
Brauch *(m.)*, **̈-e** practice
brauchbar practical, useful
brauchen to need, require
brav well-behaved, good
brechen (brach, gebrochen; bricht) to
    break
breit broad, wide
brennbar combustible
brennen (brannte, gebrannt) to burn
Brief *(m.)*, **-e** letter
bringen (brachte, gebracht) to bring
Brot *(n.)*, **-e** bread
Bruder *(m.)*, **̈** brother
Buch *(n.)*, **̈-er** book
Buchbesprechung *(f.)*, **-en** book review
Buchhandlung *(f.)*, **-en** bookstore
Bühne *(f.)*, **-n** stage
Bundeskanzler *(m.)*, **–; Bundeskanzlerin**
    (f.), **-nen** Federal Chancellor
Bundesregierung *(f.)* federal government
Bundestag *(m.)* parliament
Bürger *(m.)*, **–; Bürgerin** *(f.)*, **-nen** citizen
Bürger *(pl.)* middle class, bourgeois, citizens
bürgerlich middle class, bourgeois; civic
Bürgerkreig *(m.)*, **-e** civil war
Büro *(n.)*, **-s** office, bureau
bzw. = beziehungsweise alternatively, or,
    respectively

Chef *(m.)* **-s; Chefin** *(f.)* **-nen** boss,
    chief
Chemie *(f.)* chemistry
Chemiker *(m.)*, **–; Chemikerin** *(f.)*, **-nen**
    chemist
Chirurgie *(f.)* surgery
christlich Christian

da since; there; then
dabei thereby, in this case
dadurch thereby, thus; by this, by that
dafür for this, for it; instead of it; therefore
dagegen on the other hand; against it
daher therefore, hence, for that reason
damalig then, of that time
damals then, at that time, in those days
damit therewith; with it/them; so that
danach thereafter
dankbar thankful, grateful
danken to thank
dann then
dar/bieten (bot ... dar, dargeboten) to
    offer, present to
dar/stellen to represent, depict
Darstellung *(f.)*, **-en** representation
darüber over it, about it; **darüber**
    hinaus beyond this, above that
darum therefore, for all that
das heißt (d.h.) that is, that means
Daten *(pl.)* data
Dauer *(f.)* duration
dauerhaft lasting
dauern to last
dazu in addition, additionally
Decke *(f.)*, **-n** ceiling
demnächst shortly, soon
denken (dachte, gedacht) to think;
    denken an to think about
Denkmal *(n.)*, **̈-er** monument, memorial
denn for, because
dennoch nevertheless, yet, however
derart in such a way, to such an extent
dereinst some day, one day
desgleichen similar, suchlike, just so
deshalb therefore
deswegen for this (that) reason, therefore
deuten to interpret, construe
deutlich clear
deutsch German
Deutschland *(n.)* Germany
d.h. = das heißt i.e., that is
d.i. = das ist i.e., that is
dicht dense, packed
Dichter *(m.)*, **–; Dichterin** *(f.)*, **-nen** poet,
    creative writer
Dichtung *(f.)*, **-en** poetry, literature
dienen to serve, be used for

Diener *(m.)*, –; **Dienerin** *(f.)*, **-nen** servant
Dienst *(m.)*, **-e** service
dieser, diese, dieses this, this one, the latter
diesseits on this side of
Ding *(n.)*, **-e** thing, object
doch however, indeed, yet, nevertheless
Dom *(m.)* cathedral
doppelt double, twice
dort there
draußen outside, outdoors
dringend urgently
dringlich pressing, urgent
Droge *(f.)*, **-n** drug
drohen to threaten
Druck *(m.)*, **-e** print, pressure
duften to smell (sweet)
Dummheit *(f.)*, **-en** folly
dunkel dark
Dunkelheit *(f.)* darkness
durch through, by
durchaus clearly, certainly
durch/dringen (drang ... durch, ist durchgedrungen) to penetrate, permeate
durch/führen to carry out, execute
durchgängig throughout
durch/machen to experience, undergo
durchschlagend effective
Durchschnitt *(m.)*, **-e** average, cross section
durchschnittlich average, on the average
durch/setzen to push through, bring about
dürfen (durfte, gedurft; darf) to be permitted, may; can; *(neg.)* must not

eben just now, now
ebenfalls also
ebenso wenig just as little
echt real, true
edel noble
ehe before
Ehe *(f.)*, **-n** marriage
ehemalig former
Ehepaar *(n.)*, **-e** married couple
eher earlier, rather, formerly
Ehre ein/bringen (brachte ... ein, eingebracht) to win honors and fame
ehren to honor
Ei *(n.)*, **-er** egg
eigen own, individual
eigenartig peculiar, original
eigenhändig single-handedly
eigennützig selfish
Eigenschaft *(f.)*, **-en** property, quality
Eigentum *(n.)*, **-̈er** property, belongings

eilen to hurry
ein/beziehen (bezog ... ein, einbezogen) to include
Einblick *(m.)*, **-e** insight
ein/brechen (brach ... ein, ist eingebrochen, bricht ... ein) to enter, break into
eindeutig clear
ein/dringen (drang ... ein; ist eingedrungen) to penetrate
eindrucksvoll impressive
einfach simple
ein/fallen (fiel ... ein, ist eingefallen; fällt ein) to invade; to occur (in one's mind)
Einfluss *(m.)*, **-̈e** influence
ein/führen to introduce, import
Einführung *(f.)*, **-en** introduction
Eingang *(m.)*, **-̈e** entrance
eingeboren native
ein/gehen (ging ... ein; ist eingegangen) to go into, enter
eingehend thoroughly, in detail
ein/halten (hielt ... ein, eingehalten; hält ... ein) to observe, adhere to
einheimisch native
Einheit *(f.)*, **-en** unity, unit
einige some, several; **einige wenige** only a few
ein/kaufen to shop (for)
Einklang *(m.)*, **-̈e** harmony, accord
Einkommen *(n.)*, – income
ein/laden (lud ... ein, eingeladen; lädt ... ein) to invite
ein/leiten to introduce
Einleitung *(f.)*, **-en** introduction, prelude
einmal once; **auf einmal** all at once, suddenly; **einmal ... zum andern** on the one hand ... on the other hand; **nicht einmal** not even
einmalig singular
Einmarsch *(m.)* invasion
ein/nehmen (nahm ... ein, eingenommen; nimmt ... ein) to take in, collect
ein/ordnen to arrange
ein/richten to install, arrange, order
Einsatz *(m.)*, **-̈e** mission
ein/schalten to switch on
Einschätzung *(f.)*, **-en** estimation
ein/schließen (schloss ... ein, eingeschlossen) to include
Einschränkung *(f.)*, **-en** limitation, limiting
ein/schüchtern to scare off, intimidate
ein/setzen to engage, use; **sich ein/setzen für** to support, champion
Einsicht *(f.)*, **-en** knowledge, insight
ein/steigen (stieg ... ein, ist eingestiegen) to enter, get into
ein/stellen to cease, discontinue

Einstieg *(m.)*, **-e** entry
ein/teilen to classify, divide
Einteilung *(f.)*, **-en** division, arrangement
ein/treten für (**trat ... ein, ist eingetreten;
  tritt ... ein**) to side with
ein/wandern to immigrate
Einwanderung *(f.)*, **-en** immigration
Einwohner *(m.)*, **–**; **Einwohnerin** *(f.)*,
  -nen inhabitant
Einzelgänger *(m.)*, **–** loner
Einzelheit *(f.)*, **-en** detail
einzeln individual, single
einzelne a few
ein/ziehen (**zog ... ein, ist eingezogen**) to
  enter, move in
einzig only, single
Eltern *(pl.)* parents
empfangen (**empfing, empfangen;
  empfängt**) to receive; to greet
empfehlen (**empfahl, empfohlen;
  empfiehlt**) to recommend
empfinden (**empfand, empfunden**) to
  perceive, feel
empfindlich sensitive
empfindsam sensitive, sentimental
empören to outrage, cause indignation
Ende *(n.)*, **-n** end, limit, result
endgültig final, conclusive
endlich finally
endlos endless
eng narrow
Engel *(m.)*, **–** angel
entdecken to discover, disclose
Entdeckung *(f.)*, **-en** discovery, disclosure
Entfaltung *(f.)*, **-en** development
entfernen to remove
Entfernung *(f.)*, **-en** distance
Entfremdung *(f.)* alienation
entgegengesetzt opposite
entgegen/wirken to counteract, check
enthalten (**enthielt, enthalten; enthält**) to
  include, contain
entkommen (**entkam, ist entkommen**) to
  escape, flee
entlang along
entscheiden (**entschied, entschieden**) to
  decide
Entscheidung *(f.)*, **-en** decision; **... -en
  treffen** to make decisions
entspannen (**sich**) to relax
entsprechen (**entsprach, entsprochen;
  entspricht**) to correspond to, match,
  be in accordance with
entstehen (**entstand, ist entstanden**) to
  come about, begin
entweder either; **entweder ... oder**
  either . . . or

entwerfen (**entwarf, entworfen;
  entwirft**) to design, plan
entwickeln to develop; **sich entwickeln** to
  develop, evolve
Entwicklung *(f.)*, **-en** development
Entwicklungsland *(n.)*, **⸚er** developing
  country
Entwurf *(m.)*, **⸚e** sketch, draft
erblich hereditary, inheritable
Erde *(f.)* earth
Ereignis *(n.)*, **-se** event
erfahren (**erfuhr, erfahren; erfährt**) to
  learn, find out
Erfahrung *(f.)*, **-en** experience
erfinden (**erfand, erfunden**) to invent
Erfindung *(f.)*, **-en** invention
Erfolg *(m.)*, **-e** success
erfolgreich successful
erfordern to require, call for, need
Erforschung *(f.)*, **-en** investigation, study
ergänzen to complete, expand
ergeben (**ergab; ergibt**) to yield, give,
  show
Ergebnis *(n.)*, **-se** result
ergreifen (**ergriff, ergriffen**) to take hold
  of, seize
erhalten (**erhielt, erhalten; erhält**) to
  preserve
erhältlich available
erheben (**erhob, erhoben**) to raise, elevate
erheblich considerable, weighty, important
Erhebung *(f.)*, **-en** elevation
erhoffen to hope for, expect
erhöhen to increase, raise
erinnern an to remind about/of; **sich
  erinnern** (**an**) to remember, recall
Erinnerung *(f.)*, **-en** memory
erkennen (**erkannte, erkannt**) to recognize, perceive
Erkenntnis *(f.)*, **-se** perception, knowledge
erklären to explain
Erklärung *(f.)*, **-en** explanation
erkundigen (**sich**) to inquire, make
  inquiries
erläutern to comment
erleben to experience
Erlebnis *(n.)*, **-se** experience
erleiden (**erlitt, erlitten**) to suffer
erlernen to learn, acquire
erleuchten to illuminate, enlighten
erlöschen (**erlosch, ist erloschen;
  erlischt**) to wipe out, extinguish
ermöglichen to make possible for, enable
ermutigen encourage
Ernährung *(f.)* feeding, food, nourishment
erneuern to renew
ernst earnest

Di-Er

ernten to harvest
Eroberung *(f.)*, **-en** conquest
eröffnen to open
Erörterung *(f.)*, **-en** discussion, debate
errechnen to calculate
Erreger *(m.)*, **–** cause, producer
erreichen to reach, attain
erscheinen (erschien, ist erschienen) to appear; to be published
erschrecken to frighten
ersehen aus (ersah, ersehen; ersieht) to see from, to understand from
ersetzen to replace
erst first, only
erstatten to give, make
erstaunlich amazing
erstrecken to stretch, extend
erwähnen to mention
erwarten to expect
erwerben (erwarb, erworben; erwirbt) to attain
erweisen (erwies, erwiesen) to show, render
erweitern to expand, broaden
erzählen to tell, relate, report
Erzbischof *(m.)*, **ᵘe** archbishop
erzeugen to produce
Erzeugnis *(n.)*, **-se** product
erziehen (erzog, erzogen) to train, educate
Erziehung *(f.)* education, upbringing
es gibt there is, there are
Essen *(n.)*, **–** food, meal
essen (aß, gegessen; isst) to eat
etwa about, perhaps
etwas something, some, somewhat
europäisch European
Evangelium *(n.)*, **-lien** Gospel
eventuell possible, perhaps
ewig eternal
Ewigkeit *(f.)* eternity
Exemplar *(n.)*, **-e** copy

Fabrik *(f.)*, **-en** factory, plant
-fach times, -fold
Fach *(n.)*, **ᵘer** profession, trade; academic subject
Fachhochschule *(f.)*, **-n** advanced technical college
Fachmann *(m.)*; **Fachfrau** *(f.)*; **Fachleute** *(pl.)* expert, specialist
fähig capable
-fähig capable of, -able, -ible
Fähigkeit *(f.)*, **-en** talent, capacity, ability
fahren (fuhr, ist gefahren; fährt) to ride, travel, go, drive

Fahrrad *(n.)*, **ᵘer** bicycle
Fahrt *(f.)*, **-en** trip
Fahrzeug *(n.)*, **-e** vehicle
faktisch de facto, factual
Fall *(m.)*, **ᵘe** case, situation; **auf jeden Fall** in any case, by all means; **in diesem Fall(e)** in this case
fallen (fiel, ist gefallen; fällt) to fall
falls if, in case
falsch false, wrong
Familie *(f.)*, **-n** family
fangen (fing, gefangen; fängt) to catch
Farbe *(f.)*, **-n** color
farbig colored
farblos colorless
Fassung *(f.)*, **-en** version
fast about, almost
Feder *(f.)*, **-n** pen (plume), feather
fehlen to lack, be absent
Fehler *(m.)*, **–** error, mistake
feiern to celebrate
Feind *(m.)*, **-e; Feindin** *(f.)*, **-nen** enemy, opponent
Feld *(n.)*, **-er** field
fern far, distant
ferner further, farther, besides
Fernsehprogramm *(n.)*, **-e** television program
fertig/stellen to complete
festlich festive
fest/stellen to ascertain, determine
Feststellung *(f.)*, **-en** establishment, confirmation
finden (fand, gefunden) to find; **finden (sich)** to turn out to be
finster dark
Finsternis *(f.)*, **-se** darkness
Firma *(f.)*, **Firmen** firm, company
Fläche *(f.)*, **-n** area, surface
flächenmäßig according to surface measure
flächig flat, two-dimensional
fliegen (flog, ist geflogen) to fly
fliehen (floh, ist geflohen) to flee, escape
fließend running, flowing, fluent
Flüchtling *(m.)*, **-e** refugee
Flug *(m.)*, **ᵘe** flight
Flughafen *(m.)*, **Flughäfen** airport
Flugzeug *(n.)*, **-e** airplane
Fluss *(m.)*, **ᵘe** river
Flüssigkeit *(f.)*, **-en** liquid
Flut *(f.)*, **-en** flood
Folge *(f.)*, **-n** (as a) consequence
folgen to follow
Folgendes the following; **im Folgenden** in the following
folgendermaßen as follows

fordern to ask, demand
fördern to further, promote
Forderung (*f.*), **-en** demand, request
Förderung (*f.*), **-en** promotion
Form (*f.*), **-en** form, shape, type
forschen to research
Forscher (*m.*), **–**; **Forscherin** (*f.*), **-nen**
  researcher
Forschung (*f.*), **-en** research
fort/fahren (fuhr ... fort, ist fortgefahren;
  fährt ... fort) to proceed
fort/schreiten (schritt ... fort, ist
  fortgeschritten) to progress
Fortschritt (*m.*), **-e** progress
fort/setzen to continue
Fortsetzung (*f.*), **-en** continuation
Fracht (*f.*), **-en** freight
Frage (*f.*), **-n** question; **eine Frage**
  stellen to ask (pose) a question
fragen to ask
Franzose (*m., n-noun*), **-n; Französin** (*f.*),
  -nen Frenchman/woman
Frau (*f.*), **-en** Mrs., Ms.; woman; wife
Fräulein (*n.*), **–** Miss; young lady
frei free, unconnected
Freiheit (*f.*), **-en** freedom
fremd foreign
fremdartig unusual, strange
Fremdverkehr (*m.*) tourism
freuen (sich) auf to look forward to;
  freuen (sich) über to be happy about
Freund (*m.*), **-e; Freundin** (*f.*), **-nen** friend
Friede (*m., n-noun*), **-n** peace
fromm devout
früh early
Frühjahr (*n.*), *also* **Frühling** (*f.*) spring
fühlen (sich) to feel
führen to lead
Führung (*f.*), **-en** tour; leadership
Fülle (*f.*) abundance, profusion
füllen to fill
Fund (*m.*), **-e** finding, find, discovery
für for; in favor of
Furcht (*f.*) fear
fürchten (sich) vor to be afraid of
Fürst (*m.*), **-en; Fürstin** (*f.*), **-nen** ruler,
  prince/princess
füttern to feed

Gang (*m.*), **⁼e** path, way, action; gait
ganz whole, quite
Ganze, Ganzes (*n.*) whole, entirety; **im**
  Ganzen on the whole
gar even, very, quite
Gastarbeiter (*m.*), **–; Gastarbeiterin** (*f.*),
  -nen immigrant worker

Gebäude (*n.*), **–** building
geben (gab, gegeben; gibt) to give; **es**
  gibt there is, there are
Gebiet (*n.*), **-e** area, region, field
gebildet educated
Gebirge (*n.*), **–** mountains
geboren born
Gebot (*n.*), **-e** commandment
Gebrauch (*m.*) usage, employment
gebrauchen to use, employ
gebräuchlich common, customary
Geburt (*f.*), **-en** birth
Geburtstag (*m.*), **-e** birthday
Gedanke (*m., n-noun*), **-n** thought
gedeihen (gedieh, ist gediehen)
  to flourish
gedenken (gedachte, gedacht) to com-
  memorate
Geduld (*f.*) patience
geeignet suited, qualified, suitable
Gefahr (*f.*), **-en** danger
gefährdet endangered
gefährlich dangerous
gefallen (gefiel, hat gefallen; gefällt) to
  please, be pleasing
Gefangen- (*m./f. adj. as noun*), **-e/-en**
  prisoner
Gefühl (*n.*), **-e** feeling
gegen against; toward
Gegend (*f.*), **-en** area, region, district
gegenseitig each other, one another
Gegenstand (*m.*), **⁼e** object, subject
gegenüber as compared to, opposite
Gegenwart (*f.*) present, the present time
gegenwärtig present, contemporary
Gegner (*m.*), **–; Gegnerin** (*f.*), **-nen**
  opponent
Gehalt (*m.*), **-e** content; proportion; salary
geheim secret
Geheimnis (*n.*), **-se** mystery
geheimnisvoll mysterious
gehen (ging, ist gegangen) to go, walk;
  vor sich gehen to take place
gehorchen to obey
gehören to belong to
Geist (*m.*), **-er** spirit
geistig intellectual, mental, spiritual
geistlich religious, pertaining to church
geistreich ingenious, gifted
gekonnt skillfully
Gelächter (*n.*) laughter
Gelände (*n.*), **–** tract of land
gelangen to arrive at, reach
gelb yellow
Geld (*n.*), **-er** money
Gelegenheit (*f.*), **-en** opportunity

Gelehrte *(f. or m.)*, **-n**   scholar, scientist
gelingen (gelang, ist gelungen)   to succeed; **es gelingt mir**   I succeed
gelten (galt, gegolten; gilt)   to be valid, to be true; **gelten als**   to be regarded as, be seen as
Gemälde *(n.)*, **–**   painting
gemäß   according to
gemein   ordinary, vulgar
Gemeinde *(f.)*, **-n**   community
gemeinsam   mutual, joint, common
Gemisch *(n.)*, **-e**   mixture
genau   exact
genießen (genoss, genossen)   to enjoy
genug   enough
genügen   to suffice
geprägt   characterized
gerade   just, recently
Gerechtigkeit *(f.)*   justice
Gericht *(n.)*, **-e**   court of law
gering   small, slight, minimal
gern   gladly, willingly; **gern** + *verb*   to like to + *verb*
gesamt   total, entire
Gesamtheit *(f.)*   entirety
Gesamthochschule *(f.)*, **-n**   comprehensive university
geschehen (geschah, ist geschehen; geschieht)   to happen, take place
Geschenk *(n.)*, **-e**   present, gift
Geschichte *(f.)*   history
Geschichte *(f.)*, **-n**   story
geschickt   adept, talented
Geschlecht *(n.)*, **-er**   gender
Geschwindigkeit *(f.)*, **-en**   speed
Gesellschaft *(f.)*, **-en**   society, company
Gesetz *(n.)*, **-e**   law
Gesicht *(n.)*, **-er**   face
Gesichtspunkt *(m.)*, **-e**   point of view, aspect
Gespräch *(n.)*, **-e**   conversation
Gestalt *(f.)*, **-en**   figure, character
gestalten   to fashion, form
gestehen (gestand, gestanden)   to admit
gestern   yesterday
gesund   healthy
Gesundheit *(f.)*   health
Gewalt *(f.)*   power, dominion, might
gewerbsmäßig   occupational
Gewicht *(n.)*, **-e**   weight
Gewinn *(m.)*, **-e**   earnings, profit
gewinnen (gewann, gewonnen)   to win
gewiss   certain
Gewohnheit *(f.)*, **-en**   habit
gewöhnlich   usual, customary, common
gierig   eager, greedy
Gift *(n.)*   poison

Glaube *(m.)*   belief
glauben   to believe
gleich   same, equal
gleichen (glich, geglichen)   to resemble, be like
gleichermaßen   to the same extent
Gleichung *(f.)*, **-en**   equation
gleichwohl   nevertheless, for all that
Glück *(n.)*   happiness, luck, good fortune
glücken   to succeed
glücklich   happy, fortunate
Gott *(m.)*, **ü-er**   god, God
Gottesdienst *(m.)*, **-e**   religious service
Grab *(n.)*, **ü-er**   grave
Graben *(m.)*, **ü-**   rift, division, trench
Grabmal *(n.)*, **ü-er**   tombstone
Grenze *(f.)*, **-n**   boundary, border
Grieche *(m., n-noun)*, **-n; Griechin** *(f.)*, **-nen**   Greek
groß   large, great, tall
  Großartigkeit *(f.)*   grandeur
Größe *(f.)*, **-n**   size
Großeltern *(pl.)*   grandparents
Großmacht *(f.)*, **ü-e**   superpower
Großraum *(m.)* **ü-e**   metropolitan area
grün   green
Grund *(m.)*, **ü-e**   ground, reason; **auf Grund**   on the basis of, on the strength of; **aus diesem Grund**   for this reason; **dem liegt zu Grunde**   this is based on; **im Grunde**   basically, fundamentally
gründen   to found, organize
Grundlage *(f.)*, **-n**   basis
grundlegend   basic
gründlich   thorough
Grundsatz *(m.)*, **ü-e**   principle
grundsätzlich   fundamental(ly)
Grundstück *(n.)*, **-e**   property, piece of land
Grundzug *(m.)*, **ü-e**   main feature, characteristic
Gruppe *(f.)*, **-n**   group
gültig   valid
Gunst *(f.)*   favor
günstig   convenient
gut   good, well
Gymnasium *(n.)*   college preparatory high school

Hab und Gut   worldly possessions
haben (hatte, gehabt; hat)   to have
halb   half, semi-
halber   for the sake of
Hälfte *(f.)*, **-n**   half
halten (hielt, gehalten; hält)   to hold; to stop; **halten für**   to consider
Handel *(m.)*, **–**   trade

handeln to act, trade, deal
handfest strong
Handlung (*f.*), **-en** action, deed; act (theater)
Handwerk (*n.*) craft, trade
hart hard
häufig frequent
Häufigkeit (*f.*), **-en** frequency
Haupt (*n.*), **⁼er** head, chief
Hauptfach (*n.*), **⁼er** major field (of study)
Hauptrolle (*f.*), **-n** main function
hauptsächlich main(ly), chief
Hauptstadt (*f.*), **⁼e** capital city
Haus (*n.*), **⁼er** house; **zu Hause** at home
Hausaufgabe (*f.*), **-n** homework, assignment
Haut (*f.*), **⁼e** skin, hide
heben (**hob, gehoben**) to raise
hebräisch Hebrew
heilig holy
Heilmittel (*n.*), **–** medicine
Heimat (*f.*) native land, homeland
heimisch native, indigenous
heiraten to marry
heiß hot
heißen (**hieß, geheißen**) to be called, be named
heizen to heat
Held (*m., n-noun*), **-en** hero; **Heldin** (*f.*), **-nen** heroine
helfen (**half, geholfen; hilft**) to help
hell bright, clear
heran/ziehen (**zog ... heran, herangezogen**) to bring up, refer to
heraus/geben (**gab ... heraus, herausgegeben; gibt ... heraus**) to publish; **herausgegeben von** published by
herbei/führen to bring about
Herbst (**m**) fall, autumn
herein/fallen (**fiel ... herein, ist hereingefallen; fällt ... herein**) to fall for
Herkunft (*f.*), **⁼e** origin
her/leiten to derive
Herr (*m.*), **-en** Mr., lord, gentleman
Herrschaft (*f.*), **-en** rule, dominance
herrschen to rule, prevail, govern
her/stellen to produce, make
hervor/heben (**hob ... hervor, hervorgehoben**) to call special attention to, emphasize
hervorragend outstanding
hervor/treten (**trat ... hervor, ist hervorgetreten; tritt ... hervor**) to step forward, stand out, be prominent
Herz (*n.*), **-en** heart

Herzog (*m.*), **⁼e; Herzogin** (*f.*), **-nen** duke; duchess
heute today
heutig present (today's, current)
hier here
Hilfe (*f.*), **-n** help, aid
Himmel (*m.*) heaven, sky
Himmelskörper (*m.*), **–** celestial body
hin there, thither
hinauf up, upward
hinaus away, outside
hinderlich hindering, obstructive
hin/geben (**gab ... hin, hingegeben; gibt ... hin**) to give up; **sich hin/geben** to resign oneself to
hingegen on the other hand, on the contrary
hin/nehmen (**nahm ... hin, hingenommen; nimmt ... hin**) to put up with
hinreichend sufficient
hinsichtlich with respect to
hintereinander one behind the other
hinunter down, downward
Hinweis (*m.*), **-e** tip, information
hin/weisen auf (**wies ... hin, hingewiesen**) to refer to, point to
hinzu/fügen to add, supplement
hinzu/kommen to be added to
Historiker (*m.*), **–; Historikerin** (*f.*) **-nen** historian
hoch, hoh- high
Hochmut (*m.*) pride, arrogance, haughtiness
Hochschule (*f.*), **-n** university, college
höchst highest, extremely, very, maximum
höchstens at most, at best
hochwertig high-grade
Hof (*m.*), **⁼e** (royal) court; yard
hoffen (**auf**) to hope for
Hoffnung (*f.*), **-en** hope
Höhe (*f.*), **-n** height, elevation
Holz (*n.*), **⁼er** wood, timber
hören to hear
hrsg. = herausgegeben edited

Idee (*f.*), **-n** idea
illustrieren to illustrate
immer always, ever; **immer reicher** richer and richer; **immer wieder** again and again; **war schon immer** has always been
immerhin nonetheless
imstande sein (**war, ist gewesen; ist**) to be able
indem while; as; since; in that
infizieren (**sich**) to become infected
infolge on account of, because of

Informatik (*f.*), – computer science
Inhalt (*m.*), **-e** content, contents
inmitten in the middle of
inner inner, interior, spiritual
innerhalb within
insbesondere especially
Insel (*f.*), **-n** island
insgesamt all together
insofern als in so far as, in that
Intendant (*m., n-noun*), **-en; Intendantin**
  (*f.*), **-nen** theater director
interessant interesting
Interesse (*n.*), **-n** interest
interessieren (sich) für to be interested in
inzwischen meanwhile, in the meantime
irdisch earthly, human
irgend any, some; **irgend etwas**
  anything, anything at all, something;
  irgendein any(one), some(one);
  irgendwelch- any, any kind of;
  irgendwie somehow, in some way
Irrsinn (*m.*) insanity, nonsense
Irrtum (*m.*), **⁻er** error, misake

Jagd (*f.*), **-en** hunt
Jahr (*n.*), **-e** year
Jahrestag (*m.*), **-e** anniversary
Jahreszeit (*f.*), **-en** season
Jahrhundert (*n.*), **-e** century
jahrhundertelang for centuries
-jährig -year-old
Jahrzehnt (*n.*), **-e** decade
Jammer (*m.*) misery
je ever; every; per
je ... desto the ... the
je nach depending on, according to; **je
  nachdem** depending on whether
jedenfalls in any case, at any rate
jeder each, every
jederzeit any time, at all times, always
jedoch however, nevertheless
jemand somebody, anybody
jener that, the former, the one
jenseits on that side of
jetzt now
jeweilig respective
Jubel (*m.*) jubilation, joy
jüdisch Jewish
jung young
Junge (*m., n-noun*), **-n** youth, boy, young one
Jura (*no article*) law

Kaiser (*m.*), **–; Kaiserin** (*f.*), **-nen**
  emperor/empress
kalt cold
Kampf (*m.*), **⁻e** battle, fight
kämpfen to fight, battle, struggle

Kapital (*n.*), **-e, -ien** capital, funds
Kapitel (*n.*), **–** chapter
kassieren to receive money
Kauf (*m.*), **⁻e** purchase
kaufen to buy
kaum hardly
kein no, not any
keinesfalls in no way
keineswegs in no way
keinmal never
kennen (kannte, gekannt) to know, be
  acquainted with
kennen lernen to get to know, become
  acquainted with
Kenntnis (*f.*), **-se** knowledge
kennzeichnen to characterize, typify
Kind (*n.*), **-er** child
Kino (*n.*), **-s** cinema, movie theater
Kirche (*f.*), **-n** church
klagen to complain
klar clear
klären to clarify
klein small
klettern to climb
Klima (*n.*) climate
klingen (klang, geklungen) to sound,
  resound
knapp exactly, precisely; barely
Kollege (*m., n-noun*), **-n; Kollegin** (*f.*),
  -nen coworker, colleague
kommen (kam, ist gekommen) to come
kompliziert complicated, complex
Komponist (*m., n-noun*), **-en; Komponistin**
  (*f.*), **-nen** composer
komprimieren to compress
König (*m.*), **-e** king; **Königin** (*f.*), **-nen**
  queen
konkurrieren to compete
können (konnte, gekonnt; kann) to be
  able to
konsequent consistent, ongoing
Konsum (*m.*) consumption
konzentrieren (sich) auf to concentrate on
Konzepte (*pl.*) notes
Kopf (*m.*), **⁻e** head
Korb (*m.*), **⁻e** basket
Körper (*m.*), **–** body
körperlich physical, bodily, corporal
Kosten (*pl.*) cost, expenditure, expense
kosten to cost; *also* to taste or try
kostspielig expensive
Kraft (*f.*), **⁻e** power, force, strength
kräftig powerful
Kraftwerk (*n.*), **-e** power plant
krank ill, sick
Krankenhaus (*n.*), **⁻er** hospital
Krankheit (*f.*), **-en** illness, disease

Kreis *(m.)*, **-e**   circle
Krieg *(m.)*, **-e**   war
kriegen   to get
Krise *(f.)*, **-n**   crisis
Kritik *(f.)*, **-en**   criticism, review
kritisch   critical
krönen   to crown
Kultur *(f.)*, **-en**   culture
kulturell   cultural
Kulturgeschichte *(f.)*, **-n**   history of
   civilization
kümmern (sich) um   to mind, worry
   about
künftig   henceforth, in the future
Kunst *(f.)*, **̈e**   art
Künstler *(m.)*, **–**; **Künstlerin** *(f.)*, **-nen**
   artist
künstlich   artificial, man-made
kurz   short
kürzlich   recently
kurzsichtig   shortsighted, nearsighted
Küste *(f.)*, **-n**   coast

lächeln   to smile
lachen   to laugh
laden (lud, geladen; lädt)   to load
Lage *(f.)*, **-n**   position, situation
Lager *(n.)*, **–**   camp
lähmen   to cripple, paralyze
Laie *(m., n-noun)*, **-n**   novice, layperson
Land *(n.)*, **̈er**   land, state, country
Landschaft *(f.)*, **-en**   landscape
Landwirt *(m.)*, **-e**; **Landwirtin** *(f.)*, **-nen**
   farmer
landwirtschaftlich   agricultural
lang   long; **drei Jahre lang**   for three years
Länge *(f.)*, **-n**   length, duration, longitude
langsam   slow
längst   long ago, for a long time; **längst
   nicht**   by far not; **längst vorbei** long
   gone
langweilig   boring
Lärm *(m.)*   noise
lassen (ließ, gelassen; lässt)   to let, leave,
   yield, permit, cause; **sich lassen**   can
   be, may be
Last *(f.)*   burden, load
Lauf *(m.)*   course; **im Laufe**   in the
   course of
laufen (lief, ist gelaufen; läuft)   to run
laut (+ Objekt)   according to (+ *object*)
lauten   to say, read
Leben *(n.)*, **–**   life
leben   to live
lebendig   lively, alive
Lebensdauer *(f.)*   life span
Lebensführung *(f.)*, **-en**   lifestyle

Lebensmittel *(pl.)*   food, victuals
Lebensunterhalt *(m.)*   livelihood
Lebewesen *(n.)*, **–**   living being, creature
lebhaft   lively, vivacious
lediglich   only, merely
leer   empty
legen   to lay, place; **sich legen**   to lay
   down
Lehre *(f.)*, **-n**   theory, teaching
lehren   to teach
leicht   light, easy
Leiden *(n.)*, **–**   suffering
Leidenschaft *(f.)*, **-en**   passion
leider   unfortunately
leisten   perform
Leistung *(f.)*, **-en**   work, performance,
   achievement
leiten   to conduct, lead
Leiter *(m.)*, **–**; **Leiterin** *(f.)*, **-nen**   leader
lernen   to learn
lesen (las, gelesen; liest)   to read
letzt   last, final
letztendlich   in the final analysis
Leute *(pl.)*   people
Licht *(n.)*, **-er**   light
lieben   to love
lieber   rather, preferably
lieblich   lovely, sweet
Lieblings-   favorite . . .
Lied *(n.)*, **-er**   song
liefern   to supply
liegen (lag, gelegen)   to lie, be lying
   down
Linie *(f.)*, **-n**   line; **in erster Linie**   primarily, in the first place
links   left
loben   to praise
Loch *(n.)*, **̈er**   hole
locker   loose
Lohn *(m.)*, **̈e**   reward, pay
lösbar   solvable
lösen   to solve, dissolve
**los/lassen (ließ ... los, losgelassen,
   lässt ... los)**   to let go
Lösung *(f.)*, **-en**   solution
lügen (log, gelogen)   to tell a lie
Luft *(f.)*, **̈e**   air
Lustspiel *(n.)*, **-e**   comedy

machen   to do, make, cause
Macht *(f.)*, **̈e**   power, might, force
mächtig   powerful, mighty, huge
Mädchen *(n.)*, **–**   girl
mahnen   to remind, warn, admonish
mal   times
Mal *(n.)*, **-e**   point of time, time
malen   to paint

In-Ma

Malerei *(f.)*, **-en** painting
man (some)one, they, we, people
manch some, many a
manchmal sometimes
Mangel *(m.)*, ÷ deficiency, lack
Mann *(m.)*, ÷**er** man; husband
mannigfaltig varied, manifold
männlich male
Mannschaft *(f.)*, **-en** team, crew
Mantel *(m.)*, ÷ coat
Märchen *(n.)*, – fairy tale
Markenzeichen *(n.)* trademark
Maß *(m.)*, **-e** measure, measurement
massig big, heavy
Maßnahme *(f.)*, **-n** measure, precaution
Maßstab *(m.)*, ÷**e** criterion, measure
Mauer *(f.)*, **-n** wall, outdoor enclosure
Meer *(n.)*, **-e** ocean, sea
mehr more; **immer mehr** more and
    more; **nicht mehr** no more, no longer
mehrere several, some, a few
mehrfach several times
Mehrzahl *(f.)* majority
meinen to state an opinion; to mean,
    intend
Meinung *(f.)*, **-en** opinion
meist most
meistens mainly, mostly
Menge *(f.)*, **-n** amount, quantity
Mensch *(m., n-noun)*, **-en** mankind;
    human being, person
Menschheit *(f.)* mankind, humanity
menschlich human, humane
Merkblatt *(n.)*, ÷**er** leaflet, handout
Merkmal *(n.)*, **-e** characteristic
messen (maß, gemessen; misst) to measure
Milliarde *(f.)*, **-n** billion
Minderheit *(f.)*, **-en** minority
mindestens at least
missbrauchen to misuse, speak in vain
mit with
Mitarbeiter *(m.)*, –; **Mitarbeiterin** *(f.)*,
    -nen coworker
Mitglied *(n.)*, **-er** member
**mit/halten (hielt ... mit, mitgehalten;
    hält ... mit)** to keep up with
Mitte *(f.)*, **-n** middle, center
mit/teilen to tell, communicate, impart
Mitteilung *(f.)*, **-en** report, communication
Mittel *(n.)*, – means, aid, middle
Mittelalter *(n.)* Middle Ages
mittels by means of
mittlerweile in the meantime, meanwhile
modisch popular, in vogue
mögen (mochte, gemocht; mag) to like
    (to)
möglich possible

Möglichkeit *(f.)*, **-en** possibility
Monat *(m.)*, **-e** month
Mond *(m.)*, **-e** moon
Mord *(m.)*, **-e** murder
morgen tomorrow
Mühe *(f.)* trouble, effort
Mund *(m.)*, ÷**er** mouth
mündig responsible
müssen (musste, gemusst; muss) to have
    to, must, be obliged to
mutig brave
Mutter *(f.)*, ÷ mother
Mythos *(m.)*, **Mythen** myth

nach to, toward; after, according to; **nach
    und nach** gradually, little by little
Nachbar *(m., n-noun)*, **-n; Nachbarin** *(f.)*,
    -nen neighbor
nach/bilden to copy, imitate
nachdem after
nachfolgend following
Nachfrage *(f.)*, **-n** demand, request,
    inquiry
**nach/gehen (ging ... nach, ist
    nachgegangen)** to pursue
Nachlass *(m.)*, ÷**e** literary remains
Nachmittag *(m.)*, **-e** afternoon
**nach/schlagen (schlug ... nach, nachge-
    schlagen; schlägt ... nach)** to look up
nächst next, nearest
Nacht *(f.)*, ÷**e** night
Nachteil *(m.)*, **-e** disadvantage
nächtelang for nights at a time
Nachweis *(m.)*, **-e** proof, determination
**nach/weisen (wies ... nach,
    nachgewiesen)** to prove, show
Nachwirkung *(f.)*, **-en** consequence,
    after-effect
nah(e) near
Nähe *(f.)* vicinity, nearness; **in der
    Nähe** near
**nahe/legen (lag ... nahe, nahegelegen;
    liegt ... nahe)** to suggest
näher more closely, in greater detail
nähern (sich) to approach
nahezu nearly
Nährstoff *(m.)*, **-e** nutrient
Nahrungsmittel *(pl.)* food
Name *(m., n-noun)*, **-n** name
nämlich namely, that is
Nase *(f.)*, **-n** nose
Natur *(f.)*, **-en** nature
Naturforscher *(m.)*, –; **Naturforscherin** *(f.)*,
    -nen scientist
natürlich of course, naturally
Naturwissenschaft *(f.)*, **-en** natural science
neben beside, in addition to, near

Nebenfach (*n.*), **-̈er** minor field (of study)

nehmen (nahm, genommen; nimmt) to take

nein no

nennen (nannte, genannt) to name

neu new

neuartig novel, new-fashioned

neulich recently

nicht not

nichts nothing; **gar nichts** nothing at all; **nichts als** nothing but

nie never

Niedergang (*m.*) decline

Niederlage (*f.*), **-n** defeat

nieder/lassen (sich) (ließ ... nieder, niedergelassen; lässt ... nieder) to settle down, establish oneself

niedrig low

niemals never

niemand nobody

noch still, even; **noch einmal** once again, once more; **noch immer** still; **noch nicht** not yet

Nord, Norden (*m.*) north

nördlich northern, northerly

Not (*f.*) need, necessity

nötig necessary, needed

Notizbuch (*n.*), **Notizbücher** notebook

notwendig necessary

Notzustand (*m.*), **Notzustände** state of emergency

Nüchternheit (*f.*) sobriety, dullness

Nummer (*f.*), **-n** number

nun now

nunmehr henceforth, now, by this time

nur only; **nur dem Namen nach** in name only

nützen to help

nützlich useful

Nutzung (*f.*), **-en** yield, revenue, utilization

ob whether, if

oben above

oberhalb above, overhead

Oberhaupt (*n.*), **Oberhäupter** head, ruler

obgleich although

obwohl although, though

oder or

offen open

offenbar apparent

Offenheit (*f.*) openness, frankness

offensichtlich obvious, apparent

öffentlich public

Öffentlichkeit (*f.*) public

öffnen to open

oft often, oftentimes

öfters frequently, quite often

ohne without

Ökologie (*f.*) ecology

Oper (*f.*), **-n** opera

Opfer (*n.*), **-** victim, sacrifice

opfern to sacrifice

Orgel (*f.*), **-n** organ (mus.)

Ort (*m.*), **-e** village, place, site

Ost, Osten (*m.*) east; Orient

Ostern (*n.*) Easter

Österreich (*n.*) Austria

Ostküste (*f.*) east coast

östlich eastern, oriental, easterly

Palast (*m.*), **-̈e** palace

Papier (*n.*), **-e** paper, document

Papst (*m.*), **-̈e** pope

Partei (*f.*), **-en** political party

Partikel (*f.*), **-n** particle

pathetisch lofty, solemn, expressive

Periode (*f.*), **-n** period, interval

Persönlichkeit (*f.*), **-en** personality

Pflanze (*f.*), **-n** plant

Pflege (*f.*) care, cultivation

pfeifen (pfiff, gepfiffen) to whistle

Pflicht (*f.*), **-en** duty

pflücken to pick

Pfund (*n.*), **-e** pound

Phänomen (*n.*), **-e** phenomenon

Platz (*m.*), **-̈e** place

plötzlich suddenly

plump clumsy, awkward

Politik (*f.*) politics, policy

politisch political

Polizist (*m.*, *n-noun*), **-en; Polizistin** (*f.*), **-nen** police officer

prägen to shape, coin, mint

praktisch practical

Prinzip (*n.*), **-ien, -e** principle

pro per

profund thorough, solid

Prozentsatz (*m.*) percentage

Prozess (*m.*), **-e** process

prüfen to test

Prüfung (*f.*), **-en** test, examination

Quadrat (*n.*), **-e** square

quälen to torture

Quelle (*f.*), **-n** source, spring

Rad (*n.*), **-̈er** bike or wheel

Rahmen (*m.*), **-** frame; **im Rahmen** within the framework, scope

rasch rapid, fast

Rat (*m.*), **Ratschläge** advice; **um Rat bitten** to ask for advice

Rate (*f.*), **-n** rate

raten (riet, geraten; rät) to advise
rationell efficient, rational, economical
rauchen to smoke
Raum *(m.),* **Räume** room, space, volume
reagieren auf to react to
rechnen mit to count on
Rechnung *(f.),* **-en** calculation, bill
recht right, true; quite
Recht *(n.),* **-e** right, permission
rechtfertigen to justify
rechtlich legal
Redakteur *(m.),* **-e; Redakteurin** *(f.),* **-nen**
  editor
Rede *(f.),* **-n** speech, talk
Redefreiheit *(f.),* **-en** freedom of speech
Redewendung *(f.),* **-en** figure of speech
Redner *(m.),* **–; Rednerin** *(f.),* **-nen**
  speaker, orator
Regel *(f.),* **-n** rule; **in der Regel** as a rule,
  ordinarily
regelmäßig regularly
Regen *(m.),* **–** rain
regen (sich) to cause a stir, set in motion
regieren to rule, govern; to prevail
Regierung *(f.),* **-en** government
Regisseur *(m.),* **-e; Regisseurin** *(f.),* **-nen**
  director (movie, theater)
Register *(n.),* **–** index
regnen to rain
reich rich, abundant
Reich *(n.),* **-e** empire, state, realm
reichlich sufficiently
reifen to ripen, mature
Reihe *(f.),* **-n** series
Reihenfolge *(f.),* **-n** order, sequence
reihenweise by the dozen, in series
rein pure, clean
Reise *(f.),* **-n** trip
reisen to travel
reiten (ritt, ist geritten) to ride (an animal)
renommiert well-known, respected
reparieren to repair, mend
Repräsentant *(m., n-noun),* **-en; Repräsen-**
  tantin *(f.),* **-nen** representative
Rest *(m.),* **-e** remains
restaurieren to restore
Resultat *(n.),* **-e** result, findings
retten to rescue, save
Rettung *(f.),* **-en** rescue
richten (sich) nach to conform to
richtig right, correct
riesig gigantic
ringen (rang, gerungen) to struggle
Rohstoff *(m.),* **-e** raw material
Rolle *(f.),* **-n** role
Roman *(m.),* **-e** novel
Römer *(m.),* **–; Römerin** *(f.),* **-nen** Roman

rot red
rücksichtslos inconsiderate, reckless,
  ruthless
rufen (rief, gerufen) to call
Ruhm *(m.)* fame, honor, glory
rund round, about; approximately

Sage *(f.),* **-n** legend, fable, saga
sagen to say
sammeln to collect
Sammlung *(f.),* **-en** collection
sämtlich all, entire
Satz *(m.),* **-̈e** sentence, theorem; movement *(music)*
Säugling *(m.),* **-e** infant
Schaden *(m.),* **-̈** damage
schaffen (schuf, geschaffen) to produce,
  formulate, create
schaffen (schaffte, geschafft) to do, work
Schall *(m.),* **-e or -̈e** sound
Schaltjahr *(n.),* **-e** leap year
scharf sharp
schärfen to intensify
Schatz *(m.),* **-̈e** treasure
schätzen to estimate; to value
Schau *(f.),* **-en** show, exhibition
Schauspieler *(m.),* **–; Schauspielerin** *(f.),*
  -nen actor/actress
scheiden (schied, geschieden) to separate, divide
scheinen (schien, geschienen) to shine;
  to appear, seem
schenken to give, award
schicken to send
Schicksal *(n.),* **-e** fate, destiny
Schild *(n.),* **-er** sign
schildern to describe
schimpfen auf to complain about
Schlacht *(f.),* **-en** battle
schlagen (schlug, geschlagen; schlägt)
  to hit, to nail to, to fasten to
Schlagfertigkeit *(f.)* quick wit
schlecht bad, ill, poor, evil
schlicht plain, simple
schließen (schloss, geschlossen) to close,
  finish, conclude
schließlich finally, in conclusion,
  after all
schmackhaft tasty
schmal slim, slender
schmecken to taste
Schnee *(m.)* snow
schnell rapid, fast
schon already
schön beautiful, nice
schöpferisch creative
Schreck *(m.),* **-e; Schrecken** alarm, fright

schrecklich frightful, terrible, dreadful
schreiben (schrieb, geschrieben) to write
Schrift (*f.*), **-en** work, writing
Schriftsteller (*m.*), **–**; **Schriftstellerin** (*f.*), **-nen** writer, author
Schritt (*m.*), **-e** step
Schuld (*f.*), **-en** guilt, blame, debt
Schule (*f.*), **-n** school
Schüler (*m.*), **–**; **Schülerin** (*f.*), **-nen** pupil
Schuss (*m.*), **¨e** shot; **Schüsse fielen** shots were fired
schützen to protect
schwach weak, feeble, slight
Schwäche (*f.*), **-n** weakness
schwächen to weaken
schwarz black
schwimmen (schwamm, ist geschwommen) to swim, float
schweben to hover
schweigen (schwieg, geschwiegen) to be silent
schwer heavy, difficult, severe
Schwester (*f.*), **-n** sister
schwierig difficult
Schwierigkeit (*f.*), **-en** difficulty
See (*m.*), **-n** lake
See (*f.*), **-n** sea
Seele (*f.*), **-n** soul, spirit
seelisch psychic, spiritual, emotional
sehen (sah, gesehen; sieht) to see
sehnen (sich) nach to long for
Sehnsucht (*f.*) longing, desire
sehr very, very much
sein (war, ist gewesen; ist) to be; **es sei denn, dass** unless
seit since
Seite (*f.*), **-n** page
selber: er selber -self: he himself
selbst -self; even
Selbständigkeit (*f.*) independence
Selbstbekenntnis (*n.*), **-se** self-revelation, confession
Selbstbewusstsein (*n.*) self-assurance, self-confidence
Selbstmord (*m.*), **-e** suicide
Selbstüberwindung (*f.*) self-control
selbstverständlich self-evident, obvious
Sendung (*f.*), **-en** broadcast
Senkung (*f.*), **-en** decrease, lowering
sensibel sensitive
sensitiv hypersensitive
setzen to set, place, put; **sich setzen** to sit down
sicher safe, secure; definite, sure, certain
Sicherheit (*f.*), **-en** security
sichern to protect
sichtbar visible

Siedlung (*f.*), **-en** settlement
Sieger (*m.*), **–**; **Siegerin** (*f.*), **-nen** victor
siegrich victorious
Sinn (*m.*), **-e** meaning, sense
Sitte (*f.*), **-n** custom, tradition
sittlich moral, ethical
Sitz (*m.*) seat of government
sitzen (saß, gesessen) to sit
so so, such, thus, then; **so wie** just as
sofort immediately
sogar even
sogenannt so-called
Sohn (*m.*), **¨e** son
solch such
Soldat (*m., n-noun*), **-en**; **Soldatin** (*f.*), **-nen** soldier
sollen shall; to be said to, be supposed to, should, ought to
Sommer (*m.*), **–** summer
sonderlich particularly
sondern but (rather)
Sonne (*f.*), **-n** sun
sonst otherwise, else
sonstig other
sooft as often as
Sorte (*f.*), **-n** kind, variety, type
soviel so far as, to the extent that
so viel wie as much as, as good as
sowie as well as, just as, as soon as, as also
sowohl ... wie/als auch both . . . and, not only ... but also, as well as
sozusagen so to speak, as it were
Spaltung (*f.*), **-en** splitting
spannend exciting
Spannung (*f.*), **-en** tension, excitement
spät late
Speicher (*m.*), **–** data bank, (computer) memory
speichern to store
Spiegel (*m.*), **–** mirror, looking glass
Spiel (*n.*), **-e** play, game
Spielfilm (*m.*), **-e** feature film
Spielzeug (*n.*), **-e** toy
Spitze (*f.*), **-n** point; **an der Spitze** at the front/top
Sprache (*f.*), **-n** language
sprechen (sprach, gesprochen; spricht) to speak
Sprichwort (*n.*), **¨er** saying, proverb
springen (sprang, ist gesprungen) to jump
spürbar detectable, perceivable
Staat (*m.*), **-en** state, country, nation
staatlich state, civil, national, public
Staatsangehörigkeit (*f.*) citizenship
Stadt (*f.*), **¨e** city
Stadtführer (*m.*), **–** guide (book) to a city
Stamm (*m.*), **¨e** tribe, stem

stammen to come from, stem from
Stand *(m.)*, **⁻e** position, stand
ständig constant
Standort *(m.)*, **-e** position
Standpunkt *(m.)*, **-e** position, standpoint, perspective
stark strong
statt instead (of)
statt/finden (fand ... statt, stattgefunden) to take place, occur
stehen (stand, gestanden) to stand
stehlen (stahl, gestohlen; stiehlt) to steal
steigen (stieg, ist gestiegen) to rise, increase, climb
steigern to increase, raise
Stein *(m.)*, **-e** stone
Stelle *(f.)*, **-n** place, location, passage
stellen to place, put, set
Stellung *(f.)*, **-en** position, situation
Stellungnahme *(f.)*, **-n** opinion, point of view
sterben (starb, ist gestorben; stirbt) to die
Stern *(m.)*, **-e** star
stets constantly
Steuer *(f.)*, **-n** tax
steuern to steer
Stichwort *(n.)*, **-e** catchword, keyword
Stil *(m.)*, **-e** style
still calm, silent
Stimme *(f.)*, **-n** voice
Stimmung *(f.)*, **-en** mood, emotion
Stoff *(m.)*, **-e** substance, material
stolz proud
stören to disturb, disrupt
stoßen (stieß, gestoßen; stößt) to kick, bump, run into
Strafe *(f.)*, **-n** punishment
Strahl *(m.)*, **-en** ray, beam
Straße *(f.)*, **-n** street
streben to strive
streiten (stritt, gestritten) to fight/ struggle for
Strom *(m.)*, **⁻e** stream, flow
Stück *(n.)*, **-e** piece
Studienabschluss *(m.)*, **⁻e** academic degree
Studienanfänger *(m.)*, **–; Studienanfängerin** *(f.)*, **-nen** first-year student
Studiengang *(m.)*, **⁻e** course of study
studieren to study at a university
Studium *(n.)*, **Studien** study, studies (at university)
Stuhl *(m.)*, **⁻e** chair
Stunde *(f.)*, **-n** hour; lesson, class
Sturm *(m.)*, **⁻e** storm
stürmisch stormy, turbulent
Suche *(f.)*, **-n** search

Süd, Süden *(m.)* south
südlich southern, southerly
Sünde *(f.)*, **-n** sin
sympathisch engaging

Tabelle *(f.)*, **-n** table, summary, chart
Tag *(m.)*, **-e** day
Tagebuch *(n.)*, **⁻er** journal, diary
Tageslicht *(n.)* daylight, sunshine
täglich daily
Tagung *(f.)*, **-en** convention, meeting
Tanz *(m.)*, **⁻e** dance
tanzen to dance
Taschenbuch *(n.)*, **⁻er** paperback book
Tat *(f.)*, **-en** deed, act
tätig active, engaged, busy
Tätigkeit *(f.)*, **-en** activity
Tatsache *(f.)*, **-n** fact
tatsächlich in fact, actual, factual
Teil *(m.)*, **-e** part; **zum Teil** in part, partly
teilen to divide
Teilnahme *(f.)* participation
teil/nehmen (nahm ... teil, teilgenommen; nimmt ... teil) to take part, participate
Teilnehmer *(m.)*, **–; Teilnehmerin** *(f.)*, **-nen** participant
teils partly, in part
Teilung *(f.)*, **-en** division
teilweise partly, partially
Teppich *(m.)*, **-e** carpet
teuer expensive
Theaterstück *(n.)*, **-e** theater play
Thema *(n.)*, **Themen** topic, theme
tief deep, low
Tier *(n.)*, **-e** animal
Titel *(m.)*, **–** title
Tod *(m.)* death
tödlich lethal
tot dead
Tote *(m., f.)* dead person
töten to kill
tragen (trug, getragen; trägt) to carry, bear, wear
Träger *(m.)*, **–; Trägerin** *(f.)*, **-nen** winner, recipient, bearer
Traum *(m.)*, **Träume** dream
treffen (traf, getroffen; trifft) to meet
Treffen *(n.)*, **–** meeting
treiben (trieb, getrieben) to drive
trennen to separate
Trennung *(f.)*, **-en** separation
treten (trat, getreten; tritt) to step, move
trinken (trank, getrunken) to drink
trotz in spite of
Trümmer *(pl.)* ruins
Truppe *(f.)*, **-n** troop

Tugend (*f.*), **-en** virtue
tun (tat, getan) to do
Tür (*f.*), **-en** door
Turm (*m.*), **⁻e** tower, steeple

u.a. = unter anderem, unter anderen
  amongst other things, among others
u.a.m. = und anderes mehr and others,
  and so forth
üben to practice
über over; about
überall everywhere
überaus extremely, exceedingly
Überblick (*m.*), **-e** overview, survey
überdies moreover, besides
Übereinstimmung (*f.*), **-en** agreement
überfällig overdue
Überflutung (*f.*), **-en** flood
Übergang (*m.*), **⁻e** changeover,
  transition
überhaupt generally, on the whole, at all
überlegen (sich) to think about, ponder
Übermensch (*m., n-noun*), **-en** superman
übermorgen day after tomorrow
**übernehmen (übernahm, übernommen;
  übernimmt)** to take over
überqueren to cross (over)
überraschen to surprise
Überraschung (*f.*), **-en** surprise
überreichen to hand over
**überschreiten (überschritt,
  überschritten)** to exceed, go beyond
übersetzen to translate
Übersetzung (*f.*), **-en** translation
Übersicht (*f.*), **-en** view, survey, digest,
  summary
überstehen (überstand, überstanden) to
  withstand, survive
**übertragen (übertrug, übertragen;
  überträgt)** to transfer (to)
übertreiben (übertrieb, übertrieben) to
  exaggerate
überwältigen to overcome, overwhelm
überzeugen to convince
überziehen (überzog, überzogen) to
  overstate, exaggerate
üblich usual, customary
übrig (left) over, other
übrigens by the way, moreover
Übung (*f.*), **-en** exercise, practice
Uhr (*f.*), **-en** clock; **um acht Uhr** at eight
  o'clock
um around, about; at (+ time); by; for;
  um mehr als by more than; **um ...
  willen** for the sake of . . .
um ... zu in order to
um/arbeiten to rewrite, revise

Umfang (*m.*) extent
umfangreich extensive
umfassen to encompass
**umgeben von (umgab, umgeben;
  umgibt)** surrounded by
Umgebung (*f.*), **-en** environ, surrounding
  area
um/gestalten to reconfigure
Umkreis (*m.*), **-e** circle
um/setzen to implement
um/siedeln to relocate
umso ... je the . . . the
Umstand (*m.*), **Umstände** circumstance,
  situation
**um/steigen auf (stieg ... um, ist
  umgestiegen)** to switch to,
  transfer to
umstritten contested, controversial
Umwelt (*f.*) environment
Umweltschutz (*m.*) environmental
  protection
um/ziehen (zog ... um, ist umgezogen)
  to move; **sich um/ziehen (hat sich
  umgezogen)** to change clothes
unabhängig independent
unbedingt absolutely
unbegrenzt unlimited
unbestritten indisputably
undurchsichtig opaque
unergründlich unfathomable
unerlässlich indispensable
unerträglich unbearable
Unfall (*m.*), **⁻e** accident
ungeeignet unsuitable, unfit
ungefähr about, approximately
ungeheuer huge, colossal, enormous
ungekannt unknown
ungenau inaccurate
ungewöhnlich unusual
unglaublich unbelievable
unmittelbar direct
unmöglich impossible
Unruhe (*f.*), **-n** unrest, upheaval
unsichtbar invisible
unten below
unter under; among
**unter/gehen (ging ... unter, ist
  untergegangen)** to set, sink
**unternehmen (unternahm, unternommen;
  unternimmt)** to carry out, undertake
Unternehmen (*n.*), **–** enterprise, large
  company
Unternehmer (*m.*), **–**; **Unternehmerin** (*f.*),
  -nen entrepreneur, contractor
Unterricht (*m.*) instruction
Unterschied (*m.*), **-e** difference,
  distinction

unterscheiden (unterschied, unterschieden) to distinguish
unterstellen to place under
unterstreichen (understrich, unterstrichen) to emphasize, underline
unterstützen to support
Unterstützung (f.), -en support
untersuchen to examine, investigate
Untersuchung (f.), -en investigation, examination
Unterwerfung (f.), -en submission
unterzeichnen to sign
unverantwortlich irresponsible
unvergesslich unforgettable
unvermeidlich unavoidable
unverständlich unintelligible
unverwechselbar unmistakable
unzählig countless
Ureinwohner (m.), –; Ureinwohnerin (f.), -nen native inhabitant
Urkunde (f.), -n document
Ursache (f.), -n cause
Ursprung (m.), ̈-e origin, source
ursprünglich original(ly)
u.s.w. = und so weiter and so forth, etc.
u.U. = unter Umständen under certain circumstances

Vater (m.), ̈- father
väterlich paternal
v.Chr. = vor Christi (Geburt) B.C.
verachten to despise
veraltet outmoded
verändern to change
Veränderung (f.), -en change
veranlassen to bring about, occasion
verbannen to ban
verbergen (verbarg, verborgen; verbirgt) to hide
verbessern to improve
verbieten (verbot, verboten) to forbid; verboten forbidden
verbinden (verband, verbunden) to combine, connect
verbindlich binding
Verbindung (f.), -en connection
verbrauchen to consume
verbreiten to spread, disseminate
verbrennen (verbrannte, verbrannt) to set fire to
verbringen (verbrachte, verbracht) to spend, pass time
Verbundenheit (f.) bond, solidarity
verdanken to owe, be indebted to
verdienen to earn
verdrängen to displace

verehren to worship
Vereinbarung (f.), -en agreement
Vereinigten Staaten (pl.) United States
Vereinigung (f.) unification
verewigen to perpetuate
Verfahren (n.), – process
Verfasser (m.), –; Verfasserin (f.), -nen author
verfolgen to persecute
Verfügung (f.), -en disposal, order; zur Verfügung haben to have available; zur Verfügung stehen to be available
Vergangenheit (f.) past
vergessen (vergaß, vergessen; vergisst) to forget
Vergleich (m.), -e comparison; zum Vergleich as a comparison
vergleichen (verglich, verglichen) to compare
vergrößern to enlarge
Verhältnis (n.), -se ratio, relation; relationship; situation
verhältnismäßig relative, comparative
verhelfen (verhalf, verholfen) to help/assist toward an end
verherrlichen to glorify
verkaufen to sell
Verkäufer (m.), –; Verkäuferin (f.), -nen salesman/woman
Verkehrsmittel (n.) means of transportation
verkommen (verkam, ist verkommen) to decay, come down in the world
verkörpern to embody
verkünden to proclaim
Verkündigung (f.), -en announcement
Verlag (m.), -e publisher
verlangen to demand, claim, desire
verlassen (verließ, verlassen; verlässt) to leave
verletzen to injure; sich verletzen to get hurt, injure oneself
verlieren (verlor, verloren) to lose
Verlust (m.), -e loss
vermehren (sich) to multiply
vermeiden (vermied, vermieden) to avoid
vermerken to annotate, note, remark
vermischen to mix, combine
vermitteln to convey, give
Vermögen (n.), – wealth
vermuten to suspect, assume
vermutlich presumable, possible
vernichten to destroy
Vernichtung (f.) total destruction
Vernunft (f.) reason
Veröffentlichung (f.), -en publication
verpönt taboo, despised

verschieben (verschob, verschoben) to postpone

verschieden various, different

verschollen disappeared

verschweigen (verschwieg, verschwiegen) to keep secret, conceal

verschwinden (verschwand, ist verschwunden) to disappear

versehen (versah, versehen; versieht) to equip, provide, furnish

versetzen to transplant

versichern to insure; to assure

Versicherung *(f.),* **-en** insurance

versöhnen to reconcile

versorgen to provide, supply

versprechen (versprach, versprochen; verspricht) to promise; **sich versprechen** to mispronounce

Verstand *(m.)* mind, reason

verstandesmäßig rational

verständigen to inform, make understood

verständlich intelligible

Verständnis *(n.)* understanding

verstehen (verstand, verstanden) to understand

verstorben deceased

Versuch *(m.),* **-e** experiment, attempt

versuchen to try

vertauschen to exchange

verteidigen to defend

Verteidigung *(f.)* defense, vindication

verteilen to distribute; **verteilen lassen** to divide up

Vertrag *(m.),* **⸚e** treaty, contract

vertreiben (vertrieb, vertrieben) to exile

vertreten (vertrat, vertreten; vertritt) to defend, advocate

Vertreter *(m.),* **–; Vertreterin** *(f.),* **-nen** representative

verurteilen to condemn

Verwaltung *(f.)* administration

verwandeln (sich) to change, transform, metamorphose

Verweigerung *(f.),* **-en** denial, refusal

verwenden to use, employ

verzeichnen to record, list

verzichten (auf) to forgo

v.H. = vom Hundert percent

viel much; **vieles** much

viele many

vielfach manifold, various, frequent

Vielfalt *(f.)* variety, diversity

vielfältig varied, manifold

vielleicht perhaps

Vogel *(m.)* **⸚** bird

Volk *(n.),* **⸚er** people, nation

vollbringen (vollbrachte, vollbracht) to perform, accomplish

vollenden to complete, end, finish

völlig fully, completely

vollständig complete, entire

vollziehen (vollzog, vollzogen) to accomplish

Vollziehung *(f.)* execution, achievement

Vollzug *(m.)* completion

von of; from; about; by; on; upon

vor before; in front of; for; **vor allem** above all; **vor zehn Jahren** ten years ago

voran/gehen (ging ... voran, ist vorangegangen) to precede

voraus before, in advance, ahead

voraus/sagen to predict

Voraussetzung *(f.),* **-en** assumption, hypothesis; prerequisite

vor/bereiten to prepare

Vorbild *(n.),* **-er** model, example

Vordergrund *(m.),* **⸚e** foreground

vor/dringen (drang ... vor, ist vorgedrungen) to advance, penetrate

Voreingenommenheit *(f.)* prejudice

vor/finden (fand ... vor, vorgefunden) to find

vor/führen to bring up, present, demonstrate

Vorführung *(f.),* **-en** demonstration, presentation, show

Vorgang *(m.),* **⸚e** procedure

Vorgänger *(m.),* **–** predecessor

vorhanden sein to be present

vorher before, previously

vorher/gehen (ging ... vorher, ist vorhergegangen) to precede

vor/kommen (kam ... vor, ist vorgekommen) to occur, happen

vorläufig for the time being, temporary, preliminary

vor/legen to produce, present

Vorlesung *(f.),* **-en** lecture

vorletzt next to last

Vorliebe *(f.),* **-n** preference

vor/liegen (lag ... vor, vorgelegen) to be available, be under discussion

vor/nehmen (nahm ... vor, vorgenommen; nimmt ... vor) to undertake, do

Vorschlag *(m.),* **⸚e** suggestion

vor/schlagen (schlug ... vor, vorgeschlagen; schlägt ... vor) to suggest, propose

vor/schreiben (schrieb ... vor, vorgeschrieben) to dictate, prescribe

Vorschrift *(f.)*, **-en**   rule, instruction

vor/sehen (**sah … vor, vorgesehen; sieht … vor**)   to consider, provide for

vor/stellen   to introduce, present; **sich vor/stellen**   to introduce oneself; to imagine

Vorstellung *(f.)*, **-en**   imagination, idea

Vorurteil *(n.)*, **-e**   prejudice

vor/werfen (**warf … vor, vorgeworfen; wirft … vor**)   to reproach

vor/ziehen (**zog … vor, vorgezogen**)   to prefer

vorzüglich   excellent

wachsen (**wuchs, gewachsen; wächst**)   to grow

Wachstum *(n.)*   growth

Waffe *(f.)*, **-n**   weapon

Wagen *(m.)*, **–**   wagon, vehicle, car

Wahl *(f.)*, **-en**   choice, vote

wählen   to choose, select; to vote

Wahlkampf *(m.)*, **⁼e**   election campaign

wahr   true

während   during, while; for; whereas

wahrhaft   truly

Wahrheit *(f.)*, **-en**   truth

wahr/nehmen (**nahm … wahr, wahrgenommen; nimmt … wahr**)   to perceive

wahrscheinlich   probably

Wald *(m.)*, **⁼er**   forest, woods

Wand *(f.)*, **⁼e**   wall

Wandel *(m.)*   change, transformation

wandeln   to change

wann   when

Waren *(pl.)*   goods, merchandise

Wärme *(f.)*   warmth, heat

warum   why

was   what; that, which; whatever; **was für (ein)**   what kind of

(sich) waschen (**wusch, gewaschen; wäscht**)   to wash

Wasser *(n.)*, **–**   water

Weber *(m.)*, **–**; **Weberin** *(f.)*, **-nen**   weaver

Wechsel *(m.)*, **–**   change, changeover, exchange

wechseln   to change

weder … noch   neither . . . nor

Weg *(m.)*, **-e**   way, path, course

wegen   because of, on account of

weh/tun (**tat … weh, wehgetan**)   to be painful

Weib *(n.)*, **-er**   woman

weiblich   female, feminine

weich   soft

Weihnachten *(pl.)*   Christmas

weil   because, since

weinen   to cry, wail

weise   wise

Weise *(f.)*, **-n**   way, manner; **auf diese/in dieser Weise**   in this way

weiß   white

weit   wide, far, extensive

weiter   further

weiter/gehen (**ging … weiter, ist weitergegangen**)   to continue

weithin   widely, largely

welch   who, which; what

Welle *(f.)*, **-n**   wave

Welt *(f.)*, **-en**   world

Weltkrieg *(m.)*, **-e**   world war

Weltstadt *(f.)*, **⁼e**   metropolis

Wende *(f.)*, **-n**   turning point, new era

wenden (sich) an   to appeal to

wenig   little, few

wenigstens   at least

wenn   if, when; whenever

wenn auch/auch wenn   even though, although

wer   who, which; he who, whoever

werben (**warb, geworben; wirbt**)   to advertise

werden (**wurde, ist geworden; wird**)   to become; **werden zu**   to turn into

werfen (**warf, geworfen; wirft**)   to throw

Werk *(n.)*, **-e**   work, plant

Werkzeug *(n.)*, **-e**   tool

Wert *(m.)*, **-e**   value, worth

Wesen *(n.)*, **–**   being, nature, essence

wesentlich   essential, important, considerable; **im Wesentlichen**   essentially

weshalb   why

West, Westen *(m.)*   west, Occident

westlich   west, western, occidental

Wetter *(n.)*   weather

wichtig   important

Wichtigkeit *(f.)*   importance

wider   against

widerlich   repulsive, revolting

widerrufen (**widerrief, widerrufen**)   to deny, recant

widersprüchlich   contradictory

Widerstand *(m.)*, **⁼e**   opposition, resistance

widmen (sich)   to be dedicated

wie   as, like; how

Wiederaufbau *(m.)*   rebuilding, reconstruction

wieder/geben (**gab … wieder, wiedergegeben; gibt … wieder**)   to reproduce

wiederholen   to repeat

wiederum   in (his/her) turn, in return

wiegen (**wog, gewogen**)   to weigh

wie viel   how much

wie viele   how many

Wille *(m.)*   will

willig willing
willkürlich arbitrary
Winkel *(m.)*, **–** angle
wirken to work, be engaged; to have an effect
wirklich actual, real, true; really
Wirklichkeit *(f.)*, **-en** reality
wirksam effective
Wirkung *(f.)*, **-en** effect, consequence
Wirtschaft *(f.)*, **-en** industry, economy
wirtschaftlich economic, industrial
Wissen *(n.)* knowledge, learning
wissen (wusste, gewusst; weiß) to know (facts); **wir wissen es schon lange** we have known it for a long time
Wissenschaft *(f.)*, **-en** science, scholarship
Wissenschaftler *(n.)*, **–; Wissenschaftlerin** *(f.)*, **-nen** scientist, scholar
wissenschaftlich scientific, scholarly
wo where
Woche *(f.)*, **-n** week
woher where from
wohin where to
wohl well; perhaps; probably; indeed; no doubt
Wohnplatz *(m.)*, **̈e** living space
Wohnraum *(m.)* living quarters
Wohnsitz *(m.)*, **-e** abode, domicile
wollen (wollte, gewollt; will) to want to, intend to, be about to, wish
Wort *(n.)*, **-e; ̈er** word
Wörterbuch *(n.)*, **̈er** dictionary
Wunde *(f.)*, **-n** wound
wünschen to wish
würdigen to appreciate, value

Zahl *(f.)*, **-en** number
zählen to count; **zählen zu** to belong to, be classed with
zahlen to pay
zahlreich numerous
z.B. = zum Beispiel for example
Zeichen *(n.)*, **–** sign, symbol, mark, token
zeigen to show, demonstrate; **sich zeigen** to appear, prove to be
Zeile *(f.)*, **-n** line (of text)
Zeit *(f.)*, **-en** time; **im Laufe der Zeit** in the course of time; **in neuester Zeit** most recently; **zur Zeit (z.Z.)** at the time, at present, now
Zeitalter *(n.)*, **–** age, era
zeitgenössisch contemporary
zeitlos timeless, universal
Zeitraum *(m.)*, **̈e** period of time
Zeitschrift *(f.)*, **-en** journal, magazine
zeitweise at times, from time to time
Zelle *(f.)*, **-n** cell

Zentrum *(n.)*, **Zentren** center
zerdrücken to crush
zerreißen to rip into pieces
zerschlagen (zerschlug, zerschlagen; zerschlägt) to beat up
zerstören to destroy
Zerstörung *(f.)*, **-en** destruction
ziehen (zog, gezogen) to move, pull
Ziel *(n.)*, **-e** goal, aim
ziemlich fairly, rather
zigmal over and over, repeatedly
Zimmer *(n.)*, **–** room
Zitat *(n.)*, **-e** quote
zu to; in; for; at; in addition to, too
zu/bereiten to prepare, mix
zuerst at first, first of all, first
Zufall *(m.)*, **̈e** coincidence
zufrieden satisfied
zu/fügen to do unto, inflict upon
Zug *(m.)*, **̈e** train
zu/geben (gab … zu, zugegeben; gibt … zu) to admit
zugleich also, at the same time
zu/hören to listen to
zu/kehren to turn to
Zukunft *(f.)* future
zum Beispiel *(also* **z.B.)** for example
zumindest at least
zunächst next, first of all, to begin with, above all
Zunahme *(f.)*, **-n** increase
zu/nehmen (nahm … zu, zugenommen; nimmt … zu) to increase, grow
zurück back
zurück/kehren to return
zurück/treiben (trieb … zurück, zurückgetrieben) to drive back
zusammen together
Zusammenarbeit *(f.)* cooperation
zusammen/bringen to combine
Zusammenbruch *(m.)*, **̈e** collapse
zusammen/drängen to compress
zusammen/fassen to summarize
Zusammenhang *(m.)*, **̈e** connection, relationship
zusammen/hängen mit (hing … zusammen, zusammengehangen) to be connected with
Zusammensetzung *(f.)*, **-en** composition
zu/schauen to observe, watch
Zuschauer *(m.)*, **–; Zuschauerin** *(f.)*, **-nen** spectator
Zustand *(m.)*, **̈e** condition
zustande kommen (kam … zustande, ist zustande gekommen) to come about, produce

zu/stimmen to agree, be in agreement
Zustimmung *(f.)*, **-en** agreement
zuvor previously
Zuwachs *(m.)* growth
zu/wandern to immigrate
zwar indeed, to be sure; **und zwar** that is, they are

Zweck *(m.)*, **-e** purpose
zweifeln to doubt
Zweig *(m.)*, **-e** branch
zwingen (zwang, gezwungen) to force, coerce
zwischen between
Zwischenzeit *(f.)*, **-en** meantime

INDEX

verbs (*cont.*)
  past tense, meanings of, 29
  past tense of strong verbs, 45
  past tense of weak verbs, 29
  perfect tense, 87–89
  present tense, 16–18
  present tense of strong verbs,
    irregularities, 36–37
  reflexive, 147–148
  with inseparable and separable
    prefixes, 78–80

während, 177
was as relative pronoun, 187–188,
  203–204
was für (ein), 5–6
wenn auch, 178
welch-, 185
wer as relative pronoun, 203–204
werden
  auxiliary of future tenses, 123–124
  auxiliary of passive. *See* passive
    voice infinitive +, 122–123

present and past tense of, 46–47
  three uses of, 131–132
wo(r)-compounds, 246
worden, 138
word order
  finite verb separated from
    participle, 92
  formula for word order, 47–48,
    Appendix A
  important element at end of
    clause, 47
  normal and inverted, 15,
    48–49
  of indirect object, 23–24
  of information questions, 5–6
  position of verb, 47
  in subordinate clauses, 47

zu
  with infinitive, 211–213
  with **ist (war)** + infinitive,
    236–237
  with present participle, 234–235

CREDITS

READINGS

Kapitel 3 from *Bertolt Brecht: Leben des Galilei.* Frankfurt am Main: Suhrkamp 1963. (15 scene titles) © Suhrkamp Verlag Berlin 1955. Reprinted by permission of Suhrkamp.

Kapitel 4 based on *Tatsachen über Deutschland*, www.tatsachen-ueber-deutschland .de; reprinted by permission of Societäts-Verlag.

Kapitel 5 based on information from http://www.cs.uni.magdeburg.de/~toepel/ dom/dom_hi~1.html.

Kapitel 6 © 1974 by Stefan Heym: *5 Tage im Juni*, C. Bertelsmann Verlag, a division of Verlagsgruppe Random House GmbH, Munich, Germany. 1974; excerpted from pp. 168–186; reprinted by permission of Mohrbooks AG Literary Agency, Zurich.

Kapitel 7 based on *Schüler Duden: Das Wissen von A bis Z*, Duden, Mannheim, 1992; p. 436; reprinted by permission of Bibliographisches Institut & F.A. Brockhaus AG.

Kapitel 13 references to Goethe und *Werther* from *Sturm und Drang und Zeitgenossen* Katalog 13, J. Voerster, 1996; p. 46.

Kapitel 14 based on "Frauen verzweifelt gesucht," *sueddeutsche.de*, May 30, 2007. Reprinted by permission of *Süddeutsche Zeitung* GmbH.

Kapitel 17 from Richard Hofbauer "Größter Raub-Saurier in Patagonien entdeckt," © www.ExpeditionZone.com; reprinted by permission of ExpeditionZone.com.

Kapitel 19 introductory paragraph based on "Karl-May—Leben und Werk," from the Karl-May-Stiftung website http://www.karl-may-stiftung.de/.

Kapitel 20 based on review of Jürgen Mirow's *Geschichte des deutschen Volkes* in *Wissenschaftliche Buchgesellschaft Jahreskatalog 95*; p. 168, and online review © 2002 Casimir Katz Verlag, Gernsbach; reprinted by permission of Casimir Katz Verlag.

Wiederholung 4 adapted from "Im wilden, wilden Westen blüte die Fantasie," at www.nz-online.de, Aug. 8, 2007; reprinted by permission of Nordbayerische Verlagsgesellschaft mbH.

Kapitel 21 from Renate Schostack's "Robert Schumann: Original-Partitur wiedergefunden," *Frankfurter Allgemeine Zeitung*, Oct. 27, 1994; reprinted by permission of FAZ.

Kapitel 24 shortened and adapted from Stephan Reinhardt's "Carl von Ossietzky: Vom Idealismus getragene Leidenschaft," *Rowohlt Revue*, Spring 1995; p. 7; reprinted by permission of Rowohlt Verlag.

Wiederholung 5 adapted from the original by Albert Gier, "Über die Familie Mendelssohn," *Neue Zürcher Zeitung*; Dec. 19, 1995; p. 44; reprinted by permission of the author.

Kapitel 26 from Margaret Wertheim's "Ehre sei Gott im Cyberspace"; *Die Zeit* 22, May 31, 1996; p. 19, translated by Regine Reimers from the original "The Medieval Consolations of Cyberspace," *The Sciences*, vol. 35, Nov./Dec. 1995; pp. 24–25; reprinted by permission of The New York Academy of Sciences.

Kapitel 28 adapted excerpt from Toralf Staud's "Ossis sind Türken. 13 Jahre Einheit: In Gesamt-Westdeutschland sind die Ostdeutschen Einwanderer," *Die Zeit*, Oct. 2, 2003, Nr.41; reprinted with permission of the author.

Kapitel 29 shortened from Werner Spies, *Frankfurter Allgemeine Zeitung* 1/96; pp. 12–13; reprinted by permission of the author.

Kapitel 30 from Ingeborg Braa and Sigrid Kumm, *Städteporträt: Berlin*, InterNationes, Bonn, 1992; pp. 16–17; reprinted by permission of the Goethe-Institut e.V.

Wiederholung 6 excerpted from Ina Boesch's "Entgrenzung: Gedanken zu einer transnationalen Literatur" in *Küsse und eilige Rosen: Die fremdsprachige Schweizer Literatur. Ein Lesebuch*, edited by Chudi Bürgi, Anita Müller and Christine Tresch, Limmat Verlag, Zurich, 1998; reprinted by permission of the author.

REALIA

Kapitel 6 from *Collins German Unabridged Dictionary,* 5th Edition, London 2006; p. 655.

Appendix C from *Collins German Unabridged Dictionary,* 5th Edition, London 2006; back cover.